THE CYBER THREAT AND GLOBALIZATION

●

THE IMPACT *on* U.S. NATIONAL *and* INTERNATIONAL SECURITY

●

JACK A. JARMON

Rutgers University

PANO YANNAKOGEORGOS

Air University Cyber College

ROWMAN & LITTLEFIELD

LANHAM · BOULDER · NEW YORK · LONDON

Executive Editor: Traci Crowell
Assistant Editor: Mary Malley
Senior Marketing Manager: Amy Whitaker
Interior Designer: Ilze Lemesis
Cover Designer: Sally Rinehart

Published by Rowman & Littlefield
An imprint of The Rowman & Littlefield Publishing Group, Inc.
4501 Forbes Boulevard, Suite 200, Lanham, Maryland 20706
www.rowman.com

Unit A, Whitacre Mews, 26-34 Stannary Street, London SE11 4AB, United Kingdom

British Library Cataloguing in Publication Information Available

Library of Congress Cataloging-in-Publication Data Available

ISBN 978-1-5381-0430-9 (cloth: alk. paper)
ISBN 978-1-5381-0431-6 (pbk.: alk. paper)
ISBN 978-1-5381-0432-3 (electronic)

∞™ The paper used in this publication meets the minimum requirements of American National Standard for Information Sciences—Permanence of Paper for Printed Library Materials, ANSI/NISO Z39.48-1992.

Printed in the United States of America

Contents

Preface

The application of military power has taken on new purpose and significance in the twenty-first century. The change in the order of world affairs has been driven by disruptive technologies, an ever-expanding global economy, a dispersion of power, and a clash with embedded institutions, interests, and worldviews. Adjustment will continue to be a process of trial, reorientation, missteps, and lapses. Despite the integration of information and communication technologies (ICTs) onto military platforms and the rise of cyber commands worldwide, militaries find difficulty in resisting the drift to organize, train, and equip using organizational methods adopted in the twentieth century. Further, the nature of the use of the raw power of the military as "an instrument of policy" is no longer the convenient definition of global conflict it was when Carl von Clausewitz lived and wrote. In today's postindustrial age, information is more valuable than territory and has become the main commodity influencing geopolitics. The reliance of societies on cyberspace and ICTs for economic prosperity and of national security on data flows represents a new domain of human activity and conflict. Cyberspace has become both an economic enabler and also a source of global instability. Its potential as a tool of social disruption in mobilizing populations and the low cost of entry into asymmetric conflict have forced a paradigm shift unknown to man since, as General Michael Hayden has remarked, the invention of human language.

In addressing the paradigm shift in national security and global conflict, this book is co-written and designed as a text for courses and students of security studies and international relations who want a better grasp of the nature and existential threat of today's information wars. Additionally, security professionals and practitioners will find it a useful tool. The work is a conceptual and practical book, not a theoretical work. It explains the relevant concepts as well as structural challenges and responsibilities with which policy makers struggle and practitioners must work. The text interweaves chapters with pedagogy boxes that illustrate the challenges and issues for both. For members of the lay public with an interest in cyber-related security issues and security affairs, the book is written to make policy and technical concepts user friendly and, hopefully, enjoyable to read. Ultimately, it will increase the level of understanding of readers of all audiences who are concerned about cyber threats and their impact on society, including at the level of our daily routines.

The ultimate goal of the book is to enable students and concerned citizens to have a better understanding of the complex nature of the morphing cyber threat vector as it relates to national security, commerce, and the everyday things we often take for granted. It is intended for upper-level undergraduate and graduate-level advanced courses in national and international security. However, security professionals will also find the work a valuable resource and reference book. Although this is not necessarily a textbook for specialists in computer technology, practitioners in supply-chain logistics, legal consultants, public policy administrators, and criminal justice professionals will find it a worthwhile tool in communicating relevant concepts and definitions in a way that is accessible and less esoteric.

Scholarly/popular audiences who want an understanding of our overdependence on networks and the vulnerabilities to which they are subject should find the book educational and clarifying. For these readers, it will become clear how the U.S. economy, our political system, and our quality of life are under attack. The threats from disgruntled employees, hacktivists, criminals, terrorists, and hostile governments are described, and security vulnerabilities are explained in a structured and coherent way. It is the wish of the authors, the contributors, and the publisher that all groups will regard the book as a constructive, timely text and a worthy addition to their library. Any student is likely to encounter cybersecurity in disciplines like public administration, public policy, criminology/criminal justice and policing, emergency management, political science and international studies, international relations, global affairs, security studies, and military or defense studies. Cybersecurity is fundamental to many fields as societal institutions and conventions adapt to the information age and consequential new patterns of change.

Moreover, as the state-centered international system is under immense pressure, security frameworks become more outmoded. Yet, in the face of the challenges from offensive cyber capabilities being developed by terrorist groups, criminal gangs, and other substate actors, the primary competitors of the Cold War are still major players and pose the most significant threat to national and global security. In addressing the nonsymmetrical onslaught, this book offers an analysis of the altering landscape of warfare and economic competition. Using recent events and documented experiences as examples, the book reveals truths about our dependence on networks, the fragility of these networks, and the programs, policies, technological advancements, and other efforts to defend against adversarial use of cyber.

To further augment the text, pedagogy boxes include vignettes and case studies. Noted subject matter experts also amplify the topics through opinion pieces, essays, and extended quotes from testimonies and scholarly articles. Their opinions are their own and are not influenced by the views of the authors. Therefore, their purpose is to offer different perspectives on a variety of debatable issues and subjects and to give the reader exposure to independent thought pieces within the structure of an organized work. We are fortunate to have contributors who are recognized authorities, and their insights add depth and breadth to a book that attempts to make clear some truths and facts on a range of technological and policy issues against the backdrop of a mutable environment and a complex and developing world order.

Defining Cyberspace 1

A World at War with Itself

On April 1, 2001, a U.S. EP-3 reconnaissance and surveillance plane was conducting operations along China's Hainan Province via the South China Sea. When the EP-3 approached Chinese airspace, two Chinese F-8 fighter jets scrambled to meet it. A mid-air collision forced the reconnaissance plane to land in Hainan and resulted in the death of one of the fighter pilots. The clash and the death of Wang Wei, the Chinese jet pilot, was not only an international incident—it provoked discussions in chat rooms in China and the United States which eventually spanned the globe.

In China, the outrage found vent in messages such as the following: "This is the third time the American imperialists have dumped crap down China's neck." "We can forego joining the WTO but we cannot afford to lose face." "Why can't the U.S. show any human rights concern to the poor missing pilot?" "The whole nation is waiting to see if China can play hardball with the U.S."[1]

Within two weeks, an exchange of cyberattacks arose across the Pacific. A cyber war was even declared for the dates of April 30 through May 8 between hackers in China and the United States. These "unauthorized enthusiasts" launched denial-of-service attacks and defaced websites. Fortunately, the attacks inflicted little damage since participants chose not to launch malicious codes or target servers.

Three Chinese groups bore primary responsibility for most of the defaced websites. The Honker Union of China, Hacker Union of China, and China Eagle Union—a civilian nonprofit organization of part-time network fanatics—vandalized such targets as the White House home page and the websites of the U.S. Department of Labor, the U.S. Department of Health, and UPI (United Press International).[2] By the time hostilities ended, Chinese hackers had defaced about a thousand American sites, often with images of waving Chinese national flags and anti-American slogans.

For their part, the Americans not only targeted Chinese government sites, but also universities and nonprofit organizations.[3] With a tinge of hauteur and characteristic self-assurance, one American defacement read, "bagel—morning coffee—and a Chinese website. Nice little routine."[4] At the center of these attacks were two American hacker groups identified as Pr0phet and Poizonb0x.[5]

Both the Chinese (PRC) and U.S. governments took the cyber "war" seriously. During the aggressions, the National Infrastructure Protection Commission Watch and Warning Unit established a hotline. The U.S. Navy also announced that it was at INFOCONALPHA, a cyber-equivalent status of a physical threat condition. Meanwhile, the Chinese Communist Party (CCP) urged citizens to show "collective displeasure" by defacing American sites. By the time the U.S. crewmen were released and the two governments declared the episode closed, thousands of young Chinese hackers had joined in the attack on targets as diverse as military installations and public libraries. Further, before the attack's end, hackers from all corners of the planet took sides and participated. Individuals from India, Pakistan, Brazil, Indonesia, Malaysia, Argentina, South Korea, Saudi Arabia, and Japan took part in what today would be described as a global "cyber riot."

However, after the U.S. issued a "letter of sorrow" and paid reparations, Chinese hackers continued to ply their craft, even under the threat of arrest. In response, the CCP seized the moment to bring this community under control by converting these groups of "net warriors" into more formal organizations. In 2003, the People's Liberation Army (PLA) began conducting surveys and competitions to identify talent. Today, some estimate that as many as two hundred thousand work in labs and commercial firms with the support of the Chinese military.[6] Reflecting on the events of April and May 2001, Professor Zhang Zhaozhong, at the Chinese National Defense University and director of its Military and Equipment Teaching and Research Center, commented that the cyber conflict

> presented a modern format of warfare, alive and kicking, before the eyes of the netizens, and invented many a combat method through practice, amassed abundant experience, expanded the contingent of hackers, tempered their mettle for cyberspace fighting, and made an impressive show of the wisdom and abilities of the Chinese netizens to the netizens around the world.[7]

Beyond being a platform for a "modern format of warfare" as Zhang hypothesized, the British technologist and journalist Ben Hamersley declared, "[The Internet had become the] dominant platform for life in the 21st Century." The social networking phenomenon at work in the EP-3 incident has grown enormously over the past decade. The processes and relationships that govern it are complex. The benefits to national security are significant, even critical. Social media (also referred to as Web 2.0) is recognized as a connective tool and an intellectual force multiplier.[8] However, as telling as the EP-3 episode was, it is only a scant glimpse of the density and impact of cyber on today's arena of conflict.

The notion that the application of military power has been transformed in the twenty-first century finds acceptance in even the most sclerotic of conventional wisdom. Yet despite the integration of information and communication technologies (ICTs) into military platforms and the rise of cyber commands worldwide, militaries continue to organize, train, and equip personnel using organizational methods adopted in the nineteenth century and used throughout the twentieth. Raw military power as "an instrument of policy" is a departed strategic response mechanism in today's arena of conflict. As General David Petraeus, former commanding general of the International Security Assistance Force in Afghanistan and CIA director, commented, "to kill or capture our way to victory" is no longer a strategic opportunity.[9] Disorienting features of the new conflict are the unfamiliar objectives that dominate a new strategy of warfare and competition by state and nonstate actors. In these new wars, mass disruption rather than destruction can be acceptable goals. The preference for endless conflict over final victory is another strategic objective that forces a reshaping of the accepted wisdom on preparedness and offensive planning. Because of our reliance on technology, we are highly vulnerable to these threats. Therefore, the cyber domain represents the most critical field of conflict.

What, Then, Is Cyber?

Prior to the terms *cyberspace, cybersecurity, cybercrime, cyberwar*, etc., there was the subject area of *cybernetics* (from the Greek word *kubernētēs* [κυβερνυ], "steersman," from *kubernan*, "to steer"). Cybernetics is the study of communication and control systems in living beings and machines. Beginning in the late 1940s, specialists from fields as diverse as biology, engineering, and social science took up the question, "How do systems work?" and hence a new morpheme appeared in the modern lexicon. Earlier natural variations included *cyber cubicle, cyber friend, cyber lover, cyber snob*, and even adverbs like *cyber-sheepishly*.[10]

The word *cyberspace* was first coined by the science fiction author William Gibson. He expresses "cyberspace" in the novel *Neuromancer* as a "consensual hallucination . . . a graphic representation of data extracted from the banks of every computer in the human system." Ultimately, the word *cyberspace* is at best a lax term, an attempt to describe an information environment while conveying the evolutionary and unrestrained nature of its substance and essence. Through time, the Pentagon has offered up at least twelve definitions of what it believes is the definition of *cyberspace*.[11] Ultimately, the operational definition we use must confer a meaning of *cyber* and attendant concepts in the same terms that we use to understand, pen, and verbalize our notions about the oceans, outer space, the ecosystem, and other frontiers of human endeavor where serious challenges co-exist alongside grand opportunities for cooperation. For the purposes of this discussion, we can defer to the U.S. Joint Chiefs of Staff:

> The domain characterized by the use of electronics and the **electromagnetic spectrum** to store, modify, and exchange data via network systems and associated physical infrastructure.[12]

Thus, cyberspace is both logical (virtual) and physical. It encompasses digitally networked information and information technologies, which include computer terminals, servers, and mobile devices connected to remote or hard drives (servers) via a digital network.[13] Although man-made, cyberspace is bound by physics. Cyberspace exists where the wave-particle duality of radiation, when modulated with bits, creates an information flow. Most attention focuses on the

Box 1.1 Electromagnetic Spectrum

What is known as the electromagnetic spectrum is the combination of electric and magnetic fields. The reciprocal relationship between electricity and magnetism forms the medium. When these forces are unified mathematically, they create electromagnetic (EM) waves of radio and light. The oscillation of atomic interaction determines wave frequencies, which govern such properties as visibility and energy and can create the separate pathways, or wavelengths, along which information streams.

logical elements of cyberspace. However, the importance of the electromagnetic spectrum (EMS), cyberspace's physical element, will increase as broadband and mobile technologies continue to converge.

It is the "logic" elements of cyber that permits information to flow across networks and appear within applications to create effects in the real world, which are bound only by the limits of human innovation.

The two main types of media, or digital networks, are the Internet and intranets. *Intranets* refers to private or restricted networks created using Internet software. Internet, or the World Wide Web, is the global network that permits access to computers worldwide and users the ability to connect and exchange information. As is the nature of all technology, the World Wide Web has gone through generations of evolutionary processes. It began with Usenet, a computer-based distributed discussion system first devised in 1979. Currently, we are on the cusp of Web 3.0, or the semantic web. The beginnings of this technological era date roughly between 2010 and 2012 and will intensify in 2020.[14] Historically, the evolutionary trajectory of the Internet is as follows:

- *Web 1.0* was the static web, where people would go and read information without interacting with the media. Referred to, also, as the personal computer era from 1980 to 1990.
- *Web 2.0* is the interactive and social web. The trend toward this started circa 2000 but did not fully take off until later in the decade with the popularization of services such as YouTube and Facebook. Users interact across many devices and fluently transfer between author and audience states—in real time. Information retrieval (Google) and speech recognition (IBM's ViaVoice) also belong to this era of web development.
- *Web 3.0*, or the semantic web, is about machines connecting data, which was not previously linked.[15] The semantic web will teach the computer what the data means, and this will evolve into artificial intelligence that can utilize that information.[16] Semantic web technologies enable people to create data stores on the web, build vocabularies, and write rules for handling data. The question-answering system (e.g., IBM's Watson, which appeared on episodes of the TV quiz-show *Jeopardy!*) is an example of Web 3.0 technology.

Figure 1.1 Users with Access to the Internet

In 2012 | 2 billion users | 12 billion devices

As the number of people with access to the Internet rises, total Internet traffic is expected to more than double from the 2012 level by 2017.

Source: U.S. Department of Homeland Security, 2014 Quadrennial Homeland Security Review.

The World Wide Web is a planetary marvel. From 2007 to 2013, the number of Internet users doubled to about 2.27 billion. From 2011 to 2016, experts estimated that global network connections increased from 10.6 billion to 18.9 billion. The number of connected devices will be 31 billion in 2020, compared to only 2 billion in 2011.[17] The main drivers of these trends are technologies referred to as Internet of Things (IoT) and Bring Your Own Device (BYOD).

IoT is still in its infancy. It is the network of routinely used objects such as Fitbits, smart TVs, home security and thermostats, alarm systems, and health monitoring devices. They contain embedded technologies that communicate and sense or interact with their internal states or the external environment. BYOD refers to the policy of permitting employees to bring personally owned mobile devices (laptops, tablets, and smart phones) to their workplace and to use those devices to access privileged company information and applications. With the growing ubiquity of such machines and expansive usage, there are significant security concerns, which will be discussed later in greater detail.

The History of the Internet

Steve Jobs once observed, "Creativity is just connecting things." In 1968, the Advanced Research Projects Agency (ARPA), which later became the Defense Advanced Research Projects Agency (DARPA), began "connecting things" by working on what eventually would become the modern-day Internet. ARPA was founded as a result of the national trauma created by the Soviet Union in 1957 with the launch of *Sputnik 1*.[18] To counter the USSR's new position of advantage, the agency's reason for being was to identify key challenges in science and technology that would allow the United States to retake and maintain a lead in these fields.

By the late 1960s (at the height of the Cold War and the "space race"), the use of computers was bourgeoning. The demand from researchers was beginning to outstrip availability. Therefore, the project's main goal was to find a way to allow scientists from disparate locations to have reliable access to unused computer time. Dedicated connections were expensive and subject to disruption. A second project aim was to invent a communications network that was scalable, could sustain physical attacks, and was able to survive malfunctions occurring at other points along the system. The solution was a shared network of data links and computational resources.

This linkage meant a changeover from traditional circuit-switched telephone networks to a revolutionary packet-switched network. A packet is a digital envelope of data. Outside the envelope is what is known as a header, which contains information about the network source, destination, and limited detail on the packet's contents. Along the network are devices called interface message processors (IMPs), or packet-switch nodes, to facilitate connections—what we refer to today as "routers." Electronic messages are disaggregated into bits of data at the origin point—contained and sent in the form of small packets that have routing information on packet headers. Routers along the network read the packet headers and relay the packets toward their destination. At the destination point, the data is re-assembled as packets arrive to form the original message. The first successful link ran between UCLA and Stanford in 1969, and lo, ARPANET was born.

However, in order to achieve scale, a system must be able to accommodate many different networks with varying underlying technologies. In cyberspace, circuits that information travels can be physical (copper wiring, optical cable) or radiation based (microwave, WiFi). Therefore, a data packet system connecting numerous and assorted networks relies upon standardized communication protocols to assure operation and control. In 1973, researchers at Stanford and ARPA found a solution in a model called Transmission Control Protocol (TCP). The Transmission Control Protocol/Internet Protocol (TCP/IP) is the common set of protocols that govern the transmission of data between devices. Communication is disaggregated into independent layers. The critical information in the IP header allows the transport layer of the TCP/IP, or "protocol stack," to operate across networks. The IP header is simply a string of numbers that routers read to direct packets toward their destinations and, hence, form connections. At the receiving end, the header carries information that also instructs the destination computer how to re-create the message from the incoming packet data. Once deployed, TCP/IP became the "vital lingua franca between previously incompatible computer networks."[19]

In addition, the model allows systemic integrity. A breakdown or interruption of transmission at any place along the network will not cause a system failure. The data packets are simply rerouted. Unless messages are encrypted or transmitted over virtual private networks (VPNs), information flows according to this mode of transport. The system's openness contributes to this resiliency as well as to its vulnerability.[20]

Shortly after the inception of ARPANET, the U.S. National Science Foundation (NSF) realized the potential impact this technology could have on university research throughout the nation. Unfortunately, to have access to ARPANET an institution had to have a research contract with the Department of Defense. In 1985, the NSF removed this restriction by creating NSFnet, which linked to ARPANET and connected existing supercomputing centers around the country. A TCP/IP "backbone" was later added to manage traffic between the different regional networks (see figure 1.2). The objective of the architecture was to create an "inter-net"—a "network of networks." The new blueprint connected to DARPA's own internet, which included the ARPANET. The result would offer users the ability to access remote computing resources from within their own local computing environment.[21] As NSFnet became the successor system to ARPANET, it became an instantaneous success and quickly overloaded. The NSF realized it could not continue financing the build-out indefinitely and therefore set plans for its commercialization.[22]

During the late 1980s, ground was being laid for the commercialization of NSFnet. In 1989, Senator Al Gore introduced a bill to accelerate the network's privatization. Although he was wrongly accused by political foes for claiming to have "invented the Internet," his legislation was instrumental in NFSnet's upgrade and commercialization. At the twentieth anniversary of the NSFnet in 2007, one attendee remarked,

> In the 2000 election, Al Gore, then the vice president, was derided by opponents who claimed that he had said he "created" the Internet. But many of the scientists, engineers and technology executives who gathered here to celebrate the Web's birth say he played a crucial role in its development, and they expressed bitterness that his vision had been so discredited.[23]

By the 1990s, Internet service providers (ISPs) overtook an Internet once dominated by government, university, and industrial researchers. ISPs competed in regional areas based on price and quality of service—and in the process signed up millions of customers. Despite the calls for limited government from various political corners, the creation of the Internet represents an extraordinary example of the possibilities of public-private partnership. In the final accounting, it was the federal government through the Department of Defense and the National Science Foundation that created the infrastructure that formed the basis of the Internet and then handed it over to industry to operate.[24]

The commercialization of NSFnet also overlapped with technological innovations. Al Gore may have been unjustly mocked for claiming to have invented the Internet, but Tim Berners-Lee can be justifiably credited for inventing the World Wide Web. In 1989, while working as a contractor at the European Organization for Nuclear Research (CERN), Timothy Berners-Lee (now Sir Timothy) proposed a "universal linked information system" that allowed academics across the globe to upload immense amounts of information on the web and assign locations for accessing it. His HyperText Transfer Protocol (HTTP)

Figure 1.2 Backbone Network

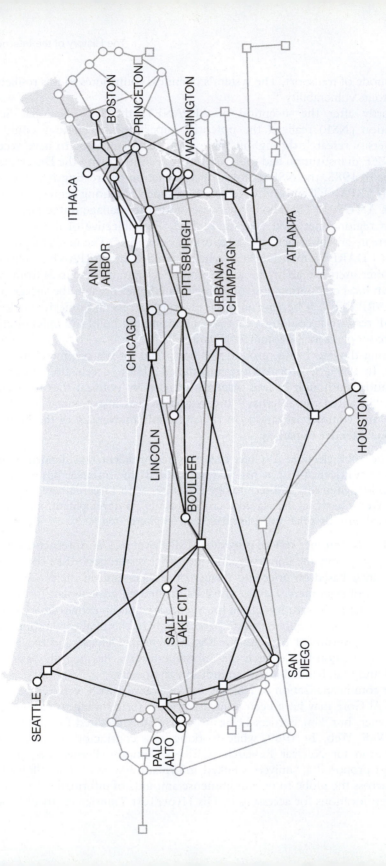

SEATTLE

PALO
ALTO

SAN
DIEGO

SALT
LAKE CITY

BOULDER

LINCOLN

HOUSTON

CHICAGO

ANN
ARBOR

PITTSBURGH

URBANA-
CHAMPAIGN

ITHACA

ATLANTA

BOSTON

PRINCETON

WASHINGTON

is the networking interface, or the computer language, used to communicate hypertext documents over the "web" of information—the Internet.

The World Wide Web (WWW) exists only because computers are interconnected via MAC and IP addresses using HyperText Transfer Protocol (HTTP), which can communicate data and information via a Uniform Resource Locator (URL), and the Domain Name System (DNS). The Uniform Resource Locator is the directory of domain names. Applications are then built on top of this platform to organize data and provide services such as Facebook and Google.

The URL is the protocol for specifying global addresses on the web. The URL is another string of numbers, which are read by machines and translated (resolved) into letters by the Domain Name System (DNS) for easier understanding by humans. Therefore, rather than having to type 66.249.90.104 when accessing a search engine, you can enter the more user-friendly URL "google. com." Domain Name Resolvers are the computers, commonly located with ISPs or in institutional networks, used to respond to a user request to "resolve" a domain name.

Thirteen root servers house the DNS databases, which facilitate translation between IPs and URLs. The former U.S. Department of Commerce agency, Internet Corporation for Assigned Names and Numbers (ICANN), allocates top-level designations such as .com, .org, .edu, .gov, .mil, and so on and maintains and updates the data. ICANN is now a private entity and as a result of international pressure has facilitated the movement from a less English-centric system of domain naming to accommodate other languages. However, the rollout of new top-level domain names for non-Roman script languages such as Chinese, Arabic, Persian, and Russian has been delayed, and the pause in this effort creates a new round of accusations against the United States and the European Union of "Internet imperialism" and "Western mercantilism."[25]

In the backdrop to these issues are other problems. While DNS allows for a free and open Internet to function, the standards and protocols that ICANN uses to maintain the domain name registries can be used by individuals, ad hoc networks,

Box 1.2   Hypertext, HTTP, and HTML

- Hypertext links allow readers to alternate from one digital document to another.

- HyperText Transfer Protocol (HTTP) is the underlying protocol used by the World Wide Web. HTTP defines how messages are formatted and transmitted and what actions web servers and browsers should take in response to various commands. When you enter a URL in your browser, this actually sends an HTTP command to the web server, directing it to fetch and transmit the requested data.

- HyperText Markup Language (HTML) is the authoring language used to create documents on the World Wide Web. HTML defines the structure and layout of a web document by using a variety of tags and attributes.

Source: www.webopedia.com.

and nation-states to design and deploy an alternative domain name system that can either be independent of or "ride on top of" the Internet.[26] When a group wishes to ride over the global DNS root but incorporate its own pseudo top-level domain, core operators of the pseudo-domains can use specific software resources to resolve domains that are globally accessible within their alternative DNS system. When appraising cybersecurity, these alternative domain name systems (altDNSs) are another critical concern of the threat matrix as adversaries develop ways to mask their presence and any problematic or illegal activity on the Internet.

In addition to the rise of altDNSs, there is also a trend of non-Latin-character URLs as well as generic top-level domain names (gTLDs). Top-level domain name extensions such as .com or .org have been limited by ICANN. In 2011, ICANN opened up a process for applicants to create their own domain name extensions, such as. culture. If organizations run their own top-level domain names, they may operate them as they wish, thus making the gTLD either as open or as closed to the public as the organization wishes.

The use of non-Latin script on the Internet is rising. Whereas today Latin characters from A to Z are used to resolve URLs, ICANN has launched an effort to introduce non-Latin scripts, such as Arabic, Chinese, and Greek, into the Domain Name System. This will allow more users to access the Internet in their own language.[27] The Internet will thus be open to masses of new users who may not have entered the space because of the English-language barrier. This presents a significant human capital challenge as the cultural and linguistic challenges facing the cyber profession today will only intensify.

Unfettered Growth and Challenges

The sheer growth of the Internet has opened the system to greater risk. By the mid-1990s, business took over the role as the driving force behind the design and future direction of the Internet. ISPs were quick to realize the benefit of having a voice communication over Internet protocol (VoIP). Advances in technology allowed connections between the Internet and traditional phone lines (PTN—public telecommunication network) and resulted in further consumer demand. This revolution in ICT forced greater interdependency between PTNs and the Internet. It also increased our reliance on computer networks as these systems became more software driven. Over the years, the epidemic demand for larger-scale operations and more access points has been transformative in its impact on communication and commerce. The ceaseless expansion of the web has further elevated the risk of vulnerability.[28]

Today when we refer to the Internet, we are not discussing a monolithic framework of connections but rather a complex network of hardware, software, protocols, and phantasmagoria of evolving technology. A 2007 report estimated that at least 80 percent of U.S. commerce flowed through the Internet.[29] Content-wise, it is a domain with three billion users and, as of 2014, has an economic impact of $6.3 trillion.[30]

At the core of cyberspace are the standards and protocols that allow for interoperability and functionality. As the most potent manifestation of cyberspace, the Internet works seamlessly. The protocols and standards that allow computers to interoperate permitted this technological wonder to catalyze innovation and prosperity globally.

Despite the vastness of these numbers, the current conception of the Internet is a simple modality expressed by a structure with a stack of four layers (protocol stack or TCP/IP, see above), each with separate functions. The four layers of the Internet are:

- infrastructure layer
- logical layer
- application layer
- content layer

The **infrastructure layer** is mostly hardware and includes routers, switches, Internet exchange points (IXPs—physical intersections between networks), and transmission facilities such as fiber optic cable, cellular systems, IoT structures, and systems. The majority of this infrastructure is owned and operated by the private sector, particularly telecommunications companies.

The **logical layer** of the Internet includes Internet Protocol (IP) addresses and domain names, as well as the Domain Name System (DNS). The logical layer also includes Internet standards, such as TCP/IP, HTTP (HyperText Transfer Protocol), and HTML (HyperText Markup Language)—in other words, the core protocols and standards that permit information to travel across different software and hardware platforms.

The **application layer** contains the software with which end users and IoT devices interact directly. Mobile apps, voice-over-IP applications, search engines, social media platforms, and platforms for sharing user-generated content are examples of applications found within this layer of the stack.

The **content layer** of the Internet is the most apparent. Alphanumeric text (messaging, IoT data, e-mail, web content, and books), audio (music and voice calls), pictures (photographs, diagrams, digitized art, and illustrations), video (user-generated video, video conferencing, and streaming movies), and multimedia of all kinds (video games, virtual reality, and IoT environments) reside here.

Synoptically, the Internet has been described as "part town square (where people engage in politics and speech), part Main Street (where people shop), part dark alleys (where crime occurs), part secret corridors (where spies engage in economic and military espionage), and part battlefield."[31] It connects half the world's population and is still in its infancy. As it expands, it compounds. The future for all of us will be based on a digital superstructure, which will underlie and shape our modes of production, commerce, trade, and governance.

From its beginnings as a closed military project, the Internet has undergone several cycles of evolution. The surges in efficiency, reduction of cost, and ease of access have boosted commerce while testing the resilience of public policy. At the same time, security remains a challenge for the national defense establishment and the private sector. At its inception as a U.S. military project, the Internet's security concerns were minimal. It was a closed system because it was closed to others outside its small circle of users with authorized access to specific government-owned and -sponsored mainframe computers. Due to the government's original intension to keep the function and system limited and proprietary, many of the security issues faced today are inherited traits of a previous generation of development.[32] Despite the hopes expressed by the original developers of the Internet and others that the digital age would bring with it new access to empowerment and a spirit of democracy, the trend is that these hopes often give way to misuse and exploitation. From the welter of globalization and disruptive technologies, an ominous era of competition between states and non-state actors frequently emerges.

Information Technology versus Operational Technology

Cyberspace infrastructure is the critical underpinning of the global economy. We depend on this critical infrastructure to conduct business, power our households, access financial assets, and provide and receive health care. Hence, the security of these networks is central to our daily life and national defense. The reliance of societies on cyberspace and the data flows that information communication technologies afford us is essential for our current economic prosperity and national security. These dependencies also represent a new domain of human activity and conflict.

In today's conflict arena, the threats and sources of attacks are myriad. Cybercriminals, disgruntled employees, terrorists, activists, organized crime syndicates, and state actors all have their own resources and motivations. In order to understand the cyber threat, however, we need to understand what makes something a target—the apparatus, properties, and functionalities that create an "exposure." We also need to understand how these elements interoperate and where they disconnect. Such insights reveal how security gaps are created through the flaws of legacy systems, conventional approaches to system/network management, and the economic pressures that drive investment.

Information technology (IT) is a broad term. It basically refers to the use and study of systems that store, send, receive, and process data. Excluded from references to IT are personal or home computing and networking. On the other hand, operational technology (OT) is the hardware and software systems that manage and monitor the physical equipment that operates the critical infrastructure, automated manufacturing processes, and defense networks. Although these two environments share some commonality, they historically remain separate domains and are managed as independent silos within organizations.[33] Not only are they distinct in their functionally, but they differ culturally and strategically as well. Traditionally, commercial enterprises view IT as a cost center and a support unit, while OT more directly aligns with the core business and return on assets and investment.

Critical infrastructure sectors such as utilities, water, oil and gas, energy, and transportation rely on OT systems for operation, support, and upgrade. The same is the case for the vast defense industrial base and manufacturing and pharmaceutical firms. These enterprises require a system to perform limited functions but over a widely distributed environment. The value is placed on reliability across long time periods without the need for human involvement. A white paper by the cybersecurity firm NexDefense notes,

> While enterprise computers are largely considered obsolete within two to five years, operational equipment is expected to be in place a minimum of 10–20 even in harsh manufacturing, refining and outdoor settings. It is not uncommon to find legacy equipment as much as 50 years old, still in place and functioning.[34]

Supervisory control and data acquisition (SCADA) systems, which monitor industrial control systems (ICSs), are OT systems with origins that go back to the 1960s. SCADA systems can be found in public and private sector operations from transportation and recycling to manufacturing and energy. Refineries, supermarkets, and households rely on some type of SCADA. The acronym refers to the function of acquiring data from remote devices such as pumps, valves, transmitters, sensors, etc., and transmitting the information to computers with SCADA software for analysis and graphical display. The technology is ubiquitous. Unfortunately, wide-area network SCADA systems often rely on tenuous communication links.[35] Data is sent "in the clear," or over open pathways that rely on the Internet and often require no authentication.[36] This feature brings to focus another distinction between the two domains.

By nature, IT and OT technologies have separate approaches to security and attitudes toward risk tolerance. An unplanned OT outage or failure is a crisis. It can result in a high-impact event with severe economic repercussions and possibly personal injury or loss of life. Even planned outages for upgrade are challenges to OT environments because of the apprehension linked with unwanted downtime. Upgrades can take months of advance planning, require suspension of operations, and sometimes result in declining revenues and harm to corporate reputation. Although preferable to a disaster event, these stoppages more immediately affect the OT unit's bottom line than they do that of an IT unit, which regards such procedures as a cost of doing business. In contrast to OT, downtime to upgrade software, install firewalls, or run system audits in IT environments is acceptable and routine. Lost data can be restored or re-created with minimal cost. Contrariwise, product and supply cannot. A lost transformer or downed production line is not the same as a failed server. Cloud computing and server clusters (also known as a virtual server farm, which is a collection of servers that can provide a network environment and backup capability) reduce the impact of system interruption for the IT group. There is no corresponding mitigating feature in the OT domain.

Despite some parallel development owing to OT adaptation of IT-based technologies, these environments still basically function by different standards, using dissimilar infrastructures, unrelated processes, and managerial departments.[37] However, IT/OT convergence may be an issue that can no longer be deferred. Pressures and calls for a more integrated and holistic approach are mounting. These pressures are regulatory as well as organizational. As we move on to smart power grids, smart manufacturing plants, smart distribution systems, and even the use of automated weapons systems, the encroaching connectivity of intelligent devices will force a more robust dependence on IT functions. These trending architectures rely on networks of self-monitoring transformers, remote meters, and sophisticated sensor systems.[38]

In the area of national defense, the future "large-scale weapons environment" that the U.S. military envisions will involve complex systems engineering and integration. They include the global deployment of unmanned operations, undersea warfare and supply, and extended air operations.[39] At the core of this strategy are lethal and nonlethal distributed systems. These systems will rely on artificial intelligence technologies that support a global network of sensors, refueling capabilities, and strike operations on aerial and marine platforms. In sum, the pressures on commerce, the guardians of our critical infrastructure, and the military give no alternative choice but to adapt to changing conditions. Reducing personnel costs, cybersecurity risks, and the benefits of enhanced performance represent forces too powerful to resist. To that end, IT/OT discipline convergence is a self-organizing function.

Vulnerabilities

SCADA systems are security problem areas. When they were developed over forty-five years ago, the designers of these software applications sought a model that was scalable, easy to operate, and able to link together decentralized facilities. In this environment, security concerns ran second to interests of Internet expansion and accessibility. Therefore, standardized technologies and open solutions seemed more corresponding to the original vision. Today's standardization of software products, hardware products, and connectivity with other networks are both problematic and seminal. The escalating threat from cyberattack has put at risk these control systems and the critical national infrastructure facilities that rely on them.

The chief defense against cyberattack for SCADA systems has been their relative remoteness and separation from major networks. "Remote locations and proprietary industrial networks used to give SCADA systems a considerable degree of protection through isolation."[40] However, that defense is compromised through Internet and enterprise network connections, from the level of network nodes to remote field devices. Furthermore, no network is completely segregated, or "air gapped." A completely isolated system would exclude software and certification updates and restrict file uploads.[41] The extension of smart grids and smart metering makes the notion of a disconnected critical infrastructure counterproductive to the goals of cost efficiency and service/product reliability.

The most publicized and advanced SCADA malware to date is Stuxnet. Known within official circles as "Olympic Games," Stuxnet attacked the Iranian nuclear facility at Natanz over a period between 2008 and 2011, disabling 3,700 of the 9,000 centrifuges at the facility[42] and setting back the Iranian uranium enrichment program by one year. Stuxnet, which is believed to be a joint operation between the United States, Israel, and the UK, contained multiple **zero-day exploits** that took advantage of a number of Windows vulnerabilities. It preyed on widely used Siemens industrial control software and databases and Vacon and Fararo Paya PLCs (programmable logic controllers). Once activated, it caused rotor failure of centrifuge operations, forcing centrifuges to dump contents.

Box 1.3 Zero-Day

A day zero or zero-day is an exploit that takes advantage of a security flaw in software that is unknown to the code's developer. Software companies may make public a bulletin or security advisory when the exploit becomes known. However, their ability to offer a solution or "patch" may not be available until sometime in the future. The term *zero-day* refers to the moment or day that the vulnerability becomes known.

Zero-day exploits are rare. Only a dozen may surface during a single year. The Stuxnet worm contained four exploits. A malware program this highly developed might attract a price of approximately $500,000 on the black market, according to the producers of the documentary film *Zero Days*.

As the delicate, finely tuned instruments spun uncontrollably from sixty-three thousand RPMs to eighty thousand RPMs, vibrations damaged equipment. The system then lowered the rate to two RPMs, causing further deterioration. While this was occurring, the control center was reporting that all systems were operating normally.

Although the vast majority of incidents are concentrated in Iran, Stuxnet first surfaced in Belarus in 2010 and is believed to have spread throughout the world. According to the cybersecurity firm Symantec, it may have spawned a trend and been the precursor of other malware attacks known as Duqu, Shamoon/Disttrack, and Night Dragon.[43] Both Russia and China have versions of the worm, and Iran may not have been its only victim. Since its release, there has been an increase of attacks on U.S. banks, American energy companies in the Middle East, and the Saudi oil company Aramco. Infections resulted in a range of effects, from distributed denial-of-service (DDS) attacks to an unexplained pipeline explosion.

Generally, security in legacy systems still depends on what is known as commercial off-the-shelf (COTS) components. These products serve as "patches," rather than holistic solutions. Enterprise OT departments avoid the cost and delays of an overall system upgrade by using COTS. Their installation requires no extended period of suspended services. The downside, however, is a less tenable framework medley of patch updates. Rather than an integrated, whole-cloth design, such repairs weaken system integrity. A common fear is when industrial controllers and SCADA software systems are replaced and updated, hardware may be compromised.[44] The use of COTS may even violate manufacturer certification.[45] Additionally, COTS under certain conditions could open the operator up to litigation. In summary, patched SCADA systems may be more cost effective in the short term than whole-cloth solutions, but come with perils. They also are an additional risk factor for critical infrastructure facilities, turning them into attractive targets for malicious hackers, criminals, or potential terrorist agents looking to exploit security gaps. Their vulnerability, criticality to infrastructure and defense operations, and the general awareness of the lack of security used in their design and support can open them up as tempting exposures for any state or nonstate actor.[46]

The Internet of Things (IoT)

A White House press release in 2015 describes the Internet of Things as "a ubiquitous network of connected devices, smart sensors, and big data analytics."[47] However, as with the term *cyber*, there is no recognized standard definition for the term *Internet of Things*. Yet its economic impact over the next decade will be measured in trillions of dollars. For consumers and enterprises, IoT remains, by and large, invisible. Nevertheless, billions of tiny data pipes from a multitude of devices, from the common to the extraordinary, infiltrate our world owing to the vastness and density of these networks of devices. Also known as **ubiquitous computing**, IoT has been used to describe the full universe of devices that, combined together in the near future, will drastically modify the way our societies function. It represents a paradigm shift from networked laptops and desktops toward a paradigm of networked objects sensing their environments and communicating what they see among themselves.

Smart TVs, health monitoring systems, home appliances, thermostats, and NASA hard drives sitting on home and business networks are all part of a network of "things" that communicate with computers and other objects through the Internet. Virtually any object that uses remote control or remote data collection falls within the panoply of IoT. This is more than an extension of the Internet to mobile and other devices, as it could include independent systems that operate on their own infrastructure and have only partial reliance on the Internet. These objects, from books to cars, from electrical appliances to food, create the Internet of things. These objects may have their own IPv6 addresses (discussed below) or be embedded in complex systems and use sensors to obtain information from their environments (such as food products that record the temperature along the supply chain). As in other fields, the trend of the Internet is of an ecology that is becoming more fragmented while at the same time more closed.

The Internet of Things is an opportunity and a challenge. A quick scan of the potential number of sensors embedded in everything from Fitbits to smart cars, and you reach a trillion sensors with reservoirs of information to be mined. No more secrets due to the distribution of data that has not been captured in the past. Now data is flowing out of objects. For example, your "dumb" oven is currently being used but is not recording and distributing data about the use. A smart oven would have a data link between the cook and the oven so that the cook can monitor from a wireless device what the temperature is in the oven in real time to create efficiency in the cooking process. That data, now collected, could be distributed back to the oven manufacturer to solicit information about oven performance. With lots of data links containing information that was previously digitized and automatically sent between machines and between humans, several issues arise.

For instance, how does our relationship with data change? We have had too much data coming at us for a generation. How do we find the most important thing? What if an adversarial actor were to turn the spigot off in order to deny access to vital information? What if the same actor chose to flood the system with false data? For national security concerns, the issue becomes a grave problem if that data is the most important fact for protecting the country. If this becomes the case, then data is a weapon and perception war is a weapon in itself.

Cloud Computing

The National Institute of Standards and Technology (NIST) has defined cloud computing as a model for "enabling ubiquitous, convenient, on-demand network access to a shared pool of configurable computing resources (e.g., networks, servers, storage, applications, and services) that can be rapidly provisioned and released with minimal management effort or service provider interaction."[48] Put more briefly, cloud computing is access from remote terminals to shared software or data.

Cloud computing and IoT, though separate technologies, are becoming more integrated.[49] However, IoT is becoming so systemic that it is outgrowing the transport apparatus it travels and the databases it accesses. This fact, combined with an increasing trend within the commercial sector of locating many independent services on one physical host, is forcing further research and development.

The paradigm, from an operational perspective, allows for a greater tolerance to operate resiliently in a contested environment, enabling a system to transparently continue operation in the face of one or more faults that would otherwise cause the system to fail. Highly resilient systems are ones that could restart quickly and restore data. In a virtual environment, a sensor will be able to detect a virtualized machine's failure and conduct a replacement of the virtual machine with a duplicate backup based on the snapshot of a trusted virtualized environment. All of the data that had not been backed up within the trust configuration would be lost, but system functionality would be restored.

One might argue that centralizing management of virtual assets may lead to an increased risk of a single point of failure that would not have existed before. Yet the virtualized environment can also enable a protected environment for deploying security services. This would enhance efforts to mitigate the risk of rootkits and social engineering attacks. However, there are still problems of the virtual machine understanding of how to detect whether or not a guest application is behaving in an anomalous manner. Thus, the potential for false positives will persist.

Virtualization also makes installation operations and managing instances of a specific operating system configuration under one authority easier. This lends itself to automating the installation of the same operating system across several virtual machines. Such massive deployments create software monocultures that could facilitate the spread of malicious software, but also creates a uniform ecosystem that would make deploying patches to vulnerabilities more efficient and effective.

Lastly, among other issues connected with the explosive growth of IoT is the matter of **latency**. Latency is the term to describe the time it takes for the data to be transferred from the device or sensor to the remote public cloud. The sluggish rate of broadband deployment in comparison to the growth of IoT is creating bottlenecks. Latency, therefore, continues to be an issue and prevents full functional synthesis between the two technologies.

Nevertheless, our energy grids, transportation infrastructure, manufacturing facilities, Fitbits, and automobiles connect to an integrated system of appliances, machines, and equipment that essentially share and analyze data. The future, some predict, may be one where cyberspace and human space will merge. The consequence could be a scenario in which cultural and societal norms are transformed.[50] We are in the middle of a paradigm shift from networked laptops and desktops toward a new pattern of networked objects sensing their environments and communicating what they see among themselves.[51] Aside from the boon to our quality of life, it also intensifies our dependence on IT/OT technology and opens us up to an environment of increased vulnerability. Signs of the new technological era and the new risks to security are beginning to appear.

At the same time, this trend essentially creates a difficult operating environment for the United States in that, if effectively deployed by extremist organizations, secure virtualized environments combined with ad hoc pseudo-DNS systems will become hard to penetrate and possibly be invisible unless invited to the network. Countering this should be a top technical priority for the computer science field.

A Two-Edged Sword

Various examples of how these risks can seep into our daily routines are both self-evident and quite subtle. In 2010, researchers demonstrated that they could directly control the locks, brakes, and engine of an automobile by connecting a computer into the onboard diagnostics ports of the automobile. They successfully bypassed the independent driver and automated controls that operate the vehicle. They later proved that they could take control wirelessly through cellular radio, Bluetooth, audio compact-disc players, navigation systems, and emergency communications. There is no documentation or studies on the number of auto accidents that have been caused by cyberattacks. However, the average luxury car has up to 100 computers and at least seven networks controlling everything from entertainment to performance and location detection.[52] Considering their frequency and what is known to be technically feasible, the threat of a car accident as a violent crime or assassination attempt rather than an unintended collision can be deemed within the realm of possibility instead of a mere unfortunate coincidence.[53]

Consider also personal health and health-care system threats. Thanks to breakthroughs in telemedicine, doctors can assess our physical well-being by checking our blood chemistry with implanted chips and pills that monitor how we are responding to treatment. Pacemakers also offer reads on our health status. Unsettlingly, in 2008, researchers demonstrated that implantable cardioverter defibrillators and pacemakers with electronic circuits theoretically could be accessed wirelessly. Not only can hackers acquire personal health information,

| Box 1.4 | **Brief Examples of Cyberattacks on Public Services** |

- In March 1997, a teenager in Worcester, Massachusetts, used Internet access to disable control systems at the local airport control tower.
- Over three months in 2000, a former worker on a sewage control system in Queensland, Australia, hacked into the system and released more than 264,000 liters of raw sewage at different locations, polluting the environment.
- In August 2006, two striking traffic engineers logged into a road traffic management center using their manager's identity and caused gridlock at an airport, a freeway ramp, and other key intersections.
- In January 2008, in Łódź, Poland, a fourteen-year-old boy rewired a television remote control to control wireless switch junctions on the city's tram system. His actions caused the derailment of four trams, resulting in minor injuries to more than a dozen passengers.

but the experiment revealed that they could also reprogram the device to deliver a deadly 830-volt shock within a range of twelve meters.[54] Similarly, blood chemistry results might be manipulated the same way unless data traveled along a closed circuit with an air gap that hackers could not leap.

The 2015 announcement of President Obama's Smart Cities Initiative is another indicator of how technology impacts and interacts with a changing society. While revolutionary trends in technology continue, a mass global migration on a scale never before known is also currently taking place. More than 50 percent of people worldwide are living in cities and that number is on track to increase to 70 percent by 2050. To address these changing patterns, the Obama administration declared plans to fund grants and investment for urban infrastructure development, which will "continuously improve the collection, aggregation, and use of data." Through research collaboration, investment in low-cost sensor technology, and even the creation of "living labs," the government's plan is to harness emerging technology in order to address a set of challenges, which range from improving the delivery of municipal services to managing the effects of climate change. The emerging vision is for an entirely new infrastructure and technological paradigm that will enable the monitoring and management of traffic, emergency responses, electricity, utilities, repairs, and "other myriad but minute optimization tasks that make a city run more efficiently."[55] An additional challenge, however, is how to implement cybersecurity with the new onslaught of information to be acquired, processed, and transmitted as we undergo and manage this paradigm shift.

The complexity of networks and the need for additional automated functions complicate the security element for IoT. Additionally, the interconnectivity of IoT devices also provides an expanded world of entry points for malicious actors to potentially exploit. Access to databases, remote meters and sensor devices, surveillance cameras, and restricted areas presents a world replete with risks of compromise and intrusion for critical infrastructure and private networks. The control of smart objects would allow hackers to launch cyberattacks to commit data and intellectual property theft, conduct espionage operations, and inflict physical damage. Stuxnet showed that smart objects and systems can be hacked even if they are not connected to the Internet and that no air gap is completely impenetrable.

IoT is two edged. On the one hand the implications for it to improve our quality of life are far ranging and full of possibility. But so is its potential to make more unsafe our efforts to manage our health care, conduct business, facilitate communication, operate transportation systems, and secure the homeland. The complexities of these systems leave them susceptible to malfunction and sabotage.[56] As our dependency grows and this next generation of the Internet becomes more ubiquitous, so does the exposure to risk as breach points and application flaws populate systems. In order to protect our privacy and assure our safety, the future Internet will require new state-of-the-art norms and collaboration among stakeholders.

The Next-Generation Internet (IPv6)

This lurch into the future comes with a tectonic shift in the cyberworld—from its crust to the core. It also comes with a price for extant Internet technology. Any "thing" or device of IoT has a chip that gives that object a unique identifier and connectivity to the Internet. The growth of these "smart devices" will be epidemic and exponential. Internet traffic will accelerate because of the uncontrollable demand for these objects, and as it spreads these smart devices continually consume IP (Internet Protocol) space. The lack of available addresses and the restricted availability of wireless and high-speed connections strains the system. Consequently, the growth of the Internet from a small government project to a global experience requires the next leap in technological evolution.

First deployed in the spring of 1978, Internet Protocol version 4 (IPv4) has been the underlying protocol that allows computers to internetwork. IPv4 is now reaching its limit. It accommodates 4.2 billion unique addresses while the population of the earth is currently 7.3 billion and growing.[57] Present data suggests that more than twenty-five billion IoT objects will be in use by 2020, and possibly fifty billion by 2050.[58] The saturation point is at hand, and the move to the next generation Internet is as well.

Indications of the obvious constraints appeared early during the "dot.com" boom. Realizing that the future of the Internet was at stake in the mid-1990s, the Internet Engineering Task Force (IETF) undertook an effort to engineer a new version of the Internet Protocol to assure that the rapid explosion of Internet growth would not outpace the availability of IP addresses. The new protocol adjusts for a monstrous increase in the number IP addresses. The empyrean standards of IPv6 will allow for over 10^{38} addresses—more than a trillion trillion per person.[59] Precisely, the new address range number is 340,282, 366,920,938,463,463,374,607,431,768,211,456.[60]

Available since 1999 and officially launched in 2012, IPv6 is no longer hypothetical—nor is the transition from IPv4. Today's Internet is already in the process of conversion. Once the shift is complete, it will be the first time in the Internet's history that the underlying protocol (TCP/IP) will have changed. The impact of this transition will affect U.S. and global commerce and security for the next twenty to fifty years.[61]

Outside the United States, the transferral has begun and has been gathering momentum. In August 2012, the European Internet registry exhausted its supply of addresses, resulting in the European Internet registry only giving carriers IPv6 addresses.[62] In April 2011, the Asia-Pacific region was no longer able to meet IPv4 demand, and IPv6 became mandatory for building new Internet networks and services as the final IPv4 spaces are rationed out to the Asia Pacific Network Information Centre (APNIC).[63]

The United States is at a disadvantage for transition. Because we pioneered the Internet, we own legacy technology that is IPv4. Thus, the cost of transitioning is higher than for most other countries that do not have this legacy infrastructure and can migrate directly to IPv6-compatible infrastructure without dual-stacking during the transition period and then shutting off IPv4 (a dual-stack device is a device with network interfaces that can originate and understand both IPv4 and IPv6 packets). Security issues and availability of replacement applications and other system resources also inhibit the conversion process in the United States.

Meanwhile, IPv6 transition is strongest in the Asia-Pacific region given that its IPv4 allocation expired in 2012. In fact, the China Education and Research Network is the largest IPv6 network in the world. The Asia-Pacific region now effectively becomes the first IPv6-enabled region. Hence, there is a greater operational understanding of how IPv6 implementations operate in the wild outside the United States.[64] At the present time, the adaption rate in the United States is approximately 20 percent.[65] However, the conversion has been sporadic and uneven. Some reports hint that it may have plateaued, raising doubts about whether the adaption rate will be sufficient to accommodate the anticipated growth of IoT.[66]

As mentioned above, a contributing inhibitor is the lag time between the growth of IoT and the expansion of high-speed Internet and advanced telecommunication services. The deployment of IPv6 and its massive address space, in conjunction with the convergence of industrial sensing systems with the Internet, is also driving the third major change in the cyber landscape: the intensification in the use of broadband mobile devices. While urban centers and their surrounding areas are well networked, rural locales lack infrastructure. They also lack the economic incentive for private sector investment. Low-density population rates and the high cost of wiring an expansive geographic area limit development. While commercial enterprises dither, government programs are not yet in place to adequately fill all needs.[67] The result is a supply-demand gap that slows the infrastructure build-out.

The lag time for upgrading to IPv6 also inhibits the process of creating a more secure cyber environment by delaying the incorporation of "traceback" mechanisms, which would reconstruct the path from the source of traffic and across intermediate locations to the final destination. Technologists submit that with IPv6 there is the opportunity to map logical addresses to their physical counterparts.[68] The advancement would go a long way in helping to address attribution issues and to bake in a deterrent against advanced persistent threat and other cyberattacks.

As IoT continues to expand, the risk of exploitation and opportunities for cybercrime grows as well. In some cases, particularly in underdeveloped countries where security regimes are weaker, broadband carries a natural exposure for cybercrime. On the other hand, industrial nations have more sophisticated cyber defenses but are much richer target environments. They attract more sophisticated hackers and are also the focus of espionage efforts. The growth of IoT is especially problematic, because devices are small and are designed to be disposable. Therefore, they have limited capacity for software updates. If a device cannot be updated securely and in a timely way, it is at risk of being compromised. An exploitation can spread across a network and infect any hardware and software that comes within contact.

BYOD—bring your own device—refers to the organization policy of allowing employees to bring personally owned mobile devices such as laptops, tablets, and smart phones to their workplace. In using those devices to access privileged company information and applications, employers benefit from higher productivity rates and cost savings. Employees, in turn, enjoy the benefits of convenience. However, the security concerns are obvious. Information systems become subject to the possibility of unauthorized use and mal-intent as interconnectivity opens up other parts of the network and potential breach points to determined hackers.[69] The cost to organizations can be critical and also hard to detect. Without any sort of governance or recognized agreement over the application of standards and best practice norms concerning IoT, the situation will remain perilously static.[70]

Cybersecurity

Estimating the cost of cybercrime is difficult. Experts at Sandia Laboratories describe the loss valuation of cyber threat as "immature." The domain of cyber threats is "nebulous," the report further asserts, and one that "tends to resist easy measurement, and in some cases, appears to defy measurement."[71] Its impact on economic activity is gauged in various ways. In order to comprehend its full effect, it must be computed in terms other than simply hard dollars due to cyberfraud or monetary theft. There are collateral, long-term social effects as well.

Cybercriminals can secure inside information on business plans, merger and acquisition strategies, unpublished reports, or other sensitive data that could impact a company's stock prices or bottom line. Once in possession of this information, criminals can take advantage of the market through illegal inside or arbitrage trading (simultaneously purchasing and selling securities in separate exchanges and profiting from unequal prices). These manipulations are difficult to detect and even harder to prosecute, often because of their complexity and the legal restraints of extraterritorial jurisdiction. Stockholders and businesses suffer financially, and national economies can be affected when their exchanges are exposed to loss of reputation and loss of investor confidence. Melissa Hathaway cites a 2011 study which claims that "the Group of Twenty (G20) economies have lost 2.5 million jobs to counterfeiting and piracy and that governments and consumers lose 125 billion USD annually, including losses in tax revenue."[72]

Cybercrime also impacts economies by redistributing assets away from core business activities by forcing enterprises to reallocate funds to security. In this way cybercrime shifts employment toward jobs of lesser value. Opportunity costs also occur when enterprise budgets divert funds away from research and development or pursue other lines of business in order to earn and protect shorter-term profits. The result is a slower rate of innovation and lesser returns on investment.[73] Stolen intellectual property can also completely destroy companies and ruin careers. Nortel Networks was the victim of cybercrimes for years. The firm once was a global leader in the telecommunications industry and one of the biggest employers in Canada in the late 1990s. Sadly, as a result of cyber corporate espionage (presumed to have been China), the vast majority of its one hundred thousand–plus workforce departed, and the company was forced into bankruptcy in 2007.

According to a 2014 study sponsored by the cybersecurity firm McAfee and the Center for Strategic and International Studies (CSIS), cybercrime exacts between 15 and 20 percent of the value of economic activity created by the Internet. By those estimates, the cost to the global economy is anywhere between $400 billion and $575 billion per year.[74] In the cyber environment the advantage is to the attacker. Rewards can be high while the risk of detection and prosecution is low. The opposite correlation is true for the victim. Meanwhile, the cyber threats to society are outpacing our defenses.[75]

Furthermore, enterprises may not detect an attack or their vulnerability at the time of an infiltration. They often only become aware once the damage has been done, which could be several years later and usually through a third party. Frequently, because of manpower and technical skills deficits, cybercrime goes on undetected and with no ill consequences for the perpetrator. Once the loss of a market or competitive advantage occurs, it may also be too late to react. Another problem for estimating and combating cybercrime is underreporting. Reports are obviously lacking when victims are unaware of electronic intrusions. Deliberate intent is another factor in underreporting. When cybercrimes do surface, there are incentives for the injured party to keep these incidents out of the public realm. The consequences for a victimized organization can be dismaying. The fear of negative publicity is always a concern for private sector enterprises as well as public offices and organizations. In the case of a security breach of a business firm, the incident can open an organization to lawsuits and adverse market impact.

Public disclosure of a security failure can also be a signal to attackers that vulnerabilities exist and an organization may be ripe for exploitation. With these circumstances also come fears of job loss and the demise of reputations. In weighing the costs and impact of reporting such incidents, it is easy to understand why many organizations opt to remain silent about their situation rather than draw public attention. Additionally, the allocation of time and resources, as well as the poor record of prosecution, creates further disincentive to report such offenses. The era of cybercrime has created a new set of legal problems and issues. Theft infers possession, which is a difficult, delicate, and more complicated argument when the property is intellectual rather than tangible. Furthermore, the information disclosed during the process of cross-examination can run the risk of being as damaging to the plaintiff's self-interest as the original crime. The outlook for controlling cybercrime and the adverse "incentive equation" may be summed up by a passage in the McAfee/CSIS report:

> As people, businesses, and governments become more reliant on computer networks and devices, as more economic value is digitized and stored on networks, as manufacturing capabilities increase around the world, losses from cybercrime will grow if there is no improvement in international cooperation.

Overview of the Attack Matrix

The Cyber Emergency Response Team (CERT) describes a cyber threat as an attempt by persons "[to gain] unauthorized access to a control system device and/or network using a data communications pathway. This access can be directed from within an organization by trusted users or from remote locations by unknown persons using the Internet. Threats to control systems can come from numerous sources, including hostile governments, terrorist groups, disgruntled employees, and malicious intruders."[76]

CERT (also known as CSIRT—Computer Security Incident Response Team) refers to groups of computer experts who handle computer security incidents. CERT's inception originated with the early appearance of self-replicating computer worms. (The first "team" was formed in 1988 in reaction to the Morris Worm—named after its author, Robert Tappan Morris, a Cornell graduate student.) Around the world, more than 250 organizations using the name CERT or CSIRT focus on cybersecurity threat issues and response. US-CERT acts independently of these organizations yet maintains relationships for information-sharing and coordination purposes (see table 1.1).

US-CERT works with its partners to control the abuse and misuse of technology across cyberspace. Those partners include private sector cybersecurity vendors, academia, federal agencies, Information Sharing and Analysis Centers (ISACs), state and local governments, and domestic and international organizations. Its network of participating individuals and organizations represents how deep and expansile the threat is.

Nation-states are far less numerous than private actors. Although their capacity and strategic purpose exceed most others, they are much less active compared to nonstate actors. Verizon Enterprise Solutions discovered that of more than six hundred breaches that occurred in twenty-seven countries in 2012, more than 75 percent could be sourced to someone in an identifiable country. Of those attacks, only 19 percent of data breaches were attributed to state-affiliated

TABLE 1.1	Cyber Incidents Involving American Cyber Infrastructure as Reported to the U.S. Computer Emergency Readiness Team	

Year	Incidents
2006	5,503
2007	11,911
2008	16,843
2009	29,999
2010	41,776
2011	42,854
2012	48,562

Source: U.S. Government Accountability Office, "Attack Sources," 2013.

actors. Brazil, Colombia, Germany, Armenia, and the Netherlands were each the source of about 1 percent of breaches. Russia at 5 percent, Bulgaria at 7 percent, Romania at 28 percent, and China at 30 percent rounded out another 70 percent of detected intrusions. The United States accounted for 18 percent of the total.[77] Altogether, forty countries formed the list of active states that targeted the United States.

Most of the attacks were financially motivated, except the Chinese-sourced breaches, which were almost all espionage. Chinese sources accounted for 96 percent of all espionage cases in the data set.[78] In recent years, U.S. officials referred to **advanced persistent threats** (APTs) as code for national threats in general, and Chinese threats in particular.

Unofficially, some U.S. officials have stated that about 140 foreign intelligence and security services target the United States. Fifty are estimated to have serious capacity to harm the United States, and five or six are severe threats.[79] The commonly identified national cyber threats are China, Russia, Israel, Iran, North Korea, and France. These sources are not necessarily official; they could be private activists, private actors with official support, or disguised official actors. Due to globalization, the lines between state and nonstate actors have become blurred. This ambiguity clouds attempts to establish attribution and formulate appropriate responses. For example, the CSIS/McAfee report claims European sources maintain "20 to 30 cybercrime groups in the former Soviet Union that have 'nation-state level' capacity." This means that such groups not only have the requisite resources and skilled staff to conduct a high-impact event; they also have repeatedly shown that they can overcome almost any cyber defense. Making matters even more Byzantine, their affiliation with official Russia, the Russian Federation, is conveniently veiled. The report further asserts that "financial crime in cyberspace now occurs at industrial scale."[80]

Ultimately, most cyberattack sources are not affiliated with any state and act privately. Fewer than ten of the nearly two hundred sovereign governments in the world are commonly cited as having most of the capacity or intent for cyberattacks. These operations are usually under the authority of intelligence or military agencies—designated by the U.S. government as either foreign intelligence services (FISs) and/or foreign intelligence and security services (FISSs).

Yet it is important to note that as national borders become blurred by the imperatives of global commerce and manipulated by the lure of transnational crime, so do the roles of state and nonstate actors become complex and transformative. The dependence on interlocking networks for commerce, financial services, communications, utility grids, government, and military logistical needs puts all countries at risk. Without some form of global governance that establishes the scope of legitimate responses to cyberattacks and norms about the use of cyberweapons, the grand hope of a vast public good will diminish.[81] Undermining that hope is the prospect of a post–Cold War remilitarization. Many believe it is a likelihood, which has earnestly and irrevocably begun.

For-profit criminals account for approximately 75 percent of cyberattacks.[82] Of that category, as much as 80 percent of digital crime involves some form of organized activity.[83] Other estimates claim the percentage is as high as 90 percent.[84] These acts include computer-related fraud, forgery, and identity offenses. Although the definitions of *cybercrime* and *organized crime* impact these numbers, the involvement of some sort of organized effort continues to drive activity.[85] The size of these groups may range from small criminal units to loose ad hoc networks or organized crime that operates on a larger scale. Regardless of their size, organized cybercrime is an expanding global phenomenon.

On the whole, transnational organized crime (TOC) benefits from globalization and technology much the way global businesses do. Access to technological innovation and the formation of global goods and financial markets have offered opportunities to criminal organizations. Exploiting markets, taking advantage of capital and exchange rate spreads, and moving funds and personnel are not limited to the world of licit business. In cybercrime, TOC finds another field of operations to exploit. What is more, criminals do not need complex skills, formal education, or training to ply their craft in this area.

Organized crime is aided by an accelerated and robust black market that facilitates cybercrime growth and allows for a vibrant exchange of sophisticated and new exploitable technologies. Malware tool kits, or exploit kits, are available online. These packets offer capabilities to nontechnical types who are looking to deliver a malware payload and control an infected system remotely. They often include user-friendly web interfaces for creating Internet platforms for future exploitation.[86]

The cyber black market is responsible for a cycle of malware creation that includes a niche for zero-days. As mentioned earlier, there already is an established market and going price for Stuxnet products. Computer infection, harvesting of personal and financial data, data sale, and "cashing out" of financial information are all part of the manufacturing and service economy that drives its expansion. Additionally, as players/customers tend to be extremely specialized, they can find products and "consultants" that customize "solutions" to the demands of the criminal market.[87] Many experts expect the underground market to continue to grow and even become more relevant as it adapts to changing demands, continues to mature, and even spurs innovation.[88]

A common instrument for crime is the **botnet**. Botnets, short for "robot networks," are large numbers of computers infected to perform automated tasks to attack other networks with spam, denial-of-service commands, viruses, and other forms of malware. They are often used to attack information systems to steal data. Botnet rentals are popular among criminals. Offered at relatively low cost by benefiting from the turnover from one group or individual to another, a server with stored malware, exploit kits, or botnet components costs anywhere from $80 to $200 a month.[89] The return on this investment can be within the range of tens of thousands to tens of millions of dollars.

The largest cybertheft involved an attack on more than 100 banks and other financial institutions. The thefts began in late 2013 and were not revealed until February 2015. Over the span of two years and across thirty nations, hackers penetrated systems and transferred money digitally. ATMs responded to prompts and dispensed cash. Through a network of accomplices, a slow drip of account leakage occurred undetected as thieves limited the withdrawals to relatively small amounts. However, by the time officials uncovered the operation, a total theft of around $1 billion had taken place.[90]

As the number of connected devices begins to outnumber people and broadband subscriptions approach 70 percent of the world's population by 2017, it is hard to imagine a hyperconnected world not imperiled by an expanding cybercrime threat. In truth, it may be hard to envision any crime without a cyber component. Quoting a United Nations report, "In the hyperconnected world of tomorrow, it will become hard to imagine a 'computer crime,' and perhaps any crime, that does not involve electronic evidence linked with internet protocol (IP) connectivity."[91] Moreover, the threat comes not solely from nation-states and organized crime groups. Disgruntled employees, malicious hackers, and political activists all contribute to a morphing threat matrix.

Insider threats are personnel who are employed, authorized, or granted privileges by an organization but who intentionally or inadvertently harm the organization. Theft and lapse of security compliance result in the loss of a numberless amount in bottom-line dollars and opportunity costs. Current and former employees, consultants, suppliers, contractors, and even business partners all fall within the scope of the insider threat.

Further, information/communication technology has given insiders more capacity to steal data. The explosion of IoT and the growing popularity of "bring your own device" policies facilitates the ease and speed with which employees can move data across multiple programs and applications. Regardless of intent, these technology breakthroughs increase the population of malicious or inattentive insiders with increased access to sensitive information such as pending patents, trade secrets, merger and acquisition plans, and other competitive and market intelligence. The globalization of the economy also contributes to the disorder. Employee turnover results in lax or competing loyalties.[92] Skilled workers and managers frequently cross national borders seeking opportunity and may be influenced by financial gain or sense of patriotism to a home country or activist cause. Lifetime employment is a thing of the past when corporations are global and the workforce is essentially migratory.

A report sponsored by PricewaterhouseCoopers and the Center for Responsible Enterprise and Trade found examples of the cost insiders inflict on companies with high-value trade secrets. They included:

- In 2012, a former employee of a North American automotive company and the employee's spouse were found guilty of stealing trade secrets related to hybrid vehicle technology worth $40 million. The couple intended to sell the information to a Chinese competitor.
- An employee of a large U.S. futures exchange company pleaded guilty in late 2012 to stealing more than ten thousand files containing source code for a proprietary electronic trading platform. Prosecutors estimated the value of these trade secrets at between $50 million and $100 million. The employee said he and two business partners had planned to use this source code to develop their own company.
- In 2011, a former employee of an automotive company was sentenced to seventy months in prison for copying some four thousand documents on the design of engine transmission and electric power supply systems. The employee intended to take these documents to a new job with the China branch of another North American company.

By 2010, some companies had added to employment contracts an agreement that noncompliance would be a dismissible offense (after two or three breaches, say). Nondisclosure agreements (in which the employee promises not to release sensitive information, even after separation) became commonplace in the 1990s.[93]

Insiders could be naturally motivated or enlisted by external actors. They might also be willing accomplices or unwitting abettors. The inadvertent leaker may be a victim of malware and spyware exploits rather than tempted by the lure of bribes. The incident record suggests that the causes are divided evenly. The US-CERT noted the increasing role of external actors in insider threats after finding that half of insider threats from 2003 to 2007 in the United States had been recruited by outsiders, including organized criminals and foreign governments. New mergers and acquisitions also increase the chance of insider threats.[94] A Verizon report confirmed similar data in 2015.[95]

Bradley Manning may have summed up the problem of insider threat with his correspondence to an online hacker who eventually betrayed him: "Weak servers, weak logging, weak physical security, weak counter-intelligence, inattentive signal analysis . . . a perfect storm."[96] Before his arrest by the FBI, Manning, who was a private in the U.S. Army working as an intelligence analyst in Iraq, stole more than 260,000 U.S. diplomatic cables and more than 500,000 military reports about or from Iraq and Afghanistan. It was the largest amount of restricted data ever leaked from one source.

Economic relations and notions of governance have felt the pressures of globalization and the breakneck speed of technological advancement. While technology hurls populations, cultures, and institutions headlong into the information age, in many ways we are still organized to fight industrial age conflicts. Knowledge of and familiarity with the new battle landscape that takes form in cyberspace is always evolving. The battle terrain is blurred, the weaponry is in a constant state of upgrade, and the enemy is indistinct and ubiquitous. The rivalry is among states, tribes, crime organizations, corporate interests, religious and political sects, and even allies. Sometimes it also includes neighbors and co-workers.

The cyber landscape of town squares, Main Streets, dark alleys, secret corridors, and open battlefields referred to earlier is not a static environment. It is dynamic, and instability is an accepted condition—for now. As the metaphor implies, cyber conflict ensnarls many actors, on varying levels, and in many ways. Finally, because the United States is so target rich, the establishment of order may require new partnerships between the public and its government, a rewriting of legal codes, and new mechanisms for mobilizing society.

Key Terms

electromagnetic spectrum	ubiquitous computing
infrastructure layer	latency
logical layer	BYOD
application layer	advanced persistent threat
content layer	botnet
zero-day exploit	insider threat

Notes

[1] Timothy L. Thomas, "The Internet in China: Civilian and Military Uses," *Information & Security: An International Journal* 7 (2001).

[2] http://www.popsci.com/scitech/article/2009-04/hackers-china-syndrome.

[3] http://www.foxnews.com/story/2001/05/01/it-all-out-cyber-war-as-us-hackers-fight-back-at-china.html.

[4] Thomas.

[5] Ibid.

[6] P. W. Singer and Allan Freidman, *Cybersecurity and Cyberwar* (New York: Oxford University Press, 2014).

[7] Thomas.

[8] Mark Drapeau and Linton Wells II, "Social Software and National Security: An Initial Net Assessment," Center for Technology and National Security Policy, National Defense University, April 2009.

[9] Christopher Paul, "Winning Every Battle but Losing the War against Terrorists and Insurgents," in *The Long Shadow of 9/11: America's Response to Terrorism* (Santa Monica, CA: Rand Corporation, 2011).

[10] http://blog.oup.com/2015/03/cyber-word-origins.

[11] Singer.

[12] Panayotis Yannakogeorgos, 2009, www.jcs.mil/Portals/36/Documents/Doctrine/pubs/jp3_0_20170117.pdf .

[13] Bruce Newsome and Jack Jarmon, *A Practical Introduction to Homeland Security and Emergency Management from Home to Abroad* (Los Angeles: Sage Publications/CQ Press, 2015).

[14] Panayotis A. Yannakogeorgos and John P. Geis II, *The Human Side of Cyber Conflict: Organizing, Training, and Equipping the Air Force Cyber Workforce* (Maxwell AFB, AL: Air University Press, 2016).

[15] Tim Berners-Lee, "Linked Data," http://www.w3.org/DesignIssues/LinkedData.

[16] Nigel Shadbolt, Wendy Hall, and Tim Berners-Lee, "The Semantic Web Revisited," *IEEE Intelligent Systems*, May/June 2006, 96–101.

[17] Newsome.

[18] http://www.darpa.mil/about-us/timeline/where-the-future-becomes-now.

[19] John Markoff, "The Team That Put the Internet in Orbit," *New York Times*, December 9, 2007.

[20] Jack Jarmon, *The New Era in US National Security* (Lanham, MD: Rowman & Littlefield, 2014).

[21] https://www.nsf.gov/about/history/nsf0050/internet/launch.htm.

[22] Andrew Tannenbaum, *Computer Networks*, 4th ed. (Upper Saddle River, NJ: Prentice Hall PTR, 2003), 56–58.

[23] Markoff.

[24] Tannenbaum.

[25] Sinan Ülgen, *Governing Cyberspace: A Road Map for Transatlantic Leadership* (Carnegie Endowment for International Peace, 2016), 38.

[26] Panayotis A. Yannakogeorgos, "Internet Governance and National Security," *Strategic Studies Quarterly* 6, no. 3 (2012): 102–25.

[27] Internet Corporation for Assigned Names and Numbers, "Internationalized Domain Names," http://www.icann.org/en/resources/idn.

[28] Hedieh Nasheri, *Economic Espionage and Industrial Spying* (Cambridge: Cambridge University Press, 2005), 98.

[29] John Doyle, "Air Force to Elevate Status of Cyberspace Command," *Aerospace Daily & Defense Report*, March 22, 2007.

[30] Global Commission on Internet Governance, Centre for International Governance Innovation, and the Royal Institute for International Affairs, 2016, v.

[31] "Securing Cyberspace for the 44th Presidency," Center for Strategic and International Studies Commission Report, Washington, DC, December 2008.

[32] Jarmon.

[33] Derek R. Harp and Bengt Gregory-Brown, "IT/OT Convergence: Bridging the Divide," nexdefense.com, 2015.

[34] Ibid.

[35] Schneider Electric white paper, March 2012.

[36] "Making the Nation Safer: The Role of Science and Technology in Countering Terrorism," National Research Council of the National Academies, Washington, DC, 2002, 140–41.

[37] Harp.

[38] Ibid.

[39] Robert Martinage, "Toward a New Offset Strategy," Center for Strategic and Budgetary Assessments, 2014, 27.

[40] Bonnie Xia Zhu, "Resilient Control and Intrusion Detection for SCADA Systems," PhD diss., University of California, Berkeley, 2011.

[41] Candid Wueest, "Targeted Attacks against the Energy Sector," Symantec, January 13, 2014.

[42] Edward Turzanski and Lawrence Husick, presentation to the Foreign Policy Research Institute, October 12, 2012.

[43] Ibid.

[44] Larry Husick and E. A. Turzanski, "Why Cyber Pearl Harbor Won't Be Like Pearl Harbor" (presentation to the Foreign Policy Research Institute, Washington, DC, October 2012).

[45] Alvaro A. Cardenas et al., "Challenges for Securing Cyber Physical Systems" (report prepared for the Department of Electrical Engineering and Computer Sciences, University of California, Berkeley, and the Department of Electrical Engineering, Carnegie Mellon University, 2009).

[46] Newsome, 364–65.

47 https://www.whitehouse.gov/the-press-office/2015/09/14/fact-sheet.

48 Peter Mell and Timothy Grance, "The NIST Definition of Cloud Computing" (Washington, DC: National Institute of Standards and Technology, 2011), 2.

49 David Linthicum, "Traditional Cloud Architecture Has Too Much Latency for Many IoT Applications: Welcome to the Edge of the Cloud," Infoworld.com, 2016.

50 Eric A. Fischer, "The Internet of Things: Frequently Asked Questions," Congressional Research Service, October 13, 2015.

51 Yannakogeorgos, 2016.

52 Rick Hutley, "Technologies That Will Change Your World," in *Cyberspace: Malevolent Actors, Criminal Opportunities, and Strategic Competition*, ed. Phil Williams and Dighton Fiddner (Carlisle, PA: Strategic Studies Institute and U.S. Army War College Press, 2016).

53 S. Applegate, "The Dawn of Kinetic Cyber" (paper presented at the 5th International Conference on Cyber Conflict, Tallinn, Estonia, 2013).

54 Newsome.

55 Michael Chi, "Big Data in National Security: Online Resource," Australian Strategic Policy Institute, 2017, 12.

56 Fischer.

57 Ibid.

58 Cisco, "The Zettabyte Era—Trends and Analysis," May 2015.

59 Ibid.

60 Hutley, 80.

61 Panayotis A. Yannakogeorgos, "The Rise of IPv6: Benefits and Costs of Transforming Military Cyberspace," *Air & Space Power Journal* 29, no. 2 (2015): 103.

62 C. D. Marsan, "Europe's Supply of IPv4 Addresses Could Be Exhausted This Month," Network World U.S., 2012.

63 A. Shukla, "Asia Pacific Internet Registry Unable to Meet IPv4 Address Demand," MIS Asia, 2011.

64 Yannakogeorgos, 2015, 103.

65 Akamai, "IPv6 Adoption by Country and Network," State of the Internet, September 16, 2015, https://www.stateoftheinternet.com/trends-visualizations-ipv6-adoption-ipv4-exhaustion-global-heat-map-network-country-growth-data.html.

66 Fischer, 12.

67 Lennard G. Kruger and Angele A. Gilroy, *Broadband Internet Access and the Digital Divide: Federal Assistance Programs*, CRS Report RL30719, 2013.

68 Joshua Gruenspecht, "Cyber Security and Identity," in *Cyber Infrastructure Protection*, vol. 2, ed. Tarek Saadawi, Louis H. Jordan Jr., and Vincent Boudreau (Carlisle, PA: Strategic Studies Institute and U.S. Army War College Press, 2013), 166.

69 Fischer, 15.

70 http://www.mcafee.com/us/resources/reports/rp-economic-impact-cybercrime2.pdf.

71 M. Mateski et al, *Cyber Threat Metrics* (Albuquerque, NM: Sandia National Laboratories, 2012).

72 Newsome, 448.

73 McAfee.com.

74 Ibid.

75 Hathaway *sic* Newsome, 488.

76 https://ics-cert.us-cert.gov/content/cyber-threat-source-description.

77 Verizon Enterprise Solutions, *2013 Data Breach Investigation Report*, 2013, 3.

78 Newsome, 388.

79 Ibid.

80 McAfee, 15.

81 Ülgen, 62–67.

82 Newsome, 380.

83 BAE Systems Detica and London Metropolitan University, "Organized Crime in the Digital Age," 2012.

84 Norton Cybercrime Report, 2011.

85 United Nations Office on Drugs and Crime (UNODC), "Comprehensive Study on Cybercrime," February 2013.

86 https://zeltser.com/what-are-exploit-kits.

87 UNODC.

88 Lillian Ablon, Martin C. Libicki, and Andrea A. Golay, *Markets for Cybercrime Tools and Stolen Data: Hackers' Bazaar* (Santa Monica, CA: RAND Corporation, 2014), 39.

89 Ibid.

90 Kaspersky Lab, "The Great Bank Robbery: Carbanak Cybergang Steals $1bn from 100 Financial Institutions Worldwide," February 16, 2015, http://www.kaspersky.com/about/news/virus/2015/Carbanak-cybergang-steals-1-bn-USD-from-100-financial-institutions-worldwide.

91 UNODC, xxvii.

92 PricewaterhouseCoopers, "Economic Impact of Trade Secret Theft: A Framework for Companies to Safeguard Trade Secrets and Mitigate Potential Threats," 2014.

93 Newsome.

94 Dawn Cappelli, Andrew Moore, Randall Trzeciak, and Timothy J. Shimeall, *Common Sense Guide to Prevention and Detection of Insider Threats*, 3rd. ed. (Carnegie Mellon University, 2009), 6.

95 Verizon Enterprise Solutions, 2015, 46.

96 B. Bennett, "Witnesses in WikiLeaks Case Describe Lax Security," *Los Angeles Times*, December 21, 2011, http://articles.latimes.com/2011/dec/21/nation/la-na-manning-hearing-20111222.

The Mutable Domain 2

What Is Cryptology?

Cryptology has been a science for at least four thousand years. The Egyptians and later Assyrians, Hebrews, Greeks, and Romans all used some form of encryption to secure communication in government and commerce. Codes employed systems of secret symbols, word scrambling, and intaglios (flat stone imprints) to transmit messages in secret. In modern times, cryptology relies on math theory to transfer data. Mathematical algorithms are the core of cryptology. Three types of cryptography algorithms exist: hash functions, private key, and public key.

A **hash function** maps data of arbitrary size to data of fixed size by taking a group of characters and creating a string of numbers or a **"key,"** which is normally smaller than the original string of numbers. Essentially, the contents of a file are processed through a cryptographic algorithm to produce a unique numerical value—the **hash value**—that identifies the contents of the file. Called keys or simply "hashes," these numeric values are commonly used for indexing and rapid data retrieval from databases. The hash value is representative of the original string of characters, but its compressed size makes locating data faster and more efficient. Hashes can also be thought of as fingerprints for files.[1]

Sometimes referred to as one-way encryptions, hash functions can turn text messages into strings of large fixed numbers to verify that input data (the message) maps to a specific hash value. These types of abbreviated hash values are also called **message digests** in encryption terminology. The hash function similarly transforms a **digital signature** into a small block of data that authenticates digital messages or documents. The digital signature and the message digest transmit to the receiver. The message digest and the signature are sent in separate transmissions. The addressee then uses the same hash function to reproduce the message digest and compares it to the one they also derived from the digital signature. If the hash values/keys are the same, it is likely that the message was transmitted without errors and is authentic, because they are linked by the same hash function. The "one-way" prefix to the *one-way encryption* term refers to the fact that it is extremely difficult to invert the large fixed string of numbers back into the text message.

A second type of algorithmic key is called a private or secret key. A **private key** is an encryption/decryption method where the algorithm is known to the parties that exchange the coded message. The communicators share the key so that each is able to encrypt and decrypt messages. Because each trusted party shares the same key, the method is known as symmetric encryption. The security risk is the threat of someone outside the system or exchange loop gaining access to the key.

The solution to the security dilemma of private key schemes took a radical turn in 1976 when two Stanford cryptologists, Whitfield Diffie and Martin Hellman, publish a paper titled "New Directions in Cryptology." Until that time, a fundamental problem of the field involved methods of distributing cryptographic keys. The new solution, which became known as the Diffie-Hellman key exchange, proposed a protocol in which the transfer cannot be seen by observing the communication. This is explained by the fact that rather than sharing information, correspondents are actually creating a key together. This is done by creating two mathematically linked numbers and using them as separate keys—referred to as a private key and a **public key**. The public key in the pair can be shared with everyone; the private key is kept secret. Either of the keys can be used to encrypt a message; the opposite key from the one used to encrypt the message is used for decryption. In other words, what one key encrypts only the other can decrypt. A crude example would be the semi-prime number 15 as the public key, with the private keys being prime number factors (3 × 5), which are used to encrypt/decrypt. In reality, the numbers in the key exchange are very large, and though paired together, they are not identical and hence are asymmetric.

The communication exchange between two correspondents is thus: Each party of a communication has a pair of public and private keys. Each shares their public key with the other while maintaining control of their private key. Only the recipient's private key can decrypt the sender's message, which the sender encrypts with the recipient's public key. If this seems confusing, try thinking of asymmetric cryptography in terms of these five steps:

1. Alice and Bob establish communication by making available their public keys and keeping their private keys secret and secure.
2. Alice puts a secret (encrypted with Bob's public key) in a box and locks it with a padlock, which is a digital signature she created with her private key.
3. She then ships the box to Bob.
4. Bob receives the box and decrypts the message with his private key that corresponds with his public key, which Alice used to encrypt her message.
5. He then uses Alice's public key to verify her signature (padlock), which she encrypted with her private key.

Hence, Bob can decipher the message and also be assured it came from Alice. To communicate back to Alice, Bob repeats the process. Since the box has always had at least one lock on while in transit, the opportunity to see what's inside and steal the secret does not exist.[2] In cryptographic terms this means that even if someone intercepted and recorded the traffic in order to analyze it later, it would be impossible to decipher the public/private key. Having possession of only one of the keys is not enough information to allow an infiltrator to deduce the value of the complementary key. Despite the fact that exchanges may have been visible, the entire public/private key was never saved, never transmitted, and never itself made visible.

Since the encryption/decryption of public and private keys is interchangeable, the private key also encrypted a digital signature. The shared public key decrypts and verifies the signature, which the recipient generates from the message or document.

How then are the keys, which are large numbers, linked? There are several ways of pairing numbers. In cryptology, the dominant standard is the RSA algorithm. *RSA* stands for the Massachusetts Institute of Technology researchers who created the math scheme, Ron Rivest, Adi Shamir, and Leonard Adleman. A year after Diffie and Hellman published their article, Rivest, Shamir, and Adleman published a piece in *Scientific American* called "A New Kind of Cypher That Would Take a Million Years to Break." The cypher draws its security from the complexity of factoring large whole numbers that are the product of two large prime numbers. These semi-prime numbers, as they are known, are easy to create but almost impossible to factor back to arrive at the original prime numbers. Furthermore, the larger the semi-prime, the more difficult the factoring. The largest prime number known has 17.5 million digits. It is infeasible to determine the original primes of the RSA algorithm owing to the time it takes, even using today's supercomputers. According to James Lyne, global head of security research at the security firm Sophos, "It would take thousands of computers millions of years" to calculate the numbers that could have been multiplied together to form the semi-prime to get back to the original values.[3] For this reason, the RSA algorithm is essentially still the prevailing standard for encryption over the Internet. It is built into many software products, including Netscape Navigator and Microsoft Internet Explorer. The technology is so powerful and resilient that the U.S. government restricts exporting it to foreign countries.[4]

Despite the impressive statistical probability surrounding RSA, the search for more complex integers continues. In fact, RSA may be on the verge of being superseded by alternative approaches to factoring. Elliptic curve cryptology (ECC) is gaining support, with many researchers seeing it as an alternative to RSA. ECC is a public key encryption technique based on elliptic curve theory. Its attraction for many security experts is that it can generate faster, smaller, and more efficient cryptographic keys. The elliptic curve discrete logarithm presents a considerably more challenging code-breaking problem for would-be hackers than factoring. Furthermore, ECC key sizes can be significantly smaller than those required by RSA and yet provide equivalent security with lower computing power and battery resource usage. The result is that ECC becomes a more efficient encryption method for mobile applications.[5] This feature is particularly attractive as we consider the approaching explosion in IoT usage.

The entire arrangement of key exchanges, distribution, and verification is known as the **public key infrastructure** (PKI). The topography of PKI consists of hardware, software, and policies and standards to manage the creation, administration, distribution, and revocation of keys and digital certificates. A digital certificate is sometimes referred to as a public key certificate and is central to PKI. These units of data are in the form of attachments to the electronic message. They confirm the identity of the certificate holder and tie that identity to the public key, which is also contained in the digital certificate. Digital signatures are issued by organizations called CAs. *CA* stands for **"certificate authority"** or "certification authority," which are "trusted third parties" that produce signed digital certificates. VeriSign and DigiCert are examples. In some cases, companies and organizations create their own in-house CAs.

Digital certificates usually contain the owner's public key (used for encrypting messages and digital signatures), the expiration date of the certificate, the owner's name, and other pertinent data about the public key owner. The system relies on CAs to create a trusted chain of information exchange for Internet traffic.

However, while a reliable CA can ensure the security of data traffic, the security of the CA itself is not always a guarantee. In 2011, several CAs were victims of hacks. Hackers compromised user accounts and fraudulently exploited digital signatures. In a noted case, someone (or some entity) stole a Dutch CA's signing keys. The thieves used the keys to intercept Iranian users' access to Google's Gmail. The prime suspect was the U.S. National Security Agency. Within weeks of the discovery, DigiNotar, a privately owned Dutch certificate authority, had its operational management transferred over to the government and shortly thereafter declared bankruptcy.[6] The same year, the Stuxnet operation also used stolen certificates to infiltrate the computer system at Natanz.[7]

Criminals and governments can and have used stolen certificates to launch man-in-the-middle attacks. These techniques intercept or redirect traffic to counterfeit sites as they deceive users into thinking their communication is confidential. Malware imbedded with stolen digital signatures, as was used in Stuxnet, escapes detection by installers and opens systems to manipulation and possible ruin. Malware, or malicious software, varies according to technique, purpose, and sophistication. They are the weapons in the cyber arsenal of information age warfare. Their complexity intensifies and their dispersion advances hourly.

Exploiting the System

As covered in chapter 1, computer networks are dependent on the use of internationally standardized communications protocols (TCP/IP) to send and receive data packets and information. TCP/IP allows for the flow of data packets and information across computer networks, including the Internet. The way machines identify each other on the Internet is through Internet Protocol (IP) and media access control (MAC) addresses. MAC is a hardware address that uniquely identifies each node on a network. Recalling the previous discussion, IP was not intended to function as the backbone of the global project that became the Internet. Designed and deployed for military and research purposes in the late 1960s, the ability to track and trace user behavior in a highly untrustworthy computing environment was not embedded into the design of communications protocols.[8] It is this foundational protocol on which the Internet runs that is too weak to provide reliable security mechanisms.[9] According to Internet expert Tom Leighton, the DNS, ports, and IP address systems are plagued by flaws that "imperil more than individuals and commercial institutions. Secure installations in the government and military can be compromised as well."[10]

Consequently, the current flaws in the network architecture of the Internet are a result of relying on the protocols that were built thirty-five years ago when the Internet was not a global entity but a closed research network. When it did become global, there was no shift to create stronger security mechanisms. To better understand the functioning of TCP/IP, a brief recount and description of how information is sent across networks is necessary.

Data packets are the basic units of network traffic. They are the standard way of dividing information into smaller units when sending information over a network. A significant component of computer networks is the IP header, which contains information pertaining to the source and destination addresses. Machines require these strings of numbers to connect with other computers on the Internet or other networks.[11] All networked hardware must have a valid IP and MAC address to function on the network. Data packets are re-created by the receiving machine based on information within the header of each packet that tells the receiving computer how to re-create the information from the packet data. Without international standards, such as TCP/IP, there would be no assurance that packets could be read by a receiving machine.[12]

Manipulating TCP/IP to spoof identities (when an unknown source sends a communication while disguising itself as a source known to the receiver) has become a norm in cyberspace. In the past, a significant understanding of networking was required to spoof one's IP address. However, over the past fifteen years, there has been a proliferation of tools for the layman to anonymize his Internet activities. "Onion routing" networks (discussed below) are one example that allows for the masking of a data packet's point of origin. Activists may enter the Internet from unsecured WiFi networks or cyber cafés or dial into ISPs across the planet to hide their identity from the prying eyes of government censors. Most malicious actors may propagate zombies to serve as proxies for cyberattack. Actors may spoof IP addresses to inject malicious data into critical infrastructures, commit fraud, or bypass authoritarian censors.

These spoofing attacks are the foundation of the attribution challenge. Masking one's location on the Internet strikes at the root of trust in identity and security in cyberspace. An individual may manipulate various layers of the TCP/IP protocol in order to create a false appearance of a user, device, or website. Given the global nature of the Internet, it is possible for a malicious actor to exploit software vulnerabilities in such a way that makes computers appear is if they are located elsewhere in the world. This technique gives skilled attackers the ability to evade cybercrime investigations. Dorothy Denning aptly points out that in order to "trace an intruder, the investigator must get the cooperation of every system administrator and network service provider on the path."[13] This is the root of the attribution problem, but not an impossible challenge to surmount with the appropriate global policies in place.

> ### Box 2.1   Internet Freedom Program
>
> The **Internet Freedom program** is a program run by the U.S. Department of State's Bureau of Democracy, Human Rights, and Labor. The aim of the program is to promote fundamental freedoms, human rights, and the free flow of online information through collaboration for anti-censorship and secure communications technology, advocacy, digital safety, and research.

While the ability to spoof an individual's or entity's location is a critical element of cybercrime, espionage, and sabotage, tools are currently being developed by the U.S. Department of State that utilize the vulnerability in IP protocol and network design to promote freedom of speech in closed regimes via the Internet. Such efforts complicate the attribution of cyberattacks as people are being actively trained to anonymize their Internet activities. It also inhibits prospects of international cooperation since some closed regimes view breaching of censors as a form of cyberwarfare and thereby withhold information during investigation.

As part of its Internet Freedom Agenda, the State Department in cooperation with Internet companies is distributing tools and running seminars on how to mask identities in cyberspace. While the goal is the free flow of information, the tools and tactics can be used to attack U.S.-based information systems as well. This, unfortunately, does not contribute to a safe cyber ecosystem.

The Onion Router (TOR)

One powerful method for achieving anonymity is the use of technology such as "the Onion Router," a technology first developed by the U.S. Naval Research Laboratory to protect data packets on open networks. The Onion Router system is a distributed anonymous network of proxy servers connected by virtual encrypted tunnels.

In 1995, employees at the U.S. Naval Research Laboratory began work to develop an anonymous network system to shelter and secure online U.S. intelligence communications. The Onion Router system, more commonly referred to as TOR, was first developed by mathematician Paul Syverson and computer scientists Michael G. Reed and David Goldschlag. After turning the project over to DARPA, the venture eventually became operational in 2003. By 2004, the government released the TOR code under a free license, and since 2006, the project has been maintained and developed as a Massachusetts-based 501(c)(3) nonprofit. TOR Project Inc., and its staff of about thirty people, receives financial support from private donors and organizations as well as public sources. Its sponsors include the Bureau of Democracy, Human Rights, and Labor of the U.S. Department of State; DARPA; and the National Science Foundation, to name a few.[14]

The TOR system draws its anonymity from two foundational elements. One is the TOR enabling software, which users can download freely. The other is a network of volunteers who maintain their computers as relays for TOR traffic. Data is encrypted in multiple layers, like an onion, which are peeled away one layer at a time as it passes through a computer, or node, on the TOR network. Across the globe, approximately six thousand computers[15] supported by three thousand volunteers[16] maintain the TOR anonymity system.

A computer linked to a TOR network transmitting data sends the data through a series of randomly selected proxy servers that strip away one layer of encryption along with the IP identification information. As communication snakes along its path, the information is encrypted between relays.[17] The onion servers replace the IP identification information with new IP information and direct it to another proxy server to repeat the same process before connecting to the final server to distribute the information being sent from the point of origin. In this scheme, each relay decrypts a layer of encryption to reveal only the next relay address in the circuit. From that point, the relay passes on to the subsequent node the remaining encrypted data. The final relay, referred to as the "exit relay," decrypts the innermost layer of encryption and sends the data of the original source to its destination without revealing, or even knowing, the source IP address or intermediate addresses. The effect of this is that if someone is observing the network traffic on any of the proxy servers, the observer will not be able to discern the true location of point A, nor will the observer be able to tell what the destination of the data is, unless he or she is observing the final transmission point.

Because the routing of the communication is partly concealed at every hop in the TOR circuit, this method eliminates the possibility of revealing the identity of all communicating peers at any single point. Each node in the path records the preceding node and the immediate destination node, but the other nodes along the path remain concealed. An observer at point B will not know where the data is really coming from, as he will only be able to detect the location of the proxy server from which the data arrived at point B. Hence, no single part of the system can be used to establish traffic links with communication partners. In this way, a network address is masked, and there is no direct link between point A and the final destination of the data packet.

A revision and enhancement to the TOR protocol included untraceable websites hosted on TOR nodes. These sites are only accessible via the TOR network and are known as "TOR hidden services" (THS). Referred to as rendezvous nodes, specific nodes within the network store contact information needed to reach a TOR hidden service site. In addition to acting as intermediary points, they also function as encryption keys in a distributed hash table (DHT) that resolve normal DNS addresses such as .com, .org, .gov, .ca, and .uk to .onion— the TOR hidden services URL address format.[18] The THS protocol has the ability to thwart any third-party effort to investigate or obstruct the traffic. However, for users with fewer privacy concerns, there is a software project called **Tor2web**. Tor2web allows TOR hidden services to be accessed from a standard browser without being connected to the TOR network, but it does not anonymize activity.

Within the TOR network, THS real locations are concealed from each other, making the system more cryptic.[19] There is also no indexing by common search engines such as Google and Yahoo!. Although some directories are found on the "dark web,"[20] there is no central record of all existing THSs, and some THS addresses are not published. (Yet THS search engines such as ahmia.fi are emerging and allow users to identify THS related to specific content.)[21]

Since its beginning as a government research project, the TOR network has grown. Studies estimate that there are about forty-five thousand .onion addresses populating the TOR hidden service on any day.[22] These sites are random and temporary, and therefore no accurate accounting of them exists. Nor are they restricted to lawful activity. According to a study sponsored by the UK Parliament in 2015, "Almost half of them were not accessible at the time of the analysis and about a third linked to sites generated automatically by computers infected with a botnet malware."[23] Criminal activity accounts for almost half the traffic flowing over the THS network. Drugs, weapons, counterfeit products, and illegal pornography are the most common illicit items available for sale.

The black market site Silk Road was the most notorious TOR hidden service. Between February 2011 and July 2013, the site processed over $1.2 billion worth of sales and supported 4,000 vendors and 150,000 customers.[24] After the authorities terminated its operations, others quickly filled its position in the hidden marketplace. Silk Road 2.0 was up and running within one month (although that site was also taken down once authorities uncovered flaws in its computer code). When Silk Road's founder, Ross William Ulbricht (aka Dread Pirate Roberts) was arrested, the cyber black market drew public attention around the world. Successor sites populated the TOR system and began offering vendors such value-added features as feedback metrics from customers. Customer satisfaction ratings included product quality and time-to-delivery scores.[25]

Not all traffic along TOR is malicious. TOR hidden sites also offer a haven for whistleblowers and dissidents. The *New Yorker* magazine maintains a THS known as Strongbox that allows informants to share messages and files anonymously with the publication.[26] Similarly, the *Washington Post*'s SecureDrop and the Hermes Center's GlobalLeaks are tools for journalists to share files while protecting their sources.[27] In another THS example, Italian citizens banded together to form MafiaLeaks. The developers established this site to subvert the Mafia code of silence (omertà) that protects gang members from prosecution. By providing citizens with the means to submit information about Mafia activity anonymously, the site helps to weaken the ability of Italian organized crime to honor their "code" and operate freely.[28]

Nonetheless, despite the extra anonymity offered by the TOR hidden services platform, the vast volume of TOR traffic moves through the surface web. According to TOR Project Inc., over 98 percent of TOR users access the network in order to reach public sites and social media but want or need the anonymity to protect their privacy and maintain free speech.[29] Dissident movements during the Arab Spring and in Iran and China were aided by TOR, which helped to conceal the communications and locations of activists. Both businesses and individuals rely on the TOR protocol to safeguard sensitive information. Firms can shield information on projects and corporate strategies from competitors and spies.

Forums and chat rooms for discussing private issues related to abuse, illness, or crime victimization can use TOR to assure confidentiality among chat group members.[30] Law enforcement agencies have found TOR to be an effective tool for surveillance operations directed at criminal websites. Online and undercover, authorities can track the movements and activities of not only criminal organizations but also terrorist groups. To these ends, TOR Project Inc. works with law enforcement and counterterrorist efforts across the world to develop tools for pursuing and prosecuting perpetrators.

Data on the scope and stripe of the users and usage of anonymous networks such as TOR are sparse and nonspecific. Movements are random, and the sites themselves are evanescent. Consequently, as encryption technology advances, the challenges of attribution remain. Meanwhile, the friction between the imperatives of security and the rights of privacy and freedom of speech also creates tensions. Many private citizens, businesses, government authorities, and media organizations depend on the anonymity of networks like TOR to communicate sensitive information. Unfortunately, so do criminals and terrorists.

TOR, despite the original intentions of the U.S. government, is the primary network for underground illegal marketplaces.[31] The technology to create an anonymity network in order to veil intelligence communications and protect contact between military command-and-control centers and field operations may have extended benefits to law enforcement, commerce, political activism, and advocates of free speech and privacy rights, but it has also facilitated the rise of privately maintained sites that traffic in illegal goods and services. Contraband drugs, weapons, hired assassins, exotic animals, child pornography, stolen or counterfeit documents, etc., can be found either on underground message boards, with prices and contact information, or on sites offering full e-commerce solutions, including purchase/checkout, payment management systems, and escrow services.[32] Moreover, the shadows of the dark web, where TOR users navigate, not only allow criminals, state-sponsored spies, and terrorists to conduct business transactions, but they offer them an opaque platform to participate in untraceable forums to deploy malware and botnet attacks, coordinate operations, and recruit.

The multifaceted implications for anonymizing technology, together with the hidden environment, challenge the imagination of researchers, policy makers, security experts, and even popular culture. Despite the interest and fascination by authorities and the public, progress in policy and legal codes still lags behind the technological advances. The transnationality of these networks and the challenges they create for traditional law enforcement make these anonymity networks problematic. Furthermore, the unindexed environments below the surface web where they maneuver are another frustration for authorities who are more accustomed to conventional investigative and prosecutorial techniques.

TrendMicro studied the private sites available on the TOR system and compiled a table of offerings that can be purchased with a credit card. Table 2.1 gives only a partial list of goods, prices, and addresses. The more antisocial services such as botnet rentals, malware services, weapon purchases, assassinations, and the like are omitted for obvious reasons.

TABLE 2.1 Prices of Various Goods on TOR

Site Name	Address	Type of Good	Cost	Normalized Cost (US$)
CloneCard	http://kpmp444tubeirwan.onion/board/int/src/1368387371226.jpg	EU/U.S. credit cards	1 BTC	US$126
Mister V	http://wd5pd4odd7jmm46.onion	EU credit cards	€40–80	US$54–100
CC-Planet Fullz	http://tr36btffdmdmavbi.onion	EU/U.S. credit cards	UA$40	US$54
CC 4 ALL	http://qhkt6cqo2dfs2llt.onion	EU/U.S. credit cards	€25–35	US$33–47
Cloned credit cards	http://mxdcyv6gjs3tvt5u.onion.products/html	EU/U.S. credit cards	€40	US$54
NDS CC Store	http://4vq45ioqq5cx7u32.onion	EU/U.S. credit cards	US$10	US$10
Carders Planet	http://wihwaoykcdzab.add.onion	EU/U.S. credit cards	US$60–150	US$60–150
HakPal	http://pcdyurvcdiz66wg.onion	PayPal accounts	1 BTC for US$1,000	US$126 for US$1,000
Onion identity	http://abbujjh5vqtq77wg.onion	Fake IDs/passports	€1,000–1,150 (ID) €2,500–4,000 (passport)	US$1,352–1,555 (ID) US$3,380–5,400 (passport)
U.S. citizenship	http://ayjkg6ombrsahbx2.onion/silkroad/home	U.S. citizenship	US$10,000	US$10,000
U.S. fake driver's licenses	http://en35tuzqmn4lofbk.onion	Fake U.S. driver's license	US$200	US$200
U.K. passports	http://vfqnd6mieccqyiit.onion	U.K. passports	£2,500	US$4,000
Guttemberg prints	http://kpmp444tubeirwan.onion/board/int/src/1366833727802.jpg	Counterfeit money	1/2 of the monetary value	1/2 of the monetary value
High-quality euro replicas	http://y3fpieiezy2sin4a.onion	Counterfeit euro banknotes	€500 for 2,500 CEUR €1,000 for 3,000 CEUR €1,900 for 6,000 CEUR	US$676 for 2,500 CEUR US$1,352 for 3,000 CEUR US$2,570 for 6,000 CEUR

Source: TrendMicro.

Attackers, Facilitators, Defenders, and Targets

Responding to any cyber incident requires the ability to answer the following questions within acceptable levels in order to select appropriate responses: Who is the threat agent? What motivated the agent and what were his objectives? What methods and techniques were used? What were the causes of the effect, which services were affected, and what impact did the event have?[33]

Attack agents can be states, substate actors such as Chinese privateer hackers or Romanian computer criminals, regional/global organizations such as the Russian Business Network (believed to be sponsored and supported by the Russian government), and ad hoc networks such as LulzSec or Anonymous. There are also malicious individuals, such as an unreformed Kevin Mitnick (who served five years in prison for various computer-related crimes and now runs a cybersecurity firm) and the proverbial and ever-threatening insider.

While all attack agents within information systems pose a threat, not all attack agents are likely to produce an effect in cyberspace that would pose a threat to national security. An advanced-level attack agent who could mount a complex attack with effects of national significance while taking advantage of Internet ambiguity to stall attribution of the event would require the following capabilities: (1) expert-level programming and cryptographic skills, (2) detailed knowledge of industrial control systems, (3) mastery of multiple open and closed operating systems, and (4) detailed knowledge of telecommunications and legal regimes.

The motivating factors for an attack are also important when gauging the intentions of the attack agent. Identity theft, espionage, zombie propagation, extortion, sabotage, and widespread destruction are common motives. The first four of these often indicate economic incentives, where the perpetrator of an attack judges that an investment of time and other resources would bring about a payoff. The goals and objectives of an attack include the corruption, fabrication, destruction, disclosure, or discovery of information. System subversion or disruption can be additional goals. The methods by which cyber events occur are through system or protocol compromise, resource exhaustion, hardware failure, or software crashes. The techniques used to achieve these objectives include the targeted exploitation of a system, social, or protocol vulnerability. The overload of network or system resources and the autonomous self-propagation of malware are other techniques used. A cyber incident is caused by all of the preceding variables.

Attack incidents range from organized cyberattacks and zombie propagation to uncontrolled malicious code. Cyber events of national significance are those that result in extensive damage to critical infrastructure or key assets.

Targets and effects include human targets for social engineering campaigns that aim to exploit trust relationships among computer users. The 2011 attack on RSA Security (a cybersecurity and computer firm founded by the creators of the RSA algorithm) is only one example in which employees interacted with a malicious e-mail message that gave the attack agents access to RSA's networks. Other targets include critical infrastructures and financial networks. A cyber-related event will produce effects that depend on the perpetrator's motivation for launching an attack. Cyber events can be either discrete and finite events, or they can be advanced and persistent. An example of a discrete and finite event is an operation aiming to degrade the operation of critical infrastructure by attacking a SCADA. Advanced persistent threats (APTs) are those linked with espionage and criminal activities that aim to gain as much information about the functioning of a system as possible and can remain active over time.

Malware

The harmful software we refer to as malware proliferates at an exponential rate around the world. Criminals, state actors, researchers, and hobbyists create malware with malicious intent, for amusement, and sometimes by mistake. At present, nearly one million new releases of malware occur every day. Their functions and targets vary. However, attackers narrow their use to any of three tracks: stealing data, misuse of credentials, and hijacking resources.[34] At risk are a target's competitiveness in war or commerce, the ability to protect civilian or national assets, and the capability to maintain communication with operational branches or the public. As the attack matrix expands and becomes denser, the trend in malicious code is a more silent and deeper design. These upgrades allow attackers to more regularly and remotely control the target's computer in order to launch massive attacks or "exfiltrate" (infiltration and extraction of data) sensitive information from networks.[35]

Although *malware* is a broad term, there are nuances. Malicious code is often considered a separate threat. Malicious code is technically not software but refers to scripts or code designed to create vulnerabilities in computer systems and on websites. These implants exploit unanticipated sequences of multiple, often noncontiguous faults (referred to as byzantine faults) throughout the software.[36] "Infection" may be the result of various methods or pathways. The source might be a USB drive, an e-mail, a link to a malicious online site, or a message in a social network. Once compromised, malware (malicious software) can be uploaded through the entry points. An implanted malicious code can beacon out to a server for commands from inside the system. **Shell code** is the term used to refer to the payload in the exploitation of software. They may also function autonomously by lying dormant until a designated time or a particular system event occurs before activating.

In a world of expanding connections and momentous swelling demand, commercial software becomes more complicated. This transformation not only makes software products more sophisticated and complex, but it also increases the chances of inherent software flaws and vulnerabilities to the hardware. Although only a small fraction of flaws may become actual malware entry points,[37] the spread and stretch of software vulnerabilities in the application layer of computer systems is still an enormous challenge for cybersecurity. Problematic is not only the way we address the problem but also how we even detect and measure it. For benchmarking purposes, a 2005 report by the U.S. National Institute of Standards and Technology estimated that there were twenty flaws for every line of code (LOC).[38] Considering that the Microsoft 2000 operating system contains thirty-five million lines, it is easy to understand the level of vulnerability and fear potential for exploit. However, the flaw per LOC, or defect density, is hard to estimate. More recent evaluations have placed the number below one flaw per LOC.[39]

Yet approximations are elusive despite the progress made to limit defects and improve software reliability. This is because of the changing nature of the threats and the targets. Also, as system administrators reconfigure software to establish different permissions, misconfigurations create a logic gap between design specification and the actual code.[40] Thus, vulnerabilities result from the modified configuration of the software or its execution environment.[41] As Martin Libicki explains,

> Statistics on the inevitability of so many flaws per thousand lines of code suggest that vulnerabilities are nearly infinite (because they may arise through an indefinite combination of bugs). . . . Between what design specifications say a system will do and what the code says it will do lie potential *vulnerabilities*.[42]

Below is a brief list of various categories of malware.

Malware Categories

Computer viruses are the most common form of system infection. They are usually a contagious program or malicious code that attaches itself to another piece of software and then reproduces itself when that software is run. Most often this is spread by sharing software or files between computers. Computer viruses earned their name due to their ability to "infect" multiple files on a computer. They spread to other machines when infected files are sent via e-mail or when carried by users on physical media, such as USB drives.

Bacteria do not carry malicious code. Bacteria replicate and damage device storage reserves by overloading disks and memory capacity. Commonly, bacteria cause denial-of-service attacks (an attempt to make a machine or network resource unavailable to those attempting to reach it) by consuming large volumes of system resources.

Worms are a program that replicates itself and destroys data and files on a computer. Worms can "eat" the system operating files and data files until the drive is empty. Olympic Games (Stuxnet) is an example. Unlike viruses, worms are stand-alone programs. They do not require human help in order to spread and infect: they infect once and then use computer networks to spread to other machines—without the help of users. During transmission, they may also spawn additional malware. By exploiting network vulnerabilities—such as weaknesses in e-mail programs—worms can send out thousands of copies of themselves in the hope of infecting new systems, where the process begins again. Worms simply "eat" system resources, thus reducing performance. Most now contain malicious "payloads" designed to steal or delete files.

Denial-of-service attacks/distributed denial-of-service attacks disable a computer system by taking up a shared resource, leaving none of the resource available for legitimate users. A DDoS (distributed denial-of-service) attack is a variant of a denial-of-service attack that uses a coordinated attack from a distributed system of computers, such as a botnet (see below), rather than a single source.

Adware is the least dangerous and most lucrative malware. Adware displays ads on your computer. One of the most common online nuisances is adware. The programs automatically deliver advertisements to host computers. Familiar types of adware include pop-up ads on web pages and in-program advertising that often accompanies "free" software. While some adware is relatively harmless, other variants use tracking tools to glean information about your location or browser history and serve up targeted ads to your screen. They also have the capability to disable antivirus software.

Spyware is software that can detect what you are doing at your computer. It tracks your Internet activities in order to send back adware, which collects data such as keystrokes, browsing habits, and even login information. Your information is forwarded to third parties, usually cybercriminals. It may also modify specific security settings on your computer or obstruct network connections. Legitimate companies use forms of spyware to track consumer behavior across multiple devices. Although it does so without user consent, it is legal.

Botnets (short for "robot networks") are an array of computers that run applications that spy on and disable networks. They involve programs (bots) designed to automatically carry out specific operations. Although they may be useful for many legitimate purposes, they also are often repurposed as a type of malware. Bot programs can execute specific commands without the user's approval or knowledge to steal sensitive data, to spy on the victim's activities, to distribute spam automatically, or to launch devastating DDoS attacks on computer networks. When hackers infect multiple computers with the same bot, they create a "botnet," which is then used to remotely manage compromised computers.

Rootkits corrupt an operating system by allowing the installation of hidden files and processes that enable remote access or control of a computer by a third party. Rootkits go unnoticed and functionally hide their presence. They intercept data from terminals, keyboards, and network connections. Identity information from a computer can be compromised without detection, and therefore rootkits are the hardest of all malware to uncover. Because it activates before the infected system boots, its stealth features make it not only the most difficult to detect but also the most difficult to remove. Manual monitoring for anomalies and patching operating systems and software to eliminate potential infection routes is the most effective detection method. Despite their threat as a virulent form of malware, IT professionals also find rootkits a useful tool in troubleshooting for network issues.

Trojan horses are malicious programs that mask their true function by appearing legitimate or useful. Trojans carry out malicious activities without the knowledge or consent of the victim. Their purpose is to grant unauthorized access for hackers into systems for either stealing data or to inflict damage. Trojans can access a victim's financial information, take command of a computer's system resources, and in larger systems conduct a denial-of-service attack.

Flaws are defects in software code. They are not a type of malware but rather programming errors. As mentioned above, they provide pathways for attackers to infect machines with malware. While better security and quality control by developers helps eliminate software defects, also critical is the continual application of software patches and updates that address specific flaws as they become known.

Logic bombs are similar to software defects in that they are embedded code. Logic bombs activate upon a specific time and date or may be triggered by an event. They can be spread or be spawned by a Trojan horse. Once embedded into a system, they damage circuitry or cripple operations at critical points or times.

Backdoors are much the same as Trojans or worms, except that they open a "backdoor" into a computer, providing a network connection for hackers or other malware to enter or for sending viruses or spam.

Keyloggers record keystrokes in order to gather login names, passwords, and other sensitive information. The information transmits to the source of the keylogging program. These programs are also used legitimately by corporations and suspicious parents to acquire computer usage information.

Browser hijackers redirect your normal search activity by altering browser settings. Users find themselves on websites in which they have no interest or any intention of visiting. As users are forcibly made to access websites, developers capture your surfing interests. This is particularly precarious for users who bank or shop online. Browser hijacker programs may also contain spyware and keylogger programs.

Ransomware is a malware variant that can encrypt sensitive data such as personal documents or photos and demands a ransom for their release. Unless payment is made, cybercriminals threaten to delete the data. Some ransomware will deny access to the computer. Victims may have a message appear on their screens claiming that the action is on behalf of a legitimate law enforcement agency such as the FBI. It suggests that the user has been caught doing something illegal and locks out the computer. In return for resolving the situation, the hackers demand payment. There are two types of ransomware. The locker type blocks access to the infected device but does not destroy files. The second is crypto-ransomware, which encrypts files on computers and mobile devices. The program scrambles the contents and requires a decryption key to restore normal usage.

According to the cybersecurity firm Symantec, ransomware attacks are reaching a new level of sophistication and expertise.[43] Furthermore, the trend indicates a continuous increase of attacks on organizations rather than consumers, where attackers deploy the kinds of tactics seen in APTs (advanced persistent threat). As organizations become more frequent targets, ICSs and SCADA software may be at risk from future ransomware attacks. A crypto-ransomware infection at a critical infrastructure facility could have a devastating outcome.

Cryptocurrencies

The rise of cryptocurrencies, also referred to as virtual currencies, has facilitated trafficking in ransomware. Cybercriminals require a transfer payment system that is untraceable, accessible, and convertible. Because there is no single entity governing the oversight and verification of transactions, cryptocurrencies such

Box 2.2 Cryptocurrencies

Cryptocurrencies are digital assets and a medium of exchange that uses cryptology to secure financial transactions. Cryptocurrency exchanges are collectives where users can conduct business in these digital units of account, as well as exchange them for traditional currencies. Because they exist outside the traditional banking system, participants in cryptocurrency markets benefit from minimal transaction fees and faster transaction time.

Mechanics—the transfers are peer to peer and employ public and private keys. The recipient provides their currency address to the sender, who authorizes the transaction with their private key. Users' addresses and private keys are stored in corresponding wallets to facilitate verification and maintain secrecy. Records are maintained on a public ledger, known as a "blockchain," which contains address, transaction date, time, and amount information. The blockchain is essentially a distributed database of shared data spread geographically across multiple sites, institutions, and countries. Because transactions do not require the disclosure of identities, traders enjoy some degree of anonymity. Some virtual currencies (VCs) such as Bitcoin are semi-anonymous, whereas other cryptocurrencies have encryption software that provides additional anonymity and further assurance to those seeking to keep their identities and transactions secret. Although the threat from hacking is limited, a system crash can be disastrous if there is no central repository.

Macro issues—since these public systems are free from government control, seizure, and regulatory constraints, they are also free from the influences of monetary policy or fiscal policy. Because there is no central government to impose monetization, inflationary disruptions are not an investment risk. There is often a limit on the amount of currency that will be in circulation, and therefore, for this reason, cryptocurrency exchanges are similar to the precious metal markets and susceptible to built-in market risk.

Since 2009 (when Bitcoin first appeared) there are now thousands of other cryptocurrencies in circulation. Often referred to as altcoins, these digital currencies have user benefits and disadvantages. As mentioned above, the transfer of funds is faster and less expensive. Users avoid fees charged by banks and other financial institutions as well as whatever advantages they derive from anonymity. Although the currencies are not subject to valuation swings due to monetary and fiscal policies, they are subject to the laws of supply and demand. Therefore, prices between currencies, whether digital or fiat (national currencies), can fluctuate markedly.

---

as Bitcoin, Litecoin, Quarkcoin, etc., offer an allure to ransomware attackers. Bitcoin is the current most popular cryptocurrency and, according to the RAND Corporation, ransomware is among the most common criminal uses of these currency systems.[44] Meanwhile, exchanges and marketplaces are becoming more common on the Internet, as are exchange services and buy-and-sell websites.

Many banks and other financial institutions have business relationships with legitimate companies that exchange these virtual currencies into government-issued currencies. Therefore, due to this interaction, virtual currencies are part of the real economy.[45] As their usage surged, many consumers discovered the benefits of the new payment system. At the same time, these math-based, digital currencies also created challenges for law enforcement and regulatory agencies. The anonymity offered by many virtual currency networks poses obvious difficulties for law enforcement and counterterrorism efforts. Tax evasion, money laundering, terrorist financing, and the illegal trafficking of drugs, weapons, and other banned goods and services favor transactions that conceal identities. Consequently, agencies as diverse as the FBI, the IRS, USAID, the Drug Enforcement Administration, the Treasury Department, the Department of Homeland Security, the Department of Justice, the Financial Crimes Enforcement Network (FinCEN), the Security and Exchange Commission, and the Prudential banking regulators (FDIC, Federal Reserve, National Credit Union Administration, and Office of the Comptroller of the Currency) all work and collaborate to address the criminal potential and use of these currency collectives.

Advanced Persistent Threat (APT)

The U.S. Air Force coined the term *advanced persistent threat* in 2006. As mentioned earlier, *APT* originally referred to national security threats, specifically those from China. Until recently, most experts believed that only about 5 percent of the world's sovereign states have the technical capacity and likely intent for serious cyberattacks against the United States. It is not only traditional rivals with which the United States has concerns. Allies, as well, constitute the growing cyber threat vector. According to the National Intelligence Estimate of January 2013, Israel and France are among the most aggressive in cyber espionage. Nonetheless, APT attacks from these countries against the United States may "pale in comparison to China's effort" and are mostly economically motivated.[46] The electronic intrusions our society undergoes are serious issues and call attention to the nature of the competition, which reveals the overlap and clash of global politics and economics.

While the United States may be the most targeted country for cyberattacks, it is often accused of being the most active in conducting such attacks. In the application and art of cyberwarfare, many countries regard the United States as the primary menace. Former RAND analyst and lecturer at the University of California, Berkeley, Bruce Newsome cites the Office of the National Counter Intelligence Executive admitting that, "In 2010, the German government assessed the US and France as Germany's primary economic espionage threats 'among friends.' In 2011, France's Central Directorate for Domestic Intelligence described the US and China as the leading 'hackers' of French businesses."[47] The United States has also been accused of cyberattacks on an array of foreign countries that span from Russia, China, North Korea, Iran, and Syria to Hungary, Canada, and Australia.

However, as the costs and risks involved with launching APTs become lower, the term has evolved to represent not only other state sources of these prolonged network attacks but also APTs conducted by nonstate actors. Because the ability to fund APTs is no longer restricted to foreign powers, the methods used for the purposes of cyber espionage are increasingly found in attacks on private sector enterprises, particularly financial institutions.[48] Since its entrance into the modern lexicon as a military term, *advanced persistent threat* is now a buzzword with a definition and functionality with grander sweep. APT attacks can originate from any number of states, global corporations engaged in industry espionage, criminal groups, and possibly terrorist organizations as well.[49] They not only collect data, but can also potentially cause considerable damage and panic.

When addressing an APT in connection with a foreign government, attribution is a particularly complex and problematic issue. The perpetrator might be a hostile state or involve surrogates. Governments can claim plausible deniability if the sources of the attack are private actors who mask their linkages with official authorities. The shadows of cyberspace offer excellent cover for states who use hackers "as part of their weapons system."[50] The targets (whether governmental or private) of an APT find themselves in a perilous position of having to conclude whether the attack was an act committed by a group of cybercriminals or an act of war committed by a private actor with official support. The agent can also be an official actor masquerading as a criminal unaffiliated with a regime.

The source of an APT determines what warrants a justifiable and legal appropriate response. If the boundaries between the government and its proxies blur, options for the victim fall into the same gray zone of ambiguity. This type of asymmetric warfare has been tracked and documented. Since its earlier days as a phenomenon, APTs have become a nightmare scenario for the cybersecurity industry. Beginning in 2003, investigators believed cyberattacks originating in China were systematically and routinely launched against government targets in the United States. Within five years, according to the 2008 Report to Congress of the U.S.-China Economic and Security Commission, there were 250 hacker groups operating in China with either government support or encouragement.[51] Chinese hackers have been credited with electronic intrusions against the State Department and the Departments of Defense, Energy, Agriculture, Treasury, and Health and Human Services. For obvious reasons, the Pentagon and its sprawl of private contractors are particularly targeted. Boeing, Raytheon, General Dynamics, General Electric, and Lockheed Martin have all experienced attacks from cyber spies looking for sensitive information. By 2012, as the attack surface became more expansive and dense, Secretary of Defense Leon Panetta cautioned the country of the threat from APTs:

> They could derail passenger trains, or even more dangerous, derail passenger trains loaded with lethal chemicals. They could contaminate the water supply in major cities, or shut down the power grid across large parts of the country.[52]

During this time, analysts mainly focused on China's activity. Meanwhile, Russia's cyber initiatives were becoming more strident and obvious. As reported in a 2016 *New York Times* article, the Russian brand of hybrid warfare employs a means in which unofficial cyberwarriors "serve a multitude of goals, including espionage, [and] the disruption of vital infrastructure."[53] In another article, Eugene V. Kaspersky, founder of Kaspersky Labs, a cybersecurity firm based in Moscow, describes the breadth and depth of cybercrime activity emanating from Russia: "They don't just hack the victims, they trade the technology to other gangs," he said. "Now there are hundreds of victims, in the United States and Asia."[54]

An APT attack begins with reconnaissance to uncover system vulnerabilities. This preliminary stage uses various techniques. A favorite method is **spearphishing**. Spearphishing is an exploitation tactic that uses e-mails that appear to be from a trusted individual or organization. In order to scam their victim, hackers will use as cover the names and fake online addresses of legitimate financial institutions, colleges, charities, or merchandisers. They often use organizations familiar to the target, which they obtain by hacking into the victim's company network or by searching authentic websites, blogs, and social media. The target will unwittingly click on the link to the sham website containing malware. The website might request sensitive information such as passwords, PIN numbers, access codes, or user IDs. Once ensnared, the website tricks the victim into downloading malware designed for exfiltrating proprietary or secret information for the purposes of government or corporate espionage. This is also a method for hijacking systems as zombie computers or botnets (see above).

Similar to spearphishing are "watering holes." **Watering holes** also use websites to attack network systems. This is done when hackers detect vulnerabilities in legitimate websites and inject malicious code that redirects the target to a corrupt site that hosts the malware. They lure victims to these websites by profiling targets based on their online habits. Employees of corporations, government offices, and nongovernmental organizations (NGOs) frequently visit industry websites with affinity content[55] and therefore are opportune targets.

Another common attack vector is **"island hopping**." Island hopping, also referred to as "leapfrogging," is a borrowed term from World War II. The U.S. Navy used island hopping in the Pacific to attack strategically important but less well defended Japanese-held islands. The strategy allowed the Allies to control a series of islands and form a network of landing strips and supply bases that led to Japan's containment and ultimate defeat.[56] In general, island-hopping strategies concentrate their attack on entities that are not the ultimate targets. Attackers use these units to leverage their assaults on the original primary target. Similarly, in a cyberattack, hackers act against their target's less well protected affiliates or vendors in order to exploit breaches in the main target's system. Targeted companies might be of any size and represent any industry. In addition to research and development, payroll, human resources departments, health-care firms, and law firms all retain sensitive information that might be of interest to criminals and hostile governments.

Regardless of method, once the attacker implants the malware, the network is compromised. However, "compromised" does not mean the system has been breached—yet. Before activating the exploit, the installed malware also probes for further access points and vulnerabilities in the network. By exposing additional access points, hackers establish alternative entries into the system if the primary pathway closes. This assures that the cyberattack can continue despite detection by network security. Even if monitors remove evidence of the APT attack, the network remains compromised. The cybercriminal can return at any time to continue the breach operation.

Having gained entry, the malware beacons out to command-and-control (C2 or CC) servers requesting additional instructions or malicious code. The malware then updates code and distributes the malware payload to other machines. Firmly implanted, the exploit gathers data, including account names and passwords for decryption. The attacker identifies and accesses information from the penetrated system and collects it on a staging server. Once the network falls under the control of the attackers and they begin receiving data, the co-opted network is considered breached.

Carbanak—in 2013 an APT attack targeted over one hundred banks in Ukraine, Russia, Germany, China, and the United States. By the time it was uncovered, experts estimate that over one billion U.S. dollars had been stolen. Cybercriminals drained the financial system by either transferring funds into false accounts or dispensing cash via ATMs where affiliates, or "mules," waited to make the collection. The mules would collect the money and transfer it over SWIFT (Society for Worldwide Interbank Financial Telecommunications) to accounts belonging to other affiliates.[57] The name Carbanak refers to the cybercriminal group credited with the attack and the malware used in the scam. As of 2016, many security experts believe that not only is the scam still active, but it is now targeting the hospitality industry.[58]

The opening attack used spearphishing e-mails sent to employees of the target banks. The e-mails appeared as legitimate banking communications from a co-worker, often containing a news clip as an attachment. Once the attachments were clicked on, the malware downloaded. Sometimes e-mail recipients were redirected to websites containing **exploit kit** software. These exploit kits ran on web servers and identified vulnerabilities in targeted machines, with which they eventually communicated, uploading and executing malicious code. Once that code was uploaded, attackers began trawling the bank's network to identify employees who administered cash transfer systems or could remotely connect to ATMs. These accounts then became compromised.[59]

The reconnaissance component to Carbanak also allowed attackers to take control of video capabilities on the target systems. Remote access tools captured video and screenshots of system administrators and other employees' computers and thereby allowed attackers to conduct long-term surveillance. Gradually the cyberthieves gained insight into their victims' operational picture. As an understanding of the protocols, workflow, practices, and tools of their targets came to light, exploitation methodologies and mechanisms were developed and tailored to each victim. Cybercriminals impersonated legitimate users with the permissions to perform actions, which were later used to process fraudulent transactions.[60] Unfortunately, even when evidence of an APT attack has been removed, often the network remains compromised. As a result, the hackers can return at any time to continue exploiting the breach. The exploit is long term in its implementation and execution.

APTs represent an evolving weaponry of the cyber conflict arena. In the new virtual warscape, actors are bound by electronic connections rather than regional jurisdictions and state borders. These circumstances benefit those outside the law and create obstacles for law enforcement, who generally are rooted territorially. The "de-bordering" of the world map as a result of globalization pertains to commerce in far more practical terms than it does to governance. As technology blurs the contours of previously established boundaries and norms, policies and legal codes scramble, as do authorities, in order to keep pace with events.

Whether associated by cultural and traditional ties or motivated by unembellished economic self-interest, the new order of battle is an alternating pattern of states, corporations, terrorists, criminals, and social activists. These actors attack, interact, and often secretly affiliate in a domain that remains ungovernable. Adding further disorder to the attempt to maintain order are the clashes between the requirements of security versus the rights of privacy and civil liberty. In these affairs, solutions have been elusive and comprise a delicate balancing act.

Box 2.3 Defending against APTs

Tom Kellermann

On May 10, 1940, the French realized the ineffectiveness of the Maginot Line against Nazi Germany's invasion. We must accept the reality that perimeter defense is ineffective against the exploit kits, RATs [Remote Access Trojans], and application-based attacks of today. Our traditional architectures and controls for cybersecurity are inadequate. As the recent Verizon Data Breach Report noted, most breaches are not discovered for at least one hundred days. This damning reality necessitates a paradigm shift. Given the fact that the cybercriminal has a footprint within a company network for an extended period, organizations must alter their security posture accordingly; the metric by which we should assess the potency of a cyber countermeasure is how effectively it can decrease an adversary's dwell time. Decreasing dwell time is the measurable metric by which we can value a return on investment for an enterprise. Diving down into what decreasing dwell time affords the enterprise requires an examination of what the costs are to the enterprise when exfiltration of their data occurs. The proper strategy for your organization is to build a structure that inhibits the free movement of the adversary once they penetrate your system. We must transform our castles into prisons via intrusion suppression.

Intrusion suppression requires clandestine detection, deception, diversion, and eventual containment of a cyber adversary. It involves three steps that aim to detect cybercriminals by decreasing their dwell time and lateral movements.

A. Deploy a deception grid to enhance situational awareness per the latest techniques to deceive and divert the adversary unbeknownst to them.

B. Deploy adaptive authentication with contextual verification to eliminate an access an adversary has to your network.

C. Deploy user entity behavior analytics, which provides contextual analysis on the activity and lateral movement of the adversary.

We must spin the chessboard. In order to combat the cyber spy of tomorrow, the intrusion suppression architecture must be embraced.

Tom Kellermann is CEO of Strategic Cyber Ventures, a Wilson Center fellow, and a former member of the Commission on Cyber Security for the 44th president of the United States.

The Deep and Dark Webs

The terms *Internet* and the *World Wide Web* are often used interchangeably. Yet the two are not synonymous. The Internet is a massive network of networks connecting millions of computers together. It is a global networking infrastructure in which any computer can communicate with any other computer as long as they are both connected to the Internet. The Internet refers to the network of networks where all the information resides. Things like file transfer protocol (FTP), Internet gaming, live online discussions, and e-mail are all part of the Internet. They are, however, separate from the World Wide Web.

Specifically, the World Wide Web, or "the web," is an information system on the Internet that allows documents to connect to other documents. As discussed in chapter 1, it was the initial creation of Timothy Berners-Lee's "universal linked information system" that allowed academics across the globe to upload immense amounts of information on the web and assign locations for accessing it—all owing to his HyperText Transfer Protocol (http) and the Uniform Resource Locator (URL) system.

The "surface web," on the other hand, describes only the portion of the World Wide Web that is readily accessible to the general public through browsers like Internet Explorer and Firefox and traditional search engines such as Google, Yahoo!, etc. Generally, the surface web is made up of static and fixed pages, which means they reside on servers as HTML files (HyperText Markup Language; see chapter 1) waiting to be retrieved. These are the sites whose domains end in *.com*, *.org*, *.net*, *.edu*, etc., and no special configuration, such as TOR, is required for access.

The surface web grows every day. Estimates conclude that after the number of sites that go offline is subtracted from the number of new registers, thirty thousand websites are added daily.[61] Yet, despite its growth, the surface web is a fraction of what the deep web is believed to be. The algorithms used by commercial search engines, such as those named above and others, only capture approximately 5 to 16 percent of the total Internet.[62]

The "deep web," however, refers to content that is not indexed and that traditional search engines cannot access. It includes private sites, blocked sites, unlinked sites, and non-HTML sites. Put simply, it is "a class of content on the Internet that, for various technical reasons, is not indexed by search engines."[63] The volume of data on the deep web has been growing exponentially. While earlier estimates suggested that the deep web might be as much as four thousand to five thousand times greater than the surface web,[64] other calculations put its volume more modestly between four hundred and five hundred times as much. Regardless of the differences in numbers, current evaluations concede that the rate of growth may be unquantifiable.[65]

What we do know is that there is a vast amount of information below the layer of the surface net (see figure 2.1). It includes Twitter and Facebook posts, information in databases, and data under the layers of content of a website retrieved in a standard search. Some are reachable through custom queries made on a specific website. For example, if you want to look up information about the "deep web" on the surface web, begin by doing a simple Google search.

Figure 2.1 Layers of the Internet

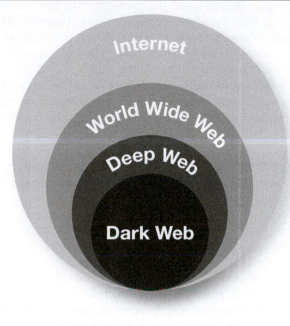

Note: Proportions in the figure are not to scale.

Source: Congressional Research Service.

You can sort through the many hits or you could go directly to publicly available sites such as the Department of Homeland Security's Digital Library, found at https://www.hsdl.org. When you reach the site, you are still on the surface web. There, you can request access to the complete database by submitting your e-mail address and identifying yourself as a member of the government or military, or a researcher at a college, university, or think tank. Once you log in and enter your search criteria, you have gone below the surface web and successfully accessed the world of the deep web. Basically, one enters the deep web when one navigates away from a typical search engine to do a search directly in a website.[66] BrightPlanet is a firm that specializes in "harvesting" deep web data, and it explains the deep web thus:

> The Deep Web isn't found in a single location. It consists of both structured and unstructured content—a huge amount of which is found in databases. This content has often been compiled by experts, researchers, analysts and through automated processing systems at an array of institutions throughout the world. All of the content is housed in different systems, with different structures, at physical locations that can be as far apart as New York and Hong Kong.[67]

Traditional search engines use "web crawlers" to navigate the surface web. Also known as spiders, web search engines use these programs to index all the pages on a site by following the links from page to page. The search engine encapsulates the content and adds the links to their indexes. They can also locate web pages that sell a particular product or find blogs that have opinions about a product. According to BrightPlanet, the problem with this technology is that search engines return links based on popularity, not content.[68] As the surface web grew, the utter volume of these sites forced the information to be managed through automated systems with databases. The result is an evolved web of database-centric design rather than one of static sites.

The main growth in web traffic occurs here as larger, more dynamic sites come online. Dynamic sites are capable of producing different content for different visitors from the same source code file. This is a distinction from static sites whose content does not change unless edited by an administrator. Interactive online shopping sites are examples of dynamic websites. Other examples are blogs and any e-commerce site used to make a reservation, check an account balance, or submit a form. Practically every time we go online we use the resources of the deep web unconsciously, at work, at home, and at leisure.

Within the deep web is a small segment of content called the dark web. There is no standard definition for the dark web. In some circles, the dark web is simply a term for data that has been intentionally hidden and is inaccessible through standard web browsers.[69] By this definition, the hidden sites trafficking in illegal goods and services, and the secure command-and-control centers that operate nuclear power plants, are both technically part of the dark web. Sometimes the word *dark* implies a reference to the more disturbing and malevolent aspects of the Internet, and therefore distinctions are drawn in the literature between "deep" and "dark." But as noted above, not all of this content is as sinister as the name implies. Still, some subject matter experts insist that the dark net only refers to sites that can be accessed anonymously.[70] Further, in order to make the debate over definitional language as esoteric and confusing as possible, many commentators simply use the terms interchangeably.

Definitional distinctions aside, the deep web and the dark web contain the largest pool of replacement and fresh data on the Internet.[71] Additionally, these subsurface webs lend themselves to searches that are more targeted and subject relevant because custom queries are often made via content-specific websites. But because websites on the deep web are unindexed, a knowledge of their specific URL addresses is needed for access. Alternative search engines can help users access corners of the deep web that are unreachable with normal search tools. These subscription search engines allow users to locate different parts of the deep web for specific content. Content ranges from scientific and political topics to issues of concern for communities devoted to pet care and figure skating.

In the anonymous dark web, visitors mainly use TOR to navigate through the population of sites. The Invisible Internet Project, known as I2P, is another distributed communication network designed for anonymity. However, rather than being a tool to connect with and create hidden sites like TOR is, I2P's sole purpose is as a mechanism to host services such as e-mail, online discussions (IRC—Internet Relay Chat), and hidden I2P network websites called "eepsites." Similar to I2P is Freenet, a predecessor network with parallel but more limited capabilities.

As noted above, these anonymous realms within the dark net are refuges and covers for those on both sides of the law. Its conception, rise, and continuance reflect the needs of commerce, national security, human rights advocacy, and crime. As put by another observer, "The Darknet is nothing more than a mirror of society. Distorted, magnified, and mutated by the strange and unnatural conditions of life online."[72] While contributing to social welfare, it also facilitates crime. Yet, rather than constraining it, policy makers concentrate on shaping its progression. To that purpose, initiatives and technology are moving forward to oppose bad actors who exploit the anonymity of the dark net.

An example of this effort is CAUSE (Cyberattack Automated Unconventional Sensor Environment), a project of IARPA (Intelligence Advanced Research Project Activity). In general, cybersecurity has been mostly reactionary—relying on resilience and redundancy to stop infiltrators from doing maximum damage and mitigating losses. The developers of CAUSE hope to introduce a more proactive approach by creating a framework for a "probabilistic warning system" that anticipates and identifies new attack vectors before they emerge.[73] Because cyberattacks, like those in the physical world, progress in phases, "observations of earlier attack phases, such as target reconnaissance, planning and delivery, may enable warning of significant cyber events prior to their most damaging phases."[74] These unconventional "sensors" will filter data streams from social media, economic trend reports, and political and cultural news. These subjects and sources might be nondirectly related to cybersecurity, but they might reveal probable impact by potential bad actors and their shifting motives and methods.

We already know how social software can track political situations worldwide. It is a valuable enabler of information sharing and connectivity and an intellectual force multiplier.[75] While it is useful as a general networking apparatus for expressing dissent and advocating policy, it can also identify emerging trends and influencers. Social media can mobilize sympathizers, associates, and armed insurgents into action in support of causes or combat. Hopefully, with CAUSE's other data sources, it can help to merge information flows into a single automated system that allows authorities to anticipate and get ahead of cyberattacks well before they materialize.

The transnational dynamic of the anonymous web frustrates legitimate society and law enforcement. The lack of functioning markets in economically depressed regions of the world forces them to seek alternative commercial practices and opens them up to exploitation. Meanwhile, international consensus on the definition of cyberwar, cyber espionage, and cybercrimes remains elusive with respect to official policy and law. As well, accurate data on the volume, usage, and very character and scope of dark web content is tenuous. The shadowy world of underground markets, failed states, and opaque and anonymous cyberspace has resulted in momentous change. These forces have changed roles and rules for states, opened opportunities where crime and terrorism can fester, altered the impact of nongovernmental organizations (NGOs) on civil society, and created new spheres of authority among populations. The shifting phantasmagoria is a pageant with which the global security establishment's history and experience is only relatively recent.

For additional understanding of the challenges of cybersecurity, it might be wise to refer to a mythical dialogue between Socrates and a Greek slave called

Meno. Meno poses a question to the philosopher: "How will you look for something when you do not know what it is?" suggesting that rational inquiry is impossible. Socrates's reply is that, generally, the nature of a solution is not fully known, but it is not totally unknown either. We may not know the right answer to a problem, but we are able to recognize the wrong answers. Eventually, through continuous trial and inquiry we come to the right conclusions. In the current arena of conflict, solutions are elusive. The competition over political and economic control by state and nonstate actors and the expanding web of criminals, terrorists, disgruntled workers, hacktivists, and so on, add to cybersecurity's version of that paradox. In an environment where the combatants are indistinct and their motives are often vague or intentionally masked, new threats take shape that do not comfortably conform to previous patterns of activity, analysis, and protocols for response.

Inhibiting the ability to interdict is not only the lack of experience with this kind of threat but also the paucity of data that could help create predictive modeling methods and tools. These new opponents create a multivariate network of plotters. In some cases, they may be unrelated, stateless, and widespread, and in other cases not. As a result, Meno's question becomes a troublesome and persistent dilemma for the security and defense communities as a simple hypothetical query from the past evolves into a somber global concern.

Fortunately, our experience with the virtual world grows ceaselessly, and the lessons we gain from that experience allow us to better prepare for the increased onslaught of cyberattacks and new-generation malware. Unfortunately, as technological advances occur and contribute to the stealth and expansion of the dark web, policy-making and law enforcement efforts lag behind due to an absence of broad consensus. The deep web and the dark web grow deeper and darker every day. The situation, therefore, is too critical to leave the solutions solely to the experts. An extensive public debate is necessary in order to address the threat from an expanding array of plotters and a range of complex issues that are constantly morphing.

The Lexicon of Cyber Conflict

If there is ever a war between great and emerging great powers, we must assume that cyberweapons will be used and apply the Law of Armed Conflict to their use until a more formal treaty or convention can be negotiated, signed, and ratified. Consistency of definitions is essential. There cannot be a system of definitions for legal scholars and a conflicting system of definitions for the policy maker, technologist, and layperson. It is the clarity of common definitions and language on which domestic policy and global norms of behavior can be built. Clarifying definitions on technological grounds allows for the distinction of legitimate military targets and permits for the establishment of policy tools such as escalatory ladders. Embargo and trade sanctions might be the correct approach in milder cases of gross intellectual property theft and serve as a warning and token of severe penalties to come should something escalate from cyber espionage to attack. It is in the early scale of malicious cyber events that the United States should diplomatically address criminal disputes. Claiming all malicious actions as cyberwarfare could result in threats of retaliation which, in a real cyberwar, could be discounted as a bluff. Vigorously grasping at the situation that we are in, rather than fearfully reacting and making desperate pronouncements, will prevent misperception by our adversaries and the public alike.

Participants in debates about air, land, sea, and space power all know what they mean by armed attack and the use of force. Definitions and a common lexicon are the basis of all debates on warfare. What little argument takes place about definitions usually revolves around two or three assertions that more or less mean the same thing.

The United States, its allies, and other nations around the world invest vast sums into cyberspace, a domain that is identified not only as a critical national infrastructure with myriad vulnerabilities, but also a war-fighting domain that is increasingly critical to delivering military capabilities and operations. The purpose here is to encourage a formal debate to forge common cyberspace definitions that are rooted in technological realities that will eventually lead to more coherent domestic and international cyber policy, strategy, and doctrine. This is not a topic of mere academic semantics. In 1911, the British maritime theorist Sir Julian Corbett wrote about the importance of definitions thus: "Without such an apparatus no two men can even think on the same line; much less can they ever hope to detach the real point of difference that divides them and isolate it for quiet resolution."[76]

The absence of a clear understanding of what cyberwarfare is—and more importantly, what it is not—continues to present challenges. This is largely due to an absence of understanding of the underlying technologies and expertise required to mount, and the tools, techniques, and procedures that would result in, an incident qualifying as an armed attack in cyberspace. Experienced professionals all too often contribute to confusion by focusing concepts of cyberspace on information and communication technologies (ICTs), while not understanding their difference from industrial control systems (ICSs). ICTs are those technologies used daily by people globally for socioeconomic purposes. ICSs control the physical systems on which modern societies also depend. However, there, cyber and physical boundaries blur. Actions associated with systems, instrumentation, and controls—through and by means of cyberspace—can have actual physical effects.

Not making this distinction between targets leads to the conflation of incidents that target malicious actions on corporate functions, such as e-mail servers, with cyber-physical effects, such as Stuxnet. In short, ICT views security through the lenses of Windows, the Internet, malware, botnets, etc., which are used for espionage, crime, and disruption. While these may also be issues for control systems, the vulnerabilities that can cause significant physical effect, such as **Aurora**, are on ICS proprietary platforms and software that are not exploitable by malicious software targeting ICTs.

Not making this distinction between ICT and ICS leads to very different incidents treated as a single concept: cyberwar. Illustrative of this is a proclamation by the *Washington Post*'s editorial board that "China is waging a quiet,

Box 2.4 Operation Aurora

Aurora is an advanced persistent threat operation attributed to the Chinese People's Liberation Army (PLA). It first appeared in 2009 and targeted dozens of organizations that ranged from Yahoo!, Adobe Systems, Juniper Networks, and Symantec to Northrop Grumman, Morgan Stanley, and Dow Chemical. In total, as many as thirty organizations had become targets. When Google realized that it, too, was under attack, it took unprecedented action by announcing publicly that the attacks against its network originated in China. The disclosure fueled diplomatic tensions between the People's Republic of China (PRC) and the United States.[77]

Google further claimed that the attacks were directed at Gmail accounts of human rights activists and individuals, whom the Chinese government considered to be political dissidents. Equally grave for Google were the Chinese intentions to compromise Google's source code. The source code is a vital corporate asset and critical piece of intellectual property. "If the hackers had been able to alter the source code while remaining undetected, they could have built vulnerabilities directly into Google's product plans."[78] Officials at the security firm McAfee said the principal goal of Operation Aurora was to access the source codes at high-tech security and defense contractors with the possible aim of modifying them at some point in the future.

Google's defensive action meant tracing the path of attack and entering a privately owned and listed Taiwanese server. The response could have opened the company to lawsuits under the U.S. Computer Fraud and Abuse Act (CFAA). However, rather than level charges against Google, U.S. federal agencies chose to publically laud Google and reprove the PRC. The episode evinced two salient points: (1) without clear evidence of an identifiable victim, such countermeasures likely escape lawsuit, and (2) attribution is not impossible.[79]

---

mostly invisible but massive cyberwar against the United States, aimed at stealing its most sensitive military and economic secrets and obtaining the ability to sabotage vital infrastructure."[80] Theft of information and conducting espionage for the purpose of hypothetical future sabotage operations do not rise to the level of armed attack in the lexicons of kinetic warfare, and thus they should not be conflated in the cyber domain. Discussions of cybercrime and cyber espionage must be clearly separated from discussions of cyberwarfare. While we are certainly in a cyber Cold War, we are not in an international armed conflict in cyberspace. By continuing to employ terms interchangeably, the current discussion drifts from issues of information security to issues of national security that warrant a military response.

Cyber espionage, crime, and attack are very different and necessitate responses that fall under mutually exclusive sections of the U.S. Code. This makes it increasingly important that we clearly define what the targets and potential effects of cyberattack are. Existing definitions work; what is lost is the technological understanding that underpins cyber operations to create effects. To offer clarity on the kinds of events that take place in cyberspace, we distinguish between organized crime, cyber espionage, crime, disruption, and attack:

Cyber espionage: the act of securing information of a military or political nature that a competing nation holds secret.

Cybercrime: any interference with the functioning of a computer system, with fraudulent or dishonest intent of procuring, without right, an economic benefit for oneself or for another person.[81]

Cyber disruption: the serious hindering without right of the functioning of a computer system by inputting, transmitting, damaging, deleting, deteriorating, altering, or suppressing computer data.[82]

Cyberattack: a cyber operation, whether offensive or defensive, that is reasonably expected to cause injury or death to persons or damage or destruction to objects.[83]

The paradigms required for addressing cybercrime and cyber espionage are not the same as those required to succeed in cyberwarfare. Developing a clear distinction at the technological level between various types of malicious cyber activity is critical to assuring that policy makers appropriately adopt existing international law or develop global norms. As will be discussed later, there are separate definitions and perceptions for the concept of "cybersecurity," as well. Indeed, the word *cyber* has no direct semantic equivalent in every language. While the West uses the word *cybersecurity* to refer to the technical domain, other governments understand cybersecurity as a concept that also embraces content. Content is an element of the cyber domain that needs securing, but in some cases, this interpretation can mean censorship and/or weaponization of information. These differences between the technical terminology and the more holistic understanding form barricades and inhibit treaties, obstruct progress in the codification of international law and the setting of global norms, and aggravate contentions between political systems. Therefore, the time for gross generalizations and sweeping assertions may be at an end for a variety of reasons and at various levels.

Unfortunately, international norms related to cyberspace are currently scant. Guidance and collective action for the advancement of global norms has been wanting. This frailty in international governance of cyberspace exists in arrant opposition to the rushing pace of technological innovation and its diffusion. The lack of multilateral rules, policies, and agreements represents an underdeveloped system and opportunity loss to create not only a more secure international environment but also a more prosperous one.[84]

Key Terms

hash function	public key
key	public key infrastructure
hash value	certificate authority
message digest	Internet Freedom program
digital signature	Tor2web
private key	attack agent

shell code

computer virus

bacteria

worm

denial of service attacks/distributed denial of service attack

adware

spyware

rootkit

Trojan horse

flaw

logic bomb

backdoor

keylogger

browser hijacker

ransomware

spearphishing

watering hole

island hopping

Carbanak

exploit kit

Aurora

Notes

1. https://www.trendmicro.com/vinfo/us/security/definition/hash-values.
2. http://security.stackexchange.com/questions/45963/diffie-hellman-key-exchange-in-plain-english.
3. http://www.pbslearningmedia.org/resource/nvrh-sci-algorithm/rsa-algorithm.
4. http://www.webopedia.com/TERM/R/RSA.html.
5. http://searchsecurity.techtarget.com/definition/RSA.
6. http://securityaffairs.co/wordpress/647/cyber-crime/2011-cas-are-under-attack-why-steal-a-certificate.html.
7. *Zero Days*, documentary film, Alex Gibney, director (2016).
8. Howard F. Lipson, *Tracking and Tracing Cyber-Attacks: Technical Challenges and Policy Issues*, CERT Special Report, 2002.
9. Tom Leighton, "The Net's Real Security Problem," *Scientific American*, September 2006, 44.
10. Ibid.
11. Robert E. Molyneux, *The Internet under the Hood: An Introduction to Network Technologies for Information Professionals* (Westport, CT: Libraries Unlimited, 2003), 85–86.
12. Ibid., 27.
13. Dorothy E. Denning, "Activism, Hacktivism, and Cyberterrorism: The Internet as a Tool for Influencing Foreign Policy," in *Networks and Netwars: The Future of Terror, Crime, and Militancy*, ed. John Arquilla and David Ronfeldt (Santa Monica, CA: RAND Corporation, 2001), 35.
14. "The Darknet and Online Anonymity," POSTnote no. 488; Parliamentary Office of Science & Technology note no. 488, UK Houses of Parliament, 2015.
15. Vincenzo Ciancaglini, Marco Balduzzi, Max Goncharov, and Robert McArdle, "Deepweb and Cyber Crime: It's Not All about TOR," TrendMicro research paper, 2013, 6.
16. Ibid.
17. Kristin Finklea, "Dark Web," CRS, July 7, 2014, 4.
18. Ibid.; "The Darknet and Online Anonymity."
19. Ibid.
20. Gareth Owen and Nick Savage, "The TOR Dark Net," Global Commission on Internet Governance, Chatham House, September 2015, 5.
21. Ibid.
22. "The Darknet and Online Anonymity."
23. Ibid.
24. Ibid.
25. Daniel Sui, James Caverlee, and Dakota Rudesill, "The Deep Web and the Darkweb: A Look Inside the Internet's Massive Black Box," Woodrow Wilson International Center for Scholars, August 2015, 9.
26. Finklea, 8.

27 Sui, 9.
28 Ibid.
29 Ibid.
30 Finklea, 8.
31 Ciancaglini, 9.
32 Ibid., 14.
33 For the taxonomy of cyber events, see Keith Harrison and Gregory White, "A Taxonomy of Cyber Events Affecting Communities," in *Proceedings of the 44th Hawaii International Conference on System Sciences* (2011). It should be noted that the paper included natural events; however, for the purpose of this paper, chipmunks chewing through fiber optic cables are not deemed to be relevant to state responsibility for cyberattacks.
34 Singer, 39.
35 Panoyotis Yannakogeorgos, "Privatized Cybersecurity and the Challenges of Securing the Digital Environment," in *Crime and Terrorism Risks: Studies in Criminology and Criminal Justice*, ed. L. W. Kennedy and E. F. McGarrel (New York: Routledge, 2012), 261.
36 "Software Security Assurance, State-of-the-Art Report," Defense Technology Information Center, July 31, 2007, 30.
37 Martin C. Libicki, *Cyberspace in Peace and War* (Annapolis, MD: Naval Institute Press, 2016).
38 U.S. Government Accountability Office, *Critical Infrastructure Protection: Department of Homeland Security Faces Challenges in Fulfilling Cyber Security Responsibilities*, GAO-05-434, Washington, DC, 2005.
39 http://www.coverty.com/library/pdf/open_source_quality_report.pdf.
40 Libicki.
41 Software Security Assurance, 30.
42 Ibid.
43 "Ransomware and Businesses 2016," Symantec, 2016, 4.
44 Joshua Baron, Angela O'Mahony, David Manheim, and Cynthia Dion-Schwarz, *National Security Implications of Virtual Currency: Examining the Potential for Non-State Actor Deployment* (Santa Monica, CA: RAND Corporation, 2015), 19.
45 *Virtual Currencies*, GAO report, May 2014, 5.
46 Ellen Nakashima, "U.S. Said to Be Target of Massive Cyber-Espionage Campaign," *Washington Post*, February 10, 2013.
47 Bruce Newsome and Jack Jarmon, *A Practical Introduction to Homeland Security and Emergency Management from Home to Abroad* (Los Angeles: Sage Publications/CQ Press, 2015).
48 Kaspersky Lab, "The Great Bank Robbery: Carbanak Cybergang Steals $1bn from 100 Financial Institutions Worldwide," February 16, 2015, 23, http://www.kaspersky.com/about/news/virus/2015/Carbanak-cybergang-steals-1-bn-USD-from-100-financial-institutions-worldwide.
49 Merete Ask, "Advanced Persistent Threat (APT): Beyond the Hype," Gjøvik University College, 2013, 2.
50 Andrew Higgins, "Foes of Russia Say Child Pornography Is Planted to Ruin Them," *New York Times*, December 8, 2016.
51 2008 Report to Congress of the U.S.-China Economic and Security Commission, 164.
52 Elizabeth Bumiller and Thom Shanker, "Panetta Warns of Dire Threat of Cyber Attack on U.S.," *New York Times*, October 11, 2012.
53 Higgins.
54 Neil MacFarquhar, "A Russian Cybersleuth Battles the 'Dark Ages' of the Internet," *New York Times*, June 10, 2016.
55 http://searchsecurity.techtarget.com/definition/watering-hole-attack.
56 http://america-at-war-wwii.weebly.com/island-hopping.html.
57 Kaspersky Lab, 3.
58 http://securityaffirs.co/wordpress/53486/breaking-news/carbanakhospitality.html.
59 http://www.controlrisks.com/en/our-thinking/analysis/the-carbanak-hack-a-warning-to-all.
60 Kaspersky Lab, 4.
61 Ibid., 2.
62 Ibid., 13; Sui, 6.

63 Michael Chertoff and Toby Simon, "The Impact of the Dark Web on Internet Governance and Cyber Security," Global Commission on Internet Governance, paper series no. 6, February 2015, 1.

64 BrightPlanet, "Deep Web: A Primer," http://www.brightplanet.com/deep-web-university-2/deep-web-a-primer.

65 Ciancaglini, 13.

66 BrightPlanet, "Clearing Up the Confusion: Deep Web vs Dark Web," https//brightplanet.com/2014/03/clearing-confusion-deep-web-vs-dark-web.

67 BrightPlanet, "Deep Web: A Primer."

68 Ibid.

69 BrightPlanet, "Clearing Up the Confusion."

70 Sui, 6.

71 Ibid.

72 Ibid., 12.

73 http://www.federaltimes.com/story/government/cybersecurity/2015/07/20/iarpa-cyberattack-unconventional-sensors/30415367.

74 Ibid.

75 Mark Drapeau and Linton Wells II, "Social Software and National Security: An Initial Net Assessment," Center for Technology and National Security Policy, National Defense University, April 2009, 34.

76 Julian S. Corbett, *Some Principles of Maritime Strategy* (Annapolis, MD: Naval Institute Press, 1988; first published in 1911), 7.

77 http://www.computerworld.com/article/2489451/malware-vulnerabilities/-elderwood--hackers-still-setting-pace-for-zero-day-exploits.html.

78 "Into the Gray Zone: The Private Sector and Active Defense against Cyber Threats" (Project Report, Center for Cyber & Homeland Security, George Washington University, October 2016), 14.

79 Ibid.

80 http://www.washingtonpost.com/opinions/chinascyberwar/2011/12/15/gIQA2Aw1wO_story.html.

81 Council of Europe, *Convention on Cybercrime*, ETS no. 185, 2001.

82 Ibid.

83 Michael N. Schmitt, ed., *Tallinn Manual on the International Law Applicable to Cyber Warfare* (Cambridge: Cambridge University Press, 2013).

84 Sinan Ülgen, *Governing Cyberspace: A Road Map for Transatlantic Leadership* (Carnegie Endowment for International Peace, 2016), 72.

Global Cyber Risk and Access Vectors 3

The Globalization Process

The term *globalization* throughout the text refers to the highly connected state and manner by which populations link economically and politically. Technological advancement has resulted in a compression of time and space. The consequence has meant an unprecedented interconnectedness and interdependence never before known among peoples and locales. As the world transforms, as it moves toward a mode of existence resembling a single space, the possibilities of market relations and political responses are heightened and intensified. This new geography that pressures commerce to respond to exact quality and price demands of the market similarly imposes a historical transformation on the national security establishment to adapt to the precision weaponry and information technology of modern warfare. In the current lexicon, *cyber* and *globalization* are lax terms. Definitions can be politicized or have no direct equivalent as they cross into other languages and cultures. However, a relative constant is the fact that whether the target or objective is a market or a battlefield, no territory is beyond reach at, ideally, any time. As James Mittelman puts it, globalization is more than a process of forming a new structure of international relations. It is also a "domain of knowledge." Cyberspace, William Gibson's "consensual hallucination," is another domain of information where structures are formative and mutable.

For commerce and the defense and national security community, the impact has been seismic. The integrity of the global marketplace, and the responsibilities for securing the homeland and advancing U.S. interests overseas, are under new pressures. In the post–Cold War environment, globalization has meant a reenvisioning of priorities, creating modern disaggregated enterprises, adapting the force structure, and devising new ways to network with civic society, the private sector, and other organs of government—at home and abroad.

In his 1960 book *International Politics of the Atomic Age*, John Herz wrote, "Political authority is based upon the power of protection." The ability to assure

U.S. survival by protecting the nation's economic strength and competitiveness is no longer in defending the strategic markets in Western Europe and Japan and the remote territories from which we access valuable resources to feed the economic engine. The prime target is the economic engine itself. It includes the critical infrastructure, intellectual property, and stability of the markets. The ironic twist to the argument is Herz's claim that the "permeability of the state" is due to an exploitation of a different kind of onslaught, an asymmetric offensive that exists despite the advantage a nation may have in strategic nuclear weapons. The primary differentiator is that asymmetric attacks do not aim for total annihilation or to establish an area of pacification as security regimes of previous eras did. Rather, the goals are either parasitical, as often is the case with cyberattacks, or to drain a country ("the protection unit," as Herz would say) financially and psychologically through unending conflict. The pacification of an area or a group is unproductive and plays into the hands of any adversary who seeks unending war. The erosion of markets means the erosion of political influence.

The United States, its allies, and its adversaries have entered a new age and face a new generation of weapons. The struggle is not in fending off annihilation but rather in avoiding marginalization. In addition, the scope of the threat matrix not only includes the nation-state; it spans the arc of criminal syndicates, entrepreneurial terrorists, and the disgruntled employee or the hubristic hacker seeking to add to his reputation. Therefore, national governments and militaries are limited in their capacity to provide a "protection force." The onus is upon all sectors of society, including an educated citizenry.

Adjustment to the new order of world affairs will continue to be a process of trial, reorientation, missteps, and lapses. Inhibiting progress are not only the present institutions and embedded interests, but also a policy-making apparatus and a preference for large-scale maneuver warfare, which are rooted in a fluctuating inter-state system. As mentioned above, it is a system that has been reshaped by technology and the demands of an ever-expanding and intensifying global economy. The advanced skills revolutions in science and commerce require harmony with a global marketplace that operates by the requirements of "just-in-time processing" and disregard for borders. These same "megatrends" have made information accessible in waves of tsunami proportion. Today, we do not mine data; we are bombarded by it. Management of information on such a grand scale is key.

The riches of information come with an underside, however. These resources can be used for either empowerment or in exploitation of one group over another. As these developments have drawn populations closer, they simultaneously create opportunities for collaboration and tension. At the same time, emerging technologies and the undermining of borders compel militaries to adapt force structures to a new generation of weaponry and the need to be more flexible, to operate in smaller units, to adjust objectives, and to maneuver by different rules of engagement and definitions of war. Similar demands are put on diplomatic efforts, but also include the imperatives of economic and social corporate responsibility as the private sector confronts its revised role in national security.

These developments have given way to a different structure and level of interaction. For the national security establishment, it involves a break from the state-centered international system and contending more with national and sub-national governments, quasi-states, ethnic groups, rivalries among traditional allies, criminal gangs, diasporas, nongovernmental organizations, and the new phenomena in media. In the post–Cold War arena of conflict, the security frame-work of past power alliances and strategies based on a notion of collective security has become outmoded in the context of how a cyberattack would raise such an event to the level of an act of war. The organizing principles of U.S. national security strategy reflect less a threat from peer military competitors and more of an "all hazards" approach to counter transnational forces that emanate from criminal enterprises, terrorists, pirates, and events caused by natural catastrophes.

Yet, while these emerging threats exist, the primary competitors of the Cold War are still major players. Russia and China are participants and innovators in this asymmetric war. They compete politically and economically with the United States and continue to prosecute the remains of a conflict born from the previous era, but with variation in mission and rationale adapted to the realities of the post–Cold War period. Adding to the enigma and burden of the American security establishment is the need for the U.S. hegemony to support global commerce and defend the global commons. The Pacific Rim countries, including the People's Republic of China and despite its military buildup in recent years, still rely on the U.S. Navy to protect global shipping lanes. Other nations, particularly Saudi Arabia and Japan, have bought U.S. federal debt instruments as indirect payment for a security force. At least until now, these and other governments have justified the investment as being more favorable than the alternative of developing their own capabilities and militarizing their domestic economies.

The result of these upheavals is that the familiar ground of a few decades ago has become a changing landscape. Furthermore, we now see trends developing and events unfolding at a historic pace. Yet, before they have a chance to take hold, we have watched as they reverse their course or, in some cases, disappear altogether. It is prudent to recall that most of the U.S. national security establishment was taken by surprise by the fall of the Soviet Union at the time, and no one could have predicted how much the world has changed since September 11, 2001. The prospect of unforeseen circumstances and disruptive technologies is even greater now as we uncover advancements in artificial intelligence and develop emerging Third Offset weaponry.

Further, the array of failed states, the crime-terrorist nexus, jurisdictional arbitrage, attribution and response, and the role of multinational firms are only some of the issues that create and impact the global security paradigm. The pattern shift signals the emergence of a new and perilous world. The reorientation in national security portends an era of an asymmetric environment that is in effect non-asymmetric. Disorienting features of the new conflict are the unfamiliar objectives that dominate a new strategy of warfare and competition by state and nonstate actors. In these new wars, mass disruption, rather than destruction, can be acceptable goals. The preference of endless conflict over final victory is another strategic objective that forces a reshaping of the accepted wisdom on preparedness and offensive planning.

The impact of technology has been the key driver. The compressing of time and space has made populations more accessible, whether they are markets or political constituencies. Just as economic globalization has opened the field of play to new actors and opportunities ·for creating wealth, global warfare has given many competitors frequent openings for plunder and exploitation. The motives can be political or economic. In addition, radicalization via the Internet is creating a crisis environment, nationally and globally. The risks can be low for the attacker, and the losses to the targeted group can be substantial.

On these subjects, much has been written. Modern weaponry, cyberterrorism, corporate espionage, the corruptibility of failed states, and other various themes are often discussed as instruments of hard power. Each topic has specific issues, vernacular, and a circle of noted authorities and subject matter experts.

Cyberspace is the new field of battle. Because it is the core of critical infrastructure and industrial control systems, the electronic medium is a target for adversaries, whether they be hostile states, criminals, terrorists, or disgruntled employees. The power grid is decentralized, aging, and susceptible to blackouts. The U.S. reliance on these systems and the increasing demands of the digital economy make the quality of life vulnerable. Overall, the cybersecurity threat is outpacing the attempts at a solution. Cyberwar and cybercrime employ the same weapons and require the same skills. However, the skills and weapons may now be for sale. Underscoring how the cyber threat has become so pervasive and vast, the executive director of the National Cyber Security Alliance noted in 2014 that almost every crime has a cyber aspect.[1] The world may be at the onset of an inter-state war among past Cold War rivals and, simultaneously, engaged in an asymmetric conflict of nonstate players who all have access and the means to become peer forces.

The collusion between terrorists and cross-border crime networks is a topic of growing concern and an expanding field of subject matter experts. Still, it is a critical area often given short shrift in most standard texts in courses on national security. Although there is no evidence of any grand strategy of terrorists and criminals locking arms against their legitimate counterparts, motives and opportunities exist around the world for their collusion. The growth of the global economy, communication/computer networks, and the volume of information transmitted has fueled scientific advancement, but it has also complicated the threat vector as crime insinuates itself in the political process and terrorists become more entrepreneurial. The struggle to adapt to a new and perilous environment has strained the capacity to think anew and to form efficient partnerships within government and between the private and public sectors. These changes arose from the natural and irresistible forces of technological development and advancement and high-volume trade. Obviously, those outside the law have benefited as well. Terrorists and criminals take advantage of the same tools and mechanisms of the global economy as do legitimate actors. Therefore, the opportunities to create wealth and to engage in plunder exist side by side.

In the background of these events, many population segments have become victims of poverty. Economic globalization policies from above, such as structural adjustment programs, privatization strategies, and other IMF- and World Bank–imposed reform projects, are often agents of this spreading poverty. The debt trap now being experienced by the developing world has unleashed global migration on a mass scale. Ethnic groups, indigenous populations, religious sects, and others have the ability to traverse the globe while maintaining ties with identities, cultures, belief systems, and devotions or hatreds. They remain connected with their communities and worldviews by the instruments of technology and globalization, which reduce the importance and relevance of geographic distances and the effectiveness of borders. The same tools that can inspire and empower marginalized populations can also make them prey to terrorist and criminal enterprises and conspiracies.

In the case of Russia, globalization has allowed the state to add to its arsenal of subversive activity by weaponizing the Internet and weaponizing economic corruption. The World Wide Web has given the Putin government a grander reach than anything Lenin might have imagined for his propagandist vanguard. The Soviet-style "active measure" practices plied during the Cold War found a new potency in the post–Cold War arena via the proliferation of legitimate and sham news outlets, social media, and a twenty-four-hour news cycle. Russia (as can other state and nonstate actors) uses digital technology to organize a fantastic deception. James Jesus Angleton, the founding counterintelligence chief of the CIA in the 1950s, called this sort of perverted statecraft a "myriad of stratagems, deceptions, artifices, and all other devices of disinformation . . . to confuse and split the West [with] an ever-fluid landscape, where fact and illusion merge, a kind of wilderness of mirrors."[2]

International money flow is another "weapons system," according to Marius Laurinavičius of the Hudson Institute. Through a network of "friendly firms" initially established by the Soviet security organ, Russia created an underground banking system to transfer and launder funds throughout the world. These funds were weaponized through corruption and the financing of extremist political parties, who worked to undermine policies unfavorable to Moscow and create division among Western allies.[3] Former director of U.S. National Intelligence James Clapper named Russia as a "threat actor" and an example of a nation for which "the nexus among organized crime, state actors, and business blurs the distinction between state policy and private gain."[4] Additionally, as Laurinavičius notes,

> This channel does not just operate one way, however, and local business affiliates have also been known to rely on their business connections to provide vital capital and political backing to acquire additional assets and investments in large projects in their national economies. In this way, Russia appears to have created a mutually reinforcing network of patronage that rewards loyalty with loyalty—with increased financial compensation.[5]

The private sector plays a key role in national defense across so many spheres and domains. The weaponizing of money, whether out of Russia, China, or any of the various narco-states, terrorist groups, or transnational criminal organizations, cannot occur without complicity of the international community and, particularly, partners in the West. The lure of bonuses, commissions, bribes, and directorships allows the doors and vaults of government offices and banks to remain open for criminal collusion.[6] Joint ventures and a network of domestic and foreign banks facilitate these sorts of arrangements, which lax regulatory regimes, cryptocurrencies, and affiliates at every level further enable. Mittelman refers to a "web of criminals, the rich, and politicians, [where] the holders of public office provide 'legal' protection for their partners"[7] as another ugly underside of globalization. Economic globalization has accelerated cross-border capital flows and information flows. During the era of neoliberalism, tensions always arise between political forces that demand persistent deregulation and the calls for more accountability.

Criminal intent aside, practical business pressures of just-in-time processing often crowd out concerns for security. Financial constraints, market disruptions, and the absence of regulatory control or governance to establish and enforce cyber "public health" defense often leave fallow the will and the actions necessary to commit resources to protect data or elements of the supply chain. Private firms are also hesitant to release sensitive market or competitive intelligence to the government for fear of being compromised or the loss of competitive advantages. They also sometimes feel they have an overriding responsibility to their shareholders and clients, particularly when the release of information may trigger legal consequences. Meanwhile, the infrastructure is aging. The threat is growing and morphing. Under such pressures, government and commerce are entangled partners. The convergence of functions should, therefore, reflect a confluence of policies—industrial, defense, fiscal, and diplomatic.

The forces of globalization and international trade, persistent hatreds, and an environment of economic and democratic deficits create unfamiliar security threats and smoldering tensions. National defense, worldwide, might be better served when security becomes a part of the core business process. However, in spite of awareness of the overhanging cyber threat, incentives are still lacking, and security investments are not seen as directly converting into earnings.

Motives and Sources of Attack

When Edward Snowden, a former CIA employee and NSA contractor, revealed details of the United States and Britain's mass surveillance programs in 2013, he unleashed a global controversy and had some even accusing him of treason. His revelations, nevertheless, do not focus on the core issue of these programs. The main challenge to governments is not in gathering data but, rather, in managing it. The estimated amounts of data produced each year are almost beyond comprehension. The growth of social networks has added to the situation and intensified the imperative of controlling the massive flows of information. How to sift through these immense amounts of records to find the relatively minute sets of data that could potentially have relevance for national security is more than a task—it is an industry. Tools and methods range from the obvious to the odd. Some governments, like Iran, develop official forms of social media to impose control on or gain information from social media. Less conventional means include an account by a leaked government document revealing that the U.S. and UK governments have used massively multiplayer online games (MMOGs) for surveillance purposes in tracking down potential terrorist threats.[8]

Ultimately, all attempts to access, manipulate, or change information have a human source. Botnets and other automated attacks, in the end, trace to some individual or group. These human sources include official actors (such as spies and saboteurs), profit-oriented organized criminals, terrorists, commercial competitors, ideologically motivated hackers (including campaigners for political and Internet freedoms), political operatives working on behalf of specific candidates or parties, inquisitive and curious people, and journalists. Sources can be separated into external and internal threats—those without or within the target organization. Some of the actor categories above overlap, and some are defined more by their vectors than motivations.

In its definition of *cyber threat,* the U.S. Department of Homeland Security terms it as "any identified efforts directed toward accessing, exfiltrating, manipulating, or impairing the integrity, confidentiality, security, or availability of data, an application, or a federal system, without lawful authority."[9] Taking and reviewing data from the U.S. Federal Bureau of Investigation, the Central Intelligence Agency, and the Software Engineering Institute, the U.S. Government Accountability Office[10] identifies the following list of actors as primary sources of cyberattacks.

Hackers who break into networks for the thrill of the technical challenge or to enhance their reputation in the hacker community. While remote code cracking once required a fair amount of skill or computer knowledge, hackers can now download attack scripts and protocols from the Internet and launch them against victim sites. Therefore, while attack tools have become more sophisticated, they have also become more accessible and easier to use. According to the Central Intelligence Agency, the large majority of hackers do not have the requisite expertise to threaten difficult targets such as critical U.S. networks. Nevertheless, the worldwide population of hackers poses a relatively high threat of an isolated or brief disruption causing serious damage.

Bot network operators are hackers; however, instead of breaking into systems for the challenge or bragging rights, they take over multiple systems in order to coordinate attacks and distribute phishing schemes, spam, and malware attacks. The services of these networks are sometimes made available on underground markets (e.g., purchasing a denial-of-service attack, servers to relay spam or phishing attacks, etc.).

Criminal groups seek to attack systems for financial gain. Specifically, organized crime groups are using spam, phishing, and spyware/malware to commit identity theft and online fraud (see chapter 2). International corporate spies and organized crime syndicates also pose a threat through their ability to conduct industrial espionage and large-scale monetary theft. These services are available for hire, and hacker talent can be developed as well as recruited. Many transnational criminal organizations have state-level capability. Further, there is a thriving underground market for services and products. Many of them are accessible on the dark web, where anonymous marketplaces offer customers untraceable communications and full order and payment management systems.

Foreign intelligence services use cyber tools as part of their information-gathering and espionage activities. In addition, several nations are aggressively working to develop information warfare doctrine, programs, and capabilities. Information warfare extends beyond the technical issues of networks to include psychological warfare through propaganda, the manipulation of news, and the shaping of attitudes via social media and *kompromat* that entails the use of slander. Such capabilities enable a single entity to have a significant and serious impact. Sabotage operations may disrupt or destroy the supply, communications, and economic infrastructures that support military power—impacts that could affect the daily lives of citizens across the United States and other countries across the globe.

Disgruntled organization insiders are a principal source of computer crime. Insiders may not need a great deal of knowledge about computer intrusions because their knowledge of a target system often allows them to gain unrestricted access to cause damage to the system or to steal system data. The insider threat also includes outsourcing vendors as well as employees who accidentally introduce malware into systems.

Phishers are individuals or small groups that execute phishing schemes in an attempt to steal identities or information for monetary gain. Phishers may also use spam and spyware/malware to accomplish their objectives.

Spammers are individuals or organizations that distribute unsolicited e-mail with hidden or false information in order to sell products, conduct phishing schemes, distribute spyware/malware, or attack organizations (i.e., denial of service).

Spyware/malware authors are individuals or organizations with malicious intent that carry out attacks against users by producing and distributing spyware and malware. Several destructive computer viruses and worms have harmed files and hard drives, including the Melissa Macro Virus, the Explore.Zip worm, the CIH (Chernobyl) Virus, Nimda, Code Red, Slammer, and Blaster.

Terrorists seek to destroy, incapacitate, or exploit critical infrastructures in order to threaten national security, cause mass casualties, weaken the U.S. economy, and damage public morale and confidence. Terrorists may use phishing schemes or spyware/malware in order to generate funds or gather sensitive information.

Policy Lagging Technology

In 2008, a cyberattack destroyed a CIA website created to intercept terrorist communications and monitor movements of Middle East extremists. The website was a joint venture between the Central Intelligence Agency and the Saudi government. These "honeypots" are online forums clandestinely organized to entrap participants. Plotters exchange information and assist in operational planning to conduct attacks, sabotage missions, and pass along useful intelligence to accomplices. The traffic generated over the site, in turn, is closely studied and used to support counterintelligence operations. The CIA and its Saudi partners regarded the multiyear project as a boon in their efforts to stem terrorist activity and hinder the enemy's effectiveness in the region. They claimed to have captured a good number of radicals and foiled their attacks as a result of the data retrieved from this online source. Such sites are valuable assets in today's covert wars. As pipelines of information, they can be helpful in blunting militants' attempts to marshal followers, recruit, and spread their message. They are not only a mechanism for gathering actionable intelligence but can also be a conduit for implanting misinformation. The successful attack, which took down the website, consequently "led to a significant loss of intelligence," according to CIA assertions.[11]

However, despite the value to counterintelligence operations, the project did not upend as the result of efforts of a rival group or an exploited enemy looking to dismantle the program. The assault to halt the operation came from a source far closer to home. The decision and successful attack eliminating the website originated from Fort Meade, Maryland—headquarters of the National Security Agency and home of another program, called Countering Adversary Use of the Internet.[12] In other words, the U.S. military attacked and disabled a successful U.S. intelligence operation.

Pentagon officials claimed that the program was putting the lives of American personnel at risk. As useful a tool as the website was to intelligence gathering, it was also deemed to be serving the logistical needs of foreign fighters and jihadists flowing forth from Saudi Arabia into Iraq. The internal debate over the fate of the website involved the National Security Agency, the CIA, the National Security Council, the Department of Justice, the Department of Defense, and the Office of the Director of National Intelligence. Absent from discussions were a well-defined policy for the conduct of cyberwarfare and the legal machinery for assigning proper authority to make a decision and execute a plan. As former CIA director Michael Hayden commented in a *Washington Post* article, "Cyber was moving so fast that we were always in danger of building up precedent before we built up policy."[13]

In addition to exposing the obvious anarchy in national security policy and interagency and departmental turf battles, the incident also unleashed a diplomatic storm. Saudi officials, despite being previously notified, expressed outrage. Several Saudi princes and persons within the intelligence communities were alarmed by the loss of a valuable counterintelligence tool and the impact it could have on their country's national security. Compounding these consequences was the blowback on bystander organizations. Unintended outcomes involved over three hundred affected servers in Saudi Arabia, Germany, and Texas. Diplomatic tensions arose alongside private sector collateral damage.

This clash between industrial age tactics and information age technology claimed its own casualties far apart from the global war on terrorism (GWOT). The entire episode conjures up the tableau of a circular firing squad involving state militaries, private sector interests, bureaucratic territories, diplomatic protocols, and legal jurisdictions. Adding insult to injury, the coda to the operational tragedy is that the process of mobilizing attackers and assets against U.S. forces in Iraq continued. The elimination of the website did no damage to the terrorist logistical apparatus. Within an estimated forty-eight hours, information stored in servers around the world appeared on alternate and replacement websites. Data and users migrated to new loci, and a useful terrorist tool remained in service. In the final accounting, some American lives may have been spared. However, the side effects were the rise in diplomatic tensions, the loss of a valuable counterintelligence weapon, and further damage to the war effort, which may have included the further loss of American life.

Throughout the ordeal of this incident, it becomes apparent that while we may be technically prepared to fight new-age wars, we fight them encumbered by the apparatus and machinery of a bygone era. Old protocols and a degraded security framework from the previous century prevailed over the decision-making process. Policy naturally follows precedent. However, time lag is critical along this curve. As opposed to preceding times, the ability to defend often trails the offense in efficiencies. The terms of battle have changed. Attackers can choose the time and space (either real or virtual) of attack, and the adjustment to the new logic and requirements of war has been difficult. The disconnect, frustration, and disorientation caused by the blare and brawl of foundational national security institutions struggling with the paradigm shift are, perhaps, best expressed in a simple exchange between two bloggers on the subject of cyberwar. In a comment to the *Wall Street Journal*, an unnamed military official wrote,

> If you shut down our power grid, maybe we will put a missile down one of your smoke stacks.

To which an anonymous hacker responded:

> LOLZ . . . We haz 0 smoke stacks, dude![14]

The United States has the most personal computers in use and hosts the most valuable websites, service providers, and online businesses. China, the most populous country in the world, has the second-largest national population of personal computers and the largest national population of mobile-telephone subscribers. The next largest populations of mobile-telephone subscribers are in India and Russia (personal computer ownership is relatively far lower in these countries). Japan, Canada, and Western Europe trail the lead countries, and regional lead actors such as Brazil in South America, Mexico in Central America, and South Africa in Africa basically fill out the global picture of the geographic distribution of world connectivity. It is easy to see where the greatest concentration of cyber conflict occurs. Still, the worldwide web becomes denser every hour as more citizens are connected via an expanding array and commoditization of digital devices. The migration to IPv6 continues, international norms and governance remain lax, and technology overwhelms attempts of the law and policy establishments.

Prioritizing national security interests and privacy rights simultaneously is a delicate balance. Fortunately, the technical means of making the Internet a more democratic and secure instrument of enfranchisement are constantly in development. Software is available and being perfected to protect individual rights of privacy. In addition to the methods of data extraction, integration, and analysis there are programs designed to assure anonymity. Civil liberties need not always be sacrificed for the sake of security. Techniques to anonymize data for protecting privacy and facilitating information sharing are always in development. Graph databases of social networks and privacy-preserving algorithms for data streams are standard projects in the field of algorithmic methodology. This algorithmic research can generate decision trees that allow analysts to separate useful knowledge while providing privacy to affiliated entities. It is, therefore, possible to have an effective administration for extracting valuable information for data analysis while at the same time assuring privacy rights—all efforts in the interest of national security. However, analysts, commentaries, and public opinion are divided on these issues. Cynicism may be at an all-time high as trust in government has been at historic lows—even by those who place security as the nation's principal priority.

The "Sordid Boon" of Social Media

The nineteenth-century English poet William Wordsworth used the metaphor "sordid boon" to express his lament over the obsession with materialism during the early promising days of the First Industrial Revolution. In our information age we have, perhaps, a modern variant of Wordsworth's "sordid boon." The Internet is simultaneously a tool of empowerment and exploitation. While it becomes more indispensable as a means of connecting people and ideas, it is increasingly a key variable for instability worldwide.

The example of the CIA honeypot illustrates how the transformation from industrial age war to an era of information warfare (IW) can be precariously fought and, for the security establishment as well for democratic societies in general, fraught with unexpected consequences. On a grand scale, the World Wide Web is a marvelous tool of empowerment. Social media, also known as social software or Web 2.0 (see chapter 1), adds to the dynamic. Users interact across many devices and fluently transfer between author and audience states—in real time and with outreach to millions. Electronic venues such as Facebook, Twitter, LinkedIn, etc., have become drivers of the information flow. By 2009, Wikipedia had four million articles and YouTube had about one hundred million videos.[15] Social networking services now exceed web-based e-mail usage.[16]

The potential consequences for national security are also dynamic. As the CIA honeypot episode demonstrates, too, social media can mobilize sympathizers, associates, and armed insurgents into action in support of causes or combat. The same virtual pageant functions to bring nonviolent protesters, businesspeople, and consumers together for the sake of peaceful interaction and the steady continuance of commerce. Obviously, not all influencers and outcomes are positive. While the use of social media has been responsible for the exponential growth of e-commerce and e-government, at the same time, it has been a catalyst of events in many well-noted conflicts.

Social media has become a key platform for public discourse and interaction. For younger population segments, it is an almost indispensable medium for expressing views, consuming news, and developing political consciousness and identity. On the other hand, as the power of social media becomes more evident, it has been repurposed for use as a tool for social control. Governments, corporations, and political parties employ citizens, public relations firms, private contractors, and troll farms all over the world to "generate content, direct opinion, and engage with both foreign and domestic audiences"[17] (see figure 3.1).

The power of social software not only tracked the political situation in Egypt but also influenced it. In 2008, a Facebook group launched a prodemocracy protest that attracted tens of thousands of followers and exposed the government's brutality tactics. A few years later it contributed to the forced removal of President Hosni Mubarak. Mubarak's successor and Muslim Brotherhood representative, Mohamed Morsi, fell to similar pressures in 2013. As it expands, the machinery of social media has not lost timing, and its political force only gains vigor. The Arab Spring, which was unofficially launched in 2010, can credit much of its momentum in Egypt, Yemen, Syria, Tunisia, and across the Arab world to the information-sharing functionality and activism organized through social media. However, it is a phenomenon with phantasmagoric properties that often places it astride the thin line between public empowerment and mob rule.

The cyberattack on Estonia in 2007, which was instigated and conducted by freelance Russian hackers with the collusion of government authorities, involved the same suspected sources accused of disabling and defacing Georgian government websites in 2008 while a simultaneous military invasion was in process (see chapter 5). These "cyber riots," as they are known, are a new way of waging war. The 2001 "riot" between China and the United States as a result of an incident involving a U.S. EP-3 reconnaissance and surveillance plane and Chinese F-8 fighter jets is an early instance and case in point. Other examples of social web activities with national and international security implications include the following:

- An online counterrevolution against FARC (Fuerzas Armadas Revolucionarias de Colombia) enlisted over a million participants to protest the Colombian-based guerrilla group's terrorist and criminal activities. An international event in 2008 called "One Million Voices against the FARC" drew attention and world condemnation of FARC atrocities.
- The Mumbai terrorist attacks in 2008 were streamed online and in real time. As the tragedy unfolded, unverified accounts commingled with facts. The pace of the information flow put added pressure on security services, and the element of misinformation may have hindered the government's ability to respond effectively.
- In 2007, the Pakistani government imposed a state of emergency as justification for shutting down privately owned television stations. In reaction, activists, lawyers, and professional and amateur journalists kept records of their government's actions. Once formed and mobilized, the virtual social network worked to assure accountability and in 2009 successfully helped to reinstate the nation's chief justice.[18]
- A political operative who is now serving time in a Colombian prison influenced several Latin American elections with a combination of hacking tools and computer programs that control the activity of social media accounts.[19] Social media software robots have become useful in serving the political and

Figure 3.1 Organizational Density of Cyber Troops

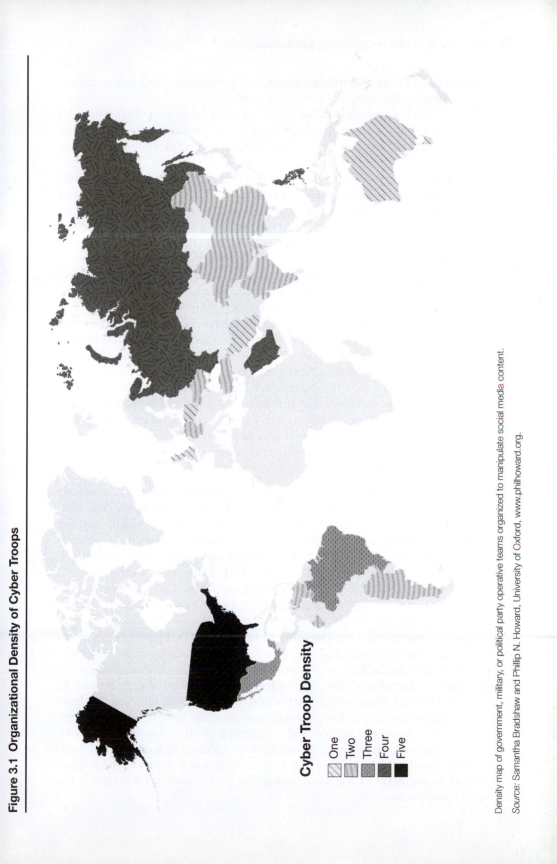

Cyber Troop Density

One
Two
Three
Four
Five

Source: Samantha Bradshaw and Phillip N. Howard, University of Oxford, www.philhoward.org.

Density map of government, military, or political party operative teams organized to manipulate social media content.

criminal aims of state and nonstate actors, terrorist groups, crime organizations, corporations, politicians, and private citizens.

- The U.S. stock market lost $200 billion of value in two minutes when the Free Syrian Army hacked the Associated Press Twitter account and used bots to broadcast fake news that there had been an explosion at the White House.[20]
- "Peñabots" is a term for hashtag spamming that supporters of Mexican president Enrique Peña Nieto used to drown out his political opponents and suppress antigovernment messaging. In addition to obscuring messaging by Peña Nieto's political opposition by manipulating social media algorithms into removing the hashtag from the trending list, the tactics also included the posting of death threats directed at dissidents.[21]
- The People's Republic of China has long appreciated the use of social media as an effective propaganda tool and an instrument of national security policy. It has not only enlisted thousands of professional propagandists to influence online blogs, chat rooms, message boards, and other types of social networking sites. It also is developing offensive capabilities to access proprietary databases, sensitive foreign government information, and infiltration into command-and-control facilities (see chapter 4).
- The Russian Federation's intelligence services regularly conduct a range of activities to gather economic and technological information from U.S. and Western targets. Further, Russia regards cyber as central to its "hybrid warfare" strategy as long as it sees itself as a powerful disruptive influence on a world stage that it can no longer impact because of its diminished economic and military roles (see chapter 5).

Over the past decade, the growth in social networks has been enormously robust. The processes and relationships that govern them are complex. The benefits to national security can be significant, even critical. It is a valuable enabler of information sharing between governments, government agencies, a government and its citizenry, individuals in government and communities of interest, and researchers and government data sources. Web 2.0 is a connective tool and an intellectual force multiplier.[22] Not only is it useful as a general networking apparatus for expressing and advocating policy, but it can also identify emerging trends and influencers. As missions overlap between the Department of Homeland Security (DHS), the Department of Defense (DoD), the Department of State, and law enforcement and emergency management agencies, these capabilities can be essential in forming a seamless connection for diverse missions.

Combat personnel and first responders rely on situational awareness to improve operational effectiveness. Extraction of geospatial information from maps and satellite images, and textual information from news articles, websites, and Twitter, can assist war fighters and emergency personnel as it can analysts. This information can be retrieved in real time and shared in a distributed manner. In this regard, social networks like Twitter form a real-time, on-the-ground distributed sensor network for whoever has the power to filter and classify the messages appropriately.

Algorithms, Software, Audience Mapping, and Targeted Messaging

In general, social networks are a resource for the intelligence community, who can use software programs to help them integrate and distill data in order to create holistic actionable intelligence. This information can reflect a particular incident at a particular time, like a revolution or earthquake, or reflect the knowledge, interests, and activities of an individual or group over periods of time. Crisis responders, emergency managers, and military leaders tend to focus on the former, while intel analysts concentrate on the latter. In both cases, natural language processing programs can be used to analyze, filter, classify, and otherwise process human language, whether it is news articles, e-mails, tweets, reports, recorded conversation, or any other medium.[23]

Eduard Hovy of Carnegie Mellon University further explains that this field includes programs that perform information retrieval (Google), speech recognition (IBM's ViaVoice), information extraction into databases, automated summarization of one or more texts, question answering such as IBM's Watson system (featured in the TV quiz game *Jeopardy!*), and many other applications.

Frequently these engines create a characterization of a word, concept, topic, person, organization, or even entire document that comprises a list of the most relevant words and phrases associated with that object, with each word or phrase being given a strength or weight score. Even though they do not fully describe the nature of the object in question, these so-called topic/word signatures are useful for a variety of purposes.[24] The field also includes so-called inference engines, which combine rules and old facts to deduce new facts to aid analysts in filling knowledge gaps and finding inconsistencies in oral or written texts. From these programs come data analytic techniques such as anomaly detection and pattern learning that help interpret subjective text, opinions, and attitudes of authors and other agents. A key approach in information retrieval and disambiguation (natural language processing that governs which sense of a word may be applicable to its use in a specific sentence) is **textual entailment**. Textual entailment captures the semantic variability of texts and performs inferences as it moves from a lexical to a relational context. Basically put, it is a relation between two natural human language sentences where readers of the "text" would agree the "hypothesis" is most likely true (*Peter is snoring* → *A man sleeps*).

Whereas textual entailment refers to the directional relation between text fragments, **sentiment analysis** is the use of natural language processing and text analysis to systematically identify, extract, quantify, and study subjective information and emotive states of the author. Sentiment analysis is broadly applied to the "voice of the customer" that ranges from marketing services, survey responses, and online and social media. It is used to uncover the attitude and mind-set of a speaker or writer with respect to a topic or the overall contextual polarity, separation, or emotional response to an interaction or event. These algorithms are also valuable tools for intelligence gathering. They have been successfully applied in accurately forecasting events that include emerging market signals, the outbreak of diseases, and political unrest. "The Intelligence Advanced Research Projects

Activity, a former Deputy Director of the CIA, and other prominent players in the national security community have publicly touted social media sentiment analysis"[25] as it has increasingly become a more relied upon technique in open-sourced intelligence operations.

However, the use and benefits of these algorithms can be undermined by any hostile state or nonstate actor who uses social media software robots, or **social media bots** (SMBs), to generate Internet traffic that targets social media accounts in order to spread misinformation. As we have seen, these online stratagems can give the appearance of false consensus, fabricate popularity, and manipulate public opinion. Their use becomes an effective means of malicious activity. Ultimately, destabilizing democracy, recruiting terrorists, disrupting markets, and complicating and hindering open-source intelligence collection are outcomes of computer coders who can access botnets and need only possess backgrounds as amateur hackers and software script writers.

Often bots can be programmed to interact intelligently and influence behavior. Political operatives use them to identify social media users who might be dissatisfied or disgruntled with their government, a political party, or a specific political figure. With the aid of proper messaging, these individuals can be recruited as activists or friendly voters. Cambridge Analytica was a data analysis firm that attracted media and investigative attention during the 2016 U.S. presidential campaign. According to some reports, the Trump campaign hired Cambridge Analytica to work with its own digital operations, headed by Donald Trump's son-in-law, Jared Kushner. A primary aim of these operations was to target voters with messages crafted to reinforce the outrage of supporters and, alternatively, nurture the apathy of Hillary Clinton supporters and independents. (The firm is involved in a lawsuit with the *Guardian*, which published a series of articles linking it to the Leave.EU campaign during the run-up to the Brexit referendum in the UK.)[26] Cambridge Analytica mapped the voter terrain to identify which parts of the Republican platform mattered most: trade, immigration, health care, etc. The subsequent phases involved producing content or narrative, identifying the audience, building the bots, microtargeting the races and voters in the most crucial swing districts and states, and finally unleashing the message with optimal timing. A reporter for the BBC who had been covering the potential coordination between the Trump campaign and Russia wrote in March 2017,

> This is a three-headed operation. Said one former official setting out the case based on the intelligence: First, hackers steal damaging emails from senior Democrats. Secondly, the stories based on this hacked information appear on Twitter and Facebook posted by thousands of automated bots, then on Russian-English language outlets, RT [Russian Times] and Sputnik, then right-wing U.S. "news" sites such as Infowars and Breitbart, then Fox and the mainstream media. Thirdly, Russians download the online voter rolls.[27]

The threat to liberal society is not only to the democratic process; the private citizen is at risk as well. Software exists to scrape information from the social media associated with a person's name. Unfortunately, while social media sites often encourage users to expand their social networks, concerns for privacy receive too little regard, and caution is too often dismissed by social media companies and the public. Some social media allow anybody to view information on anybody else, store such information in insecure domains, or even sell such information. This data can be useful to criminals, terrorists, and spies—depending on the employment or position of the targeted user.

A Belgian newspaper in November 2012 published an investigation into how many employees of the Belgian state security service listed their employer on Facebook or LinkedIn. Several French users of LinkedIn posted their employer as France's external intelligence agency. In a similar investigation, an American journalist discovered that more than two hundred users of LinkedIn claimed the Central Intelligence Agency as their employer.[28] These personal revelations are more frequent when users are looking for another job or, perhaps, a romantic relationship. Official employees upon leaving their positions or while conducting job searches have been known to distribute online photographs of themselves inside secure domains, of their official credentials, and of themselves with important persons as evidence of their professional qualifications.[29] Once exploited, victims of online abuse have difficulties finding redress in the justice system. Privacy and accuracy of information is less protected legally when online than offline. As Bruce Newsome notes,

> Private citizens face practically no criminal legal restrictions on online behavior. The tort system is usually a waste of time for claimants or victims; the few cases that have been heard in civil or criminal court usually fail to clarify responsibility or harm. In practice, cyber information and misinformation are controlled by users and hosts, motivated mostly by their intrinsic ethics and external commercial pressures, not the law. In the United States, the Communications Decency Act of 1996 makes clear that Internet service providers and online hosts are not responsible for the content of posts from outside parties, although the positive implication of this clarity is that hosts are free to moderate or delete content without legal liability.[30]

These legal obstacles encourage rampant online slander, defamation, misinformation, and abuse, including online bullying. The ambiguities in the law also allow criminals and even foreign intelligence agencies to use the anonymity of the Internet and the dark web to pursue their aims. Russian intelligence often takes advantage of cyberspace by resorting to the familiar dirty trick tactics of their predecessors in the KGB. Known as *kompromat*, these activities include the fabrication and planting of compromising or illegal material in order to discredit opponents and journalists for the purpose of shaping public opinion. Today, the "cyber mischief making" by Russia's army of official and semiofficial hackers blurs all boundaries "between truth and falsehood in the service of operational needs [and] has created a climate in Russia in which even the most serious and grotesque accusations, like those involving pedophilia, are simply a currency for settling scores."[31] Victims have found themselves defending their reputations in public against accusations that run the gamut of charges from corruption, drug trafficking, and fraud to adultery, pedophilia, and prostitution.

According to a 2016 article in the *New York Times*, "no target is too small to warrant attention, no attack too petty," and attacks are conducted by agents "trained to believe that the ends always justify the means."[32] The *Times* article adds that political opponents, environmental activists, and members of cultural societies that the regime finds offensive are among the list of *kompromat* targets. The dark web, discussed in chapter 2, is a cyber demesne where criminals, terrorists, and state-sponsored hackers and spies conduct business freely, and which at times can involve the work of ruining private lives. This Kafkaesque underworld is another dangerous reality of a globalization process driven by technology and challenging the imagination to control it equitably across jurisdictions. The dark aspect of this modern "sordid boon" might best be expressed in the boast of an advertisement by a deep web netizen:

> I'll do anything for money. [I will ruin] your opponents, business or private persons you don't like. I can ruin them financially and or get them arrested, whatever you like. If you want someone to get known as a child porn user, no problem. [A price of $600 per "account" was demanded—denominated in Bitcoins.][33]

Hindering the use of social media to combat its abuse by state and nonstate actors is oftentimes the institutionalization of old practices and the hierarchal structure of the chains of command.[34] The inflexibility of governmental bureaucratic structures can run in contrast to the self-organizing, horizontal nature of social media. There exists as well a cultural divide between many military commanders and entrenched bureaucrats, whose understanding of social software is comparatively blurred, versus junior members of the security establishment whose familiarity is more immediate and crystalline. Many observers claim that until a coherent information strategy forms, a great constructive potential of social media may remain fully unmet.[35]

In the meantime, progress pushes ahead in the fields of algorithmic methodology and cognitive security. Bot technology and bot detection technology are in an intensifying arms race. According to one expert, this competition between the opposing technologies "will only be over when the effectiveness of early detection will sufficiently increase the cost of deception."[36] At present, algorithms allow bots the ability to self-govern as they search the net for profile images and even "post messages at particular times of day, engage in conversation, and 'clone' real users' behavior."[37] The "race" becomes more intense as algorithmic research becomes more refined as methodologies move to genetic algorithmic theory from less sophisticated heuristic algorithms.

Currently, bot detection technology is expensive, and its effectiveness is as yet not convincing enough to justify investment.[38] However, as the financial industry becomes more subject to the economic and market risks of this sort of public manipulation, there may be a new awareness of the threat. Most likely this sector will be the first to commit resources, if market disruptions and eroding investor confidence are the outcomes of doing nothing.

| Box 3.1 | **Heuristic Algorithm versus Genetic Algorithm** |

Heuristic Algorithm

Heuristic algorithms find solutions among all possible options. However, the most optimum solution is not guaranteed. These algorithms approximate and are directional rather than absolute. They find a solution close to the best one, quickly and easily. However, solutions might be optimal, despite the algorithm's suppression of some of the problem's demands.

Genetic Algorithm

A genetic algorithm is a method for solving both constrained and unconstrained optimization problems based on a natural selection process that mimics biological evolution. The process continually adjusts a population of individual solutions and randomly selects ones from the current population, which at each step are used as parents to produce creations for the next generation. Over successive generations, the population "evolves" toward an optimal solution.

"Swarmcasting"—Terrorists, Protesters, and Hired Guns

The use of media platforms as a logistics and recruiting tool by terrorist groups such as ISIS, Jabhat al-Nusra, and their affiliated groups is well known and well documented. According to Ali Fisher, "media mujahedeens" avoid exposure and interdiction by platform owners and government agencies by relying on emergent and self-organizing behaviors. Working in clusters, operating through a dispersed network of accounts, constantly reconfiguring (reorganizing in midflight as bees or birds do), the new net warriors form "swarmcasts," which take advantage of the interconnectiveness of networks. The ability to repost and distribute information over a span of less time and a greater variety of locales is a key advantage over legitimate actors who attempt to remove their content.[39] A key element to these networks is the absence of a single hub point where all information must flow. The concept runs counter to the design of hub-and-spoke networks. These centralized constructs are vulnerable to debilitation if a central node is lost, whereas "these operations are emergent, collective behaviors of a complex system—much the way hurricanes and ecosystems self-organize in nature."

> Content can be domiciled "on thousands of devices around the world with copies of a film dispersed so widely it then has a permanent presence as it can be re-shared any time a copy is removed or a user requests a specific video." Media mujahedeen are also reconfiguring the mix of platform comprising the swarmcast.[40]

The parallel with guerrilla war also illustrates the similarities between kinetic operations and cyber in "irregularized" warfare against pyramidal structures. As with their predecessors from earlier ages, these net war combatants operate in small groups and have the ability to swarm, penetrate, disperse, disrupt, elude, evade, and reform (resilience). Organizationally, these challengers to established power recall past asymmetric conflict since the age of Rome. Now the same tactics are adaptable to the information age.

In contrast to ISIS and al-Nusra "media mujahedeens," **Anonymous** is a loose collective of hackers devoid of any ideological bent or core beliefs who operate similarly. Rather than a network of dedicated believers organized to create a constant presence for the purposes of spreading propaganda, planning attacks, organizing operations, and recruitment, Anonymous members, known as Anons, have no distinct profile.[41] This is a global collection of hacktivists and script kiddies where dissent is common and goals vary depending on consensus and relativity to a foundational principle. Authoritarianism is a frequent thematic target. It is a cyber mob that sporadically leverages its mass number of participants of varying skill levels to protest governments, institutions, and sometimes individuals they deem antidemocratic. Media outlets, however, are exempt from their ire and assault.

Past targets include government entities in the United States, Canada, Israel, Tunisia, and Uganda. Anonymous has also targeted the Church of Scientology and various known criminal organizations. Attacks mostly involve DDoS and website defacements against organizations the group considers antithetical to their common opposition to censorship and control of Internet platforms. Visa, MasterCard, and PayPal fell victim to them as a result of their refusal to process payments to WikiLeaks. Other high-profile prey includes websites of the U.S. Department of Justice, the FBI, Sony, the Motion Picture Association of America, and the Recording Industry Association of America in 2012. According to Anonymous, their "crime" was the effort to shut down one of the world's largest file-sharing sites, Megaupload.[42] On the other hand, the Arab Spring and the Occupy movement found support.

Since 2003, the group has been responsible for mostly nuisance and protest campaigns against its perceived foes, and sometimes it operates with an affiliated hacker group, LulzSec (short for Lulz Security). Although these attacks cause relatively little damage, "the group's construction and global membership afford it significant influence and resilience to law enforcement efforts."[43] Despite efforts by authorities to control its movement, in 2015, Anonymous claimed responsibility for attacking such high-profile targets as the World Trade Organization, Trump Towers, and an ISIS website. In 2017, Anonymous also attacked the websites of Spain's Ministry of Transportation and Ministry of Public Works in support of Catalonia's independence.[44]

Over time, it has created for itself a distinctive brand name. Its website (in nonstandard English) claims, "We will always fight for people rights. We want every citizens of the world is equal. We harm anyone at any time who doing wrong things."[45] Anonymous videos often end with the patented catchphrase: "We are Anonymous. We are legion. We do not forgive. We do not forget. Expect us." Their crest and motif is a stylized mask of Guy Fawkes, the main conspirator of the plot to blow up the British House of Lords in 1605.

Pure, unadorned crime is of course another great motivator among hacker groups. As in the legitimate world, there exists an economic service sector for contractors who provide their clients with stolen intellectual property, trade secrets, financial data, and details of business plans or merger and acquisition contracts. An example is the group Wild Neutron, or Morpho—more commonly known as the **Butterfly Group**.

Butterfly targets intellectual property and insider trading information for resale. It is a hacker-for-hire group "ready to go to work for anyone motivated enough to hire them."[46] Pharmaceutical formulas, manufacturing designs, and strategic planning details all fall within their list of targets. A 2015 report by Symantec stated, "Butterfly is financially motivated, stealing information it can potentially profit from. The group appears to be agnostic about the nationality of its targets, leading us to believe that Butterfly is unaffiliated to any nation state."[47] As of 2015 it is believed to have successfully exfiltrated corporate secrets from forty-nine organizations in more than twenty countries.

Butterfly and similar mercenary and espionage groups obtain specific knowledge of information to steal and the systems from which to steal the data through competitor sources or organization insiders. Watering hole exploits are a common attack vector. Symantec further asserts that Butterfly may not be solely profiteering from its attacks as "hackers for hire," targeting corporations on request. The group may also select its own targets and either sell stolen information to the highest bidder or use it for insider trading for its own purposes.[48] Among its victims are several multibillion-dollar companies operating in the Internet, IT software, pharmaceutical, and commodities sectors. Twitter, Facebook, Apple, and Microsoft are among the companies, to date, that have publicly acknowledged attacks.[49]

As discussed above, estimates on the extent of cybercrime are difficult to assess, and the volume of economic loss is as difficult to valuate. Ranges extend from a few billion dollars to hundreds of billions. Data collection is complicated, particularly when it concerns the theft of intellectual property. Additionally, some companies are unaware of their losses, while others make efforts to conceal them.[50] As malware commoditizes and the cost of bot rentals drops, there will be more entrants into illegal markets, and access to technology will compound.

"Psyber Warfare"

Cyberspace can be broken down into three main layers: content, connectivity, and cognition. Within the United States, we focus on cybersecurity at the connectivity layer and argue that any attempt to limit the free flow of content is against our fundamental principles. For example, in 2011, the White House International Strategy for Cyberspace was subtitled "Prosperity, Security and Openness in a Networked World," focused on promoting the Internet Freedom Agenda within international forums. Doing so focuses a suspicious international audience on the United States as being a greater proponent of using the Internet as a tool for democratization via freedom of speech rather than on the economic benefits of open networks resulting in national prosperity.

U.S. involvement in *openly* promoting and organizing "digital activists" in the fight for free flows of information has generated international friction that is counterproductive to promoting international cooperation on cybersecurity issues. The "Internet Freedom Agenda" is one example of this phenomenon. The Department of State is openly distributing "activist" software designed to circumvent cybersecurity measures within authoritarian regimes. Such technology effectively allows citizen-activists to hack past government digital sentries to spread forbidden information. Other tools allow activists to don digital disguises and organize themselves into social movements designed to topple regimes. Officials in Russia, China, and other nondemocratic countries have declared these activities as tantamount to spearheading digitized regime change. From their perspective, the United States is aiding and abetting criminal activity. This does not contribute to our national efforts to secure cyberspace. For many countries, the content the Department of State is enabling to spread is just as dangerous from their perspective as malicious code or intellectual property theft is to us. While the Internet Freedom Agenda clearly articulates a balance of security with freedom, taking worldwide Internet use out of national contexts to create a one-size-fits-all model is a flawed approach that undermines global cybersecurity cooperation and ignores the legitimate threat of what we term *psyber warfare*.

The Internet is not a luxury. It is a critical tool that when unrestricted allows information and knowledge to flow freely across the globe. This opens new possibilities for economic development and innovation. A by-product of this is freedom of thought and expression. Internet freedom is a policy that is inconsistently applied within the United States. While the U.S. State Department, the originator of the policy, advocates for freedom of speech worldwide, this policy causes unnecessary friction with allies and competitors alike. The Europeans have strong laws against xenophobic speech that are contrary to the spirit of the Internet Freedom Agenda. The Department of Defense plays whack-a-mole with terrorists, and authoritarian regimes see the agenda as a direct threat to their regime stability. Indeed, after the Russian interference in the U.S. election, it appears that "fake news" can have an impact on electoral outcomes. From Washington to Paris via Madrid, governments in democratic societies are beginning to understand that free flows of information without regard for the potential political consequences of the content may detrimentally affect societal stability. It will be a delicate balancing act not to go down a slippery slope and follow a Chinese or Russian model of censorship of information. However, the Internet Freedom Agenda as it was may no longer be that altruistic policy option that attempted to globalize the First Amendment via the Internet.

Similar challenges resulting from the misuse of the Internet occur in the United States. While our responses are not as severe as those in repressive regimes, there is some resemblance to what occurs in less democratic societies.

Although the United States has an established democracy, counterterrorist policies restrict some uses of the Internet. During the 2009 G20 Pittsburgh Summit, anarchists in New York were arrested for allegedly scanning police frequencies and using Twitter to inform the antiglobalization protesters as to the actions of law enforcement. During the 2011 London riots, the free flow of information was also cut off, citing national security. Juxtapose this with Jasmine revolutionaries protesting in China who are arrested for national security concerns for organizing themselves with similar technologies.

Broadband Mobility

The deployment of IPv6 and its massive address space, in conjunction with the convergence of industrial sensing systems with the Internet, are two trends that will drive the third major change in the cyber landscape: the use of broadband mobile devices. In the developing world, the trend is for countries to skip over the plain old telephone system (POTS) and install wireless communications infrastructures, including broadband Internet and cellular communications. Standards such as WiMAX need IPv6 to support large numbers of customers. It will be possible to create ad hoc networks that will effectively be shadow Internets on a local level. This presents both opportunities and risks for U.S. military operations. It should also be noted that extraordinarily low-priced Chinese-made computer hardware products are lucrative buys in Asia and the developing world.[51] Furthermore, Chinese entities such as Huawei are on the leading edge of developing the standards of next-generation mobile 4G LTE networks.[52]

Even under U.S. law, not all content can flow freely through the Internet. For instance, U.S. law defines *cyberbullying* as transmitting "any communication, with the intent to coerce, intimidate, harass, or cause substantial emotional distress to a person, using electronic means to support severe, repeated, and hostile behavior." Depending on circumstances and state laws, there can be legal consequences. Therefore, creating some content may be viewed as a criminal offense punishable by fine or imprisonment. Russian and Chinese officials use such examples to claim that inconsistencies between U.S. domestic and international cyberstrategies are indicative of a double standard.

A future with mobile broadband devices where interpersonal connections can be made by flipping out a device from one's pocket is indicative of the need for national security planners and operators to take into account the importance of exploiting the mind to achieve effects in the real world, and also to mitigate potential adversary operations that aim to exploit the human mind. Such efforts extend well beyond the terrorist efforts to radicalize and recruit individuals to their cause and have broader implications for U.S. operations. The question that should be asked within the national security establishment today should focus on identifying and articulating the military's and the broader intelligence community's roles and missions in the areas where cyber and neuroscience overlap to provide the United States with opportunities to counter and deter possible adversarial actions in the domain.

Box 3.2   WiMAX

WiMAX (Worldwide Interoperability for Microwave Access) is a technology standard for long-range wireless networking, for both mobile and fixed connections. WiMAX is developed by an industry consortium, overseen by a group called the WiMAX Forum that certifies WiMAX equipment to ensure that it meets technology specifications.

Source: www.lifewire.com.

Box 3.3   4G LTE

The term **4G LTE** is actually two terms. *4G* refers to the fourth generation of data technology for cellular networks, surpassing the third generation, 3G. *LTE* is short for "long-term evolution" and represents a very technical process for high-speed data for phones and other mobile devices. It is not as much a technology as it is the track and direction to achieve 4G speeds.

Another technological breakthrough with a potential underside for national security is **IPTV** and **software-defined radio**. This technology allows for the broadcasting of audio-video material over a packet-switch IP network. Currently, there is a shift toward this mode of programming with the rise of video-on-demand online services. However, IPv4 networks limit the transmission to a unicast model. That is, in terms of use experience, if someone wants to change a program, pressing "next channel" will require the device to establish a new connection, leading to a lag in load time of the next channel or program being requested. IPv6 allows for multicasting. Standards today over which IPTV services will run are emerging (such as the ITU's G.hn standard, which American companies such as AT&T support[53]).

IPTV will allow for current and new services to evolve into a format that will resemble the seamlessness of how we watch television today. It is highly likely that this will result in a paradigm shift similar to the one experienced when the television model shifted from local broadcast to satellite broadcast. As such, it will present new opportunities for the United States to broadcast messages worldwide, following paradigms from general broadcasts to targeting an individual's screen. These opportunities will exist on the open Internet. However, it is conceivable that with IPTV embedded into the closed networks described above, it will serve as another secure platform for violent extremist organizations to maintain a grip on the minds of their followers within self-referential environments.

The purpose and scope of this chapter was to provide some insight and a broad strategic estimate of several technologies. Many of these tools are already upon us. Others are being rolled out and slowly being put into practice. In a later chapter, we focus on technological trends that may shape the way the cyber environment will look by 2035. However, given current technological trends, it is a fool's errand to try to predict what even the next five years of cyberspace will bring. Considering also the rapid pace of innovation in the private sector and the unpredictability of disruptive technologies, subject matter experts in this field are best differentiated by their varying degrees of ignorance rather than their insight into the future. Thus, this chapter aimed to focus on certain changing core technologies that define cyberspace and their impact on peripheral technologies where applications will be built.

Finally, globalization has drawn populations closer together. As the process goes forward, it simultaneously creates opportunity for collaboration and tension.

Box 3.4 Cyber Risk Management: The Corporate Governance Imperative

Joseph W. McGrath

Global multinational corporations jumped to take advantage of the dynamics of globalization. They knew they could improve their financial performances by leveraging the economic benefits of using the lowest-cost labor around the globe if it delivered the same-quality results that they were accustomed to in North America and Western Europe. They moved manufacturing to China, Taiwan, Vietnam, Mexico, and other low-cost countries. They relocated call centers to India, Eastern Europe, and Latin America. They transferred software development and information technology–managed services to India where there is a vast infrastructure of engineering universities led by the Indian Institutes of Technology (IIT). It was also incredibly important that English was pervasive as a second language across all of India. They relied on a system of just-in-time supply chains to link these enterprises to a complex integrated global network.

The advances in technology served as the underpinnings of these far-flung operations. The Internet and interconnected high-speed communication networks were the digital circulatory system that linked everything and drove the information flows in this twenty-four-by-seven real-time system across six continents. Ubiquitous computing and communications in every major country involved allowed this to happen. It was this infrastructure that also proved to be its greatest weakness. This global network was its greatest vulnerability. In this far-reaching multicountry network of data centers, servers, gateways, routers, and websites, it could never be made totally secure. There were too many points of entry and too many employees, customers, suppliers, and partners who have some form of access to it. Bad actors in both the public and private sector were prepared to take advantage of it. And they did.

In 2016, reported data breaches increased by 40 percent. Yahoo! announced the largest data breach in history, affecting more than one billion accounts. At retailer Target, 110 million customers' personal and financial information was exposed. Home Depot was hacked, and credit card data was stolen from fifty million customers, which resulted in a $179 million settlement with customers. Hackers stole $81 million from the Swift payment system related to the Bangladesh Central Bank. At Blue Cross Blue Shield/Anthem, a data breach impacted eighty million customers and resulted in a $115 million settlement. Finally, Equifax, one of the three largest credit agencies in the United States, suffered a breach that affected 143 million customers, which included social security numbers and driver's license numbers. It may have been the worst breach ever. Because of the significant amount of time that elapsed between when the breach occurred and when the CEO informed his board of directors and the company's customers, the company lost total credibility, it had to testify before the U.S. Congress, and the CEO was fired. These are just the tip of the iceberg of stories regarding companies impacted by cyberattacks, intrusions, and theft.

Executives in global multinationals now realize that cyber risk may be one of the biggest challenges they face over the next decade. Nearly all of these companies had already appointed a chief information security officer (CISO) and developed a cyber risk security plan under the chief information officer (CIO), but they now recognize that these efforts fall short of what is required in the future. CEOs and their boards of directors now realize that this dilemma may be the greatest systemic existential risk to their companies.

The solution to this challenge is an end-to-end strategy that involves every employee and is the ultimate responsibility of the board of directors. There needs to be a governance process that identifies all potential risks and then addresses those vulnerabilities on a real-time basis. There needs to be an organization-wide culture of cyber awareness. The board needs to be briefed at every board meeting by either the audit/risk subcommittee or the technology subcommittee every time they meet. Ideally, they should create a cyber risk committee. They need to understand the risks to their firms and the appropriate responses. It will be a financial and reputation game changer if they do not. Senior

management and the board of directors must develop an extremely comprehensive cyber risk management strategy that is an overlay to all of their company's processes, systems, and policies and defines the responses to the challenges that they will inevitably face.

Globalization has dramatically improved the financial performance of many global multinationals. The system that has been put in place to support it has now placed it at risk. It must now invest in the cyber competencies, systems, and processes to protect it. This will ensure accountability at the most senior levels of the enterprise.

Joseph W. McGrath is retired chief executive officer of Unisys Corporation and a past member of the Technology CEO Council, the Business Roundtable, and the G100 CEO Network.

Whether associated by cultural or traditional ties or motivated by unadorned economic or self-interest, the new arena of conflict is a constellation of states, corporations, terrorists, criminals, and social activists. The cyberspace infrastructure is the critical underpinning of the global economy and human interaction, and therefore its integrity is essential to national security, public safety, and modern civic intercourse. The hyper-interconnection, which evolved parallel with globalization, expanded opportunities for all. However, as economic and democratic deficits persist, they also create smoldering tensions and unfamiliar security threats.

Key Terms

hacker
bot network operator
criminal group
foreign intelligence service
disgruntled organization insider
phisher
spammer
spyware/malware author
terrorist
textual entailment

sentiment analysis
social media bot
kompromat
Anonymous
Butterfly Group
WiMAX
4G LTE
IPTV
software-defined radio

Notes

[1] "The Role of Local Law Enforcement Agencies in Preventing and Investigating Cybercrime," in *Critical Issues in Policing Series*, Police Executive Research Forum, April 2014, 4.

[2] https://wais.stanford.edu/Governements/gov_ciajamesatleton.htm.

[3] Marius Laurinavičius, "Weaponizing Kleptocracy: Putin's Hybrid Warfare," Hudson Institute, June 2017, 35.

[4] Ibid., 13.

[5] Ibid., 16.

[6] Karen Dawisha, *Putin's Kleptocracy: Who Owns Russia?* (New York: Simon & Schuster, 2014), 340.

[7] James H. Mittelman, *The Globalization Syndrome: Transformation and Resistance* (Princeton, NJ: Princeton University Press, 2000), 209.

[8] M. Mazzetti and J. Elliott, "Spies Infiltrate a Fantasy Realm of Online Games," *New York Times*, December 9, 2013.

[9] U.S. Department of Homeland Security, "Privacy Impact Assessment for the Enhanced Cybersecurity Service (ECS)," http://www.dhs.gov/sites.default/files/publications/privacy_pia_nppd_ecs_jan2013.pdf.

[10] U.S. Government Accountability Office, *Critical Infrastructure Protection, Department of Homeland Security Faces Challenges in Fulfilling Cybersecurity Responsibilities*, GAO-05-434, Washington, DC, May 26, 2005.

[11] Ellen Nakashima, "Dismantling of Saudi-CIA Web Site Illustrates Need for Clearer Cyberwar Policies," *Washington Post*, March 19, 2010.

[12] Ibid.

[13] Ibid.

[14] Lawrence Husick, senior fellow at the Foreign Policy Research Institute, presentation in Washington, DC, July 11, 2011.

[15] Mark Drapeau and Linton Wells II, "Social Software and National Security: An Initial Net Assessment," Center for Technology and National Security Policy, National Defense University, April 2009, 1.

[16] Gregory C. Wilshusen, "Social Media: Federal Agencies Need Policies and Procedures for Managing and Protecting Information They Access and Disseminate," General Accountability Office, GOA-11-605, June 2011.

[17] Samantha Bradshaw and Phillip N. Howard, "Troops, Trolls and Troublemakers: A Global Inventory of Organized Social Media Manipulation," Computational Propaganda Research Project, University of Oxford, 2017, 4.

[18] Drapeau, 21.

[19] Matthew Bondy, "Bad Bots: The Weaponization of Social Media," Project on International Peace and Security, Institute for the Theory and Practice of International Relations, 2017, 4.

[20] Ibid., 5.

[21] Ibid.

[22] Drapeau, 34.

[23] Eduard Hovy, Language Technologies Institute, Carnegie Mellon University, conversation with author, July 17, 2013.

[24] Ibid.

[25] Bondy, 7.

[26] Kate Brannen, "Did Russians Target Democratic Voters, with Kushner's Help?," *Newsweek*, May 23, 2017, http://www.newsweek.com/did-russians-target-dem-voters-kushners-help-613612.

[27] Ibid.

[28] Bruce Oliver Newsome and Jack A. Jarmon, *A Practical Introduction to Homeland Security and Emergency Management from Home to Abroad* (Los Angeles: Sage Publications/CQ Press, 2016), 395.

[29] Ibid., 396.

[30] Ibid.

[31] Andrew Higgins, "Foes of Russia Say Child Pornography Is Planted to Ruin Them," *New York Times*, December 9, 2016.

[32] Ibid.

33 Op. cit.

34 James J. Carafano, "Social Media and National Security: A Wake Up Call," *Joint Force Quarterly*, March 2011, http://archive.atlantic-community.org/index/items/view/Social_Media_and_National_Security:_A_Wake-Up_Call.

35 Ibid.

36 Emilio Ferrara, Onur Varol, Clayton Davis, Filippo Menczer, and Alessandro Flammini, "The Rise of Social Bots," *Communications of the ACM* 59, no. 7 (July 2016): 103–4.

37 Ibid., 99–100.

38 Bondy, 7.

39 Ali Fisher, "Swarmcast: How Jihadist Networks Maintain a Persistent Online Presence," *Perspectives on Terrorism* 9, no. 3 (2015).

40 Ibid.

41 James Scott and Drew Spaniel, "Know Your Enemies: A Primer on Advanced Persistent Threat Groups," Institute for Critical Infrastructure Technology, 28.

42 Matt Peckham, "10 Sites Skewered by Anonymous, Including FBI, DOJ, U.S. Copyright Office," *Time*, January 20, 2012, http://techland.time.com/2012/01/20/10-sites-skewered-by-anonymous-including-fbi-doj-u-s-copyright-office.

43 Op. cit.

44 https://www.scmagazine.com/anonymous-hackers-launched-ddos-attacks-and-deface-spanish-government-sites/article/703115.

45 http://www.anonymoushackers.net.

46 https://www.csoonline.com/article/2947714/data-protection/morpho-group-goes-after-corporate-ip.html.

47 https://www.symantec.com/connect/blogs/butterfly-profiting-high-level-corporate-attacks.

48 Ibid.

49 Ibid.; Scott, 30.

50 "The Economic Impact of Cybercrime and Cyber Espionage," Center for Strategic and International Studies and McAfee, July 2013, 3.

51 Lieutenant Commander A. Anand, "Threats to India's Information Environment," in *Information Technology: The Future Warfare Weapon* (New Delhi: Ocean Books, 2000), 56–62.

52 "Huawei Conducts World's First Commercial Network LTE Category 4 Trial," May 9, 2012, http://www.cellular-news.com/story/54329.php.

53 Sean Buckley, "AT&T Officially Endorses G.hn Home Networking Standards," *Fierce Telecom*, June 2, 2011, http://www.fiercetelecom.com/story/att-officially-endorses-ghn-home-networking-standard/2011-06-02.

China 4

Cyberspace, and its subcomponent, the Internet, is the twenty-first century's powder keg. Competing interests and ideologies have emerged over the past decade to carve out digital spheres of influence within a domain that was supposed to represent the epitome of a project forging a global Information Society. Sadly, rather than a means of empowerment and democratization, the domain has come to be dominated by cybercriminals, terrorists, and other malicious actors who take advantage of a lack of international cyber cooperation and governance for the purposes of expanding their own agendas and influence. The absence of enforceable international standards and legal codes strains relations between great powers. Instead of focusing on ways to enhance cooperation and establish norms, states compete in the cyber domain to further their own objectives. As the world moves away from the structures and mind-sets of the industrial age and lurches into the information age, cyberspace is but another arena where states execute their geopolitical and economic strategies.

China has emerged as the foremost threat to American economic dominance and vitality in the cyber espionage arena. Utilizing the domain for intellectual property theft to drive its goals of ensured economic growth, it is also a country that wrangles with the utilization and prioritization of the cyber domain not just for the purpose of its future prosperity, but also in the service of regime stability. Therefore, the relationship between China and the United States has been strained as a result of China's intrusion and adventurism against corporate networks as it strives to meet both challenges, economically and politically. On the other hand, in the PRC's assessment, the United States' promotion of American values such as freedom of speech and the free flow of information is a direct security threat to its authority. This chapter provides an overview of these themes. Publicly uncovered data and APTs (advanced persistent threat) firmly document the PRC's activity as perhaps the world's most active source of national and industrial espionage. In these sections, the methods, motives, and capabilities come under examination and discussion. This chapter also looks into how these components fit within the PRC's effort to compensate for its relatively late arrival to the information age. In this new domain of state and nonstate activity, norms are being established through behavior and interaction among all actors. Whereas Russia has been integrating cyber across the diplomatic, informational, military, and economic levers of its grand strategy, China appears more focused (at this point in time, at least) upon utilizing cyberspace to achieve its economic developmental goals through the mass theft of intellectual property worldwide rather than using it as an offensive means for power projection.

Market Ownership: Controlling the Rules and Physics of the Domain

Because cyberspace is a man-made domain, it is possible and advantageous for states to develop products and services that are appealing and marketable to others. China's exploitation of cyberspace's natural forces for economic and strategic advantage is not limited solely to the use of it for theft of information. It is also aggressively pursuing a strategy where it seeks to vie for and ultimately usurp market share from non-Chinese firms. Companies such as Huawei and ZTE fiercely compete with American firms such as Cisco and AT&T. As the pace of technology and innovation accelerates, a battle for control of cyber infrastructure is swiftly emerging.

Along the cyberwar-scape, China is making a technical Great Leap Forward in terms of computer science and engineering. As reported by the U.S.-China Economic and Security Review Commission, "If current trends continue, China (combined with proxy interests) will effectively become the principal market driver in many sectors, including telecom, on the basis of consumption, production, and innovation." With the ascendance of China's position in these markets, there is the worry that an overreliance on it as a manufacturer of computer chips and other information and communication technology (ICT) hardware has already allowed viruses and backdoor access to equipment used by U.S.-based entities, including the military. An expanding market share might only create a further risk to U.S. cybersecurity. Extraordinarily low-priced Chinese-made computer hardware products available in Asia and the developing world are a lucrative option and prudent business decision. Competitive pressures often force U.S. companies to rely on China's outsourced production facilities to assemble and manufacture products. Western companies have long been irresistibly lured into commercial alliances with non-Western partners. These joint-venture arrangements are openings for a hostile player to implant viruses, malware, Trojan horses, and backdoors into equipment for both proprietary civilian and military use.

Malicious insider access to these products is a serious security concern. Source codes, or the software programming instructions, are particularly appealing targets. The ability to copy or corrupt these millions of lines of instructions gives hackers the capability of tunneling into information systems around the world. Once the information is accessed, there is little to prevent someone from stealing intellectual property and inserting their own code. According to Google, this is precisely what has occurred not only to them, but to at least thirty other California-based companies.[1] In addition, over the past years, counterfeit Cisco routers have surfaced. Their intrusion creates the fear that implanted software could give foreign or other unauthorized agents the capability to tap into networks with the same ease as U.S. law enforcement agencies.[2] As required of network hardware manufacturers by law, Cisco Systems produces according to specifications that allow the U.S. government wiretapping capability for investigative purposes.[3] In such a case, a corrupted router "could provide the perfect over-the-shoulder view of everything coming out of a network," according to Jeff Moss, a security expert with the Homeland Security Advisory Council.[4] In 2016, the Pentagon's Joint Staff Intelligence Directorate produced an internal paper claiming that Lenovo computers and devices might present a cyber espionage threat. The report stated that the Chinese-made products could compromise Defense Department supply chains, and further asserted that other Lenovo products were found to communicate information covertly back to Chinese intelligence agencies.[5]

As opposed to the earlier stages of China's entry into the market, it is now not only the price of Chinese products that gives them such market appeal, but also the quality of ICT manufacturing. Chinese entities, such as Huawei, are on the leading edge of developing the standards of next-generation mobile 4G LTE networks. Changsha is the home of both the fastest supercomputer in the world, Tianhe-2, and the Chinese-designed open-source software Kylin Linux operating system. While U.S.-based entities have traditionally set the standards for Internet technology, China-based entities, such as the ZTE Corporation, are increasingly taking on roles within the ITU (International Telecommunications Union) to draft important international standards that will shape the world's next-generation networks.[6]

China, naturally, has a right to compete in the global marketplace for its share of the information technology sector. Unfortunately for China, not all elements are under its control. Past events and actions have undermined trust and inhibit the building of partnerships and other market relationships. One well-known example is the incident of April 8, 2010, when Internet traffic was misrouted inadvertently or maliciously through servers based in China. The misdirection affected U.S. government and military networks. According to the U.S.-China Economic and Security Review Commission, state-owned China Telecom advertised erroneous network routes that instructed "massive volumes" of U.S. and other foreign Internet traffic to go through Chinese servers over an eighteen-minute period.[7] In their annual report, the commission claimed, "China Telecom's servers erroneously started advertising themselves as the best routes for a large chunk of Internet traffic. Such rerouting has happened before from simple configuration errors, though it can certainly be caused by deliberate actions as well."[8] Incidents such as this, and the lack of public punishment, led some in the United States to worry about Chinese companies' involvement and motives. For the United States and allied countries, such occurrences do little to ease suspicions about the PRC's activity in the telecommunications sector. Even when the source of the problem is known, these events raise to the surface the question of attribution. A variation of the usual theme is, at what point are actions and consequences the result of commercial missteps or driven by political and military interests? This example is just another facet to the many-sided and increasingly perplexing cybersecurity dilemma.

In the backdrop to these events, it is important to remember that China's long-range strategy is ambitious. The government is seeking to break the country's dependence on imports from foreign producers for two reasons: First, it wants to build an industrial sector of globally competitive semiconductor domestic firms. With this industrial base, China hopes to capture the revenue streams that currently accrue to foreign companies. Second, China feels it needs to build a bulwark against foreign threats to its national security by breaking "the technological dominance of the West and [strengthening] the country's position in the cybersecurity war," according to Dieter Ernst, senior fellow at the East-West Center.[9]

Finally, China's cyber operations reflect the leadership's priority of assuring the continuation of the Chinese Communist Party's (CCP) governing authority. Economic development, military rebuilding, border security, and domestic stabilization are, in the view of the CCP, organically linked with the hardening and enlargement of its power.[10] The philosophy stretches back to the founding days of the People's Republic of China when a Leninist military was as required to support and safeguard Chinese Communist Party rule as it was to defend China's territory. Therefore, unlike the authority exercised by counterparts in the West, PLA unit commanders are subject to control by political commissars and party committees who demand a role in all major decisions. As the PLA begins an era of reform, these issues will need to become reconcilable.

> The PLA retains features designed to maintain Party control over the military such as the CMC [Central Military Commission] (which is technically an organ of the CCP Central Committee), political commissars, and Party committees. Indeed, the reforms have emphasized the need to strengthen the "absolute leadership" of the Party. The need for Party consultation and unity could reduce the flexibility and autonomy of commanders, especially at the operational level.[11]

In 2016, China unveiled its program to reform the organizational structure of the PLA, which will carry through to 2020—and possibly beyond. However, the simultaneous goals of a more technological, flexible, and responsive force and the creation of more robust party supervision and control over military affairs appear to be and may occur at cross purposes. Leninist tradition and constructs persist today and can conflict with the PLA's need to reconfigure the system that streamlines command and control, combats corruption, and improves its ability to conduct joint operations across multiple domains. A challenge for the CCP will be how to maintain these Leninist concepts as they reenvision their cyberstrategies and restructure their security apparatus during this reorganization period.

Nation-State Economic Espionage

Experts have known for the better part of a decade that the PLA (People's Liberation Army), one of the world's largest military forces, with an annual budget of $146.67 billion, FY 2016[12] (total U.S. defense budget = $582.7 billion, FY 2017, according to the DoD[13]), has had "tens of thousands of trainees launching attacks on U.S. computer networks."[14] These trainees might not officially be act-ing on behalf of the Chinese government, thus allowing the PLA to plausibly deny its involvement in an attack. In order to fill the ranks, the government-sponsored Network Crack Program Hacker (NCPH) identifies proficient groups of hackers through competitions. Those selected receive monthly stipends from the PLA. They are recruited to not only ply their craft on foreign targets, but also to teach army cadets the tactics and tools for conducting cyberwarfare.[15] The results have been impressive. Joel Brenner, a former senior government counter-intelligence official whose past posts include inspector general for the National Security Agency and chief executive of the Office of the Directorate of National Intelligence, remarks about China's cyber threat,

> Some [attacks], we have high confidence, are coming from government-sponsored sites. The Chinese operate both through government agencies, as we do, but they also operate through sponsoring other organizations that are engaging in this kind of international hacking, whether or not under specific direction. It's a kind of cyber-militia. . . . It's coming in volumes that are just staggering.[16]

Since 2014, the picture of the spreading collusion between China's military and intelligence services, on the one hand, and private corporations on the other has become more unambiguous. Reports reveal that Chinese hacking apparatuses not only operate from the mainland, but also from third-world countries with weak cybersecurity capabilities in order to further mask the source perpetrator or true intentions of an attack.[17] Despite the globe-spanning cyber infrastruc-ture and evasion tactics aimed at hindering attribution of the perpetrator, the U.S. Department of Justice has successfully traced a number of Chinese hacks of U.S. corporate entities, which since have become well documented and the sub-ject of much global security literature. The aim of these operations was to gain unauthorized access to these computer systems in order to steal information. Despite some successful efforts at interdiction, many operations are still active, and more continue to be launched. The data that these exploits capture benefits Chinese corporations commercially and, in the longer outlook, China econom-ically. As then director of the FBI James Comey stated, "For too long, the Chi-nese government has blatantly sought to use cyber espionage to obtain economic advantage for its state-owned industries."[18]

Although collusion between official and nonofficial Chinese entities is ambiguous, the U.S. legal code is clear. National security trade secrets can be commercial trade secrets under section (a) of 18 U.S.C. § 793, "Gathering, Transmitting, or Losing Defense Information. Activity targeting this type of intellectual property meets the legal definition of espionage." Unfortunately, while the law may be well defined, enforcement and prosecution are uncertain and, at best, tenuous. In the past, these efforts were even futile. For a while, Chinese authorities have been able to claim plausible deniability regarding these intrusions. However, there are indications that diplomatic pressures and appro-priate sanctions can have an impact.

As a result of recent attacks, the U.S. government responded with punitive actions against the PLA. In 2014, for the first time, the U.S. Justice Department took the extraordinary step of indicting Chinese government personnel with the charge of conducting commercial cyber espionage. Five officials came under indictment. By the following year, in another unprecedented move, the Obama administration authorized and prepared a list of economic sanctions against specific Chinese individuals and corporations for their roles in these operations. According to the cybersecurity firm FireEye, these actions had an impact in Beijing and might have influenced events.[19] Shortly after the announcement of these threats sanctioning Chinese commerce, cybersecurity analysts noticed a marked decline of intrusion activity against the United States and other countries from China-based hacker groups.[20]

However, the larger picture in international relations also holds out some hope for pragmatism to prevail in the area of U.S.-Sino affairs. Despite the inextricable competition between the United States and the People's Republic of China on so many fronts, each nation has a vested interest in the other's future. China holds more than $1 trillion of American sovereign debt—helping to fill the shelves of Walmart and Target while employing millions of Chinese. Without diving into the balance sheets, it is important to keep this context in mind as we explore the political statements of the leaders. As their economic and financial relationship becomes more intimate, it is oftentimes evident that China and the United States can come to an understanding that their economic interdependence is threatened by a cyberwar. Therefore, the push and pull of this superpower rivalry is tempered by a need to work toward a delicate balance between the state versus state competition and the complex patterns of change in a hyperconnected globalized economy. Yet, until that delicate balance is reached, the competition will continue on various fronts and in a conflict arena that is simultaneously asymmetrical and non-asymmetrical.

Box 4.1   U.S. Indictments of PLA Hackers (2014)

Summary of the Indictment

Defendants: Wang Dong, Sun Kailiang, Wen Xinyu, Huang Zhenyu, and Gu Chunhui, who were officers in Unit 61398 of the Third Department of the Chinese People's Liberation Army (PLA). The indictment alleges that Wang, Sun, and Wen, among others known and unknown to the grand jury, hacked or attempted to hack into U.S. entities named in the indictment, while Huang and Gu supported their conspiracy by, among other things, managing infrastructure (e.g., domain accounts) used for hacking.

Victims: Westinghouse Electric Co. (Westinghouse), U.S. subsidiaries of SolarWorld AG (SolarWorld), United States Steel Corp. (U.S. Steel), Allegheny Technologies Inc. (ATI), the United Steel, Paper and Forestry, Rubber, Manufacturing, Energy, Allied Industrial and Service Workers International Union (USW), and Alcoa Inc.

Time period: 2006–2014.

Source: https://www.justice.gov/opa/pr/us-charges-five-chinese-military-hackers-cyber-espionage-against-us-corporations-and-labor.

Nevertheless, the ever-expanding application of ICT and the rise of dual-use technology have created a mesh of opportunities and risks ripe for exploitation. Since the end of the Cold War there has been a feverish and ongoing effort by the American military to adapt its forces to the emerging paradigm forced by the opening of the information age and the Revolution in Military Affairs (RMA). As expressed by the Chinese word for crisis, the confluence of these trends has offered up a convergence of opportunity and danger for China and its perceived rivals. It is a technological crisis that the PRC hopes to exploit against its adversaries on the one hand, and on the other hand, deflect attacks as it seeks to defend its national interests abroad and its authority at home.[21]

Ancient Traditions and Modern Realities

Compensating for its relatively late arrival to cyberwarfare, China attempts to gain parity with the United States and Russia through projects such as *shashoujian* (assassin's mace). Having the project code number 998, *shashoujian* is believed to be a response to America's continued efforts in RMA and an important instrument in countering U.S. hegemony in regional and global affairs.[22] Metaphorically, the term broadly refers to any action, technique, configuration of power, or technology deployed to overcome and reverse the tide of battle. For many in the military establishment, the inspiration for these efforts has origins in a Chinese proverb: "Kill with a borrowed sword." The concept has been part of the discourse on military policy in China since at least 2000.[23] In 1999, PRC president Jiang Zemin, a former chairman of the Central Military Commission, declared,

> We should set great store by stepping up high technology innovation for national defense purposes and by developing technology useable for both military and civil purposes as well, and we should also master several *shashoujian* for safeguarding our national sovereignty and security as soon as possible.[24]

The expression both corroborates and foretells a Chinese military policy that seeks to overcome technological deficiencies with superior strategies.[25] "If you are limited in your strength, then borrow the strength of your enemy." Thus said Sun Tzu, the legendary second-century BCE military strategist and traditionally recognized author of *The Art of War*. By taking the advice from an ancient text, China has girded itself to vigorously compete in the cyber conflict, both politically and economically. As part of this strategy, the PLA has been establishing and cultivating relationships with patriotic hackers, creating the NCPH, and laying the foundation for the strategic concept referred to in Chinese military literature as "virtual *shi*."

The term *shi* has no Western equivalent. The word embraces a range of meanings, interpretations, and aspects that refer to the regular order of battle, creating an overwhelming force, and maintaining the initiative. Key among these concepts is also the notion of strategic advantage for the purpose of developing a favorable situation with the potential of achieving political aims.[26] In kinetic, conventional warfare, it is parallel to the tactic of taking the high ground. In cyberwarfare, it refers to achieving strategic advantage by constantly probing networks, planting Trojan horses and viruses, using APTs, and exploiting vulnerabilities in Western systems.[27] In either domain, the objective is to "win victory before the first battle."

Taking the high ground is a military maneuver common in warfare since the time of the ancients as a way to, according to Sun Tzu, "put themselves beyond the possibility of defeat." In the post–Cold War era cyber theater of conflict, Chinese leadership and military planners reach back to the same ancient texts and traditions for guidance in an evolving twenty-first-century battle-scape. They use such expressions of thought and action to shape strategic plans in order to leverage diplomatic efforts, gain psychological advantages, apply soft power, and, eventually, close the gap in the disparities between themselves and U.S. economic and armed forces. The taking of the "digital high ground" is, therefore, a continuous sequence of historical and cultural military thinking that is central to the conceptualization of strategies and stratagems of Chinese national security. These concepts are not only a clue to understanding how the PRC hopes to revamp its military and continue their drive toward economic development,[28] but also how the CCP intends to stabilize and consolidate domestic rule.

However, ancient teachings are not enough to fully fathom the entire philosophy of the Chinese effort to compete in the twenty-first-century cyber domain. Often underemphasized in the literature about their cyberstrategy is the reality of the PRC's political structure. Ancient literature and thinking may thread together the psychological and cultural fabric of China's cyberstrategy, but the system is torn and frayed by internal rivalries and underdeveloped institutions and administrative bodies.[29] According to NATO's Cooperative Cyber Defense Center of Excellence in Tallinn, "institutional fragmentation has been a constant feature in China's cyber organization."[30] Since the regime of Deng Xiaoping, the plunge into a market economy intensified the tensions between the center and local governments and opened the system to further opportunities for both internal conflict and negotiation. The result was a political structure fraught with factionalism, departmentalism, and frequent dysfunction. These pressures also bled their way into the PRC's cybersecurity infrastructure where competing groups include government, military actors, contractors, patriotic hackers, and even criminal elements.[31] The domestic struggle over mission creep, budgets, autonomy, and priorities is unending. The interplay between cultural impulses and the political structure contributes to the dynamic equilibrium that the PRC must manage in order to service its national security interests and still continue the Chinese economic miracle.

"Win Victory before the First Battle" Abroad and at Home

The high ground in cyberwarfare means having advanced knowledge of the opponent's computer network system. This includes the mapping of hardware configuration topology and network node geography and knowledge of communication systems, encryption methods, system platforms, network protocols, and software capabilities.[32] Computer network reconnaissance is the term for gathering intelligence in the network warfare arena, which the PRC hopes will allow it to "win victory before the first battle."[33] Thus, reconnaissance operations directed at targets that could yield insight into nation-state vulnerabilities are central to China's cyberstrategy. In order to understand China's cybersecurity strategy, its objectives, the forces that influence it, and the infrastructure that allows it to stand and actuate policy, it is first necessary to establish some definitional themes and terminological distinctions.

China, similar to Russia (see chapter 5), has no direct semantic nexus or parallel for the word *cyber*. Both countries' literature refers to the term *cybersecurity* as "information security" (信息安全, *xinxi anquan*,[34] and информационное пространство, *informatsionnoye prostranstvo*). The distinction in terms is important. The West uses *cybersecurity* to specify a technical domain of physical and logical entities that attend to computer and information systems. *Information security* is a separate term generally used by Western democracies when referring to content. China, on the other hand, regards both the information systems and the content of information as inseparable constituent concepts, which fall under the term *information security, xinxi anquan*.

Although both Russia and the PRC take a more holistic view of cyber, unlike Russia, China interprets *information security* chiefly to mean the defense of data collection, its use, and its transmittal by legitimate owners. Russia, in contrast, applies the concept of information security far more unhesitatingly as a form of power projection. Cyberwar, or offensive operations, what the Chinese call "network warfare" (网络 战, *wangluo zhan*), is a separate concept. *Wangluo zhan* relates to the destruction or undermining of an adversary's network and information systems while defending the Chinese national network of information systems and information.[35] In either case, this non-Western, broader definition of *information security* expands the use of the term beyond the field of ICT-related issues and into the terrain of the cognitive/psychological realm. This more all-inclusive approach explains how the Chinese government (as is also the case with Russia and many rigid and doctrinaire regimes) views competition in the digital domain and why the PRC has been control seeking and restrictive in its cyber domestic policy as well as with its negotiations of treaties and international standards.[36]

Although China does not rely on cyber as an instrument of power projection the way Russia does, it is even more aggressive and eager to conduct cyber campaigns to target, probe, and direct espionage operations against other nation-states and private sector firms critical of its national policies and perceived as threats to its national security. According to Verizon Enterprise Solutions, 96 percent of all cyber espionage cases in 2012 were Chinese. The same 2013 report claimed that China may in fact be "the most active source of national and industrial espionage in the world today."[37] These exploit attempts go back years and span the globe. In 2007, Japan's Ministry for Economy, Trade, and Industry reported that a survey of manufacturing companies revealed that more than 60 percent of these firms had been victims of Chinese cyber operations.[38] South Korea also reported that half of all economic espionage targeted against them traced back to China. On the heels of these reports, Britain's Center for the Protection of National Infrastructure (a unit within MI5) distributed a restricted document called "The Threat from Chinese Espionage." Recipients, which included hundreds of financial service providers, were warned that agents of the PLA's Ministry of Public Safety had approached representatives of British firms in defense, international law, public relations, communications, and energy industries at trade fairs with gifts of USB and camera drives containing malware.

At the same time, the PRC sees uncontrolled information as a threat to the legitimacy and authority of its ruling elite. While it invests significant effort and resources into taking advantage of all the economic benefits of the digital world, the Chinese Communist Party's approach to the Internet is that this is a restricted global commons, "built around controlling information through real-time censorship,"[39] rather than a public good conceived for the purposes of empowerment. Put bluntly, it is an instrument of power to ensure rule. Whereas the West prefers an open cyber environment that allows individuals and private corporations to explore, express ideas, and communicate fluidly, the Chinese choose to control cyberspace through its government and military. To that end,

> China has been actively promoting a counter-narrative: justifying stringent Internet controls through propaganda, denying involvement or accountability in cyber espionage, and accusing the United States of committing similar actions against China.[40]

Still, inhibiting China's efforts to unleash its full cyber potential is the institutional fragmentation discussed above. The mixture of government institutions and military departments, hacker-for-hire threat groups, and uncoordinated action between central and local authorities creates an ungainly mechanism for collecting, harnessing, and exploiting valuable intelligence. Additionally, Chinese leadership must address an increasingly corrupt and unaccountable military establishment that is resistant to reform and slow to accept restructuring. Until the PLA successfully negotiates its way through these issues, it will be difficult for it to carry out its plans to build an effective military force capable of conducting modern joint operations on a peer level with the West.[41]

Organization and Missions

According to the NATO Cooperative Cyber Defense Centre of Excellence, "the Chinese have not established an exhaustive approach to cyber issues in the form of a strategy clearly outlining the country's cyber objectives and their execution."[42] As it searches for clearer definition, the CCP continues to control all the mechanisms regulating China's cyberspace. The struggle by the Chinese leadership to marshal in stakeholders and competing interests was begun in earnest in 2016 with a series of announced reforms to reorganize the People's Liberation Army. The restructuring of institutions, policy, and force structure will extend through, and perhaps well past, 2020.[43] As currently configured, the PRC's People's Liberation Army General Staff has three departments charged with intelligence collection and analysis. The Third Department executive body of the PLA has been the main operational force of cyber activities.

The Second Department of the General Staff chiefly uses conventional methods drawn from open-source information and a network of defense attachés. Although their tools and methods are nontechnical, the department's network of nonofficial covers is credited with obtaining valuable information on U.S. and Western weapons systems.[44] The Second Department is also not generally engaged in covert and human intelligence (HUMINT) operations. The Third and Fourth Departments are the technical departments established to conduct defensive and offensive cyber operations.

The Fourth Department's primary focus is *wangluo zhan*—network warfare. Its mission is offensive cyberwarfare rather than defensive operations.[45] The destruction of an adversary's network information systems and critical infrastructure, computer network attacks (CNA) in support of military campaigns, and countering and disrupting American C4ISR and command-and-control systems are capabilities for which the Fourth Department provides engineering and R & D support. This department also conducts electronic intelligence operations that can intersect (or conflict) with the Third Department's activity. Because its mission is more theoretical than actionable, at least at this moment in international relations, attention to Fourth Department activity is sometimes slighted by researchers. However, the Fourth Department is undoubtedly critical to PRC security. It oversees a number of the PLA's research institutions connected with electronic-based missions and countermeasures, most notably the Fifty-Fourth Research Institute and the Electronic Engineering Academy, which is an academic center in electronic warfare and training facility for junior officers. Therefore, currently, the work of the Fourth Department has its impact on and can even drive some operational and strategic planning aspects of China's overall information security community and apparatus.

As mentioned above, the Third Department of the General Staff Headquarters (3/PLA) has been the main operational cyber force. It is the PRC's security organization that most parallels the U.S. National Security Agency and is responsible for monitoring the telecommunications of foreign armies and producing finished intelligence. Cryptology, signals intelligence collection, computer security, and analysis are constituent subdivisions of the department's total mission. Although the PLA regards the Third Department as having a defensive mission, it is highly proactive. Like the Fourth Department, the Third Department has its research arms. The Fifty-Sixth Research Institute (supercomputing for the making and breaking of codes and passwords), the Fifty-Seventh Research Institute (communications intercepts, signals processing, and satellite communications), and the Fifty-Eighth Research Institute (cryptology and information security technology) support the department's R & D efforts.[46] There are currently twelve bureaus within the PLA's Third Department of the General Staff Headquarters, with a total of over 130,000 employees.[47] There are also separate technical reconnaissance bureaus (TRBs) that fall under the jurisdiction of seven military regional headquarters.[48]

The Third Department has been operative since 2002 and is believed to be responsible for the breach of at least 150 organizations. Its mission focuses on monitoring the telecommunications of foreign armies and producing finished intelligence based on this military information. A mere thumbnail sketch

TABLE 4.1	PLA Third Department General Staff Headquarters

Operational Bureaus	Mission
1st Bureau—U61786	Decryption, encryption, and other information security tasks
2nd Bureau—U61398	Regional focus—the United States and Canada, focusing on political, economic, and military-related intelligence plus APT operations
3rd Bureau—U61785	Collection of line-of-sight radio communications, including border control networks, direction finding, and emission control and security
4th Bureau—U61419	Regional focus—Japan and Korea
5th Bureau—U61565	Regional focus—Russia
6th Bureau—U61726	Political commissar (mission indefinite)
7th Bureau—U61580	Computer network defense and attack, intrusion patterns, and diverse research, e.g., the global economy, machine parsing of foreign languages, the future of the Internet
8th Bureau—U61046	Regional focus—Western and Eastern Europe and possibly the Middle East, Africa, and Latin America
9th Bureau—unknown	Strategic intelligence analysis and/or database management entity
10th Bureau—U61886	Regional focus—Central Asia or Russia-related mission, specifically telemetry and missile tracking and/or nuclear testing
11th Bureau—U61672	Regional focus—Russia
12th Bureau—U61486	Intercept of satellite communications and space-based SIGINT collection

Source: Mark A. Stokes, Jenny Lin, and L. C. Russell Hsiao, *The Chinese People's Liberation Army Signals Intelligence and Cyber Reconnaissance Infrastructure* (Arlington, VA: Project 2049 Institute, November 2011).

of organizational charts exposes the existence of overlap between the Third Department and Fourth Department, particularly with respect to research and development, intelligence collection, and joint network administration and training.[49] Table 4.1 provides a list of Third Department operational bureaus and their missions.

The sweeping restructuring of the PLA mentioned above will include changes to its cyber force. Plans call for the establishment of a new **Strategic Support Force** (SSF), which will bring China's military-related information security activities under one aegis. The Second, Third, and Fourth Departments under the General Staff will mostly be refitted to work within the SSF. Regardless of the restructuring, most assume that whatever successor agencies remain and in whatever manner they function under the new rubric, they will maintain similar corresponding goals and practices.

Espionage for National Security and Economic Advantage—"Know Yourself, Know Your Enemy"

In 2013, the *New York Times* revealed the findings of an investigation it conducted jointly with the cybersecurity provider Mandiant. The study analyzed attacks on journalists' computers and determined that the intrusions provided hackers with access to user passwords and reporters' sources. The investigation further concluded that the Chinese military was responsible for the attacks, which were prompted by the paper's story about the Chinese premier's private wealth. Mandiant later reported that in addition to linking it to attacks on nearly 150 organizations since 2006, it had identified a long-standing advanced persistent threat (later designated as **APT1** and also known as "Comment Group" and "Byzantine Candor").

Eventually experts exposed a Chinese military unit in Shanghai identified by the number 61398, otherwise known as the Second Bureau of China's Third Department. In addition to its primary focus on network warfare operations in North America, its interests in commercial objectives are intense and include financial data and intellectual property. Rather than military or state secrets, Unit 61398/Second Bureau has more often sought out business plans, proprietary documents, e-mail communications, and information on employees. Their priorities corresponded with the PRC's Twelfth Five-Year Plan (2011 to 2015), and its targets were and continue to be aerospace firms, IT companies, and public administration agencies.[50]

Unit 61398 used more than 1,000 servers and 832 Internet Protocol addresses for its attacks. In all, it attacked 141 companies, of which 115 were based in the United States; five in Britain; three each in Israel and India; two each in Canada, Taiwan, Singapore, and Switzerland; and one each in Japan, Belgium, France, Luxembourg, Norway, the United Arab Emirates, and South Africa. These companies spanned twenty major industries, of which the top ten most represented were (in order) IT, aerospace, public administration, telecommunications and satellites, scientific research and consulting, energy, transportation, construction and manufacturing, international organizations, and engineering services.[51]

Parallel with these incidents emerged a prominent cyber threat actor group known to the security expert community as **Axiom**. It is a state-sponsored group rather than a military unit. Nevertheless, its choice of targets and methodology are similar to the attacks linked to Unit 61398. Also similar are its motives, which appear to be economic rather than military. Analysis concludes that Axiom concentrated on systems, which house information also useful in advancing the PRC's Twelfth Five-Year Plan. Those same priorities seem to carry forward in the successor Thirteenth Five-Year Plan, but with an increased emphasis on creating new Chinese competitors to challenge U.S. companies abroad. The aim is to accelerate the close of market opportunities in China for U.S. and other foreign firms in important high-tech sectors.[52]

Axiom's and the Second Bureau/Unit 61398's array of strategic objectives reflects China's long-range attempt to lessen its dependency on foreign technology, particularly in the telecommunications, computing and robotics, biopharmaceutical, and energy sectors. Additionally, and in tandem with the efforts by Unit 61398, there is also evidence that the group focuses on Chinese dissidents in foreign countries and domestically.[53] A list of victims indicates that the leadership of the Chinese Communist Party is as much concerned with nonstate actors as adversary states and therefore aggressively tracks the activity and movements of activists, watchdog groups, and media organizations that could possibly create a challenge to their authority at home or undermine their agendas internationally.

In a classic APT modus operandi, Axiom compromises systems through web-based attacks, targeted attacks against public-facing infrastructure, zero-day exploits, watering hole attacks, and phishing e-mails (see table 4.2). Once the system is compromised and confirmed to be a valuable target, cyber operatives survey the network. At that point, the malware moves laterally through the network looking for additional access points for future exploitation. Finally, valuable data is identified and exfiltrated through a compromised C2 infrastructure (command-and-control server), which connects to the victim network. To mask its identity, the traffic in and out of the target system snakes through compromised proxy infrastructure in the United States, South Korea, Taiwan, Hong Kong, and Japan.

In a major breach in mid-2009, a series of cyberattacks emanating from China, dubbed Operation Aurora, targeted some of the most high-profile

TABLE 4.2   **List of Sectors Targeted by Axiom**

Asian and Western Governments	Science and Technology Sectors
communication agencies	electronics and integrated circuitry companies
law enforcement	
governmental records	networking equipment manufacturers
environmental policy agencies	Internet-based service companies
personnel management divisions	software vendors
space and aerospace exploration R&D entities	cloud computing companies
	energy firms
government audit and internal affairs divisions	meteorological service companies
	telecommunications firms
	pharmaceutical companies

Research and Analysis Organizations
journalism and media outlets
human rights NGOs
international law firms
international consulting and analysis firms
U.S. academic institutions

Source: Data compiled from James Scott and Drew Spaniel, "Know Your Enemies: Primer on Advanced, Persistent Threat Groups," Institute for Critical Infrastructure Technology, November 2015, 4.

corporations in the world. Many cybersecurity experts considered Aurora epochal.[54] The operation's attacks that began in mid-2009 became public in 2010. Its complexity and advanced capability allowed its users to exploit several zero-day vulnerabilities and infiltrate such organizations as Google, Juniper Networks, Morgan Stanley, Rackspace, Adobe Systems, Dow Chemical, Yahoo!, Northrop Grumman, and Symantec. According to cybersecurity company McAfee, the primary goal of these attacks was "to gain access to and potentially modify source code repositories at these high tech, security and defense contractor companies."[55] This access to internal systems and the software configuration management (SCM) systems allowed hackers to survey and exfiltrate intellectual property that included trade secrets, proprietary formulas, copyrights, trademarks, and source code.[56] Having this internal path gives Chinese agents the ability to eavesdrop, corrupt data, and conduct "**man-in-the-middle**" attacks (when an attacker secretly relays and alters the communications between two parties who believe they are directly communicating with each other). What is at risk are not only the fundamental assets of some of the world's most highly valuated corporations, but also U.S. national security interests and the integrity of the "invisible hand" of an equitable and fair global marketplace.

Most believe that Aurora is the creation of a Chinese-based professional hacker organization called **Hidden Lynx**. Hidden Lynx, unlike Axiom and the bureaus under the Third Department, is an independent "hackers-for-hire" group with approximately fifty to one hundred members.[57] Believed to have been operational since 2009, its particular attack expertise and MO focuses on financial firms, research and educational institutions, and government entities. Attacks on the financial sector are the most frequent (25 percent in 2011),[58] but not for the purposes of stealing funds. Rather, the group concentrates on confidential financial data such as detailed information about ongoing negotiations or business arrangements, impending and potential mergers, joint ventures or acquisitions, competitive market intelligence, or any other knowledge that might offer Hidden Lynx's client a commercial advantage.[59] Outside the financial services sector, Hidden Lynx targets government entities and contractors for technological insights for both military and commercial advantages. While half of its operations are against targets in the United States, a good percentage of activity occurs within China's "neighborhood," including Taiwan, Japan, South Korea, and even within China itself.

In 2013, Hidden Lynx attracted notoriety with its breach of Bit9, a cybersecurity firm and certificate authority based in Cambridge, Massachusetts. The intrusion, via an SQL injection, was part of a larger Hidden Lynx campaign known as VOHO that infiltrated hundreds of prominent commercial and government organizations worldwide.

Within four weeks, nearly four thousand machines downloaded VOHO's malicious payload.[60] Experts claim that Hidden Lynx has been operating against some of the most well-protected systems in the world. Some observers regard its capability to be at the leading edge of APT attacks, which the group continues to execute at the request of its clients.

> ◢ **Box 4.2** **Structured Query Language (SQL)**

SQL (Structured Query Language; pronounced "sequel") is a computer language designed to store, manipulate, request, and query data stored in relational databases (a database structured to recognize relations among stored items of information). The first SQL appeared in 1974 when a group at IBM developed the first prototype of a relational database.

SQL injection (SQLi) refers to an injection attack wherein an attacker can execute malicious SQL statements (commonly known as a malicious payload) that control a web application's database server—known as a relational database management system. Since a SQL injection vulnerability could possibly affect any website or web application that makes use of a SQL-based database, the vulnerability is one of the oldest, most prevalent, and most dangerous of web application vulnerabilities. (Therefore, it is particularly prevalent in "watering hole" exploits.)

Source: https://www.acunetix.com/websitesecurity/sql-injection.

The group makes recurring use of zero-day exploits and can rework and customize these exploits quickly. A 2013 Symantec report described Hidden Lynx: "They are methodical in their approach and they display a skillset far in advance of some other attack groups also operating in that region." Those groups include the above-mentioned Unit 61398, the military unit of the PLA associated with APT1.[61] The report further stated, "This broad range of targeted information would indicate that the attackers are part of a professional organization. They are likely tasked with obtaining very specific information that could be used to gain competitive advantages at both a corporate and nation-state level."

Espionage for National Security and Military Advantage—"Kill with a Borrowed Sword"

Beyond economic advantage for Chinese corporate interests, foreign cyber espionage provides China a means to aid its military's technological development. The Chinese government and its sprawl of military cyber units, private corporations, and unaffiliated citizens have often been identified as the primary suspect or culprit in exfiltration attacks against major Western powers as well as regional targets. The intrusions into academia, industry, and government facilities for the purpose of collecting sensitive technological secrets are in waves and occur incessantly.

During May 2007, a group of unknown cyber spies placed malware on the computer networks and mobile devices at official organizations and scientific research sites from Eastern Europe and Central Asia to Western Europe and North America, and at military-commercial and energy-sector targets in Asia outside China. As is typical of an APT, the malware was placed via phishing attacks and designed to harvest e-mails, extract online browsing histories, extract saved passwords, record keystrokes, capture screenshots, and gather information from whatever USB drives and mobile phones were connected to the target computer. The victims suggested that the sources are Chinese since they also targeted Tibetan activists. The group, referred to as **Putter Panda**, has been linked to the PLA. Specifically, it was part of the Third General Staff Department Twelfth Bureau Military Unit.[62]

In more recent salient revelations, the *Washington Post* reported that more than two dozen major weapons systems' designs have been breached by hackers, including "programs critical to U.S. missile defenses and combat aircraft and ships."[63] Such claims have become commonplace as China has expanded its cyber espionage and intellectual property theft activities over the past decade. Indeed, billions of dollars worth of intellectual property is reported to have been lost to cybertheft.

Among other high-tech secrets and weapons system designs, the Chinese successfully accessed the plans to the F-35 stealth fighter—the United States' most expensive military investment. Hackers allegedly stole over fifty terabytes of data from U.S. defense contractors in 2010.[64] In 2013, a Defense Science Board[65] report detailing the general level of cybertheft was released around the same time as the security consultancy firm Mandiant alleged that the People's Liberation Army had created a unit focused on penetrating government and corporate networks in the United States and elsewhere. The primary purpose of the group is to steal sensitive industrial and military secrets. Unlike the alleged state-sponsored corporate espionage that was highlighted in the Mandiant/*New York Times* report, the targets in this case were in the defense industry.

Another example of China's network reconnaissance effort is the Office of Personnel Management (OPM) breach. China's HUMINT agencies use cyber operations to become more effective and may have had a part in the hacking of the OPM. In June 2014, the OPM revealed (without attribution) that someone had co-opted a superuser status on its computers, giving them broad access to sensitive government data. Initially, authorities claimed that hackers compromised the records of more than four million current, former, and retired government employees. Within a week, OPM admitted that an attacker had been in the database of the government's far more sensitive security clearance system for almost a year. That presence gave them access to network manuals and two government investigative services subcontractors, KeyPoint and USIS. Anthem, a major health-care provider, was infiltrated as well.

In June 2015, officials disclosed that the Chinese-sponsored threat actor known as Deep Panda breached the OPM systems. Subsequent to these revelations, more recent and alarming estimates placed the number of people affected at up to thirty-two million. The size and scale of the theft was unprecedented. Adding to its magnitude was the significance and nature of the data stolen. The breach included data from SF-86 security application forms and involved the information of current, former, and prospective federal employees. Information about the media and people with access to federal buildings was also compromised. In addition, hackers accessed millions of images of employee fingerprints. They also obtained responses to questions regarding a broad scope of sensitive and personal topics, from foreign contacts to sexual behavior, and the details from interviews with family and friends.[66] China's access to detailed sources of personal information on U.S. personnel gives Chinese HUMINT collectors a wealth of information to target and recruit U.S. actors.[67] Such granular information about federal employees allows an adversarial state to create a veritable database of federal employees and the ability to act on data, giving them the proverbial sword of Damocles that will hang over the United States for decades.[68] General Michael Hayden laid bare the gravity of this episode with comments he wrote in a *Washington Times* opinion piece:

> We've seen breaches before, but these were particularly numbing. The massive files of American government names, Social Security numbers, dates and places of birth, jobs, training and benefits give an adversary data that can be used to coerce, blackmail or recruit U.S. sources. Access to the security clearance database would disgorge even more detailed personal information, including the foreign contacts of American officials.[69]

The purpose of these cyberoffensives is not only to gain advantage in the economic, political, and military fields to meet China's long-range strategic economic targets and strengthen national defense; it can also be intended to simply demonstrate their capability to their adversaries. In addition to eroding the public's confidence in the federal entities' ability to secure sensitive systems and data against adversarial compromise, a cyber show of force can be an application of deterrence theory in the post–Cold War era.

In military and foreign affairs, deterrence is a strategy aimed at dissuading an adversary from taking an action or incursion not yet launched—whether on its own or on behalf of another actor. In some cases, deterrence may not only be a policy instrument to deter acts but also to compel them. The policy generally refers to threats of military, hard power retaliation, but soft power instruments such as economic sanctions and "shame and blame" measures apply as well. Shame and blame are proven tactics of deterrence, often when taken by international watchdog regimes against uncompliant states that flaunt international law and accepted norms.

During the Cold War, nuclear deterrence dominated superpower strategic policy. The prospect of mutually assured destruction (MAD) was existential enough to maintain world order. In the information age, however, its relevance is debatable but still applicable in some instances. Yet issues of attribution, collective security, state sovereignty, and legal definitions as to what constitutes an act of war make discussions about the viability of **cyber or information deterrence** complex and controversial.

The Chinese, or any adversary, utilize the concept of deterrence as a means to achieve "flexibility in negotiations and gain a psychological and digital strategic advantage, perhaps through a show of force."[70] The strategy requires the gamut of cyber operations. Full execution involves extensive reconnaissance efforts to identify vulnerabilities in an adversary's cyber topology and analysis of potential attack vectors and sabotage methods to disrupt or destroy the opponent's systems.[71] The attack is logical. The threat can be physical. The pressures are psychological. The peril to the target from the onslaught is highly credible. Warning strikes on critical infrastructure, financial institutions, or e-government systems to demonstrate political will and capability would be a convincing tactic. The action might equal the effect of a preemptive strike. Finally, information deterrence can be asymmetric as well as interstatal, which is the nature of cyber conflict.

Information Control for Regime Stability

Although the Chinese have been deeply engaged in cyber espionage and state-sanctioned criminal activity for the benefit of their state-owned corporate entities, China perceives itself as a victim of information warfare. Operation Aurora, referenced above, is an example of a Chinese-linked cyberoffensive, justified in part by the CCP's perceived sovereign right to protect its governing power through information control. Among information it sought to "control" were Google user accounts of political dissidents, which the CCP believed to be sources of potential domestic unrest.[72] Operation Aurora also targeted other human rights activists' Gmail accounts and attempted to compromise Google source code. The strike impelled Google to respond with the unprecedented action of tracing the attack to its source and entering the command-and-control server in Taiwan. Google's action flirted with a possible violation of the U.S. Computer Fraud and Abuse Act (CFAA); however, no charges by the U.S. government were ever filed.[73]

In 2010, malicious data wound a path through several servers around the world before attacking components of the United States' commercial infrastructure. Forensic analysis eventually traced the attacks to China. In its denial of official involvement, the government of China bemoaned its fate and global standing as the greatest victim of cybercrime. While the individuals responsible were not caught, China received a mild censure via a State Department *note verbale* (an unsigned diplomatic communication). The incident occurred just prior to Secretary of State Hillary Clinton's February 2010 remarks launching the Internet Freedom Agenda (see chapter 2). The "Freedom Agenda" was essentially a promotion of the U.S. effort to enable democratic forces within China and other authoritarian nations. To the PRC at the time, it was akin to a declaration of cyberwar. In China, regime stability relies upon the circulation of state-approved information to assert its legitimacy and authority.

The "Great Firewall" and the "Great Cannon"—the Cyber Janus

China's argument and imperative for information control within its borders conflicts with the American value of citizens' right of free speech—their "unalienable right" to express opinions without fearing prosecution and imprisonment. China's version of the social contract frequently stands in direct opposition to Western tenets of freedom of expression. When the PRC attempts to export its content-control model, lines cross and basic canons clash.

The world's largest, most pervasive and sophisticated censorship system, the **Great Firewall of China** (often referred to as GFW) is the PRC's notion of sovereignty brought into being. Raised in 2003, the Great Firewall combines regulatory and legislative action to monitor nearly seven hundred million

Internet users and criminalize online speech and activities the CCP leadership finds objectionable. Technical controls begin with a tight grip on several layers of the TCP/IP. Blocking selected websites, filtering keywords out of searches, countering circumvention tools, obstructing anonymous overlay networks such as TOR,[74] and demanding that international online service providers store their Chinese customer's information within China are some features of the "wall."

However, the leadership's natural urge to control information and domestic sources of unrest runs counter to the imperatives of frictionless global commerce. The competitive environment of just-in-time processes, of not only goods but ideas, is a constraint on the Chinese economic miracle. The impact on cross-border Internet traffic is significant. As China is the world's leader in e-commerce, the GFW holds within its virtual borders almost one out of four Internet users.[75] In defense of this immense mechanism of censorship and surveillance, which the Chinese refer to as **"Golden Shield,"** the former head of the Cyberspace Administration of China claimed in 2016 that the apparatus represented the correct balance between "freedom and order" and between "openness and autonomy." In his buttressing argument upholding the PRC's cyber policy, Lu Wei added, "This path is the choice of history, and the choice of the people, and we walk the path ever more firmly and full of confidence."[76] However, a writer for the *Washington Post* put it another way:

> Indeed, China's Firewall is far more sophisticated and multi-tiered than a simple on-off switch: It is an attempt to bridge one of the country's most fundamental contradictions—to have an economy intricately connected to the outside world but a political culture closed off from such "Western values" as free speech and democracy.[77]

The preservation of China's Internet sovereignty is both defensive and proactive. Janus, the Roman two-headed god of passages, doorways, and transitions, is an apt metaphor. The god's two faces looked at the world from opposite directions. The deity represented a safeguard from threats outside and within the gates, and from dangers of the past and into the future. If the Great Firewall is the first face of the PRC's surveillance and censorship system, the **"Great Cannon"** is the second face. It is an attack tool colocated with the GFW. Both the Great Cannon and the Great Firewall are hosted on the same servers, and they likely share the same source code for intercepting communications. However, investigators at the University of Toronto identified the Great Cannon as more than a mere extension of the GFW. Rather, they observed, it is "a separate offensive system, with different capabilities and design." According to these researchers at the University of Toronto and their colleagues at Citizen Lab, Princeton University, and the University of California, Berkeley, the Great Cannon becomes an offensive cyberweapon by hijacking web traffic directed at Chinese sites and repurposes the same traffic to flood and disrupt targeted web servers with DDoS attacks. Acting as a "man-in-the-middle," it can arbitrarily replace unencrypted content to turn a normal Internet user into an unwitting vector of the attack. China's cyber surveillance apparatus is, thus, more than a passive censorship mechanism; it is an aggressive assault weapon as well.[78]

In March 2015, a hammering attack on a popular coding website called GitHub forced the management of the software development platform to announce via Twitter, "We've been under continuous DDoS attack for 24+ hours. The attack is evolving, and we're all hands-on deck mitigating."[79] The hosting service maintained the web pages for a target of particular interest to the CCP—GreatFire. GreatFire is a dissident organization that opposes Chinese censorship. The group uses the GitHub platform to set up mirror sites of the *New York Times*, the BBC, and Google (a mirror site is a website on a network that stores some or all of the content from another site). The group also monitors cyber-censorship activity and helps users circumvent the government's attempts to block access to politically sensitive websites.

In the attack on GitHub, the Great Cannon intercepted Internet traffic and sent it to the infrastructure servers of the Chinese web services company Baidu. Baidu runs China's largest search engine and is one of the largest Internet companies in the world. Malicious script was inserted into the traffic and aimed at the target, which overloaded GreatFire and caused damages resulting in "exceptional cost" for the organization.[80] Internet users were unknowingly "enlisted" and made involuntary requests to visit specific sites within GitHub. The Great Cannon weaponized their communications and set a disturbing precedent in its abuse of network systems and international norms.

There are equivalent content hijacking/attack tools in the West. However, their usage is restrained, so far, by legislative oversight and the rule of law. In China, the system of checks and balances is less democratic. Further, according to Alex Hern of the *Guardian*,

> The Cannon is potentially able to be more damaging still. A technically simple change in its configuration would let it target specific individuals, even if they did not reside in China, and intercept their communications the minute they communicate "with any Chinese server not employing cryptographic protections."[81]

In the meantime, as the Great Cannon continues to hijack Internet traffic to suit its purposes, people inside and outside the PRC will be subject to a weaponized suite of information systems designed to undermine the things the government opposes, such as freedom of speech.[82] While virtual private networks (VPNs) provide some loopholes by enabling users to encrypt and tunnel through different countries, these outlets from the system are mostly restricted to business elites. The remaining population, which accounts for 40 percent of all global retail sales, continues to have their voices and purchasing power held in restraint.

PLA Reform and the Strategic Support Force

As mentioned above, the PLA is in the early stages of a massive institutional overhaul. A corrupt military establishment, failures to modernize and conduct joint war-fighting operations across multiple domains, and a need by the CCP to control a fragmented and contentious association of administrative bodies while safeguarding its own interests have forced the PRC to launch the biggest organizational reform of its military establishment in decades.[83] The reorganization's official start was December 31, 2015. From an edifice with roots to the Soviet organizational style of the 1950s, a new construct of force structure and policy began to evolve and is expected to continue taking shape through 2020. The vision projects a model closer to that of the United States, where lines of authority are streamlined and operational commanders have the responsibility to organize, train, and equip their own troops. Despite the new command accountability, however, the CCP maintains control over political commissars and CCP committees in order to ensure compliance with the leadership's goals and its participation in all key decisions.[84]

These changes will impact China's cyber operations. After initial conjecture over the nature and scope of the mission of the Strategic Support Force (SSF), analysts conclude that this agency "will formulate the core of China's information warfare effort."[85] The SSF focus will be, specifically, on space, cyber, and electronic warfare.[86] Further, the General Staff's Third and Fourth Departments, the PLA's preeminent cyber intelligence and espionage units, will most likely be integrated into the SSF. These operations will involve "hacker troops" responsible for cyber offense and defense, a "space force" to conduct surveillance and satellite operations, and an "electronic force" to undertake signal interference and disinformation. The SSF might also assume the mission of the Second Department, the conventional and human intelligence arms of the PLA.[87]

The conventional wisdom is that such sweeping reorganization will unify a broad and diverse array of cyber operations under one "information umbrella." The stovepiping and competition between units would presumably yield to a single intelligence and information warfare structure, which will utilize every resource to its maximum capacity.[88] Despite the promise, rivalries, organizational cultures, allegiances, and competition over resources often persist in any bureaucracy regardless of the type of government. These reforms are ambitious, and success is hardly assured.

The political implications could also be enormous. Not only will the SSF control a substantial constituency of personnel and resources of the PRC's vast, two-million-plus military, but it will also undertake the responsibilities of protecting the expanding civilian infrastructure and China's financial institutions. In general, the daily routines and quality of life of China's citizenry will be part of its purview.[89] In addition to absorbing military personnel, the SSF will include the ranks of independent and semi-independent hacker groups and employees of commercial organizations. To put the scope and magnitude of its oversight and administration in proportional perspective, consider the unit as a fusion of military and commercial organizations. That paradigm would equal an American analog that would engulf the combined resources of government and military entities and include companies such as "Intel, Boeing and Google to the mix. Such a swath of organizations represents a U.S. equivalent model of how the SSF is conceived and constructed to operate."[90]

It still remains to be seen how much the structure will reflect the concept of the original blueprint. What roles previous units will fill and perform in the new organization and how the interaction between old regimes and developmental workforces will play out are speculative. At this point a prudent response might be found in the comments by Mikk Raud, a researcher at NATO's Cooperative Defense Center of Excellence:

> Overall, the creation of the SSF is a landmark development, giving a clear indication of the PLA's focus on informationised warfare, which raises questions of whether these actions should be seen as provocative preparations for an overt conflict, or merely to provide China with more credible deterrence in the face of technologically advanced Western powers. The developments must also be seen in political context, as it shifts control over China's most powerful and strategically important weapons from the army to the Central Military Commission, headed by President Xi.[91]

The U.S. Third Offset Strategy, whose genesis dates back to the Carter administration,[92] is an ongoing effort to maintain the United States' global power projection lead position through technology. The next-generation technologies and concepts to assure U.S. military superiority will mean development of "unmanned systems; extended-range and low-observable air operations; undersea warfare; and complex systems engineering, integration, and operation."[93] According to Eric Rosenbach, former chief of staff to Obama-era defense secretary Ashton Carter, the Third Offset threat may have been a primary inspiration behind the Chinese launch to reorganize its security structure and the creation of the SSF.[94] This undertaking to create a deeper and more multifarious fusion of its systems capabilities reveals the PLA's recognition of the current weaknesses in its force structure and the determination to resolve it. The new SSF, therefore, might be the critical integrant for China's hopes to achieve dominance in space, cyber, and electromagnetic domains. As the core element of strategic information support, the SSF might be an indispensable force in the PLA's capability to fight and win modern wars.[95] An appropriate technological, diplomatic, and collaborative response by the United States, its allies, and in concert with the private sector would appear as an indispensable counterstrategy and way forward.

Mutually Assured Deterrence

Realizing how mutually dependent each country is on the other's economy, the United States and China have been engaged in bilateral and multilateral discussions on cybersecurity cooperation and conflict mitigation. These meetings represent attempts by both sides to create and shape a global understanding of how responsible states should act, what standards of behavior states should adopt, and how to level the playing field in cyberspace for the benefit of all legitimate actors. The Sino-U.S. dialogues and roundtables on cyber matter. Despite the agreement by the United States and China that this adventurism should cease, obstacles to successful cooperation on issues of cybersecurity persist. As more and more people gain access to advanced ICT and enter the digital information society in both countries, the consequences of how states direct and respond to malicious cyber incidents targeting both business systems and critical infrastructure are unclear. As mentioned above, one of the reasons that overall prospects for U.S.-China cooperation are positive is their increasingly intimate economic and financial relationship. This dynamic is very different from the strategic competition between the Soviet Union and the United States currently and during the Cold War. Therefore, the rhetoric and the inner rhythms of this superpower relationship are neither separate nor easily grasped due to the strategic economic entanglement and competing geostrategic interests.

U.S.-Chinese Positive Engagement: Dialogue for Cyber Stability

When President Obama and President Xi met in California on June 7–8, 2013, to discuss, among other issues, cyber conflict, both leaders expressed a desire for closer cooperation. President Xi stated, "We need to pay close attention to this issue and study ways to effectively resolve this issue. And this matter can actually be an area for China and the United States to work together with each other in a pragmatic way." President Obama acknowledged that, "when it comes to those cybersecurity issues like hacking or theft, those are not issues that are unique to the U.S.-China relationship. Those are issues that are of international concern. Oftentimes it's non-state actors who are engaging in these issues as well. And we're going to have to work very hard to build a system of defenses and protections, both in the private sector and in the public sector, even as we negotiate with other countries around setting up common rules of the road." Both leaders expressed a desire to address threats, while dancing around the subject of China's use of cyberspace to engage in economic espionage.

Given their leadership in developing technology, number of users, and great power status, the Obama-Xi dialogue, or OX, began to lead by example to begin resolving the greatest security dilemma of the early twenty-first century. The two leaders concluded in September 2015 that "the United States and China agree that neither country's government will conduct or knowingly support cyber-enabled theft of intellectual property, including trade secrets or other confidential business information, with the intent of providing competitive advantages to companies or commercial sectors."[96]

The opportunity for China and the United States to make marked progress toward cyber cooperation continued in the months and years to come. Greater cyber cooperation was evident in the reduction of attempted intrusions targeting intellectual property. While areas of improvement including the timely sharing of information between China and U.S. computer emergency response teams, along with enhanced law enforcement activities, OX would serve as a clear indicator of increased cooperation on cyber concerns. These are not subject to just cyber issues but the overall strategic dialogue between the two countries. How this progress moves forward in post-Obama administrations is not yet assured.

Building toward a Cooperative Spirit

Sino-U.S. cooperation is not new. General Joseph Ralston, USAF (ret.), former vice chairman of the Joint Chiefs of Staff, makes a compelling case for the long-term benefits of building trust with China through military-to-military contacts.

A similar argument can be constructed for building trust with China regarding the areas of computer security and critical infrastructure protection. Vice Admiral Mike McConnell, USN (ret.), suggests that Sino-U.S. cooperation would help "clean up" malevolent cyber activity and minimize hostile intrusions and disruptions caused by hacking and cybercrime. The visit of U.S. Deputy Secretary of State James Steinberg to Beijing in 2010 signaled a bilateral thaw after a series of intensifying controversies over U.S. weapons transfers to Taiwan, UN sanctions on Iran, and Internet freedom—heightened by the Google flap.

The April 2013 visit of Secretary of State John Kerry to Beijing was an early sign of what was hoped would be a bilateral thaw after a series of intensifying disagreements surrounding U.S. weapons transfers to Taiwan, UN sanctions on Iran, and the United States' Internet Freedom Agenda. Kerry's visit was less successful than desired as it then did little to slow China's cyber espionage efforts, lending credence to Brad DeLong's suggestion that the balance of influence in China-U.S. relations has changed dramatically due to fundamental economic factors. Clearly, there will be fluctuations in this bilateral relationship—with the most recent "downs" linked to continued Chinese support for pervasive PLA-sponsored industrial espionage and China's growing assertiveness in the South China Sea.

Additionally, several track 2 diplomatic initiatives have been undertaken by the East-West Institute to build trust, in addition to track 1.5 dialogues. Although held at the whims of the broader strategic relations between the two countries, these meetings were launched in an April 2013 announcement by John Kerry, while in Beijing, to launch a formal initiative to begin building a foundation for cooperation between the United States and the PRC. In his statement, Secretary Kerry said,

> We will create an immediate working group because cyber security affects everybody. It affects airplanes in the sky, trains on their tracks. It affects the flow of water through dams. It affects transportation networks, power plants. It affects the financial sector, banks, and financial transactions. Every aspect of nations in modern times are affected by use of cyber networking, and obviously all of us, every nation, has an interest in protecting its people, protecting its rights, protecting its infrastructure. And so we are going to work immediately on an accelerated basis on cyber.

Dialogue has led to verifiably increased shared understanding of what kinds of state-sanctioned behavior is acceptable. If the U.S. and Chinese leadership's public statements were sincere and sustainable, this is a positive step in the U.S.-China relationship in cyberspace.

Beyond the Rhetoric

While the words of politicians are good, we can also see a positive increase in the real cooperation between U.S. and Chinese law enforcement authorities in tackling cybercrime. Chinese authorities criminalize malicious hacking, putting culprits in jail if they are found guilty of creating damage through illegal actions involving intrusions in computer systems and networks—and China's law enforcement services have cooperated with their American counterparts.

Box 4.3   China's 2017 Cyber Security Law Overview

- Create internal security management systems and operating policies, appointing dedicated network security persons.
- Adopt technological measures to prevent computer viruses, cyberattacks, network intrusions, and other harmful activities.
- Monitor and record network operational status and network security incidents and retain relevant network logs for at least six months.
- Take measures to classify data and back up and encrypt important data.
- Critical information infrastructure (CII) and CII operators must comply with more stringent requirements on top of those applicable to all network operators. The Cyber Security Law (CSL) provides for the state to implement key protections for CII in public communications.

- Annual security assessment of CII operators shall review their network security and assess potential risk at least once a year, either by themselves or through a third-party provider.
- Procurement security review: when purchasing network products and services, CII operators must sign a security and confidentiality agreement with their vendor, clearly setting out the duties and responsibilities for security and confidentiality.
- CII operators are required to keep within mainland China all personal information and important data collected and generated within mainland China. They are not allowed to transmit such data overseas without first passing a security review.

Source: Derived from: http://www.chinalawblog.com/2017/06/chinas-new-cybersecurity-law-the-101.html.

This was the case in a recent incident involving Chinese-language websites hosting child pornography, where the Federal Bureau of Investigation and Chinese Ministry of Public Security cooperated and provided each other with assistance.[97] This is indicative of selective cooperation in criminal cases. As far back as 2010, we see evidence of cooperative engagement with the Chinese on law enforcement. Congressional testimony by Larry Wortzel, a member of the U.S.-China Economic and Security Review Commission, also makes clear that cooperation in cyberspace is possible, as evidenced by supportive activities for specific law enforcement purposes: "In some areas of cybercrime, such as credit card theft rings and the theft of banking information, China's law enforcement services have cooperated with the United States." This common history of dealing with cybercrime may help increase strategic trust and pave the way for serious U.S.-China discussions (and ultimately formal bilateral negotiations) on approaches for building a strong code of conduct dealing with criminality, national security, and military operations in cyberspace.

Conclusion

Overall, U.S.-China cooperation in cybersecurity needs to encompass both military and nonmilitary aspects of cyberspace. An informed focus on the military sector is just as important as the focus on its nonmilitary counterpart in this field of interest since in the Sino-U.S. relationship, both are extraordinarily linked, presenting policy makers on both sides with a unique set of challenges to overcome. This economic entanglement could be confused with a guarantee for peace. However, history sends us a warning. When diplomacy fails, even in times of intense global economic entanglements among competitors as those that existed on the eve of World War I, war and conflict may ensue. This is why continuing efforts to establish common understanding via formal presidential agreements, diplomatic communication, law enforcement cooperation, and academic roundtable discussions are important.

Cyber conflict, ranging from access to disruption to armed attack, constitutes a new form of power. There is a common interest of all in the prevention of cyberwarfare that should overshadow any purely national interest of welfare or security. True cybersecurity will be found not only in Sino-U.S. cooperation, but in the collective efforts of all. The Sino-U.S. relationship will be seen by everyone as a positive first step. It will require, and does today require, a real renunciation of the steps by which past cybersecurity has been sought. It is clear that in a very real sense, past patterns of national security are inconsistent with the attainment of effective security in cyberspace—a domain that contains many interdependencies.

Key Terms

Strategic Support Force

APT1

Axiom

man-in-the-middle

Hidden Lynx

SQL

SQL injection

Putter Panda

cyber or information deterrence

Great Firewall of China

Golden Shield

Great Cannon

Notes

[1] John Markoff and Ashlee Vance, "Fearing Hackers Who Leave No Trace," *New York Times*, January 20, 2010.

[2] Ibid.

[3] Jack Jarmon, *The New Era in U.S. National Security* (Lanham, MD: Rowman & Littlefield, 2014), 137.

[4] Ibid.

[5] Samantha F. Ravich and Annie Fixler, "Framework and Terminology for Understanding Cyber-Enabled Economic Warfare," Center on Sanctions and Illicit Finance, February 22, 1017, 14.

[6] Panayotis A. Yannakogeorgos, "Internet Governance and National Security," *Strategic Studies Quarterly* 6, no. 3 (2012): 102–25.

[7] http://www.reuters.com/article/us-cyber-china-pentagon-idUSTRE6AI4HJ20101119.

[8] 2010 Report to Congress of the U.S.-China Economic and Security Review Commission, November 2010, 244.

[9] https://www.uscc.gov/sites/default/files/Annual_Report/Chapters/Chapter%201%2C%20 Section%203%20-%2013th%20Five-Year%20Plan.pdf (155).

[10] Amy Chang, "Warring State: China's Cybersecurity Strategy," Center for a New American Security, December 2014, 32.

[11] Phillip C. Saunders and Joel Wuthnow, "China's Goldwater-Nichols, Assessing PLA Organizational Reform," *Joint Force Quarterly* 82 (April 2016): 5.

[12] Report to Congress of the U.S.-China Economic and Security Review Commission, November 2016, 10.

[13] https://www.defense.gov/News/News-Releases/News-Release-View/Article/652687/ department-of-defense-dod-releases-fiscal-year-2017-presidents-budget-proposal.

[14] Brian Grow, Keith Epstein, and Chi-Chu Tschang, "The New E-Spionage Threat: A *BusinessWeek* Probe of Rising Attacks on America's Most Sensitive Computer Networks Uncovers Startling Security Gaps," *BusinessWeek*, April 21, 2008, 30–41.

[15] Panayotis Yannakogeorgos, "Technologies of Militarization and Security in Cyberspace," PhD diss., Rutgers University, April 2009, 28.

[16] Shane Harris, "China's Cyber Militia," *National Journal Magazine*, May 31, 2008, http://www. nationaljournal.com/njmagazine/cs_20080531_6948.php.

[17] http://en.africatime.com/kenya/articles/shocking-world-chinese-hackers-kenya.

[18] https://www.justice.gov/opa/pr/us-charges-five-chinese-military-hackers-cyber-espionage-against-us-corporations-and-labor.

[19] "Red Line Drawn: China Recalculates Its Use of Cyber Espionage," FireEye iSight Intelligence, June 2016, 8.

[20] Ibid.

[21] Jarmon, 135.

[22] Mary Kaldor, "Beyond Militarism, Arms Races, and Arms Control" (essay prepared for the Nobel Peace Prize Centennial Symposium, December 2001).

[23] Michael Pillsbury, "China's Military Strategy toward the U.S.: A View from Open Sources," U.S.-China Economic and Security Review Commission, November 2001.

[24] Alistair Iain Johnstone, "Toward Contextualizing the Concept of Shashoujian," Government Department, Harvard University, 2002, 325.

[25] Timothy L. Thomas, "China's Electronic Strategies," *Military Review*, May–June 2001.

[26] David Lai, "Learning from the Stones: A Go Approach to Mastering China's Strategic Concept, Shi," Strategic Studies Institute, U.S. Army War College, Carlisle, PA, May 2004, 2.

[27] Timothy L. Thomas, "China's Reconnaissance and System Sabotage Activities: Supporting Information Deterrence," in *Cyberspace: Malevolent Actors, Criminal Opportunities, and Strategic Competition*, ed. Phil Williams and Dighton Fiddner (Carlisle, PA: Strategic Studies Institute and U.S. Army War College Press, 2016), 183.

[28] Thomas, 2001.

[29] Chang, 10.

[30] Mikk Raud, "China and Cyber: Attitudes, Strategies, Organization," NATO Cooperative Cyber Defense Center of Excellence, 2016, 16.

[31] "Red Line Drawn," 15.

[32] Thomas, 2001, 176.

[33] Ibid., 175.

[34] Chang, 14.

[35] Ibid.

[36] Raud, 10.

[37] Verizon Enterprise Solutions 2013 data breech investigations report, 2013, http://www.verizon enterprise.com/DBIR/2013.

38 Bruce Newsome and Jack Jarmon, *A Practical Introduction to Homeland Security and Emergency Management from Home to Abroad* (Los Angeles: Sage Publications/CQ Press, 2016), 419.

39 Raud, 6.

40 Joseph Nye, in foreword to Chang, "Warring State: China's Cybersecurity Strategy," Center for a New American Security, December 2014, 5.

41 Saunders.

42 Raud, 5.

43 Saunders, 1.

44 Raud, 21.

45 Ibid., 23.

46 Thomas, 2001, 180.

47 James Scott and Drew Spaniel, "Know Your Enemies: A Primer on Advanced, Persistent Threat Groups," Institute for Critical Infrastructure Technology, November 2015, 11.

48 Ibid., 181.

49 Raud, 24.

50 Scott, 12.

51 Ibid., 422.

52 U.S.-China Economic and Security Review Commission, https://www.uscc.gov/Research/13th-five-year-plan.

53 Scott, 4.

54 http://www.computerworld.com/article/2489451/malware-vulnerabilities/-elderwood-hackers-still-setting-pace-for-zero-day-exploits.html.

55 http://securityaffairs.co/wordpress/8528/hacking/elderwood-project-who-is-behind-op-aurora-and-ongoing-attacks.html.

56 "Protecting Your Critical Assets: Lessons Learned from 'Operation Aurora'" (McAfee white paper report, 2010), 3.

57 Scott, 7.

58 Stephen Doherty, Joszef Gegeny, Bronco Spasojevic, and Jonell Baltazar, "Hidden Lynx: Professional Hackers for Hire," Symantec, September 17, 2013, 7.

59 Ibid.

60 Ibid.

61 Ibid.

62 Scott, 11; Raud, 23.

63 Ellen Nakashima, "Confidential Report Lists U.S. Weapons System Designs Compromised by Chinese Cyberspies," *Washington Post*, May 27, 2013.

64 http://securityaffairs.co/wordpress/45597/intelligence/china-hacked-us-defense-contractors.html.

65 http://freebeacon.com/national-security/china-sharply-boosts-cyber-warfare-funding.

66 Harry Krejsa and Hannah Suh, "Phishing in Troubled Waters: Confronting Cyber Espionage across the Pacific and the Strait of Taiwan," Center for a New American Security, April 2017, 9.

67 https://www.uscc.gov/sites/default/files/Annual_Report/Chapters/Chapter%202%2C%20Section%203%20-%20China%27s%20Intelligence%20Services%20and%20Espionage%20Threats%20to%20the%20United%20States.pdf (292).

68 James Scott, "The Necessity of Encryption for Preserving Critical Infrastructure Integrity: Protecting Data At-Rest, in Transit, and during Processing with Format Preserving Encryption in Next Generation Defenses for a Hyper Evolving Threat Landscape," Institute for Critical Infrastructure Technology, June 2017, 5.

69 http://www.washingtontimes.com/news/2015/jun/24/michael-hayden-opm-security-breach-blame-belongs-t.

70 Timothy Thomas, "Cyber/Information Deterrence: How Does China Understand the Concept?," March, 5, 2016, https://digital.report/cyber-information-deterrence-how-does-china-understand-the-concept.

71 Thomas, "China's Reconnaissance," 200.

72 "Into the Gray Zone: The Private Sector and Active Defense against Cyber Threats" (Project Report October, Center for Cyber & Homeland Security, George Washington University, 2016), 14.

73 Ibid.

74 Roya Ensafi, Philipp Winter, Abdullah Mueen, and Jedidiah R. Crandall, "Analyzing the Great Firewall of China over Space and Time," https://www.degruyter.com/view/j/popets.2015.1. issue-1/popets-2015-0005/popets-2015-0005.xml.

75 Simon Denyer, "China's Scary Lesson to the World: Censoring the Internet Works," *Washington Post*, May 23, 2016.

76 Ibid.

77 Ibid.

78 Alex Hern, " 'Great Cannon of China' Turns Internet Users into Weapon of Cyberwar," *Guardian*, April 13, 2015, https://www.theguardian.com/technology/2015/apr/13/great-cannon-china-internet-users-weapon-cyberwar.

79 https://twitter.com/githubstatus/status/581298353771802624.

80 Hern.

81 Ibid.

82 https://motherboard.vice.com/en_us/article/did-china-just-launch-a-cyber-attack-on-github?utm_source=mbtwitter.

83 Saunders.

84 Ibid.

85 Raud, 21.

86 Ibid., 2.

87 Adam Segal, "China's Strategic Support Force: The New Home of the PLA's Cyber Operations?," Council on Foreign Relations, January 20, 2016, https://www.cfr.org/blog-post/chinas-strategic-support-force-new-home-plas-cyber-operations.

88 https://sputniknews.com/asia/201601191033349605-china-strategic-support-forces.

89 Raud, 25.

90 Chris Bing, "How China's Cyber Command Is Being Built to Supersede Its U.S. Military Counterpart," CyberScoop.com, June 22, 2017, https://www.cyberscoop.com/china-ssf-cyber-command-strategic-support-force-pla-nsa-dod.

91 Ibid., 25–26.

92 Ibid.

93 Robert Martinage, "Toward a New Offset Strategy—Exploiting U.S. Long-Term Advantages to Restore U.S. Global Power Projection Capability," Center for Strategic and Budgetary Assessments, 2014, 2.

94 Ibid.

95 Elsa Kania, "PLA Strategic Support Force: The 'Information Umbrella' for China's Military," *The Diplomat*, April 1, 2017, http://thediplomat.com/2017/04/pla-strategic-support-force-the-information-umbrella-for-chinas-military.

96 https://obamawhitehouse.archives.gov/the-press-office/2015/09/25/fact-sheet-president-xi-jinpings-state-visit-united-states.

97 https://www.fbi.gov/contact-us/field-offices/newyork/news/press-releases/operator-of-18-chinese-language-child-pornography-websites-sentenced-to-210-months-in-prison.

Russia 5

Estonia, 2007

In April 2007, the Estonian government removed a statue memorializing the Soviet liberation of the country from the Nazis. The controversial "Bronze Soldier," known endearingly as *Alyosha* to the Russian-speaking inhabitants of the city, was a symbol of sacrifice and deliverance. To Estonians, it represented Soviet oppression. They preferred a less disarming alias—"the Unknown Rapist."[1] The history between these two peoples has been a story of mostly confrontation and strife. Tensions have existed for centuries. In the twentieth century, the annexation of Estonia by the USSR in 1940 rekindled an enduring bitterness. As the Soviets relocated hundreds of thousands of ethnic Russians there in order to "Russify" the culture and solidify the Soviet bloc, Estonian nationalism quietly entrenched. By 2007, sixteen years after the dissolution of the Soviet Union, silent ferment blossomed into open protests as the revelation of another relocation became public. *Alyosha*, the emblem of the Soviet war effort, was being reassigned from central Tallinn to a humbler post at a nearby military cemetery. The primary purpose of the transfer was to avoid the May 9 Victory Day clashes, which had become an annual tradition as Russian Estonians honored their dead and native Estonians simmered with resentment. The news of the statue's removal ignited protests in Estonia and Russia. For several days, activists in Moscow blocked access to the Estonian embassy,[2] while Russian-speaking protesters in Tallinn persisted with demonstrations and rioting.[3]

As tensions rose and protest turned to violence, events bled into the cyber domain. From April 27 to May 18, distributed denial-of-service (DDoS) attacks targeted Estonia's infrastructure.[4] Not only were Estonian government ministry websites disabled, but those of political parties, news agencies, banks, and telecommunication companies crashed as well.[5] Websites that usually received only one thousand visits per day saw their systems fail as incoming attacks reached rates above two thousand visits per second.[6] A minister of defense in this nation of 1.3 million reportedly admitted to an American Air Force general that "one million computers" attacked his country.[7] The source of the attacks was a globally dispersed botnet network of "zombie" computers. Experts believe that hacktivists in Russia and the Russian diaspora hijacked an uncountable number of personal computers over a geographic range that stretched from Russia to Egypt, Peru, Vietnam, and the United States.[8] While no permanent damage occurred, the DDoS attacks resulted in three million euros[9] in losses and demonstrated how a coordinated cyberattack could cripple an entire nation. Estonia, like many Western countries with a ubiquitous IT infrastructure, is highly vulnerable. This reliance on systems, once again, demonstrated how IT/OT networks are both a blessing and Achilles' heel of high-tech governments and societies.[10]

Because attackers used botnets and had no formal linkage with the state, attribution to the Russian government was difficult. However, a simple calculation of the motives, means, and opportunity concludes that the Kremlin probably used government agents and offices to support or inspire patriotic hackers and even criminals to attack targets in Estonia. The coordination of the cyberattacks with organized violent demonstrations in Tallinn and Moscow gave further weight to the argument that this was a synchronized strategy designed, implemented, and sanctioned by the Kremlin. While denying involvement, the Russian government made statements in praise and support of the online hackers.[11] Furthermore, Estonian officials insisted the attacks were most likely the result of a year's worth of planning by the Russian government or its military to punish Estonia for its anti-Russian policies.[12] Well before the statue became a public issue, Estonian authorities believe both the protests and the cyberattacks occurred through government initiative and with the assistance of accomplices using Russian-language forums to help prepare and coordinate the plot. The Estonian officials were aware of the chatter and reportedly even had plans to issue a notice regarding the approaching cyberstrike several days before the event actually took place. The monitoring of e-mails, chat rooms, and Internet traffic provided evidence, but, under pressure from the European Union, officials withheld the news release.[13] At the time, a meeting between Angela Merkel and Vladimir Putin was in preparation, and the backdrop of confrontational news was judged to be imprudent and would set an improper tone for the summit.

As events unfolded, the reaction by the West and NATO was weak and delayed. The electronic offensive by Russia raised alarms and cut at the core of the NATO alliance. Cries of concern about issues of collective self-defense rose to the surface and almost as quickly became mute because of a lack of definitions, precedent, a framework for resolution, and any clear policy guidance on an appropriate response.[14] Despite the evidence of a coordinated attack and Russian involvement, NATO offered no retaliatory response. In the absence of any physical damage or actual injury to Estonian citizens, NATO determined that the DDoS attacks did not constitute an act of war. A counteroffensive cyberattack would have been a violation of international norms and Russia's sovereignty. The action would have raised tensions, particularly taking into account the Kremlin's advantage of plausible deniability. Furthermore, international norms dictate that cyber actions must be deemed an act of self-defense. It is unlawful for NATO nations to conduct offensive cyber operations without authorization by a resolution of the UN Security Council,[15] of which Russia is a standing member.

In addition to its costs, however, the cyberstrike also created a call to arms for alliance members, and a rapid international response eventually emerged. NATO's Computer Emergency Response Teams (CERTs) and the EU's European Network and Information Security Agency (ENISA) helped to reestablish network operations. In addition, the incident inspired action to align European national cyber defense mechanisms and policies with NATO agencies.[16]

Ultimately, the final stage of this chess match with Estonia did not checkmate the government into changing its policy. The statue was removed and demonstrations subsided. The incident failed to coerce Estonian officials to soften their actions or attitudes toward Russia. In fact, the episode's primary effect was to raise awareness of the geopolitical threat that Russia posed and to underscore the potential of this new strain of Kremlin *machtpolitik*. While the attacks mostly involved DDoS activity, observers quickly understood the potential for far more serious exploits. Future assaults could disable military systems and critical infrastructure sectors such as energy grids, communication networks, air traffic control operations, and water purification and supply systems.

The attack was distinctive in its use of personnel, information age weaponry, and ability to take advantage of the altering attack surface. As one analyst noted, "The Estonian attack is unique in that the Russians were able to marshal the efforts of a number of criminal cyber enterprises and direct their collective efforts at a state target, while insulating official Russian institutions from culpability."[17] The strike also demonstrated, again, the impact of globalization on warfare in the information age. Represented in this conflict was a far-reaching range of actors and a strain of asymmetry heretofore unknown. It also compelled conventional thinking to reassess its notions of how to frame the definition of an "act of war."

Eventually, the Allied response resulted in moving the alliance toward harmonizing national militaries and forcing governments to react with smarter policies and processes rather than relying strictly on technology as a deterrent.[18] Subsequent outcomes included the adaptation of a unified Policy on Cyber Defense in 2008 for centralizing cyber defense planning and operations across NATO.[19] The same year, planners also founded the Cyber Defense Management Authority (CDMA) based in Brussels (later to be superseded by the Cyber Defense Management Board—CDMB)[20] and the NATO Cooperative Cyber Defense Center of Excellence (CCDCoE) in Tallinn. The primary purpose of the CDMB is to develop and coordinate cyber defenses based on technical capability, political risk analysis, and information-sharing activities.[21] The CCDCoE complements the CDMB in offering a platform for research, education, and information sharing through a suite of workshops, exercises, courses, and a staff of experts.[22] It can be argued that the silver lining to the Russian incursion has been smarter defenses and continuing organizational reform.

However, major nagging problems persist. The principle of deterrence, so fundamental to conventional and nuclear defense doctrine, *in esse*, struggles to find new relevance in today's conflict arena. The digital world requires a reimagining of established international norms. The speed of technological advancement in cyberspace strains the capacity to keep pace with legal frameworks, policies, strategies, and counterdefenses. The mechanisms of "deterrence by denial" and "deterrence by punishment" become subject to far more challenging and complex pressures.[23] These issues become particularly salient as national boundaries blur, populations link economically and politically, and attribution for an attack creates questions over legal interpretations, appropriate responses, and the legitimacy (or abuse) of state sovereignty rights.

One of the most fundamental questions for the NATO alliance remains unanswered: how to invoke the treaty's Article 5 in response to a cyberattack. Article 5, *casus foederis* (the case for the alliance), commits each member state of NATO to regard an armed attack on any other member as an act of war on all. It is the core of NATO's principle of collective security. Although cyber does not involve an armed attack, in 2016, NATO extended the term "operational domain" to cyberspace, thereby including it along with other theaters of war: land, sea, air, and space.[24] However, the question, "What would raise a cyberattack to the level of an act of war?" is thus far another unsettled issue. In addressing that subject, NATO's official response is, "NATO and its Allies rely on strong and resilient cyber defences to fulfill the Alliance's core tasks of collective defence, crisis management and cooperative security."[25] It would appear that collective security still depends heavily on a defensive strategy, while offensive and retaliatory policies remain elusive. Progress may be held captive by not only the international norms that limit cyberoffensives as a form of self-defense, but also the parlance and mind-set of nuclear warfare. Arms control planners structured negotiations and strategy around such notions as minimal deterrence, flexible response, and countervailing strategy. Adapting the same concepts to the cyber domain is proving awkward.

Meanwhile, regional tensions have remained high. In 2010, NATO cleared Estonia to develop contingency plans to protect the country in the event of a hypothetical Russian invasion. Reportedly, this included urban warfare and house-to-house defense strategies.[26] Since Russia's intrusion into Ukraine and its forced takeover of Crimea, Estonia has redoubled its training of its Defense League—an official paramilitary force of volunteers. This training includes preparation to become insurgents and instructions on how to make improvised explosive devices (IEDs) such as the ones used against U.S. forces in Iraq.[27] In assessing the all-out nature of a potential invasion by Russia, the commander of the Estonian Defense League offered, "The best deterrent is not only armed soldiers, but armed citizens, too." Consistent with Brigadier General Meeli Kiilis's advice, the government has distributed a classified number of Swedish-made AK-4 automatic rifles to Estonian households. Under this program, arms holders are instructed to hide the weapons and ammunition in a secure hideaway, such as within house walls or buried in backyard stashes.[28] As kinetic war planners make their preparations, cyber experts foresee new tensions arising in the Baltics in 2017. Russia, they predict, will create more geopolitical strife in its pivot away from the DDoS tactics of years prior toward the possible strategy of using destructive cyberattacks on infrastructure.[29]

Withal, the attacks on Estonia may have been part of a long-term and ongoing political cyber campaign by Russia. Although the cyber assaults on Estonian e-government and e-businesses did no permanent damage and might be of no more value to Russia than as a nuisance factor, there have been more serious strategies at work for some time. As early as 2004, Operation Pawn Storm has been an active pro-Russian cyber mission "as far-reaching as it is ambitious."[30] The malware operation targets rival factions and dissidents of the Russian government, but its main priorities are foreign adversaries, which include the panoply of the U.S. military, embassy, defense contractor personnel, high-profile personalities, and prominent entities such as NATO and the international media.[31] Its fingerprints prominently appeared during the 2016 U.S. presidential election when forensic analysis discovered that hackers had infiltrated the systems of the Democratic Congressional Campaign Committee and the Democratic National Committee. Experts also claim that signatures of the same APT, or some variant, surfaced in an attempt to infiltrate the campaign of Emmanuel Macron during the French elections for president in 2017.[32] Compatriot cyberattack campaigns include dozens of other cyber-enabled operations that have code names such as Snake, Turla, OLDBATE, Tsar Team, CloudDuke, Energetic Bear, Tiny Baron, Cozy Duke, etc.[33]

With the advanced digitalization of Estonia and other technologically developed nations, these threats deepen. The growth of IoT and the ubiquity of smart phones drove a Polish cyber expert to comment on the ever-looming possibility of the threat of a Russian cyberattack: "[It is] not the enemy at the gates, but the enemy in your pocket."[34] Currently and for the future, cyber defense still remains a permanent struggle in a morphing environment. Within this environment, Russia views the weaponization of information as critical and the distinction between war and politics as nonexistent.

"There Are No Absolute Rules of Conduct, Either in Peace or War"—Leon Trotsky

In 1918, the year following the Bolshevik takeover of the Russian government, Lenin appointed Leon Trotsky the leader of the Red Army. Trotsky at the time was commissar of foreign affairs. His new position involved the daunting task of transforming a sloppy network of detachments into a formidable and disciplined military. Sometimes this required managing a war effort on as many as sixteen fronts. Conscription, discipline, and the Leninist doctrine that insisted there exists a constant state of siege between and within nations and societies[35] helped earn victories against counterrevolutionary adversaries (foreign and domestic) and create the fortress state that became the USSR and the system and mindset that have endured despite its structural collapse. The belief that "conflict is a constant," found not only in Hegelian dialectics but also embedded in the Russian psyche, is a tradition that shapes and drives present government policy. In this environment of never-ending struggle, Lenin warned,

> Any army which does not train to use all the weapons, all the means and methods of warfare that the enemy possesses, or may possess, is behaving in an unwise or even criminal manner. This applies to politics even more than it does to the art of war.

In Russian military doctrine, force is one of several "instruments of policy." The Clausewitzean concept of war as a "continuation of politics by other means" turns on its head to fit within the Leninist framework. In this context, "war and politics are a single concept."[36] This constant conflict applies to enemies both external and internal. Russia longs for the Cold War framework of the 1945 international system.[37] That structure assumed Soviet superpower standing in a bipolar world and affirmed state supremacy over national internal affairs. In the post–Cold War environment, the inherited mind-sets of the Cold War era have not fundamentally changed. Russia's reduced status to a regional power and the loss of military supremacy and economic influence only raises the sense of paranoia. The Kremlin still sees the world as a sea of foreign threats—particularly, in their view, threats coming from the United States as it seeks to extend its global dominance and marginalize Russia. Russian suspicions about U.S. involvement in the color revolutions in Georgia, Ukraine, and Kyrgyzstan are enough to confirm this obsessive distrust. Even the activities of NGOs, such as Greenpeace's protests against drilling oil reserves in the Arctic, heighten their perceptions of a world mobilizing against their interests.[38] Putin railed against what he called the "instruments of soft power" when he wrote in *Rossiya i Menyayushchiyisiya Mir* (*Russia and a Changing World*), "The activities of 'pseudo-NGOs' and other agencies that try to destabilize other countries with outside support are unacceptable."[39]

In addition to its worldview, Russia also inherited from the Soviet era an underdeveloped and decaying infrastructure,[40] a corrupt and sclerotic bureaucracy, and a military resistant to reform.[41] These internal and external challenges create an insecurity among the ruling elite that they may be forced into a war in which their forces may be neither armed nor trained to win. This same angst has threads throughout Russian history. In his frequently cited memorandum to the U.S. secretary of state, known as *The Long Telegram*, George Kennan, then American chargé d'affaires in Moscow, wrote in 1946,

> Kremlin's neurotic view of world affairs is a traditional and instinctive Russian sense of insecurity. . . . Russian rulers have invariably sensed that their rule was relatively archaic in form, fragile and artificial in its psychological foundation, unable to stand comparison or contact with political systems of Western countries. For this reason they have always feared foreign penetration, feared direct contact between Western world and their own, feared what would happen if Russians learned truth.[42]

A collapsing infrastructure, an obsolete military, high levels of corruption, a faltering economy, capital flight, a brain drain, and ineffective governance contribute to the weakness of the Russian system. It is a system that cannot close itself off from the rest of the world, and the comparisons and contact with the West are unavoidable, more now than ever. Yet the same process of globalization that exposes Russia's flaws also enables Moscow to spread and exercise tactics driven by its state-of-siege doctrine. IT and OT offer opportunities to advance political struggle by means never envisioned by Lenin in his efforts to export revolution. Taking the political struggle to physical and social-political networks via information technology, as Stephen Blank says, "has vastly expanded the opportunities for almost anyone to conduct such operations in both real time and over the course of time, as well as in depth. Anyone can target anyone or anything else for as long as he or she wants and can do so more often than not with plausible deniability."[43] Surely for a Russia with a devitalized economy and a military struggling to modernize itself, cyberpower can be an ideal weapon: economical, stealthy, and opaque with respect to accountability and attribution.

The concept of defending the motherland through the spread of political struggle did not wither away with the collapse of the USSR. The use of information and communication technology as a weapon for military and political purpose is the Russian Federation state policy.[44] In fact, for President Vladimir Putin and his close circle of advisors from the military-security establishment (known as the *siloviki*, силовики), the disintegration of the Soviet Union, Yugoslavia, and the succession of "color revolutions" revealed that nonmilitary threats are far more present and pose a challenge more menacing than any foreign armed force or violent insurrection. Subversive activities from direct or indirect political, diplomatic, economic, and informational pressures are serious sources of alarm for Russian national security.[45] These strategies are actively analyzed by the national security establishment for developing defensive countermeasures.[46]

They are also assessed and aggressively placed into practice by Kremlin planners for deployment in offensive operations. As the Estonian example demonstrates, Moscow has been using such strategies to influence the "balance of power relationship in targeted countries"[47] for years. By contrast, liberal democratic societies are not fortress states. Democratically elected representative governments lack the level of centralized control needed to exert the lawful use of press/media channels and economic/market levers to coordinate such military-like operations and objectives.[48] When defending themselves against such strategies, these cultural and elemental differences put democratic societies in a position where they can come into conflict with their own rule of law. For example, the Title 10 section of the U.S. legal code that outlines the role of the armed forces might require authorizations and exceptions to conduct defensive and offensive operations.[49] This problem becomes more acute in a cyber domain where the lines between war and peace continuously change and blur.

Meanwhile, the collapse of the Soviet Union and its aftershock continue to reverberate. The promise of a post–Cold War "peace dividend" never materialized. The conclusion of the superpower hostilities left behind a string of failed states and quasi-states across the globe. As the USSR fell, new states in the region from Central Asia to Eastern Europe took their place in a ring of sovereign nations referred to by Moscow as the "near abroad." These non-Russian republics went their way according to the boundaries established prior to the founding of the USSR. By 1991, the demographic shifts that occurred over the seventy years of central economic planning and Russification programs left as many as twenty-five million ethnic Russians outside the borders of the Russian Federation.[50] Suddenly, the Russian diaspora occupied a new geopolitical terrain, and their ethnic connection was a source of friction and resistance for several newly independent states. The cries of Russian nationalism and the overwrought fears of foreign oppression toward Russians became the new pretense for interventionism—superseding the old Marxist-Leninist call for class struggle. As put by Stephen Dayspring,

> By replacing "communism" with "nationalism" or "Russian identity," the Russians may have lessened their potential appeal to a global audience, but they had strengthened their ties to the regional population whose support they must have to protect the integrity of the Russian state. The existence of this population in the near-abroad provides a necessary element for a narrative of victimization, establishment of political and irregular "separatists," and as an eventual pretext for Russian intervention.[51]

The "near abroad," the fourteen former Soviet republics and Eastern bloc states with sizable Russian-speaking populations, is a particular target of Moscow's strategy to coerce sovereign governments to align with Russian national interests.[52] Dayspring goes further to say that, not only is it part of a grand strategy, but Putin views it as a Russian version of Manifest Destiny.[53]

Georgia, 2008

In 2008, the campaign to defend nationalism and ethnic identity (although non-Russian) came to the former Soviet republic of Georgia. Several years earlier, in 2003, protests against an election that would have kept President Eduard Shevardnadze in power erupted and led to his ouster. Shevardnadze had been a major political figure for over thirty years and, although a popular figure for most of his career, his regime had come to represent the former republic's ties to the Soviet past. His downfall came when his supporters schemed to falsify the election results. The backlash turned into protests and a twenty-one-day movement, which later took the name the Rose Revolution. The gesture by students of exchanging roses for soldiers' guns symbolized the protest and gave the resulting coup its name.

The justification for Russian intervention in the South Caucasus five years later was to support two breakaway provinces seeking official autonomy. South Ossetia and Abkhazia had been functioning outside Tbilisi's control for fifteen years during a tense time of sporadic provocation, accusations, and shelling from all sides. Russia, which withdrew its military in 1991 from Georgia when it proclaimed its independence, maintained a peacekeeping force in South Ossetia and Abkhazia to ensure order. Finally, in response to an attack by Georgia against South Ossetia on August 7, 2008, Russia launched a large-scale land, air, and sea invasion the next day. In addition to supporting these demands for self-rule, a primary impulse behind Russia's actions may also have been Georgia's flirtation with joining NATO.[54]

As Russian troops, airmen, and seamen mobilized to invade Georgia, another mobilization was taking place along the digital terrain. Moscow launched a multifaceted cyberattack against the Georgian infrastructure and key command-and-control weapons systems. Simultaneously, Russians also targeted the media to spread disinformation campaigns and waged psychological warfare.[55] The cyber battlefront quickly spread to include financial companies, businesses, educational institutions, and even a Georgian hacker forum in order to preempt any retaliation efforts.[56]

The invasion was momentous as a historical marker in that for the first time a cyberstrike accompanied an armed attack. While the incursion into Georgia starkly exposed Russia's conventional military inadequacies, its success on the digital front made clear the world was entering a new era of warfare. Because Georgian infrastructure is less cyber reliant, the fear of cascading systemic failure did not pose the same threat as the attack on Estonia. However, the integration of cyber with military actions demonstrated to national security communities around the world the potential and potency of this new brand of coordinated conflict involving synchronized cyber and kinetic operations.

Although attacks remained limited to DDoS strikes and SQL injections (malware that allows attackers to manipulate web application database servers), their impact significantly hindered Georgia's ability to respond militarily and drastically degraded the means to coordinate counterattacks and control events. Hackers disrupted communications between the government and the rest of Georgian society, preventing financial transactions, promoting and circulating false news, and causing general widespread chaos. Russian trolls (see below) flooded the media with competing narratives to neutralize the Georgian news accounts. In addition to influencing narratives, Moscow even attempted to alter the reporting of facts as Russian bloggers overwhelmed "a CNN Gallup poll stating that Russia's cause was justified and to attempt to prevent Georgian media from telling Tbilisi's story."[57] Russian hacktivist websites, such as stopgeorgia. ru, posted lists of Georgian websites, downloadable malware, and after-action assessments to aid and encourage sympathizers. This crowdsourcing of warfare enlisted hackers from anywhere in the world added an extra panorama to the landscape of anonymity and a new complication for attribution efforts.[58]

Western experts believe the initial planning for the attack went as far back as 2006. Specialized software and graphic art used to deface government websites were two years old, well tested, and shelf ready by the opening of hostilities. Strategists, in order to raise the amplitude of surprise, waited until just prior to the attack before using newly registered websites and domain names.[59] The DDoS attacks first began on July 20, probably as a dress rehearsal for the all-out August campaign.[60] It is clear Russia was honing skills and refining tactics well before actual events.

By August 13, Russia ceased its military operations in Georgia and agreed to a six-point diplomatic plan for peace. President George W. Bush announced the United States' intent to send humanitarian aid the next day. Russia and Georgia completed their signing of the cease-fire agreement between August 15 and 16, and by August 22, the Russian troop withdrawal from Georgian territory was complete. During the five days of military engagement, 170 servicemen were killed, along with 14 policemen and 228 civilians from Georgia. The total wounded equaled 1,747. Russia lost 67 servicemen and 283 wounded. South Ossetian forces and civilians suffered a total 365 killed.[61] As a footnote (although hardly a final one), the International Criminal Court (ICC) in The Hague ordered a probe into charges of possible war crimes against all three combatant states. The investigation opened on January 27, 2016, and covers the period from July 1, 2008, to October 10, 2008.[62]

The failings of its conventional forces during the Georgian campaign raised tensions among military strategists in Russia. In the Ministry of Defense, officials were reeling from after-action reports on the poor level of permanent troop readiness and training, the quality and age of weapons, the flawed command-and-control system, and, not least, the social conditions in the military.[63] Wary of Western monitoring, high-ranking officers conceded with alarm the depressing performance of Russia's armed forces and formed a chorus demanding reform. Any armed confrontation with the West now seemed a circumstance charged with disaster. Yet, however obvious the distinctions in combat readiness, there were other differences between Russia and its adversarial world. Although it may appear subtle compared to the differences between Russia and the West with respect to armed conflict, the nuances in the language used to describe integrated cyberstrategy and planning are no less strategic and revealing.

Dissimilarities between the West's definition of cybersecurity and Russia's bespeak a deviation in approaches to national security—as well as a divergence of cultures. Liberal democracies generally use the term *cybersecurity* to refer to a technical domain, whereas in Russia, *information security* (информационное пространство) also includes the cognitive domain. Russia's broader definition presumes that economic and social arenas are part of the battleground, and the mission is not to steal or destroy information as much as it is to disrupt it.[64] "Information has become a weapon. It is not just an addition to firepower, attack, manoeuvre, but transforms and unites all of these," according to Russian biologist Ivan Vorobyov and physicist Valeri Kiselev.[65] The merging of military doctrine with political doctrine reflects an integrated strategy to defend Russian interests in an environment where all military conflicts involve a struggle between both armed forces and perceived truths.

The war and Georgia's threat to align closer with Europe through NATO illustrate how Russia views itself as a target of the West and a victim of these weapons, on the one hand, and, on the other, foresees itself as a preeminent exploiter of the same tools. In their theory of the world, the collapse of the Soviet Union was the first information world war, and the second information world war is occurring in the post–Cold War era.[66] The color revolutions, the Arab Spring, Syria, rumblings from the Baltic to Central Asia, and domestic dissent provoke alarm among the Russian elite, who fear that their system is vulnerable and their leadership might be unsustainable. Through this prism, Vladimir Putin construes events and makes the charge that the West's modern cries for "democratization" are merely voicing the same false outrage and code word used by the former imperial powers when they invoked their calls for "civilization" during the period of colonization. Russia's adversaries today, he believes, are the inheritors of that previous tradition.[67] In order to defend Russia from these irreconcilable differences in values, Putin also "reasons" that *Chem sil'nee gosudarstvo, tem svobodnee lichnost* (Чем сильней государство, тем свободней личность): "The stronger the state, the freer the individual."[68] Conformably, dissent is akin to treason.

Net Warriors

Sometime after the Georgian conflict, a Russian hacker posted the following on an online forum: "We will recreate historical fairness. We will bring the USA down to level of 1928–33."[69] As patriotic hackers and Russian criminal organizations become more motivated by nationalistic zeal, their usefulness to the state becomes more obvious. The exact nature and degree of collaboration between Russian cybercrime organizations and other private actors with the government is unclear. However, since Estonia, the waging of information warfare and cyberattacks aimed at disrupting operations or conducting espionage campaigns for the purposes of destabilization or subversion appears to be the long-term strategic plan, which such mergers facilitate.

The primary suspect behind the cyberattacks on major Georgian government websites during the 2007 conflict is a cybercriminal organization called the **Russian Business Network** (RBN).[70] RBN offers a complete infrastructure to undertake malicious activities. Its range of services spans an arc of activity that includes malware hosting, phishing, botnet command and control, DDoS attacks, and child pornography.[71] RBN's history may date back as far as 1996. Until 2007 it hosted an Internet service provider (ISP).[72] By that year it also operated the largest botnet in the world.[73] As its presence and notoriety expanded, so did awareness in the cybersecurity industry. Networks began blocking or blacklisting RBN IP addresses, forcing the group to restructure. Attempts to resume operations on Chinese and Taiwanese networks failed, but this did not cause the group to disband.[74] Observers believe its home remains in St. Petersburg where it enjoys political patronage and protection.[75]

The leader of RBN goes by the name "Flyman." His connections are both criminal and political. While ties with Russian organized crime are naturally assumed, the precise nature of the interaction between RBN and the Russian government is opaque. However, another principal operative within the group is Aleksandr Boykov—formerly a lieutenant colonel in the Federalnaya Sluzhba Bezopasnosti (FSB), the successor agency to the KGB.[76] Given the unique position it occupies between the Russian underground and Russian officialdom, it is easy to understand how its connections with both worlds create a potent actor in the cyber domain and a chief nexus for state and nonstate allies to wage asymmetric/hybrid war. The abandonment of the RBN ISP had no immediate impact on RBN and Russian cybercriminal activity. RBN countered by dispersing across a multiplicity of ISPs and domains. Today, the lore and scope of its activities is on such a scale that experts often refer to RBN when speaking about Russian cybercriminal organizations and their activity in general.[77] This is despite the fact that RBN's existence or extinction is sometimes still a topic of debate.

Whether it be RBN or any number of cybercrime groups, the Russian leadership recognizes their usefulness and does not hesitate to call on them to help achieve strategic goals anywhere in the world.[78] RBN surfaced not only in Estonia and Georgia as part of the attack force but also in Iran where it aided the regime in monitoring dissidents. Their assistance had a strong diplomatic subtext as

Moscow was moving to strengthen its relationship with Tehran.[79] At that time, as now, U.S. calls for "regime change" in places like Syria and other flashpoints aroused the authoritarian governments in both Russia and Iran to view such utterings as veiled threats to their own legitimacy. Russia and Iran prefer a multipolar world order united against U.S. unilateralism. In such a system, both countries see themselves as major influencers in the region, and in Russia's case, a global role.[80] Cybercriminals and hacker patriots can be critical in helping to alter the power relationship in the Gulf region, the "near abroad," and beyond. Therefore, Kremlin encouragement, sponsorship, and assistance will only grow with the weaponization of information in both the cognitive domain and technical domain. Currently, European intelligence officials estimate that as many as twenty to thirty crime groups inside Russia already have "nation-state-level" capacity to overcome virtually any cyber defense mechanism. In addition to being a force within the government's cyberwarfare arsenal, they conduct financial crimes on an "industrial scale"[81] with a blind eye from Russian law enforcement.

Energetic Bear/Crouching Yeti is a cyber threat actor that uses specialized malware focusing on strategic industrial sectors of nation-states that are politically opposed to Russia's interests. Industrial control manufacturers and energy and defense sectors are the main targets. From 2011 to 2013, the group launched a coordinated spam and malware campaign against the defense industry in the United States and Canada and the petroleum sector in the United States and Europe.[82] Cyber experts observe that the primary objective of their exploit is for espionage purposes. However, analysis of exploit kit features reveals that sabotage is another option for its highly specialized malware. Therefore, damage or disruption in critical infrastructure sectors that depend on ICS and SCADA systems is an overhanging yet heretofore uninstigated threat.[83] Restraint has tactical advantages. If hackers finally decide to launch a strike, their mark may be caught off guard as it struggles to diagnose the problem and its source. In the absence of any incident history, the perpetrators' previous self-imposed restriction might fool targets into believing they are victims of a system failure rather than the prey of a cyberattack. According to the Institute for Critical Infrastructure Technology, "Energetic Bear is uniquely positioned to assist in a combination of Digital and Physical warfare for military or political purposes. Similar to Russia's Georgian campaign in the 2008 conflict."[84] Energetic Bear has been performing massive surveillance campaigns at least since 2010, and their list of victims is in the thousands.[85] By remaining inactive as a sabotage agent, its effectiveness and destructiveness are heightened by its stealth.

In 2016, **APT28** became a subject of the U.S. presidential campaign and reports in the media. APT28 (also referred to as Fancy Bear, Sofacy, and the above-mentioned Pawn Storm) is the exploit credited with penetrating the computers of the Democratic Congressional Campaign Committee. The same exploit moved to the Democratic National Committee (DNC). Russian military intelligence, the Chief Intelligence Directorate (GRU—Главное разведывательное управление), directed the operation.[86] Unheard of prior to 2016, APT28 has been active since 2007.[87] APT28 is not related to economic crimes. Rather than obtaining financial information for financial fraud purposes or resale, it appears to collect intelligence related to Russian political goals and to propagate future cyberattacks.[88] In addition to the DNC and the Democratic Congressional Campaign Committee, NATO, media outlets, the military, and security organizations, European governments, including Georgia and Ukraine, have also been targets.[89]

Often mentioned as a companion exploit, **APT29** is believed to be the product of the Federal Security Service (FSB—Федеральная служба безопасности). **Cozy Bear**, as it is sometimes known, is a more recent exploit. It is often affiliated and even referred to interchangeably with another hacker group, dubbed **Cozy Duke**, or simply Dukes.[90] Its most notable attack occurred in 2014. That year the U.S. Department of State underwent a hack on one of its unclassified computer systems. At the time, officials and cyber experts described the system as being "owned" by its attackers.[91] Other targets include the White House and various U.S. government agencies. Although APT29's chief focus is the United States, there is evidence that government and commercial entities in Chechnya, Germany, South Korea, and Uzbekistan are also past victims.[92] Norway is a more recent prey. Officials in February 2017 publicly identified Russian sources as the perpetrator of attacks on the Norwegian Foreign Ministry, the intelligence service, the national radiation protection agency, the Labor Party, and even a school. Although the purpose of the attacks remains unclear, government representatives suggest that they are in reprisal for Norway's support of the European Union's stance on economic sanctions against Russia and to punish Norway for allowing the deployment of three hundred U.S. soldiers on its territory.[93]

Both APTs concentrate on government agencies, think tanks, universities, and corporations worldwide. Their methods are a mix of spearphishing campaigns and watering hole tactics. In 2015, APT29 delivered malware to the Democratic Party's computer systems via e-mail attachments. Once activated, the attackers were able to establish persistence, escalate privileges, specify directory accounts, and exfiltrate e-mail.[94] A year later, APT28 penetrated the Democratic Party again, this time using spearphishing and leveraging web links to malicious sites. Targeted individuals changed their passwords through a fake webmail domain hosted on an APT28 proxy server infrastructure, which permitted Fancy Bear to gain access and steal content.[95] The U.S. intelligence community eventually determined, and announced, that Russian military intelligence (under the cover name of Guccifer 2.0 and through DCLeaks.com) leaked the information publicly and in exclusives to media outlets. WikiLeaks ultimately posted the victim data online.[96]

Sandworm is another Russian state-sponsored APT group similar to APT28 and APT29 in methodology and objective. Political opponents of the Russian Federation are prime targets. Commenters note that the group most likely participated in the invasion of Georgia. In the past, Sandworm's attentions concentrated on NATO, the European Union, the European telecommunications sector, European energy companies, Poland, and the Ukrainian government.[97] In 2016, cyber experts named Sandworm responsible for attacks on the Ukrainian news media and electrical power industry.[98] A favorite malware of Sandworm is **BlackEnergy**. Originally designed for use in DDoS attacks and creating botnets,

BlackEnergy quickly evolved into a specialized tool for accessing banking information. Once established within a system, the malware can steal passwords, take screenshots, gather information on connected USB devices, and log keystrokes.[99] Later users repurposed the code to steal digital certificates and attack Cisco networking devices.

BlackEnergy has been customized to be effective in sabotage attacks against SCADA and ICS systems, as well.[100] The attack in 2014 on an energy control center in the Ivano-Frankivsk region of Western Ukraine offers some early evidence. Although it took only six hours to restore power to most of the area, months after the attack control centers remained less than fully operational.

TABLE 5.1	Reported Russian Military and Civilian Malicious Cyber Activity

Agent.btz	Havex
APT 28	MiniDionis
APT 29	MiniDuke
Black Energy V3	OLDBATE
Black Energy2 APT	OnionDuke
CakeDuke	Operation Pawn Storm
Carberp	PinchDuke
CHOPSTICK	Powershell backdoor
CloudDuke	Quedagh
CORESHELL	Sandworm
CosmicDuke	SEADADDY
COZYBEAR	Seaduke
COZYCAR	SEDKIT
COZYDUKE	SEDNIT
CrouchingYeti	Skipper
DIONIS	Sofacy
Dragonfly	SOURFACE
Energetic Bear	SYNful Knock
EVILTOSS	Tiny Baron
Fancy Bear	Tsar Team
GeminiDuke	Twain_64.dll (64-bit X-Agent implant)
GREY CLOUD	VmUpgradeHelper.exe (X-Tunnel implant)
HammerDuke	Waterbug
HAMMERTOSS	X-Agent

Source: Compiled from Joint Analysis Report of the Department of Homeland Security and the Federal Bureau of Investigation, January 29, 2016.

Technicians reestablished service by traveling to the substations and manually closing the breakers, which hackers had opened through manipulation of the management system.[101] Curiously (or not), there was an effort in the Ukrainian Parliament to nationalize privately owned power companies at that time. The legislation would have been a financial blow to a powerful Russian oligarch with close ties to Vladimir Putin.[102] His holdings included various power companies. For obvious reasons, the physical equipment and other assets of the facility were not seriously damaged, but the message to Kiev was clear.

As the attack surface advances, cyberattacks become more complex by motives and actors who enter into alliances of convenience. Sandworm/BlackEnergy is an example. Russian hacker groups, as with all cybercriminals, are complex actors who inhabit a highly mutable environment. Criminalware is constantly changing hands, being copied, customized, and updated. Vectors shift, as do strategic aims. As a result, detection and prosecution efforts are sometimes Sisyphean, as cyber spies, hacktivists, and cyberthieves maneuver to keep ahead of interdiction by lawful entities that struggle with legal and diplomatic protocols, jurisdictional conflicts, sovereignty rights, and civil rights. As a result, different private and governmental organizations assign names to malware and hacker groups based on oftentimes incomplete or slanted experiences and analysis, and other times based on the threat they pose to a specific target.

The U.S. government refers to the Russian Intelligence Service's malicious cyber activity as Grizzly Steppe. Table 5.1 provides a list of Russian advanced persistent threat actors and exploits compiled by a joint analysis team of the Department of Homeland Security and the FBI. Among these entries, the names sometimes refer to groups; other times they refer to their tools. Although the table is current as of 2017, it is always subject to change and further refinement.

Ukraine

For the Kremlin, the menacing specter of liberal democracy loomed over another region of the "near abroad." This time the "province" was much closer, historically, culturally, and psychologically. In 2014, Ukrainian president Viktor Yanukovych publicly assured the country of the government's plans to form closer ties with the European Union, when in fact he had secretly signed a sweeping economic agreement with Russia that would bind Ukraine to Moscow.

The history of distrust between Yanukovych's government and the citizenry goes back several years. A decade earlier, amid claims of ballot count fraud and manipulation from the Kremlin, Yanukovych prevailed in a highly disputed election. In 2004, the friction and chasm between him and his pro-Western opponent, Viktor Yushchenko, could not have been deeper or wider. Yushchenko's vision for Ukraine meant a move toward more economic integration with the European Union. Yanukovych (Putin's preferred candidate), on the other hand, looked eastward to the aegis of the Russian Federation and membership in its counterbalancing organization—the Eurasian Union.

As Yanukovych was being declared the winner, thousands went into the streets in protest of the election results. Thus, the "Orange Revolution" rose, taking its name from the color associated with the campaign of Viktor Yushchenko.[103] The Orange Revolution and the Georgian Rose Revolution of the previous year were seen by the Kremlin as part of a Western plot to install Western-style democratic regimes on the territory of the former Soviet Union. The Russian leadership viewed the uprising as a contagion, which if uncontrolled might possibly reach as far as Moscow.[104] Despite efforts on behalf of Yanukovych, a revote took place a month later and Yushchenko was declared the winner. However, fortunes were reversed when Yanukovych returned to office in the 2010 presidential elections. This time there was no popular uprising. Outside observers declared the election fair and the results legitimate.

Revolt, however, returned to Kiev three years later when Yanukovych refused to sign the European Union Association Agreement. In November 2013, protesters gathered in Maidan Square to demonstrate against the government's decision. The "Euromaidan" protests gained momentum through the winter and reached ignition stage on the 20th through 22nd of February 2014 when eighty-eight people were killed by government forces. Some victims were shot by rooftop snipers.[105] Protesters seized the administration buildings and on February 22 set out to form a new government. While his private residences were being seized, Yanukovych fled to Russia.

A counterblast to events in Kiev occurred on February 27 in the regional capital of Crimea. The strong pro-Russian presence on the Crimean Peninsula and in eastern Ukraine provided Moscow with just cause for intervention. The response to events in Kiev in these districts was swift and organized. Armed pro-Russia militiamen carrying Russian-made weapons and equipment took over the Parliament and headquarters in Simferopol and raised the Russian flag over both buildings.[106] The following month, Crimea opted to secede from Ukraine and join the Russian Federation. The vote was part of a political maneuver orchestrated simultaneously with a hastily prepared referendum, which the United States and Western Europe openly denounced as illegal. Two days later, on March 18, Putin signed an amendment to the Russian constitution admitting the Republic of Crimea and the federal city of Sevastopol into the Russian Federation. Thus, the coda to these events was a unilateral act of annexation of a territory by a foreign power—a milestone for Europe, which had not witnessed such political adventurism since World War II.[107]

In less than a month, tens of thousands of masked Russian soldiers (either welcomed as "friendly people," *vezhlivye lyudi*, or reviled as "little green men," *zeleni cholovichki*)[108] carrying Russian-made weapons and equipment swarmed onto the Crimean Peninsula to bolster militia forces. In a matter of weeks and without any significant loss of life, pro-Russian forces captured the seat of political power, stage-managed a referendum declaring Crimea free from Ukraine, and forced the surrender of all 193 Ukrainian garrisons. Later, Donetsk, Luhansk, and Kharkiv fell to pro-Russian rebels in April, as the conflict spread to the east. To the incredulity of the rest of the world, Putin insisted that Russia was not involved.[109]

Ukrainians and Russians have a shared ethnic ancestry and a history of intermingling. Yet tensions have endured for centuries. A state-sponsored famine ordered by Stalin in 1932–1933 resulted in the starvation of millions. Known as Holodomor (hunger plague), it was part of a policy to suppress the agricultural sector and crush any aspirations of Ukrainian nationalism. The devastation was so utter it reduced segments of the population to cannibalism.[110] Ukrainian nationalism also plays to the emotions and unforgiven past of the "Great Patriotic War." Russians still contemptibly recall that many Ukrainians collaborated with Nazis in the struggle to defeat fascism. By labeling contemporary protesters as "nationalists," pro-Russia supporters link these Euromaidans to a previous generation who took sides in the encounter with the West, which violated Russia then and, according to the pro-Kremlin narrative, represents a recidivism that looms over all that is Russian today.[111]

Unlike Estonia or Georgia, when the Soviet Union fell, Ukraine was not a small newly independent state of limited resources and strategic sway. In contrast, the country suddenly found itself with the second-largest military in Europe. However, despite its infrastructure assets and resources, it did not have the financial means to support this military.[112] To ease the financial onus and at the same time rid the world of 1,850 nuclear weapons,[113] the Russian Federation, the United States, the United Kingdom, and Ukraine signed the Budapest Memorandum on Security Assurances in 1994. The primary provision was that Ukraine agreed to dismantle its nuclear arsenal and transfer the weapons to disarmament facilities inside Russia. A second condition required that all signatories agree to reject the use of military force or occupation of one another's territory. Additionally, the diplomatic document states that all parties would "consult in the event a situation arises which raises a question concerning these commitments."[114] The legal force of the document is questionable since it is not a formal treaty. Whether the legality would have made a difference in Moscow's ultimate actions is now no more than grist for conjecture. The international opprobrium heaped upon the Kremlin for the incursion, though extreme and nearly universal, was for the leadership an acceptable public relations loss.

Ukraine's strategic place within the near abroad was a far more compelling reason to justify Russia's intervention. Its significance is unique on several levels. Not only has Ukraine been a border territory between Russia and Western European powers, but it has also been an industrial and agricultural center in its own right. It is a political buffer for Moscow as well as an economic market. Russia relies on it as part of its defensive ring against Western-style democracies, and as a consumer for its energy exports. Furthermore, the enfeebled state of its economy notwithstanding, Ukraine has the requisite infrastructural elements and population for becoming a peer to Germany, France, or the UK.[115] Therefore, for Russia, the possibility of Ukraine being part of the European Union signifies a loss of territory and an encroachment on sacred Russian space—politically, militarily, economically, ideologically, psychologically, and culturally. For these reasons, Russia views the flight of Ukraine from its orbit as an intolerable threat to its national security. The leadership also well realizes that if Ukraine had been a member of NATO, as are its Polish, Slovakian, Hungarian, and Romanian neighbors, the actions taken by Russia would have been an indisputable act of war. Until NATO membership expands to Ukraine, military action is still a relatively safe calculated risk.

Russia strives to create a military force in cyberspace that is deployable and adaptable anywhere in the world. By merging the martial and the political into a single doctrine, the strategy compensates for its inadequacies in electronic warfare (C4ISR) vis-à-vis the United States, while defending its interests behind a veil of anonymity and plausible deniability. One key element lies in part in the capacity to achieve military outcomes by nonmilitary methods. Cyberspace is a force multiplier and/or alternative for large-scale military operations. The ability to deny, destroy, exploit, corrupt, or usurp automated decision making via ICS and SCADA systems of adversaries is an ongoing industry. The manipulation of organizations and population segments of targeted societies through the deployment of public information campaigns ("psyber warfare") is, simply, ongoing.

A rootkit useful in helping to achieve parity of power was found on the Ukrainian government computer systems as early as 2010. Known as **Uroburos**,[116] this particular APT appears to be part of a widespread campaign known as "Snake"[117] (sometimes spelled "Ouroboros," the word is a reference to a mythical two-headed snake).[118] It interacts with the malicious code (described above) called **Agent.BTZ**. Once installed, typically through e-mail scams, watering hole attacks, and USB insertions, Agent.BTZ beacons out to a command-and-control computer to upload the Uroburos malware. U.S. authorities first discovered it on defense systems in 2008 and described it then as "the worst breach of military computers in history."[119]

The designers of Uroburos, who were concluded to be Russian agents, created it to scan for Agent.BTZ in order to infect entire systems and exfiltrate sensitive information. Its sophistication, flexibility, and elegance suggest the developers had access to advanced technology and funding.[120] Its targets, suitably, are intelligence agencies, businesses, government agencies, and research and education facilities. Apparently, Russians used Uroburos primarily to spy on Ukrainian government communications. However, analysts also conclude that it had the capability to take control of computers and shut down information systems.[121] Its brilliance lies in the way it propagates through networks, infecting systems as it also scans for hosts with active Internet connections. Once it locates a connected host, the information it collects can then be exfiltrated from air-gapped systems for retrieval. Because the software is complex and discreet, it is able to bypass many security controls and escape detection.[122] However, even after detection, the code remains implanted in the system and continues to search for flaws for further compromise and eventual exfiltration of data.

Tools such as these were in place to provide Russian forces "information superiority"[123] alongside military superiority. The arc of operations against pro-Ukrainian forces in Crimea and the eastern part of the country entailed attempts to manage the information flow, which ranged from compromising secure communications to overwhelming the public narrative:

> The events in Crimea that unfolded in spring of 2014 provide important clues for the interplay between IOs [information operations] and kinetic activity. The course of events—from the takeover of parliament in Simferopol and dismantling of the Ukrainian military presence on the peninsula, to the disputed referendum and the de facto annexation of the area to the Russian Federation—was

accompanied by intense activity aimed to control the flow of information. This activity extended across the entire spectrum of communication and included kinetic, cyber and IOs targeting the physical, logical and social layers of communication.[124]

Warfare in cyber includes attacks on ICS and telecommunications equipment to disable infrastructure or communications. Information warfare is influencing public opinion by the spread of disinformation and propaganda campaigns to minimize or turn the resistance. With respect to the latter, the Russian Cold War idiom **"active measures"** (*activniye meropriyatiya*) applies to operations that involve false news and accounts, the use of front groups, and forged documents to discredit individuals, institutions, and policies.[125] These practices were distinct from espionage, which are operations deployed to gather information. Active measures are operations deployed to influence events. It is a craft plied by many actors and one that not only survives but thrives in the arena of cyberwar. The technology of the information age and the process of globalization have enabled new opportunities and enriched such operations with a new potency. The Russian leadership has long recognized the potential of these tactics and, owing to traditions that go back to Leninist doctrine, have created an infrastructure of technical resources populated with hacktivists and operatives with finely honed skills. The same personnel and expertise often operates small armies of Internet trolls to deepen and amplify these campaigns. For an added splash of inspiration, a quote from Lenin, the founder of the Soviet state, contains the central pith of these strategies: "A lie told often enough becomes the truth." To be fair, the United States has also engaged in active measures of its own, but, as noted above, not with the same unbridled access to domestic economic/market levers and capability to manipulate a subservient press.

One hacktivist group engaged in active measures tactics was **CyberBerkut**. It formed during the early stages of the Euromaidan protests. The community of hackers claimed credit for attacks on the Ukrainian electronic voting system and the Ministry of Defense. In expressing their opposition to Ukrainian independence from Russia, CyberBerkut proudly posted all their assertions on their website and on social media.[126] It also attacked NATO and even Polish websites in August 2014. Nearly forty Polish government websites, including the Warsaw Stock Exchange, were defaced. Apparently, these attacks were in retaliation for Poland's involvement in NATO and support for the Ukrainian government. The defacement involved posting graphic images of the Holocaust.[127]

The Russian military revitalized and modernized the concept of "active measures" to fit the demands of the post-Soviet era. Independent hackers, criminal elements, and anonymous state security organizations with deep covers formed the shadowy cyber army to disrupt communications and disseminate propaganda and false information. Russia and pro-Russian operatives directed botnet and DDoS attacks against Ukraine through March 2014 and up to the referendum.[128]

Although the scale of the attacks was confined and the damage to the infrastructure insignificant, they substantially contributed to the annexation of Crimea. A reason for there not being a more aggressive cyber campaign was most likely due to concerns for inadvertent blowback on Russia's own networks.

Box 5.1   CyberBerkut

The group's name was derived from Ukraine's special police force, named Berkut (or "golden eagle" in Ukrainian), which was created in 1992 under the Ministry of Interior Affairs. Not only did the CyberBerkut group use the special forces' designation, but they also imitated their insignia. Below the CyberBerkut name is their slogan, "We won't forget, We won't forgive."

Source: TrendMicro.

The interdependence between Russian and Ukrainian networks had the potential to cause disruption of Russia's communication systems through widespread and uncontrolled viral contamination. For that reason, additional action would have been unwarranted given the early successes. Plus, the full extent and scope of cyber capability left the Ukrainian defense to speculate over the true potential of the threat as long as these forces remained in reserve.

Since events began, the cybersecurity firm CrowdStrike reports that "Russian-based adversaries" can include in their cyberwar operations incursions against Ukraine on the battlefield, in the civil sector, and on critical infrastructure. These strikes are accompanied by relentless disinformation operations.[129] As long as Russia forcefully demands that other countries respect its spheres of influence in the near abroad and in any region that it regards as within its security orbit, it will use all means available to counter whatever threat it perceives as existential. These means include information operations and information warfare. According to the 2013 document "Basic Principles for the Russian Federation's State Policy in the Field of International Information Security to 2020," the strategy embraces

the use of information and communication technology as an information weapon for political and military purposes with a view to interfering in the internal affairs of states, . . . undermining public order, inciting ethnic, racial or religious hostility, promoting racist and xenophobic ideas and theories leading to hate and discrimination and encouraging violence.[130]

The United States

In the mid- to late 1990s, a cyberattack began exfiltrating thousands of sensitive but unclassified documents from a swath of research institutes, universities, and government facilities that included Los Alamos National Laboratory, Sandia National Laboratory, and the U.S. Army. Similar victims appeared in the United Kingdom, Canada, Brazil, and Germany. The FBI team covering the investigation code-named the operation "Moonlight Maze." Analysts later attributed the intrusion to a hacker group known as Turla, which some forensic specialists contend may have links with the Russian Academy of Sciences in Moscow.[131] Eventually, Moonlight Maze spread to the Navy, the Department of Energy, the Air Force, and NASA. By the time of its peak, officials concluded that the total number of stolen files, if printed and stacked, would be taller than the Washington Monument.[132] The Turla group first gained notoriety when its exploit compromised classified material at the Department of Defense in 2008. The Uroburos APT that Russian hackers injected into Ukrainian government systems also may have been developed by Turla. The exploit continues to vex defense contractors, embassies, and governments around the world and establishes the odd fact that a hacking tool developed twenty years ago may still be effective against current high-value targets.[133]

Moonlight Maze may have been the first signal that the world was entering a new era of continuous cyber espionage, but by 2014–2015, it appeared that Russia was altering course. While other states and their proxies furiously stole and sold military secrets, Russia turned its cyber capabilities to include political action.[134] Targets like the U.S. State Department, the Joint Chiefs of Staff, and the White House had worth above their value as a cache of information for espionage purposes. Hackers determined that they are, in addition, valuable reservoirs of material for influence operations. To any foreign adversary, the ability to shape public opinion to impact policy or elections is a greater prize than most state or corporate secrets. Therefore, Russian hackers also coveted access to both major political parties, state and local electoral boards, and media outlets.

There are several ways of influencing U.S. elections through cyber operations. Manipulating the count and restricting voter participation are two methods. Both would be heavy lifts for a foreign adversary. Altering the vote count, although plausible, would require a rather large and costly personnel force.[135] The approximately nine thousand election districts of nonstandardized voting systems make it difficult to conduct and coordinate a nationwide cyber campaign to "adjust" vote tallies. Such an effort would entail deploying on-site agents across the country to inject malicious code. A scheme of this size and scope would be exorbitantly expensive and hard to conceal given that a small army of operatives might be too overt to avoid suspicion. Furthermore, any anomalies of historical voter patterns would raise flags. Even with the elimination of nonstrategic districts, this kind of operation requires a staff with unique expertise and resources. However, access to the voter database of a major U.S. political party or significant affiliate or campaign would make this scenario far more feasible.

Suppressing the vote by hacking into voter registration files and purging names based on party affiliation can influence the vote as well. Such a cyber operation might frustrate turnout and skew voter attrition to favor one choice at the expense of another.[136] These ploys can demobilize segments of the electorate and subdue their support for one candidate or party. However, this also might be too conspicuous, as massive delays and heavy provisional ballot demand in strategic districts would also most likely draw attention. Nonetheless, investigations could undercut confidence in the process and delegitimize results regardless of the outcome. For an adversarial actor whose aims are to spread doubt and stir controversy over any given election or the democratic process in general, this could be viewed as a victory.

Another method is by influencing the vote through active measures. Freedom of expression protects minorities, dissident voices, and artistic work, but it also gives cover to those who spread baseless claims, conspiracy theories, and the hiss of innuendo that incites racism and xenophobia. Free societies are often divided ideologically, and the same opportunity to create fissures between population segments can in some instances instigate violence. While separately these ploys come with individual risks and flaws, a combination of such stratagems might produce an effective blend of schemes potent enough to sway an election.

Because the U.S. two-party system effectively creates a winner-take-all end game, manipulation by a foreign adversary is an inviting prospect, particularly if one candidate is decidedly preferred over the other. With no experience in coalition government, and with the structure and stricture of the electoral college, the deeply divided country subjects itself to a binary choice where the outcome hangs on the voter results of a handful of strategic states.[137] Thus, despite risks of discovery, the stratagem to manipulate the U.S. election process remains a seductive temptation for influence operations.

Active measures take particular advantage of the vulnerabilities inherent in liberal democracies. These actions have a history during and since the end of the Cold War, and more recently, such actions have already delivered results—particularly in Europe. In addition to the examples described in detail above, former German chancellor Gerhard Schroeder and former Italian prime minister Silvio Berlusconi were accused of profiting from their connections with Putin and, in a like-for-like, influencing foreign and domestic policies to accommodate the Kremlin.[138] Observers also link the rise of extremist and populist parties in the Netherlands, the Czech Republic, Hungary, Switzerland, Serbia, Denmark, Austria, Finland, and France to Russian influence campaigns, financial support, and even legal assistance.[139] Attempted, but less successful, ventures include efforts to interfere with the 2014 Scottish independence referendum and a foiled hack of the United Kingdom's parliamentary elections in 2015.[140]

In the United States, Russia has relied on some tried, tested, and more tolerable methods, such as appealing to Beltway think tanks, applying diplomatic pressure, and hiring lobbying firms. Yet, as long as cyber-related influence vectors[141] represent a tempting option, the democratic process of free and open elections is always at risk of foreign interference. In the world of social media, there are no editorial mechanisms to distill factual data from white noise. Access to constituency segments is transnational and includes extremist groups, fringe elements, or any aggrieved population who feels their fears have been muted and their voice unheard. In the United States, polls reveal a single-digit approval rating of Congress by the American people, reflecting an abiding discontent with Washington. A study by the Pew Research Center during the 2016 presidential election asserted that not only were Americans more divided than at any other time in the last two decades, but their opinion of the mainstream media had reached a historic low.[142] When the background noise of outrageous assertions and "fake news" swamps attempts to elevate the truth and conduct reasonable discourse, these conditions magnify. Irrational fears amplify and fringe thought leavens to the height of legitimate election issues.[143] For Russia, the chaos presents opportunity.

A year after Barack Obama's reelection, events outside Russia were unfolding, and a new military doctrine was taking form. A Russian military forum in February 2013 featured an article attributed to General Valery Gerasimov, chief of the General Staff. It was called "Value of Science in Anticipation: New Challenges Require Rethinking of the Forms and Methods of Warfare." Despite its innocuous title, the document was groundbreaking. While it restated the elements and significance of unconventional warfare, it urged an emphasis on nonmilitary methods and instruments to achieve military effects.[144] The article went further to suggest that the use of espionage, propaganda, and cyberattacks be adapted at a four-to-one ratio of nonmilitary to military measures in order to contain the use of armed force.[145] The calculation gave the doctrine (now referred to as the Gerasimov doctrine) a new scope of opportunity during times of peace and the flexibility to adjust the ratio as situations warrant during open conflict.

Gerasimov believed that this approach, referred to as **hybrid war** in the West and **nonlinear war** by Russia, was behind the West-inspired Arab Spring and color revolutions. Despite the advantage strong central regimes have over democratic societies in mobilizing economic, media, and other nongovernmental "assets" for military objectives, the Gerasimov doctrine sees this strategy as singularly Western and proposes a Russian variant. A particular focus within the thesis of the Gerasimov doctrine is the element of "protest potential of the population."[146] This model works most effectively when the preconditions of a disaffected population are present and sympathetic to calls for mobilization. The rumbling distrust by the American public of Washington, the news media, and elites in general provided a *conditio sine qua non* for active measures and nonlinear war tactics to shape the political landscape. In his observations of events taking place during the Arab Spring, Gerasimov's essay noted that "a perfectly thriving state can . . . be transformed into an arena of fierce armed conflict, become a victim of foreign intervention, and sink into a web of chaos."[147]

Four years after the publication of this article, as if completing Gerasimov's thoughts, the office of the Directorate of National Intelligence released to the public its own document, "Assessing Russian Activities and Intentions in Recent US Elections." Its key judgment read as follows:

> We assess Russian President Vladimir Putin ordered an influence campaign in 2016 aimed at the US presidential election. Russia's goals were to undermine public faith in the US democratic process, denigrate Secretary Clinton, and harm her electability and potential presidency. We further assess Putin and the Russian Government developed a clear preference for President-elect Trump. We have high confidence in these judgments.[148]

The report goes on to say that the Russian messaging strategy was a campaign employing the resources and personnel of government agencies, third-party intermediaries, and state-funded media.[149] Activities included cyber operations by covert military units, intelligence services, and paid "trolls" who took to social media and posted pro-Kremlin propaganda under fake identities.

Box 5.2   Russian Trolls

The purpose of "trolling" is to make it appear that there are massive armies of followers across the spectrum that uphold policies favorable to Russia's position or the candidates who support those views. The word *troll* became a popular tag in the 1990s for Internet users trying to frustrate online conversations with vitriol, false news, or spam.[150] Both sides of an issue might resort to trolling to denounce politicians, harass journalists, or discredit demonstrators with false accounts of violence, rioting, or looting, all activities designed to make it as difficult as possible for the public to separate the truth from fabrication and undermine the opposition's narrative. Russian-sponsored trolls usually maintain multiple false profiles and adhere to precise guidelines.[151] Russia reportedly controls and manages a large number of bloggers through its troll farms, which it supervises through the Presidential Administration.[152] The number of people working for Russian troll farms is believed to be in the thousands.[153]

In the case of the 2016 U.S. presidential campaign, Russia planned to exploit the U.S. political process regardless of the election result. Its preference for Donald Trump was clear. However, the prospects for a Trump victory oscillated between slim and possible for most of the campaign, leaving the Kremlin to hope for the best and gird for the worst. Putin loathed Clinton and blamed her for aiding and inciting anti-Kremlin protests in Moscow in 2011–2013. He regarded her as a more hawkish threat than President Obama and believed his hopes to expand Russia's geopolitical influence and overturn economic sanctions would meet with stiffer resistance in a Clinton administration.

A 2015 International Monetary Fund (IMF) report estimated that Western sanctions and Russian countersanctions as a response to Russia's incursion into Ukraine were costing the economy 1–1.5 percent in GDP and as much as 9 percent of GDP over the intermediate term.[154] Sanctions included a restriction on the export of drilling and fracking technology, which would inhibit access to as much as $8.2 trillion in oil reserves.[155] The drop in oil prices had an added impact and was shrinking the Russian economy to the level of Spain and Australia. Putin knew the economic pressures on Russia would eventually translate into a political problem for his government. The Kremlin's best options were either a President Trump or a delegitimized President Clinton. While opinion polls unanimously projected Clinton to win, pro-Kremlin bloggers arranged Twitter campaigns to cast aspersions on a Clinton victory. Prior to the vote, an account, #DemocracyRIP, was readied. During this time, Russian trolls and diplomats publicly denounced the election process as a sham and prepared to continue the allegations of a "rigged system" after the election and during her presidency.[156]

In the run-up to the November election, Russian cyber operations not only included the intrusion into and disclosure of information from the Democratic Party's data banks (as mentioned above) but also the capture of data from state and local election boards, think tanks, primary campaigns, and lobbying groups.[157] Although the Department of Homeland Security assessed that the Russian Intelligence Service (RIS) used the information exfiltrated from election boards to further analyze the U.S. electoral process and research the technical and equipment elements involved, it found no evidence of any attempt to manipulate the actual vote count.[158] The RIS did, however, coordinate its cyber activities with the releases of sensitive information to selected media outlets and WikiLeaks through agents Guccifer 2.0 and DCLeaks. The Russian state-controlled media amplified these reports as the presidential campaigns unfolded and advanced toward Election Day. Ultimately, the results handed a victory to Donald Trump, a reversal of expectations for Democrats and a humbling acceptance of an unfamiliar political reality by most pollsters and political experts.

The U.S. presidential election was the newest post–Cold War test for Russian state-run messaging organs. The propaganda machine serves as a platform for pro-Russian messaging to Russian and international audiences. It includes a domestic media apparatus, a network of government-sponsored Internet trolls, and outlets such as Sputnik and RT (formerly, *Russia Today*), which are directed at global audiences.

RT America TV is a Kremlin-financed channel operated from within the United States. According to the Directorate of National Intelligence (DNI) report, RT "has positioned itself as a domestic US channel and has deliberately sought to obscure any legal ties to the Russian Government."[159] During the election campaign, its coverage of Hillary Clinton was consistently negative and concentrated on her e-mail leaks and allegations of corruption, poor health, and even supposed ties to Islamic terrorism. In contrast to Secretary Clinton, the same sources offered mounting and approving comments about Donald Trump throughout the primary and general election. After his victory, Russian media continued to laud Trump's success and to link it to a vindication of Putin's own campaign to discredit the West's status quo and applaud his advocacy for global populist movements.[160]

The report of the U.S. intelligence community called the Russian influence effort the "Boldest Yet in the US" and stated that the "Election Operation Signals a 'New Normal' in Russian Influence Efforts."[161] Academics and global security experts have become more resigned to referring to the post–Cold War era as "Cold War 2.0," where information can be weaponized and social media can become a weapons platform. The final assessment by the DNI was that the Russian spearphishing campaigns against U.S. government employees, think tanks, and NGOs in national security, defense, and foreign policy fields will continue, as will Russia's attempts to develop additional capabilities. It further added that the past influence campaign "could provide material for future influence efforts."[162]

Those efforts would include a mass disinformation campaign to influence American public opinion on a grander scale. According to a 2017 U.S. government counterintelligence report, Russia has already deployed the initial phases of a large-scale cyber propaganda strategy.[163] During the 2016 presidential election, Russian hackers used a command-and-control server to launch waves of e-mails carrying malware to thousands of employees of the Department of Defense and select congressional staffers. The attackers then took control of victims' phones, computers, and Twitter accounts. Not only was the authority of the U.S. armed forces compromised, but so too was the authenticity of congressional sources as tweets of false information and news flooded social media and corroborated one another in real time.

Social media platforms were also used to access and influence segments of voters. Algorithms (developed in the United States) were applied to analyze data banks of millions of consumers, voters, and activists. The data was cut and evaluated to map thousands of subgroups defined by religion, political belief, and consumption tastes. Much the way product sales organizations attempt to identify markets, Russian hackers categorized voters as followers (buyers) or susceptible individuals (potential buyers) by pinpointing polemical issues and strategic voter segments for message targeting. Claims surfaced that FBI counterintelligence agents also looked into possible collusion between these Russian influence operations and organizations linked to the Trump campaign. Far-right news outlets, such as Breitbart News and Infowars, and the data analytics company Cambridge Analytica attracted investigators' interest (see chapter 3).[164] Meanwhile, the potential to modify public sentiment by the millions and in real time remains a challenge for national security experts and defenders of the democratic process and civil liberties.

"What Is to Be Done?"

In the early days of Lenin's revolutionary career, he published a pamphlet called *Chto delat?* (*Что делать?*), *What Is to Be Done?* (1902). A central theme of the work was that Marxists needed to form a vanguard army to proliferate Marxist political ideas among the masses. It is difficult to argue against the theory that active measures and influence operations are in many ways echoes from this Leninist past. Stalin, as if doubling down on Lenin's thoughts, once posited, "Ideas are more powerful than guns. We would not let our enemies have guns, why should we let them have ideas?" This strategy of the Soviet/Russian leadership has endured periods of revolution, war, peace, détente, political collapse, regime change, and resets.

"What is to be done?" in the age of globalization and information warfare has now become a burning question for the contemporary security establishment. The digital world is a great enabler of information sharing between governments, between governments and their citizenry, and between communities of interest, researchers, and data sources. Web 2.0 is an empowering connective tool and intellectual force multiplier. It is also a means of providing access to populations for exploitation by criminal elements and hostile state actors. The Kremlin leadership appreciates well this underside and how it can be a military and political force multiplier in ways never imagined by Lenin when he sounded a call for the formation of a "vanguard." These exploitable targets include not only communities abroad but, in the Kremlin's view, population segments within Russia as well.

Circumspectly, it is important to realize that the weapons of information warfare and cyberwarfare pose risks to both the perpetrator and the intended victim. In many ways, it is analogous to the chemical weapons warfare of World War I. The use of poisonous gas, which was subject to conditions outside of any control, often resulted in unpredictable, doubtful, and even adverse consequences. Similarly, blowback is always a potential risk in the technical domain as malware and other cyberweapons spread across the Internet and circle back to inadvertently infect computers and systems that were never intended as targets.

Additionally, in the cognitive domain, active measures involving fake news and disinformation erode over time and can also have unintended results. Eventually, more facts surface and evidence comes forward to negate the false narrative.[165] Disinformation campaigns, therefore, have an element of counterproductivity as operations are exposed. Ultimately, the "tyranny of facts" becomes inescapable, population segments can become alienated and opposition groups radicalized.[166] The long-term effects of these active measures are still to be tested and analyzed, particularly in a data environment of immense and increasing volumes of information flow and twenty-four-hour news cycles.

As discovered by the members of the NATO alliance, national cybersecurity is more than a technical issue. In the cognitive domain, protecting democratic societies by assuring the integrity of a free press, upholding the right to protest, holding officials accountable, and safeguarding the legitimacy of elections is ultimately a public onus rather than another theater of war for the national security establishment. In any liberal democracy, distrust of government is healthy but certainly not enough. Ignorance can be noxious and self-consuming. It undermines social equality and corrupts through fear. Voters can resist a system they do not agree with not only by protesting but also by seeking the truth. The best defense against active measures by any actor that attempts to tamper with the democratic process or inhibit the enjoyment of our civil rights may be found in Thomas Jefferson's prescient counsel: "An educated citizenry is a vital requisite for our survival as a free people."

Key Terms

Russian Business Network	BlackEnergy
Energetic Bear/Crouching Yeti	Uroburos
APT28	Agent.BTZ
APT29	active measures
Cozy Bear	CyberBerkut
Cozy Duke	hybrid war
Sandworm	nonlinear war

Notes

[1] Casimir C. Carey III, "NATO's Options for Defensive Cyber against Non-State Actors," U.S. Army War College, 2013, 1.

[2] Kertu Ruus, "Cyber War I: Estonia Attacked from Russia," *European Affairs* 9, no. 1 (Winter/Spring 2008).

[3] Richard C. Zoller, "Russian Cyberspace Strategy and a Proposed United States Response," U.S. Army War College, 2010, 3.

[4] Stephen Herzog, "Revisiting the Estonian Cyber Attacks: Digital Threat and Multinational Responses," *Journal of Strategic Security* 4, no. 2 (2011): 49–60.

[5] "Russia Accused of Unleashing Cyberwar to Disable Estonia," *Guardian*, May 17, 2007.

[6] Clay Wilson, "Botnets, Cybercrime, and Cyber Terrorism: Vulnerabilities and Policy Issues for Congress," Congressional Research Service, 2007, 7.

[7] Shane Harris, "China's Cyber Military," *National Journal Magazine*, May 31, 2008.

[8] Ruus; Michael Connell and Sarah Vogler, "Russia's Approach to Cyber Warfare," Center for Naval Analysis, Arlington, VA, March 2017, 14.

[9] Carey, 2.

[10] Vincent Joubert, "Five Years after Estonia's Cyber Attacks: Lessons Learned for NATO," NATO Defense College, Rome, no. 76, May 2012.

[11] Connell, 15.

[12] Zoller, 3.

[13] Stephen J. Blank, "Information Age Warfare *a la Russe*," in *Cyberspace: Malevolent Actors, Criminal Opportunities, and Strategic Competition*, ed. Phil Williams and Dighton Fiddner (Carlisle, PA: Strategic Studies Institute and U.S. Army War College Press, 2016), 234–35.

[14] Jack Jarmon, *The New Era in U.S. National Security* (Lanham, MD: Rowman & Littlefield, 2014), 138.

[15] Carey, 5.

[16] Herzog.

[17] Stephen M. Dayspring, "Toward a Theory of Hybrid Warfare: The Russian Conduct of War during Peace," Naval Postgraduate School, 2015, 72.

[18] Jason Healey and Leendert van Bochoven, "NATO's Cyber Capabilities: Yesterday, Today, and Tomorrow," Atlantic Council, February 2012.

[19] Ibid.

[20] Joubert.

[21] Healey.

[22] https://ccdcoe.org.

[23] Joubert.

[24] http://www.nato.int/cps/en/natohq/topics_78170.htm.

[25] Ibid.

[26] Eric Schmitt, "US Lending Support to Baltic States Fearing Russia," *New York Times*, January 1, 2017.

[27] Ibid.

[28] Andrew E. Kramer, "Spooked by Russia, Tiny Estonia Trains a Nation of Insurgents," *New York Times*, October 31, 2016.

[29] Tom Kellermann, CEO, Strategic Cyber Ventures, conversation with the author, December 13, 2016.

[30] http://www.trendmicro.com/vinfo/us/security/news/cyber-attacks/operation-pawn-storm-fast-facts.

[31] Ibid.

[32] "Macron Was Target of Cyber Attacks by Spy-Linked Group," Reuters, April 24, 2017.

[33] "Grizzly Steppe—Russian Malicious Cyber Activity," Joint Analysis Report, NCCIC and FBI, report No. JAR 20296, December 29, 2016, 4; Lisa Sawyer Samp, Jeffrey Rathke, and Anthony Bell, "Perspectives on Security and Strategic Stability: A Track 2 Dialogue with the Baltic States and Poland," Center for Strategic and International Studies, Rowman & Littlefield, October 2016, 12.

[34] Samp, 12.

[35] Blank, 216.

[36] John J. Dziak, *Soviet Perceptions of Military Power: The Interaction of Theory and Practice* (New York: Crane, Russak, 1981).

[37] Ellie Geranmayeh and Kadri Liik, "The New Power Couple: Russia and Iran in the Middle East," European Council on Foreign Relations, September 2016.

38 Andrew Monaghan, "Preparing for War? Moscow Facing an Arc of Crisis," U.S. Army War College Press, Carlisle, PA, December 2016, 9.

39 Blank, 210.

40 Ibid., xii.

41 Matthew Kosnik, "Russia's Military Reform and Putin's Last Card," *Journal of Military and Strategic Studies* 17, no. 1 (2016).

42 George F. Kennan, *The Long Telegram* (Washington, DC: State Department, 1946), part 2.

43 Blank, 218.

44 Jolanta Darczewska, "Russia's Armed Forces on the Information War Front Strategic Documents," Ośrodek Studiów Wschodnich [Centre for Eastern Studies], no. 57, 2016.

45 Ibid., 223.

46 Ibid.

47 Ibid., 218.

48 Dayspring, 37.

49 Connell, 27.

50 Ibid., 42.

51 Ibid., 66.

52 Zoller, 1.

53 Ibid.

54 Will Englund, "Comparing the Crimea Conflict with the Georgia-Russia Situation of 2008," *Washington Post*, March 2, 2014.

55 Blank, 11.

56 Ibid.

57 Captain Paulo Shakarian (USA), "The 2008 Russian Cyber Campaign against Georgia," *Military Review*, November–December 2011, 65. Cited in Blank, 252.

58 Connell, 17.

59 Richard Weitz, "Global Insights: Russia Refines Cyber Warfare Strategies," *World Politics Review*, August 25, 2009, http://worldpoliticsreview.com/articles/print/4218, cited in Blank, 249.

60 David Hollis, "Cyberwar Case Study: Georgia 2008," *Small Wars Journal*, smallwarsjournal.com.

61 http://www.cnn.com/2014/13/03/world/europe/2008-georgia-russia-conflict.

62 Radina Gigova, "ICC Opens Investigation into Georgia-Russia War," CNN, January 27, 2016, http://www.cnn.com/2016/01/27/world/icc-investigation-georgia-russia-war.

63 Kosnik, 147–48.

64 Zoller, 7.

65 I. Vorobyov and V. Kiseljov, "Russian Military Theory: Past and Present," *Military Thought* 3 (2013), cited in Margarita Jaitner and Peter A. Mattsson, *Russian Information Warfare of 2014*, 7th International Conference on Cyber Conflict: Architectures in Cyberspace, ed. M. Maybaum, A.-M. Osula, and L. Lindström (NATO CCD COE Publications, 2015), 41.

66 Ibid.

67 Vladimir Putin, "Annual Address to the Federal Assembly," Moscow, Russia, April 26, 2007, http://en.kremlin.ru/events/president/transcripts/24203, cited in Blank, 210.

68 Vladimir Putin, "Otkrytoe pis'mo Vladimira Putina k rossiyskim izbiratelyam [An open letter by Vladimir Putin to Russian voters]," cited in Karen Dawisha, *Putin's Kleptocracy* (New York: Simon & Schuster, 2014), 237.

69 "Virtual Criminality Report 2009," Commissioned by McAfee, prepared by Paul Kurtz, Good Harbor Consulting, 2009, 12.

70 Zoller, 6.

71 David Bizeul, "Russian Business Network Study," 2007, http://fatalsystemerrorbook.net/pdf/bizeul_onRBN.pdf; Kara Flook, "Russia and the Cyber Threat," May 13, 2009, http://www.criticalthreats.org/analysis/russia/and-the-cyber-threat.

72 Ibid.

73 Carey, 8.

74 Ibid.

75 Bizeul, 6.

76 Carey, 8; Flook.

77 Flook.
78 Blank, 248.
79 Ibid.
80 Geranmayeh.
81 "Net Losses: Estimating the Global Cost of Cybercrime—Economic Impact of Cybercrime II," Center for Strategic and International Studies and McAfee, June 2014, 15.
82 James Scott and Drew Spaniel, "Know Your Enemies: A Primer on Advanced Persistent Threat Groups," Institute for Critical Infrastructure Technology, 2015, 18.
83 Ibid.
84 Ibid.
85 http://securelist.com/files/2014/07/EB-YetiJuly2014-Public.pdf.
86 Eric Lipton and David E. Sanger, "The Perfect Weapon: How Russian Cyberpower Invaded the U.S.," *New York Times*, December 13, 2016.
87 Scott, 22–23.
88 Ibid., 22.
89 Lipton.
90 Evan Osnos, David Remnick, Joshua Yaffa, "Active Measures," *New Yorker*, March 6, 2017.
91 Ibid.
92 Scott, 24.
93 http://securityaffairs.co/wordpress/55958/apt/apt-29-group.html.
94 "Grizzly Steppe," 2–3.
95 Ibid.
96 "Background to 'Assessing Russian Activities and Intentions in Recent US Elections': The Analytic Process and Cyber Incident Attribution," Office of the Directorate of National Intelligence, January 6, 2017, ii–iii.
97 Scott, 25.
98 http://securityaffairs.co/wordpress/43413/malware/sandworm-apt-ukranian-power-outage.html.
99 https://lifars.com/2014/11/kaspersky-provides-more-information-on-the-sandworm-apt-team.
100 Scott, 26.
101 Andrew Foxall, "Putin's Cyberwar: Russia's Statecraft in the Fifth Domain" (policy paper no. 29, Henry Jackson Center, Russian Studies Center, 2016, 9).
102 https://www.wired.com/2016/03/inside-cunning-unprecedented-hack-ukraines-power-grid.
103 Ariel Zirulnick, "Orange Revolution—Ukraine," *Christian Science Monitor*, January 19, 2011.
104 Dayspring, 85.
105 Ibid.
106 http://www.independent.co.uk/news/world/europe/ukraine-crisis-armed-men-hoist-russian-flag-after-seizing-crimea-parliament-9156413.html.
107 Dayspring, 103.
108 M. Maybaum, A.-M. Osula, and L. Lindström, *Russian Information Warfare of 2014*, 7th International Conference on Cyber Conflict: Architectures in Cyberspace (NATO CCD COE Publications, 2015).
109 Ibid.
110 Alexandr Solzhenitsyn, *The Gulag Archipelago* (Paris: Éditions du Seuil, 1973).
111 Jānis Bērziņš, Aivar Jaeski, Mark Laity, Nerijus Maliukevicius, Aurimas Navys, Gerry Osborne, Robert Pszczel, and Stephen Tatham, "Analysis of Russia's Information Campaign against Ukraine," NATO StratCom Centre of Excellence, Riga, 2015, 4.
112 Dayspring, 108.
113 Ibid.
114 Ron Synovitz, "Explainer: The Budapest Memorandum and Its Relevance to Crimea," Radio Free Europe/Radio Liberty, February 28, 2014, http://www.rferl.org/a/ukraine-explainer-budapest-memorandum/25280502.html.
115 Dayspring, 108.
116 Maybaum, 45.

117 *Snake Rootkit Report* (Guildford, England: BAE Systems Applied Intelligence, 2014), http://info.baesystemsdetica.com/rs/baesystems/images/snake_whitepaper.pdf.

118 Connell, 21.

119 Scott, 20.

120 Ibid.

121 Dayspring, 128.

122 Ibid., 21.

123 Maybaum, 45.

124 Ibid.

125 "Soviet Influence Activities: A Report on Active Measures and Propaganda, 1986–87," United States Department of State, August 1987.

126 http://blog.trendmicro.com/trendlabs-security-intelligence/hacktivist-group-cyberberkut-behind-attacks-on-german-official-websites.

127 "Framework and Terminology for Understanding Cyber-Enabled Economic Warfare," Center on Sanctions and Illicit Finance, Foundation for the Defense of Democracies, February 22, 2017.

128 Dayspring, 129.

129 "Fancy Bear Android Malware in Tracking of Ukrainian Field Artillery Units," CrowdStrike Global Intelligence Team, March 23, 2017.

130 Darczewska, 15.

131 Chris Doman, "The First Cyber Espionage Attacks: How Operation Moonlight Maze Made History," July 7, 2016, https://medium.com/@chris_doman/the-first-sophistiated-cyber-attacks-how-operation-moonlight-maze-made-history-2adb12cc43f7.

132 Lipton.

133 http://securityaffairs.co/wordpress/57679/apt/moonlight-maze-turla-apt.html.

134 Ibid.

135 Jacob Bund, "Cybersecurity and Democracy Hacking, Leaking, and Voting," European Institute for Security Studies, November 2016, 3.

136 Ibid., 3–4.

137 Ibid.

138 Dawisha, 6, 140–41.

139 F. Stephen Larrabee, Stephanie Pezard, Andrew Radin, Nathan Chandler, Keith Crane, and Thomas S. Szayna, "Russia and the West after the Ukraine Crisis: European Vulnerabilities to Russian Pressures," RAND Corporation, 2017, 54.

140 Mika Aaltola and Mariita Mattiisen, "Election Hacking in Democracies: The Example of the 2016 US Election," Finnish Institute of International Affairs, October 2016, 6–7.

141 Ibid., 3.

142 Osnos.

143 Ibid.

144 Dayspring, 112.

145 Ibid., 115; Osnos.

146 Valery Gerasimov, "Value of Science in Anticipation: New Challenges Require Rethinking of the Forms and Methods of Warfare," *Military Industrial Courier*, February 27, 2013, http://www.vpk-news.ru/articles/14632.

147 Osnos.

148 "Assessing Russian Activities and Intentions in Recent US Elections," Intelligence Community Assessment, ICA 2017-01D, January 6, 2017, ii.

149 Ibid.

150 Adrian Chen, "The Agency," *New York Times Magazine*, June 2, 2015.

151 Bērziņš, 23.

152 Ibid., 22.

153 Ibid., 22.

154 Rebecca M. Nelson, "U.S. Sanctions and Russia's Economy," Congressional Research Service Report, February 2017, 8.

[155] Massimo Calabresi, "Hacking Democracy: Inside Russia's Media War on America," *Time*, May 29, 2017.

[156] "Assessing Russian Activities," 2.

[157] Ibid.

[158] Ibid.

[159] Ibid., 6.

[160] Ibid., 3.

[161] Ibid., 5.

[162] Ibid.

[163] Calabresi.

[164] Ibid.

[165] Bērziņš, 5.

[166] Ibid., 33.

Violent Extremist Organizations and Terrorism in the Cyber Domain 6

To terrorize, people must feel an immediate danger. Human, physical, and apprehensive emotional reaction to terrorist operations must occur for something to be cyberterrorism proper. Although the intent to do harm against physical processes exists in terrorist tracts, the capability is currently lacking, according to Director of National Intelligence Daniel Coats's statement to the Senate Select Committee on Intelligence: "Terrorists—to include the Islamic State of Iraq and ash-Sham (ISIS)—will also continue to use the Internet to organize, recruit, spread propaganda, raise funds, collect intelligence, inspire action by followers, and coordinate operations. Hezbollah and HAMAS will continue to build on their cyber accomplishments inside and outside the Middle East. ISIS will continue to seek opportunities to target and release sensitive information about US citizens, similar to their operations in 2015 disclosing information about US military personnel, in an effort to inspire attacks."[1]

While low-hanging fruit might exist that low-skill actors could exploit, the targets that could cause events of national significance and terrorize a population are too complex for current capabilities. Furthermore, in the cops-and-robbers game between cyber offenders and defenders, the defense does not remain static, and thus the human capital of aspiring cyberterrorist organizations must remain on the cutting edge of the latest defensive posturing of critical infrastructure technology. Therefore, an emphasis of this chapter is to provide clarity on the operational realities of the misuse of cyber means by terrorist organizations to achieve operational objectives of recruitment, radicalization, fund-raising, and planning and execution of attacks in the physical environment. To understand the morphing range of limitations and competencies, it is necessary to draw a clear distinction between cyber-enabled terrorist operations and operations in cyberspace creating physical effects equivalent to an armed attack. Such categories include, but are not limited to, the following:

- Misuse of the Internet for the logistics of a terrorist network (including radicalization, recruitment, and financing).

- Cyber-enabled terrorist attacks as observed from improvised explosive devices to complex command and control and communications during an operation.
- The threat of cyberterrorism to critical infrastructure and disruption of civilian networks.
- The emergence of psyber warfare to intimidate or mobilize populations without a physical presence.

Definitions

To place these and other phenomena within their respective contexts, a spectrum of terrorist cyber operations is useful in illustrating distinctions and applying definitions. Drawing clear distinctions between cyberattacks on the one hand and the misuse of information technology for communications, reconnaissance, planning, recruiting, fund-raising, and cyber armed attacks on critical infrastructure on the other end of the spectrum is important.[2] A broad definition of *cyberattack* risks treating crime and espionage as armed attacks/threats to peace. Espionage, crime, and armed attack necessitate responses that fall under mutually exclusive sections of the U.S. Code and relevant international laws. It is increasingly important that discussions of malicious cyber activities be accurately described and differentiated. The operating paradigm required to address the terrorist misuse of the Internet to conduct espionage or criminal activities is not the same in terms of criticality or modality as that required for them to succeed in creating effects through a cyber operation that would rise to the level of an armed attack.

According to the U.S. Code, *terrorism* is defined as "premeditated, politically motivated violence perpetrated against noncombatant targets by subnational groups or clandestine agents"; *terrorist group* means any group practicing, or which has significant subgroups that practice, international terrorism. Cyberterrorism is more than just adding the *cyber* prefix to terrorist activity. For the purposes of this discussion, the definition of *cyberterrorism* is "the use of computer network tools to shut down critical national infrastructures (such as energy, transportation, government operations) or to coerce or intimidate a government or civilian population."[3]

A Spectrum of Cyber-Enabled Terrorist Operations

It would seem from headlines that the amount of power that has come into nonstate actors' hands as a result of access to cyberspace has qualitatively altered the amount of power violent nonstate actors may wield. In his 2013 statement to the Senate, former director of the National Security Agency and commander of the U.S. Cyber Command Keith Alexander reported that

cyber programs and capabilities are growing, evolving, and spreading; we believe it is only a matter of time before the sort of sophisticated tools developed by well-funded state actors find their way to groups or even individuals who in their zeal to make some political statement do not know or do not care about the collateral damage they inflict on bystanders and critical infrastructure. The United States is already a target. Networks and websites owned by Americans and located here have endured intentional, state-sponsored attacks, and some have incurred degradation and disruption because they happened to be along the route to another state's overseas targets. Our critical infrastructure is thus doubly at risk. On a scale of one to ten, with ten being strongly defended, our critical infrastructure's preparedness to withstand a destructive cyberattack is about a three based on my experience. There are variations in preparedness across sectors, but all are susceptible to the vulnerabilities of the weakest.[4]

The key point in the statement above is, as currently observed, that activity by state and nonstate actors amounts to degradation or disruption of service. This is a crucial distinction given that the effects of destruction require high-level knowledge of very specialized computer networking protocols, industrial equipment, cryptography, and computer programming. In his congressional testimony, General Alexander refers to disruption and degradation of service (including those targeting U.S. banks in 2012–13), which targets commercial information and communication technology, not industrial control systems. Thus, it is important to distinguish between the terrorist misuse of information and communication technology and the targeting of industrial control systems.

The area where cyberspace and terrorism overlap is an area with an already extensive bibliography.[5] The enhancement of terrorist organizations' capabilities for planning attacks; anonymizing their communications; recruiting, radicalizing, and inciting individuals; and financing their operations presents challenges due to the global reach and always-on nature of the Internet. The technical realities underlying all aspects of this problem will be emphasized in order to contribute to better-informed frameworks and policies.

The chart in figure 6.1 describes the spectrum across which terrorists may misuse elements of cyberspace focusing on radicalization, recruitment, fundraising/planning, espionage, disruptions, and finally armed attack. The spectrum of terrorist misuse of the Internet includes the following:

1. *Cyber influence:* the misuse of cyberspace to influence populations with propaganda. This could be to create sympathizers to the cause. Included in this category is the process of radicalization and recruitment via the cyber domain.
2. *Cyber planning:* Timothy Thomas coined the term *cyber planning* as "the digital coordination of an integrated plan stretching across geographical boundaries that may or may not result in bloodshed."[6] Thomas's definition in his work includes examples of both influence and execution of attack. One could argue that recruitment and command and control of an operation via cyberspace do not amount to planning. Planning is more akin to intelligence, surveillance, and reconnaissance.
3. *Real-time operational execution:* the misuse of cyberspace to actually cause physical destruction. This is beyond the realm of the hypothetical when it comes to detonating improvised explosive devices via cellular technologies.[7] What has still not been observed is the terrorist capability to attack industrial control systems via electronic means to cause physical effects.

Figure 6.1 Spectrum of Cyber-Enabled Operations

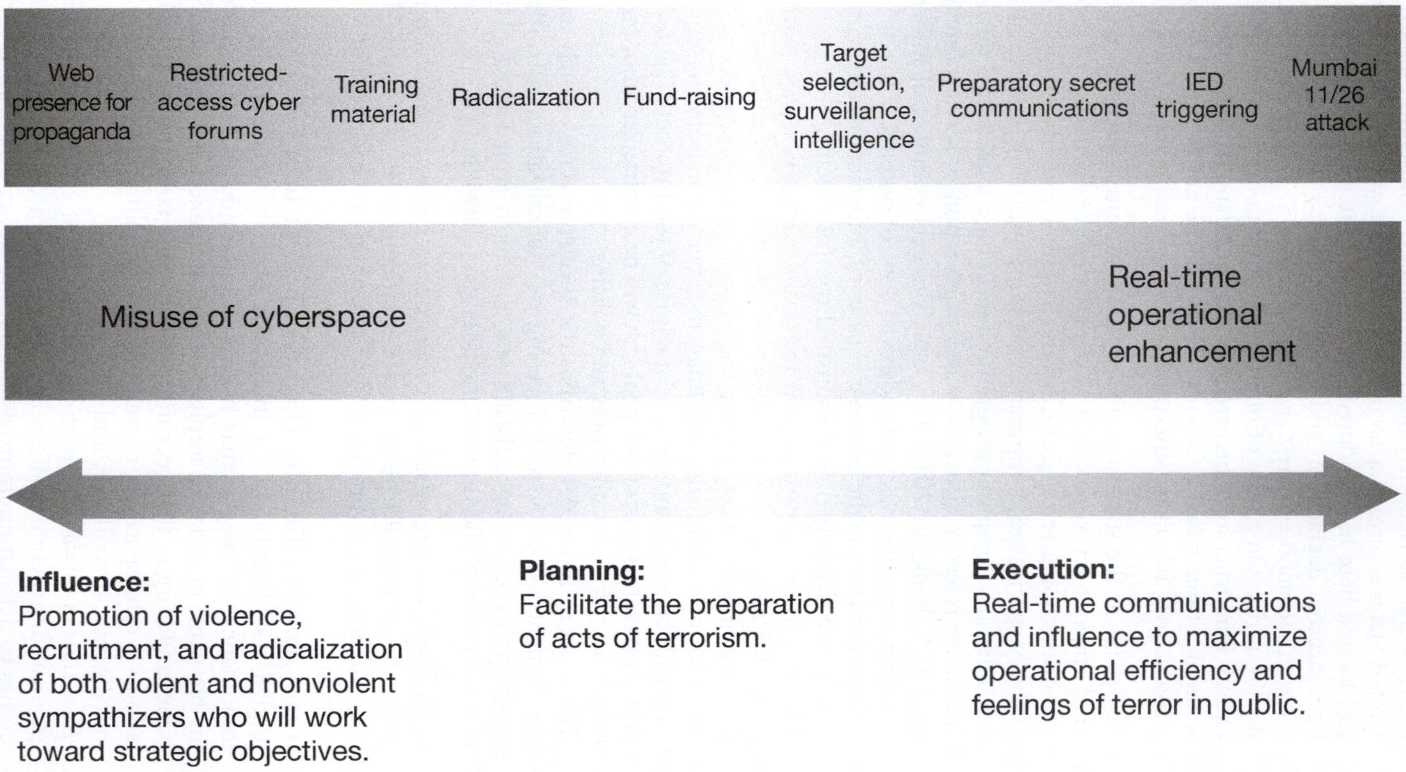

Web presence for propaganda

Restricted-access cyber forums

Training material

Radicalization

Fund-raising

Target selection, surveillance, intelligence

Preparatory secret communications

IED triggering

Mumbai 11/26 attack

Misuse of cyberspace

Real-time operational enhancement

Influence:
Promotion of violence, recruitment, and radicalization of both violent and nonviolent sympathizers who will work toward strategic objectives.

Planning:
Facilitate the preparation of acts of terrorism.

Execution:
Real-time communications and influence to maximize operational efficiency and feelings of terror in public.

Cyber-Enabled Recruitment and Radicalization

The battle against Islamist and other forms of extremism is being fought not only in the physical realm but also in the realm of the mind—the *psyberworld*. Cybersecurity experts tend to focus on spectacular worst-case scenarios in which terrorists plunge the United States into chaos with a few strokes of a keyboard. Radicalization and recruitment of individuals via the Internet is just as significant an issue.[8] Due to the "always on" nature of the Internet and the ability to direct information across the globe instantaneously, militants in Somalia and Yemen are able to influence U.S. citizens. The 2010 National Security Strategy clearly reflected the growing recognition of the security threat posed by domestic terrorism and emphasized the need to address the problem:

> Several recent incidences of violent extremists in the United States who are committed to fighting here and abroad have underscored the threat to the United States and our interests posed by individuals radicalized at home.[9]

Before the availability of Internet technology, U.S. citizens who were sympathetic to Al-Qaeda's objectives had a higher cost of entry into a terrorist organization. In today's Information Society, a plethora of terrorist recruiters are misusing the Internet with success in recruiting U.S. citizens of Muslim faith or Arab descent. Two cases, discussed below, have revealed that the Internet is a hotbed for radicalizing and recruiting individuals.

Phases of Internet Radicalization

As will be discussed, the Internet is used to recruit and incite people residing in the West to commit terrorist acts. The psychological factors in the making of a terrorist have been analyzed in depth in a multitude of sources already.[10] The intent here is emphasis rather than an analysis of the multitude of factors that could lead to an individual's radicalization either online or offline.

Prior to the widespread distribution of Internet technology, if an individual was not in a place that would expose them to terrorist propaganda, such as Somalia, it would be difficult for a Muslim living in the West to interface with radicals. The Internet changed this, facilitating the radicalization process through its misuse globally. Ordinary Muslims may now have access to content and social networks that are always available online and produced by individuals espousing an Islamist ideology intended to influence people into violent action.[11]

Internet misuse is a necessary condition for the global radicalization of ordinary people. If a terrorist did not misuse the Internet, radicalization would not occur. People who would not have otherwise come into contact with extremist content in their local environment but can now access this information on the Internet may find validity in the text and begin to support the Islamist cause in some form. Therefore, without terrorist misuse and exploitation of the Internet, the necessary radicalization catalyzed or incubated online could not occur.

The journey from reading to attempting to detonate a car full of explosives in New York City's Times Square is long. Further studies have demonstrated the linkage between ideas and action. For the purpose of this chapter, the pyramid in figure 6.2 is useful for illustrating and contextualizing the findings of

Figure 6.2 Radicalization Dynamics

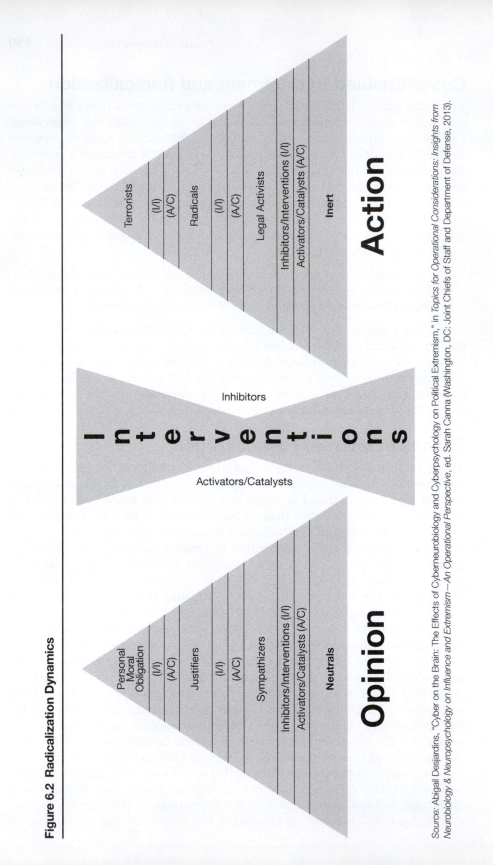

Source: Abigail Desjardins, "Cyber on the Brain: The Effects of Cyberneurobiology and Cyberpsychology on Political Extremism," in *Topics for Operational Considerations: Insights from Neurobiology & Neuropsychology on Influence and Extremism —An Operational Perspective*, ed. Sarah Canna (Washington, DC: Joint Chiefs of Staff and Department of Defense, 2013).

the McCauley two-pyramid model of radicalization.[12] The graphic represents the separation of being radicalized to sympathize with ideas and opinions from the process of being radicalized into action.[13]

The dynamics within the two-pyramid model can be correlated with four phases of radicalization, according to the New York Police Department (NYPD): the preradicalization, self-identification, indoctrination, and jihadization phases.[14]

Preradicalization: The neutral Internet user neither sympathizes with nor has motivation to conduct acts of terrorism. Reading terrorist content on the Internet is not a sufficient condition for radicalization. A person must find the content appealing, repeatedly visit a website, and reach out and lend support to the terrorists. Websites, social media, e-mail, and Internet forums are four mediums through which a radical political or religious organization can influence people. Social networks, websites, and Internet forums are areas on the Internet where people, regardless of their geographic location, can discuss a variety of topics. This includes but is not limited to radical topics in a self-referential environment where dissent is infrequent and, when it occurs, is overwhelmed with responses designed to negate the dissenting opinion. A person going into a radicalized chat room or forum with the intention of passively perusing the material or debating the ideas on a website is not misusing the Internet.

Self-identification: During this phase, a person may have been catalyzed to begin seeking information about an extremist organization by a real-world event. By beginning to browse the extremist web, the individual is exposed to the numerous sites promoting extremist ideologies that misrepresent Islamic theology. When a person first reads and begins to subscribe to the terrorist's ideology, the terrorist is not aware of the individual's metamorphosis into a violent political being. In time, a radicalized individual reaches out and offers support to the terrorist via the Internet. The terrorist accepts this and directs the individual to other websites and terrorists on the Internet. After trust is established between the terrorist and newly radicalized person, the terrorist informs the radicalized individual of other radicalized individuals in the same locale. These other individuals have also been radicalized by the terrorist via his website. This leads to the new radicals utilizing the Internet to discuss actions they can take to assist the terrorist and his cause. Since they are geographically proximate to one another, it is possible for them to continue their meetings in the real world rather than on the Internet. Thus, the terrorist has radicalized people to form a terrorist cell remotely.

Indoctrination occurs when the individual sympathizer begins to devote time to exploring terrorist websites and forming online relationships with individuals who promote extreme ideologies. Written content or speeches posted on the Internet by a militant may influence nonradicals in a way that leads to the acceptance of militant actions as legitimate recourse against perceived injustice. One expert notes that "the ability of social network sites to keep an individual embedded in multiple non-overlapping social networks reduces the leverage of any one view over an individual—organizing low-commitment movements such as Occupy Wall Street are far easier, but demanding total commitment to one cause becomes more difficult."[15] A radical website serves to lure in an ordinary person who was otherwise looking for information without the intention of joining a terrorist organization. Radical websites mix legitimate content with propaganda designed to disturb a person's psyche.

Violent extremism: Radicalization is complete when the influenced individual moves from the opinion pyramid into the realm of actively supporting a specific terrorist act, or facilitating it in some material way beyond the realm of ideas.[16] Radicalization is the transformation of a neutral person from one who is not inclined to commit or support a terrorist act to one who does. This leads to the jihadization phase, in which the online relationship between individuals serves to incite terrorist attacks by encouraging violent action and providing the material required for this action.[17]

It must be noted that radicalization is not a one-way street. Throughout the process of radicalization, there are not only drivers but also inhibitors. Intervention by family and friends and other counteractivators, such as a deeper understanding of a political event, can reverse the individual's course during the radicalization process.

Two examples illustrate the reality of online radicalization for recruitment through ideas and later action. On November 23, 2009, the U.S. Federal Bureau of Investigation announced the largest (unclassified) recruitment operation on U.S. soil. The Al-Shabab organization, an Al-Qaeda–affiliated group, successfully recruited several young men using the Internet as a propaganda distribution tool. The FBI reported that Al-Shabab does not have any significant on-the-ground presence in the United States, preferring to create Internet videos targeting a younger crowd of Muslims living in the West.[18] The recruits emigrated from Somalia to the United States over a decade ago, only to return to their homeland after being radicalized and engage in combat on behalf of Al-Shabab.

In a second, more publicized incident, Major Nidal Malik Hasan opened fire on U.S. military and civilian personnel at Fort Hood, Texas, on November 6, 2009. The gunfire and shots drew most of the media attention; however, the shooting truly began at the ideological level. Hasan's mind was influenced in part by jihadists exchanging information via the Internet.[19] Online, he was able to network with radicals whom he may have been acquainted with in the offline world. Participating in a self-referential online Islamist environment catalyzed the radicalization process, transforming Hassan into a terrorist who preferred to influence policy with violence.

There has been much coverage of Hasan's ties to the Dar al-Hijrah mosque in Great Falls, Virginia, where he attended sermons and held his mother's funeral in 2001. His presence in the mosque coincided with the attendance of two of the perpetrators of the attacks of September 11. Further, the radical cleric Anwar al-Awlaki, who has been accused of supporting attacks on troops and supporting terrorist organizations, was the imam at the mosque. While it is uncertain whether or not Hasan had begun to sympathize with Islamist ideology prior to attending services at this mosque, it has become clear from investigations that he continued to stay in contact with al-Awlaki via the Internet. Indeed, the U.S.-educated radical cleric has been described as an e-recruiter and spiritual motivator. Thus, understanding the general process of Internet misuse and how it may be used as a catalyst in the radicalization process is important in the context of how terrorists exploit the Internet. A future with mobile broadband devices and increasing interpersonal connections in the virtual world is more than a revealing indication of how terrorists plan to influence perceptions and achieve effects in the real world. It is the blueprint to their strategic planning. Such efforts, however, extend well beyond terrorist efforts to radicalize and recruit individuals to their cause. These strategies and stratagems have broader implications for U.S. operations.

There are several cyber techniques that terrorists already deploy that enable them to evade surveillance. Specifically, the **Secret Preparatory Communications VoIP** is a technology used to make telephone calls either to another computer using a VoIP application or to a traditional phone line.[20] Although counterterrorism investigators can conduct surveillance on calls that are placed from VoIP services to traditional phone services by monitoring a suspected telephone line, a computer-to-computer VoIP communication can be encrypted using features embedded in VoIP software such as Skype, Viber, or Microsoft's Instant Messenger. Thus, if law enforcement personnel intercept the data stream containing voice data packets, they will not be able to listen in on such encrypted conversations in real time. Hence, VoIP gives terrorists the secure communications capabilities that can thwart sophisticated law enforcement efforts.

As discussed earlier, the Internet Protocol is a critical Internet resource that allows for universally resolvable URLs as a result of the DNS root system that is managed by the Internet Corporation for Assigned Names and Numbers (ICANN). Although this allows for a free and open Internet to function, the standards and protocols that the ICANN uses to maintain the domain name registries can be used by individuals, ad hoc networks, and nation-states to design and deploy an **alternative domain name system** (altDNS) that can either be independent of or "ride on top" of the Internet. A corporate LAN, such as ".company name" for internal company use, is an example of the first. When a group wishes to ride over the global DNS root but incorporate its own pseudo top-level domain, core operators of the pseudo domains can use specific software resources to resolve domains that are globally accessible within their alternative DNS system.

As also mentioned above, American audiences can experience what it is like to enter an alternative DNS universe via The Onion Router (TOR) network. Downloading the TOR package and navigating to websites one would prefer to visit anonymously (the typical use of TOR), one may point the TOR browser to websites on the ".onion" domain and mingle where the cyber underworld has started shifting the management of its business operations these days to avoid law enforcement and to add another layer of protection to their personas. (Disclaimer: This is for informational use only. Any action undertaken by the reader of this research on the .onion domain is at his or her own risk, and this author is not liable for any harm caused by or to the reader.)

Should significant usage of such shadow Internets occur, it could become very challenging for counterterrorist operators to target the radicalization networks that now operate in dark corners of the open Internet. The Internet will thus be open to masses of new users who may not have previously entered the space because of the English-language barrier. This presents a significant human capital challenge as the cultural and linguistic obstacles facing the counterterrorism community today will only intensify. Thus, even finding alternative propaganda to counter or reverse the radicalization process will become more challenging.

Planning, Command, Control, and Communications

The use of information technology in an actual terrorist operation differs from its use to promote ideas and drive otherwise neutral parties into action. Today, terrorists have demonstrated that in all terrorist operations, there is some cyber element. This may range from the use of encryption technology to protect communications in the preparatory phases of an attack to the actual command, control, and communications during an operation.

Cyber Technique: Secret Preparatory Communications

Recall that voice over IP is a technology used to make telephone calls either to another computer using a VoIP application or to a traditional phone line.[21] Although counterterrorism investigators can conduct surveillance on calls that are placed from VoIP services to traditional phone services by monitoring a suspected telephone line, a computer-to-computer VoIP communication can be encrypted using features embedded in VoIP software such as Skype, Viber, or Microsoft's Instant Messenger. Thus, if law enforcement personnel intercept the data stream containing voice data packets, they will not be able to listen in on such encrypted conversations in real time. Hence, VoIP gives terrorists the secure communications capabilities that can thwart sophisticated law enforcement efforts. Encryption technology is another method that terrorists use for secret communications in the preparatory phases of an attack. Mujahedeen Secrets is one that includes 256-bit encryption, variable stealth cipher encryption keys, RSA 2,048-bit encryption keys, and encrypted chat-forum-supported instant messaging.[22] These technologies allow terrorists to plan operations that could fly beneath the radar of law enforcement agencies tasked with discovering potential plots.

Cyber Technique: Real-Time Cyber Command, Control, and Communications

The world has already witnessed the embryonic stage of the sophisticated use of information technology to enable a terrorist operation during an operation—the hotel siege in Mumbai on November 26–29, 2008. During this attack, members of the Lashkar-e-Taiba organization used information technology to not only shape public opinion and increase terror, but also to gain real-time information on the government response mid-incident to drive operational decision making.[23] Twitter in particular was an effective tool where the public could see the terrorists redirecting the operation. In tweets, the terrorists from a central command post monitoring the media noted, "See, the media is saying that you guys are now in room no. 360 or 361. How did they come to know the room you guys are in? . . . Is there a camera installed there? Switch off all the lights. . . . If you spot a camera, fire on it . . . see, they should not know at any cost how many of you are in the hotel, what condition you are in, where you are, things like that . . . these will compromise your security and also our operation."[24]

Further evidence for the use of cyber means to enable operational decision making is observed in the communications related to the decision of whether the operatives should murder a hostage who was residing in the Taj Hotel. One of the field operatives reported the identity of a hostage to a remote controller via satellite phone. Using a search engine, the remote controller was able to obtain detailed information about the target: "Terrorist: He is saying his full name is K.R. Ramamoorthy. Handler: K.R. Ramamoorthy. Who is he? . . . A designer . . . A professor . . . Yes, yes, I got it . . . [The caller was doing an Internet search on the name, and as results showed up a picture of Ramamoorthy] . . . Okay, is he wearing glasses? [The caller wanted to match the image on his computer with the man before the terrorists.] Terrorist: He is not wearing glasses. Hey, . . . where are your glasses? Handler: . . . Is he bald from the front? Terrorist: Yes, he is bald from the front."[25] Thus, the use of social media has been observed to enhance terrorist planning in the midst of an operation to challenge counterterrorist forces contributing to the response.

Distributed Denial-of-Service Disruption

Above the threshold of criminal activity but below the threshold of cyberattack are incidents and events that, while malicious and disruptive, are aggressive but do not rise to the level of attack. The oft-cited cases of distributed denial-of-service (DDoS) disruptions are an example of cybercrime, not cyberwarfare. While instances of cyber espionage may have long-term negative consequences for national security, the act of stealing the data itself is not at the level of an armed attack.

Despite private sector arguments to the contrary, industrial espionage is not an act of terrorism or war and would not require a military response by the government. Instead, a crime has occurred that may have been prevented with better information security. Federal reform to laws such as the Computer Fraud and Abuse Act would allow private sector firms to protect themselves by actively responding to thefts of data—including the destruction of what was stolen.

The Department of Defense *Dictionary of Military and Related Terms* defines a nonlethal weapon as "a weapon that is explicitly designed and primarily employed so as to incapacitate personnel or materiel, while minimizing fatalities, permanent injury to personnel, and undesired damage to property and the environment." DDoS disruptions, manipulating data in logistics networks, and other software or hardware incidents would fall into this category.

Box 6.1	**Simple Network Management Protocol (SNMP)**

Simple Network Management Protocol (SNMP) is a common protocol for network management. It is used for configuring and gathering information from network devices, such as servers, printers, hubs, switches, and routers on an Internet Protocol (IP) network. Developed in 1988 to provide network-device-monitoring capability for TCP/IP-based networks, SNMP was approved as an Internet standard in 1990 by the Internet Architecture Board (IAB) and has been in wide use since that time.

Source: https://technet.microsoft.com.

The kinds of methods that were used in Estonia and Georgia, and in the U.S. financial sector in late 2012, certainly did not rise to the level of an armed attack. These disruptions, however, were targeting the network layer of the Internet. This is not true of all denial-of-service (DOS) events. So-called "SNMP overloads" are an example of overload DOS attacks. For example, computers running Windows 2000 to program PLCs on an ICS network could be targeted by malicious code that exploited an unpatched vulnerability, causing an "SNMP overload." In this case, a computer's memory, not the network connection, would fail.

By exploiting this vulnerability, a malicious actor would cause a hiccup in the system, which would prevent *any* new processes from starting on a targeted machine. The machine would have to be powered down and restarted in order for it to operate again. In critical infrastructure, availability of systems is essential; otherwise incidents of national security concern could ensue. Thus, DOS attacks are more than just attacks targeting the network layer, leaving websites inaccessible, but also the application layer of specific targeted computers that could cause a power plant to shut down.

Armed Attack

Existing international legal frameworks provide clarity on how law and policy should treat instances of cyberwarfare. The *Tallinn Manual on the International Law Applicable to Cyber Warfare,* perhaps the most comprehensive work on the issue today, offers the definition of a cyberattack as a "cyber operation, whether offensive or defensive, that is reasonably expected to cause injury or death to persons or damage or destruction to objects."[26]

Cyber events breaching the threshold of armed attack require the use of cyberweapons, which differ substantially from Flame, Zeus, Gauss, or other malicious code. While a cyberweapon can be software code designed to attack ICSs, it can also be hardware flaws introduced into critical systems. Due to the complexity of ICSs, the skill level required to discover vulnerabilities (so-called zero-day vulnerabilities), as well as the infrastructure required to find targets, gain access, and execute the attack, necessitates significant financial and human capital. To date,

Box 6.2 Flame, Zeus, and Gauss

Flame

Flame is a highly sophisticated, malicious program used as a cyberweapon to target entities in several countries. It is designed to carry out cyber espionage and can steal valuable information—including computer display contents, information on targeted systems, stored files, contact data, and even audio conversations. It has infected systems in Iran, Lebanon, Syria, the Israeli Occupied Territories, and other countries in the Middle East.

Kaspersky.com
Wired.com

Zeus

Zeus Trojan malware is a form of malicious software that targets Microsoft Windows and is often used to steal financial data.

First detected in 2007, the Zeus Trojan, which is often called Zbot, has become one of the most successful pieces of bot-net software in the world, affecting millions of machines and spawning a host of malware built off of its code.

USA.kaspersky.com

Gauss

Gauss is a cyber espionage tool kit. Emerging in the Middle East, it "is capable of stealing sensitive data such as browser passwords, online banking accounts, cookies and system configurations. According to Kaspersky Lab, Gauss appears to have come from the same nation-state factories that produced Stuxnet."

ZDnet.com

---

only Stuxnet has risen to the level of a cyber incident that could be considered an armed attack under international law, as it caused the physical destruction of objects. One could argue for the Shamoon virus impacting the oil sector as a close second, as it destroyed virtual records, which were restored without widespread destruction or physical injury. However, the impact of Shamoon was on the business applications of cyberspace and not the ICS systems that could cause national security concerns.

Some argue that a terrorist group, with the right team of experts, could conceivably use software designed to gain illicit access to a system and, at the flip of a switch, cause destruction, which is what makes cyberwarfare "different." This oft-cited claim is groundless. Access software, such as Flame or Duqu, might serve the same function as a laser guiding a weapon to the final target. However, a targeting laser is only part of a weapons system. A missile's payload is the actual object in the weapons system creating destructive effects. Similarly, in the case of cyberweapons, operators may use previous access to guide a weapon toward a designated target. However, a separate package will have to be developed to exploit vulnerabilities resulting in physical effects that lead to death or destruction.

One might further argue that the package could be contained within the set of tools conducting reconnaissance, hence the "cyberattack at the flip of a switch" arguments. However, given the unique characteristics of an ICS, a cyberweapon could not create an effect without being tailor made for a specific target's digital and physical environment. In short, this requires ICS schematics, network maps, teams of coders, cryptographers, and a virtual environment replicating the target on which to test the effects of the weapon before deployment. To argue otherwise is akin to making a claim that a SEAL commander would turn a reconnaissance mission on its first foray at tracking Bin Laden into an all-out assault against the complex in Abbottabad and expect a high likelihood of success. Both instances require diligent preparation prior to execution.

Cyber Target: Industrial Control Systems

Industrial control systems (ICSs) are different from commercial ICT applications in business or social environments. ICSs are different because they use technologies that are largely different in organization and complexity from the technology underpinning the Internet. They are designed to automate complex physical processes on which industry, utilities, transportation management, building controls, automobiles, and so forth rely to function. By their nature, ICSs were not designed with security in mind.[27] Should ICS processes fail, physical events will stop functioning, leading to damage to equipment, physical destruction, and possibly loss of life.

Unlike Internet service and content providers, the focus of ICSs is on reliability and safety. Modern societies are dependent on their proper functioning. ICSs are comprised of distributed remote access points, which allow users to remotely connect to infrastructure connected on a particular ICS network. The systems' direct or indirect connections to the Internet allow for the remote monitoring of industrial and critical infrastructure.[28] Nations and industries rely on these computer networks to efficiently maintain the machinery on which a country depends. Thus, ICS is itself a critical system that allows countries to function.[29] Therefore, malicious software designed to cause harm to these systems poses significant threats to human and national security. Currently, terrorists have not demonstrated the necessary capabilities to conduct the vulnerability research and design the tools needed to cause effects in these highly complex systems.

The lack of capability should not be reassuring, however. Many ICSs have hardware configurations that are cyber vulnerable and cannot be patched or fixed. For example, the threat to the U.S. power grid is very tangible and has been for a very long time due to the Aurora vulnerability. During a DHS exercise, hackers were tasked with hacking into the information system of a power generator. Succeeding in gaining remote access to the generator's SCADA control system, the hackers were able to physically destroy the generator. The Aurora vulnerability, as this exploit is called, lends credence to the suggestion that the manipulation of computer code can be just as effective in destroying critical infrastructure as a missile would. Since utility companies now use SCADA to remotely monitor and access controls for their services, and because SCADA is a ubiquitous technology, U.S. utilities are just as vulnerable to these sorts of attacks. Indeed, several incidents have already occurred in which destruction of the physical elements that an ICS controlled occurred because of poor system design. One such example is the 2009 Sayano-Shushenskaya hydroelectric dam explosion due to a computer misconfiguration that resulted in the destruction of four hydroelectric turbines—the plan—in addition to the cascading effect of environmental damage.[30]

Recent events such as Stuxnet have shown that ICSs are now becoming a target of sophisticated teams of computing experts. As one expert notes, "In addition to a very broad range of more traditional computer networking attack (hacking) skills, Stuxnet required people who understood mechanical engineering (to determine the likely breaking points of centrifuges), PLC programming (to create the PLC rootkit), electrical engineering (to understand the impacts of manipulating frequency converters), human-machine interface (HMI) systems, and engineering workstations (to understand how to conceal attack symptoms from system developers)."[31] Additionally, it is not enough to be able to produce the computer code. A terrorist organization would have to develop the testing ground that simulates the target cyber-physical environment to test the malicious software to ensure that the desired effects are produced.

In comparison with crime ware or rootkits, which are easy to find and purchase for small sums of money, the operational differences between cyber operations targeting ICSs and ICTs drive up the cost in both human and financial capital. Therefore, a terrorist organization that has the intent of using cyberspace to cause physical effects in the physical world will have to either recruit or train the team of experts required to mount the operation. Hence, although ICS is more likely to be the kind of system terrorist organizations would target in order to create real-world effects akin to the often-cited "cyber 9/11," the cost of entry continues to be high. With that in mind, the following discussion will demonstrate that there is potential for the use of ICT to create physical destruction when the weapon is content and the target is the human mind.

"Psyber Operations"

The misuse of cyberspace to create effects that are destructive to person and property is not isolated to industrial control systems (ICSs) or computer systems. As has been observed in recent protest movements, such as in Iran (2009), at the Pittsburgh Summit (2009), and in Athens (2008), individuals are using converged Internet and cellular technologies, such as Twitter and Facebook, to spontaneously organize themselves into groups that begin with nonviolence but may turn to violent protest. Further, cyber means have caused more than one suicide as a result of an individual being intimidated online.[32] One study found that the Internet can facilitate protest and other antiregime activities through the formation of groups, and that there is an impact of the technology on their subsequent collective actions.[33] Thus, the human mind can be a target of influence to either mobilize, intimidate, or terrorize a targeted population. This is what I term "psyber operations": the use of social interactions to, without a physical presence, mobilize populations to cause physical effects.

The starting point of this concept is that Internet content produces emotions. As discussed above, radicalization of an individual can be the end result of this emotion. Psyber operations are not radicalization. As Aristotle noted, "In forming opinions we are not free: we cannot escape the alternative of falsehood or truth. Further, when we think something to be fearful or threatening, emotion is immediately produced."[34] A psyber operation is one in which terrorists could manipulate mass public emotion to create an effect that causes individuals or masses of people to spontaneously move in specific ways in response to messaging. This is not conjecture but has already been observed. Take, for example, the events transpiring within India in August 2012. After SMS and social media messages falsely warned of impending Muslim attacks against migrants across northeastern India, including in major cities such as Bangalore, mass panic and exodus of targeted populations ensued. Indian prime minister Manmohan Singh warned, "What is at stake is the unity and integrity of our country."[35] Thus, this is an example of a psyber operation. Hence, what occurs in the content of cyberspace can have a very real impact on a general population's perceptions of the world around them, leading them to feel terrorized and having broad implications for national security.

A Hypothetical Case of Strategic Cyberterrorism

Terrorists will target institutions regardless of whether there is a way to do it via cyberspace. Many argue that the cost of entry is low in cyberspace because it is relatively simpler to launch the digital version of a bank robbery, meddle with a hospital's HVAC system, or release the floodgates on a dam. While it is true that one requires significantly less resources to conduct a cyberattack, the reason for this has less to do with the nature of the domain and more to do with poor product development, design, and implementation. Software developers, hardware manufacturers, and network providers face no liability or responsibility for the systems they produce or operate. As a result, they have no reason to deliver secure products to the marketplace. This risk will begin to manifest more starkly as cloud computing takes hold and resulting breaches destroy multiple points within the health-care establishment rather than a single hospital. Below are some effects that a cyberattack could have.

The thought experiment described in table 6.1 better illustrates the potential of the strategic use of cyberspace by a terrorist organization during an attack to amplify the effects of a physical attack. The skill level required is high and team based. The whole goal would be to maximize carnage, delay and diminish first-responder capabilities, cause maximum fear and uncertainty among parents, and overwhelm the ability of government to protect citizens. Much of the operation requires insider knowledge of first-responder transition-to-practice (TTP) and planning, prepositioning in advance, and tailor/scale effects based on the manpower and destructive capability available.

The limited insight offered in this hypothetical case study could become a reality if the application of solutions to specific problems is not realized. Since technological skills and capability do not remain static, it is useful to be aware of the potential for the strategic use of cyberspace by terrorist organizations. Anticipating this danger means affecting the near-term future by increasing investments in cyber technology while beginning to promote legislation that would require all critical infrastructure and key resource operators to comply with

TABLE 6.1

Phase/Step of Operation	Effect
Phase Zero	A violent extremist organization has successfully recruited an unknown number of operatives to launch an attack within a medium-sized city of strategic importance. Some operatives were to be part of the actual attack, while others are sympathetic to the cause. Over several months, the plotters used cyber and noncyber means to plan a hybrid operation that combines cyber and physical means to achieve their organizational objectives.
Move Zero	False reports into 911 system flush first responders far from first target (fires/hostage situation, etc.).
Phase 1, Stage 1	Bomb at target goes boom.
Stage 2	Hack traffic signal controls to snarl traffic and delay first responders from arriving at scene.
Stage 2a	Disable cell towers near scene of attack via a distributed denial-of-service disruption.
Stage 2b	Manipulate water pressure in fire hydrant system by spoofing SCADA system monitors to indicate that hydrant has full pressure, but there is none at hydrant.
Stage 3	Broadcast video feeds from target area over Internet—stage public executions? Provide commands for Phase 2, 3 for forces; Phase 4 forces are embedded in local media (either physically or tapping into their channels and cell phones) and texting status/intel to C2 forces.
Stage 3a	Plant false updates/messages in incoming stream to crisis command center.
Stage 4	Disrupt the power grid; disable rail/metro system.
Phase 2, Stage 5	Attack local area hospitals, disable their backup generators, hack life support controls in ICU, start killing ER doctors and nurses.
Phase 3, Stage 6	Mortar rounds into elementary schools, police stations, fire stations (followed up by IEDs at chokepoints); truck bombs in local schools disguised as ambulances or school buses.
Phase 4, Stage 7	Find where they will have the news conference with mayor, etc. Preposition snipers; assassinate leaders (or bomb in podium?) on live TV.
Stage 8	If an airport nearby, mortar rounds to crater runway at five-hundred-foot intervals (prevent anyone taking off/landing); hit fuel depot, passenger terminal. Blow up as many planes as possible—especially if you can get them during takeoff/landing. Also hit National Guard armory at airport.
Stage 9	Hack into sewage treatment plant/water treatment plant controls; create mayhem (longer-term health effects—cholera, typhoid, dysentery, etc., outbreaks beyond initial attack days to weeks).

a risk-based approach to secure both legacy and next-generation network and computing environments to the highest standards.[36] No defense will be perfect. However, keeping the current status quo between nation-states and terrorist organization within ICS environments will rely on a continued commitment to maintain and increase the cost of entry for nonstate actors to conduct armed attacks in cyberspace.

Conclusion

Many terrorist organizations are advancing their use of cyberspace to meet their tactical, operational, and strategic objectives. This is evidence that cyber power is becoming increasingly important as a strategic environment for nation-states and violent nonstate actors alike. The intention of this chapter was to conduct an investigation into the role that cyberspace plays in shaping terrorist operations. By examining what is observed in the terrorist use of the domain, this discussion offers a belief that the use of cyberspace by terrorist organizations and the ability to cause physical effects via cyber are mutually exclusive. Illustrations of the difference between a spectrum of cyber-enabled operations and cyber operations confirmed this difference. The ability of Al-Shabab to recruit U.S. citizens for operations abroad, and Anwar al-Awlaki to radicalize a U.S. service member, has drawn attention to the reality of e-recruiters being able to identify, appeal to, and radicalize vulnerable individuals. The "always on" two-way transfer of information via the Internet gives terrorist organizations the ability to direct information across the globe instantaneously, encrypted and anonymously. We have seen that terrorist planning and execution are increasingly migrating toward cyberspace. Both the political and technical aspects of the Internet complicate policy responses to this emergent threat. The practical importance of all this is to craft appropriate counterterrorist policies that have the right balance between security and privacy.

Further, we are not at the point in time where terrorists can cause malicious effects of national significance against critical infrastructure. Their human capital and financing, given the complexity of the target set, is not sufficient to cause the overhyped "cyber 9/11." However, overlooked is the potential for psyber warfare. In the near term, this is the more likely use of cyber to create physical effects. When all these elements are blended together, we get the extreme example of a hypothetical strategic use of cyberspace by a terrorist organization.

Key Terms

preradicalization
self-identification
indoctrination
violent extremism

Secret Preparatory
Communications VoIP
alternative domain name system

Notes

1 https://www.dni.gov/files/document/Newsroom/Testimonies/SSCI%20Unclassified%20 SFR%20-%20Final.pdf.

2 E. F. Kohlmann, "The Real Online Terrorist Threat," *Foreign Affairs* 85 (2006): 115; M. R. Torres Soriano, "The Vulnerabilities of Online Terrorism," *Studies in Conflict and Terrorism* 35, no. 4 (2012): 263–77.

3 J. A. Lewis, "Assessing the Risks of Cyber Terrorism, Cyber War and Other Cyber Threats," Center for Strategic and International Studies, 2002.

4 Statement of General Keith B. Alexander, Commander, U.S. Cyber Command/Director, National Security Agency, before the Senate Committee on Appropriations, June 12, 2013.

5 United Nations Office on Drugs and Crime, *The Use of the Internet for Terrorist Purposes* (United Nations Publications, 2012).

6 Timothy L. Thomas, "Al Qaeda and the Internet: The Danger of 'Cyberplanning,'" *Parameters*, 2003, 112–23.

7 Larry Greenemeier, "Aftermath of Boston Marathon Bombing: How Do Terrorists Use Improvised Explosive Devices?," *Scientific American*, April 15, 2013, http://www.scientificamerican. com/article.cfm?id=boston-marathon-bomb-attack.

8 B. Braniff and A. Moghadam, "Towards Global Jihadism: Al-Qaeda's Strategic, Ideological and Structural Adaptations since 9/11," *Perspectives on Terrorism* 5, no. 2 (2011); M. R. T. Soriano, "Maintaining the Message: How Jihadists Have Adapted to Web Disruptions," *Foreign Affairs* 85, no. 5 (2006).

9 National Security Strategy 2010, 18.

10 R. Borum, "Radicalization into Violent Extremism I: A Review of Social Science Theories," *Journal of Strategic Security* 4, no. 4 (2011): 2; Lisa Blaydes and Lawrence Rubin, "Ideological Reorientation and Counterterrorism: Confronting Militant Islam in Egypt," *Terrorism and Political Violence* 20, no. 4 (2008): 461–79; Arie W. Kruglanski and Shira Fishman, "The Psychology of Terrorism: 'Syndrome' versus 'Tool' Perspectives," *Terrorism and Political Violence* 18, no. 2 (2006): 193–215; S. Helfstein, *Edges of Radicalization: Ideas, Individuals and Networks in Violent Extremism* (special report by the Combating Terrorism Center [CTC] at West Point).

11 A. Abbasi and H. Chen, "Analysis of Affect Intensities in Extremist Group Forums," *Terrorism Informatics* 18, no. 2 (2008): 285–307.

12 C. McCauley, "Group Desistence from Terrorism: Dynamics of Actors, Actions, and Outcomes" (presented at the Royal Institute for International Relations [Egmont Institute], Brussels, October 10, 2011), accessed June 25, 2013, www.egmontinstitute.be/speechnotes/11/ 111010/Clark-McCauley.pdf.

13 Abigail Desjardins, "Cyber on the Brain: The Effects of Cyberneurobiology and Cyberpsychology on Political Extremism," in *Topics for Operational Considerations: Insights from Neurobiology and Neuropsychology on Influence and Extremism—An Operational Perspective*, ed. Sarah Canna (Washington, DC: Joint Chiefs of Staff and Department of Defense, 2013).

14 M. D. Silber, A. Bhatt, and S.I. analysts, *Radicalization in the West: The Homegrown Threat* (New York: New York City Police Department, 2007).

15 Dave Blair, "Back to the Future: Understanding Radicalization through a Social Typology of Media, Past and Present," *Topics for Operational Considerations: Insights from Neurobiology and Neuropsychology on Influence and Extremism—An Operational Perspective*, Strategic Multilayer Assessment Periodic White Paper, 2013.

16 S. Canna, C. St. Clair, and A. Chapman, *Neurobiological and Cognitive Science Insights on Radicalization and Mobilization to Violence: A Review*, Strategic Multilayer Assessment, JS/J-3/ DDGO OSD/ASD (R&E)/RFD/RRTO, 2012.

17 Silber, 19.

18 Andrea Elliott, "Charges Detail Road to Terror for 20 in U.S.," *New York Times*, November 23, 2009, A1.

19 Yochi J. Dreazen and Evan Perrez, "Army Wasn't Told of Hasan's Emails," *Wall Street Journal*, November 12, 2009, A13.

[20] Federal Communications Commission (FCC), *Voice over Internet Protocol: Frequently Asked Questions*, accessed April 27, 2013, http://www.fcc.gov/voip.

[21] FCC.

[22] Liam Tung, "Jihadists Get World-Class Encryption Kit," ZDNet, January 29, 2008, http://www.zdnet.com/jihadists-get-world-class-encryption-kit-1339285480.

[23] A. Gupta and P. Kumaraguru, "Twitter Explodes with Activity in Mumbai Blasts! A Lifeline or an Unmonitored Daemon in the Lurking?," https://repository.iiitd.edu.in/jspui/bitstream/123456789/26/1/IIITD-TR-2011-005.pdf.

[24] O. Oh, M. Agrawal, and H. R. Rao, "Information Control and Terrorism: Tracking the Mumbai Terrorist Attack through Twitter," *Information Systems Frontiers* 13, no. 1 (2011): 33–43.

[25] Oh.

[26] M. N. Schmitt, ed., *Tallinn Manual on the International Law Applicable to Cyber Warfare* (Cambridge: Cambridge University Press, 2013).

[27] ICSs are composed of SCADA/EMS, DCS, PLCs, RTUs, IEDs, smart sensors and drives, emissions controls, equipment diagnostics, AMI (Smart Grid), programmable thermostats, and building controls; D. A. Kruger, "Thwarting Large Scale ICS Reconnaissance and Attacks," in *Cyberterrorism: Understanding, Assessment, and Response*, ed. Thomas M. Chen, Lee Jarvis, and Stuart Macdonald (New York: Springer, 2012), 43–62; Y. Yang, K. McLaughlin, T. Littler, S. Sezer, E. G. Im, Z. Q. Yao, and H. F. Wang, "Man-in-the-Middle Attack Test-Bed Investigating Cyber-Security Vulnerabilities in Smart Grid SCADA Systems," in *Proceedings of the International Conference on Sustainable Power Generation*, 2012 International Conference on Sustainable Power Generation and Supply (SUPERGEN 2012), http://digital-library.theiet.org/content/conferences/10.1049/cp.2012.1831.

[28] Aaron Mannes, "The Terrorist Threat to the Internet," in *Homeland Security: Protecting America's Targets*, vol. 3, *Critical Infrastructure*, ed. James J. F. Forest (Westport, CT: Praeger Security International, 2006), 339–53.

[29] M. Swearingen, S. Brunasso, J. Weiss, and D. Huber, "What You Need to Know (and Don't) about the AURORA Vulnerability," *Power* 157, no. 9 (2013); J. Weiss, "Ensuring the Cybersecurity of Plant Industrial Control Systems," *Power* 156, no. 6 (2012); Andrew Hildick-Smith, *Security for Critical Infrastructure SCADA Systems*, 1, accessed April 27, 2013, http://www.sans.org/reading_room/whitepapers/warfare/1644.php.

[30] "Insulating Oil Spreads along Siberian River after Hydro Disaster," RIA Novosti, August 18, 2009, accessed August 20, 2009, http://en.rian.ru/russia/20090818/155846126.html.

[31] Eric P. Oliver, "Stuxnet: A Case Study in Cyber Warfare," in *Conflict and Cooperation in Cyberspace: The Challenge to National Security*, ed. Panayotis A. Yannakogeorgos and Adam B. Lowther (Boca Raton, FL: Taylor & Francis, 2013), 127–60.

[32] B. K. Wiederhold and G. Riva, "Online Social Networking and the Experience of Cyber-Bullying," *Annual Review of Cybertherapy and Telemedicine 2012: Advanced Technologies in the Behavioral, Social and Neurosciences* 181 (2012): 212; B. S. Xiao and Y. M. Wong, "Cyber-Bullying among University Students: An Empirical Investigation from the Social Cognitive Perspective," *International Journal of Business and Information* 8, no. 1 (2013); D. B. Sugarman and T. Willoughby, "Technology and Violence: Conceptual Issues Raised by the Rapidly Changing Social Environment," *Psychology of Violence* 3, no. 1 (2013): 1.

[33] James D. Fielder, "The Internet and Dissent in Authoritarian States," in *Conflict and Cooperation in Cyberspace: The Challenge to National Security*, ed. Panayotis A. Yannakogeorgos and Adam B. Lowther (Boca Raton, FL: Taylor & Francis, 2013), 161–94.

[34] Aristotle, *De Anima*.

[35] J. Yardley, "Panic Seizes India as a Region's Strife Radiates," *New York Times*, August 17, 2012, A1; R. Goolsby, "On Cybersecurity, Crowdsourcing, and Social Cyber-Attack," *Commons Lab Policy Memo Series* 1 (2013): 9.

[36] J. Pollet, "Developing a Solid SCADA Security Strategy," in *Sensors for Industry Conference, 2002, Proceedings of the 2nd ISA/IEEE Conference* (Piscataway, NJ: 2002): 148–56.

Public-Private Partnerships 7

In this era of globalization, with militaries, governments, critical infrastructures, businesses, and civil society increasingly depending on the ICT composing cyberspace to operate, we are witnessing the emergence of an Information Society. The basis of this new political partnership is openness, trust, and security in cyberspace. However, this global society lacks a body of international law with the appropriate political, law enforcement, and technical regimes and institutions to govern human activity in the cyber environment. Membership in the Information Society increases as all forms of human activity are increasingly transferring into, and rely upon, cyberspace. The misuse of this domain by criminals and violent nonstate actors (VNSAs), such as terrorists, and the proliferation of strategic cyberwarfare programs among states has made the need to develop and harmonize national and cybercrime laws all the more urgent.[1]

National and international policy makers have recognized that in order to prevent the misuse of cyberspace, especially its ubiquitous elements of the Internet and the World Wide Web (WWW), all interested stakeholders must cooperate to harmonize their national legislation within the framework of existing efforts undertaken by the international community.[2] However, the framework as it stands does not emphasize the importance of a strong public law enforcement presence in cyberspace. Instead, as will be shown in a review of efforts undertaken under the auspices of the United Nations and the Council of Europe, private architectures of control, with government playing a lawmaking role, are encouraged, while its overseeing of the day-to-day operations of cyberspace, which is essential to securing the Information Society, is discouraged. It is suggested that relying on the private sector to provision cybersecurity undermines trust and security in cyberspace and hampers the distribution of justice. It is argued more that national and international law enforcement capacity building must take place in order for all public law enforcement entities to take the lead and enforce the dictates and laws created by national and international bodies.

The Information Society: An Emerging Societal Construct

Understanding the philosophical underpinnings of the role of public law enforcement for distributing justice is important when evaluating arguments calling for the private ordering of security. Since the Treaty of Westphalia, the nation-state is held as the primary provider of public security. Thus, it is necessary to briefly contemplate the conceptualization of what the responsibility of the nation-state is in developing and enforcing the laws it creates. In order to avoid contemporary debates on the nation-state,[3] this chapter examines the polis (πόλις) conceptualization in the age of Hellenic antiquity in order to deduce diachronic abstract principles of law, distributive justice, and public order that underpin the modern nation-state.

The polis in Hellenic antiquity was "an independent state organized around an urban center and governed typically by formal laws and republican institutions."[4] In essence, it is a political partnership regardless of regime. Aristotle is correct in his observation that "every partnership is constituted for the sake of some good . . . and that the partnership that is the most authoritative of all and embraces all the others does so particularly, and aims at the most authoritative good of all."[5]

The subunits in the Aristotelian partnership model are formed in a teleological hierarchy, outlined as follows:

[male/female] → [household] → [village] → [polis][6]

The partnership of the male and female is the starting point for the household, which is the starting point for the village, which is the starting point for the polis, which is the end of all the other points.[7] Each partnership is an extension of the preceding partnership, each of which "exists for the sake of living well" self-sufficiently.[8] The political system is considered the most authoritative, since the other subunits will know what is good for themselves and will manage their own affairs to suit their own interests.[9] Therefore, what distinguished the polis from the other partnerships was that it was a political partnership, which is primarily responsible for creating legislation with the interest of all its subunits so that justice exists in all the preceding social subunits. Although in practice this may be imperfect, it is more perfect that if one of the subunits were tasked with legislating. Hence, legislation and adjudication is a primary function of the polis through which regimes negate the impact of unjust actions equally throughout the political system.[10] Humans impulsively strive by nature to achieve this end state. Aristotle condemns those who do not seek to be part of a polis since they desire war.[11]

The end of the political partnership is the provision of justice to the constituents making up the whole of the community. A discussion of what Aristotle means by justice, legislation, and deliberation is necessary. In the polis, justice is that which preserves the happiness and self-sufficiency of the community, *equally* among all its members.[12] Unjust actions are those in which a person voluntarily harms another person against a victim's wish.[13] Legislation is created during a deliberative process in which the general principles of justice are set by politicians.[14] This process can be slow; however, actions on the decisions made must be quick to serve the needs of the community.[15] Lawmakers create laws which foresee possible injustices in order to prescribe corrective measures to distribute justice via adjudication. When the rulers of a polis do not treat all of its constituents equally, only an illusion of justice exists.[16]

The above discussion highlights the importance of making sure that individual interests do not guide the laws, adjudication, and distribution of justice. In this context, the role of public-private partnerships for securing the Information Society is examined.

A Global Culture of Cyber Security for the Information Society

One might suggest an update to the Aristotelian political partnership hierarchy for the Information Society as follows:

[individual/computer] → [computer/software] → [computer network] → [Information Society][17]

In this schema, individual users partner with computer hardware to benefit from the partnership between computers and software. The computer/software partnership lies in the rules governing the relationship between a computer and the computer code and protocols. For example, an individual may instruct the computer via its software to internetwork with other computers. This is done according to protocols standardized by the International Organization of Standards (ISO) for Open Systems Interconnection (OSI). These protocols are built on an open architecture designed on a cross-platform client/server model intended to minimize network traffic.[18] Computers connecting over a network depend on seven layers of standards over which computers communicate with other computers and users.[19] Without these international standards, ICTs could not internetwork, interoperate, and interconnect. The end state of the preceding units is the Information Society: the emerging political partnership being forged among a multitude of global actors as described in relevant United Nations General Assembly (UNGA) resolutions as well as the declarations and outcomes of the World Summit for the Information Society (WSIS) and the Internet Governance Forum (IGF).[20]

The establishment of a "global culture of cybersecurity" (GCC) is the main emphasis of UNGA Resolution 57/239.[21] Beginning with the fifth preliminary paragraph, the UNGA indicates its awareness that "effective cybersecurity is not merely a matter of government or law enforcement practices, but must be addressed through prevention and supported throughout society."[22] By identifying the provisioning of cybercrime as an activity separate from government or law enforcement, this element essentially relegates the traditional primary guarantor of national security to a secondary role within a broader cybersecurity framework in which other actors are tasked with preventing cybercrime. The next paragraph indicates the UNGA's awareness "that technology alone cannot ensure cybersecurity and that priority must be given to cybersecurity planning

Box 7.1   The Mechanics of the IP Layer Stack

The physical layer includes signals such as light and electricity, mechanical standards, and the signal procedures (such as the voltage and frequency of the signal). The data link is responsible for packet movement across networks. This includes protocols for the interconnection of hardware devices such as hubs, bridges, switches, and other hardware not connected to the Internet that function to move packets across a network. The network layer is a hierarchical addressing mechanism through which data is routed from machine X to machine Y. Internet Protocol (IP) is one element of the network layer. This protocol is responsible for assuring the accurate transmission of packets to their proper destination across networks. The session layer controls the establishment, maintenance, and termination of connections between applications across a network. The presentation layer delivers and formats information to the application layer; this is where the ones and zeros making up the packets are compressed, decompressed, encrypted, or decrypted in response to service requests made by the user via the application layer, which is what the user sees on his or her screen.

Source: Robert Molyneux, *The Internet under the Hood.*

and management throughout society."[23] The first part is a valid observation. However, the second part does not identify who the main actor responsible for managing and planning cybersecurity throughout society is. Not having a clearly identified government role becomes problematic in the next paragraph, where the UNGA recognizes "that, in a manner appropriate to their roles, government, business, other organizations, and individual owners and users of information technologies must be aware of relevant cybersecurity risks and preventive measures and must assume responsibility for and take steps to enhance the security of these information technologies."[24] Therefore, the trend of a broad number of actors (including governments), all of whom are responsible for securing ICT and preventing its misuse, is established in a manner that relieves government of a primary responsibility of national security in the cyber domain. Thus, in the sequence and wording of these elements, the UNGA manages to strip government of its responsibility to act as the primary mover in cybersecurity efforts. Hence, the UNGA encourages a trend of emphasizing the role of private actors in providing cybersecurity to society, rather than signifying their importance in *supporting* government and law enforcement efforts.[25]

A significant component of Resolution 57/239 is its annex, which establishes nine elements forming the basic tenets of the global culture of cybersecurity.[26] These are awareness, responsibility, response, ethics, democracy, risk assessment, security design and implementation, security management, and reassessment.[27] A brief summation of these nine elements follows. All participants in the global culture of cybersecurity should sustain a level of awareness regarding the importance of having secure information systems.[28] Each participant is responsible for securing their own information systems and reviewing the policies, practices, measures, and procedures pertaining to their own cyberspace. Timely and cooperative response is achieved with Information Society members sharing information about threats, vulnerabilities, and security incidents in order to facilitate the detection of and response to the misuse of information systems. The UNGA recognizes that cross-border information sharing may be required. The ethical basis of the GCC is founded on utilitarian grounds in that each participant is expected to respect the interests of others and to avoid actions or inaction that will harm others. Cybersecurity regimes are guided by democratic principles, identified as the freedom of thoughts and ideas, free flow of information, confidentiality of information and communication, protection of personal information, openness, and transparency. Periodic broad-based risk assessments of the security implications of technological, physical, and human factors, policies, and services should be conducted in order to determine what an appropriate level of risk is and how to best manage the risk of potential harm to information systems according to a scale based on the importance of information on the information system being assessed. Security should be incorporated during the planning, design, development, operation, and use of any information system. It is on the basis of dynamic risk assessment that security management occurs. Finally, in order to assure that all the above elements remain relevant, a periodic reassessment is required.

As with the preliminary paragraphs, the role of government is not clearly defined. It appears that members of the GCC are responsible for the protection of their own information systems and developing cybersecurity policies in a way that assures that vulnerabilities in one information system do not affect another system. Moreover, not all information systems are equal, since some information is considered more valuable than other information. It will be argued below that this approach is incorrect and does not take into account the underlying reasons pertaining to states, organizations, and individuals using ICT.

The global culture of cybersecurity grew from a previous UNGA resolution. General Assembly Resolution 56/19, entitled "Developments in the Field of Information and Telecommunications in the Context of International Security," highlights several key issues pertaining to the Information Society and the provisioning of its cybersecurity. The UNGA recognizes the global characteristics of ICT, such as the Internet and the World Wide Web (WWW), as being the basis for the Information Society, and determines that international cooperation is required to assure the peaceful use of ICT.[29]

Ongoing efforts being undertaken under the auspices of the United Nations promote what UNGA refers to in numerous resolutions as the "global culture of cybersecurity." As shown above, this is based on a P3 model of cybersecurity in which the private sector takes the lead in providing security. This section focuses on the general strategy of global cybersecurity as described in UNGA resolutions and the Council of Europe Convention on Cybercrime (CoE Convention), which aim to develop and coordinate a global cybersecurity strategy.

Recall Resolution 56/19. The UNGA acknowledges the potential misuse of ICT in ways that will "adversely affect the security of states in both civil and military fields."[30] Member states are encouraged to prevent the use of information technology for criminal or terrorist purposes while concurrently promoting its peaceful use, though guidelines for how to do so are not offered. In the operational paragraphs of Resolution 56/19, the GA calls on member states to support and contribute multilateral efforts tasked with identifying present and future threats to international security resulting from the misuse of information technology and to develop countermeasures to these threats. Cybersecurity solutions must be "consistent with the need to preserve the free flow of information."[31]

Preserving the free flow of information is a challenging objective since countermeasures tend to prevent the flow of information in one way or another. For example, when one installs a firewall on a computer network and sets it to the most secure setting, the firewall makes the use of Internet applications more of a hassle than before the firewall was installed. The free flow of information is preserved when the firewall is tweaked to fit the patterns of an individual's usage. Analogous problems exist when implementing cybersecurity solutions on a larger scale. A corporate firewall may block certain applications that are useful for some users but which present a security risk for most users. However, if one cannot afford firewalls or antivirus software, an attacker can exploit the lack of security and likewise prevent the free flow of information, among other things. Both of these examples indicate pitfalls of holding the private sector and individuals responsible for cybersecurity. A corrective measure that is explored below involves public law enforcement efforts, which allow users to not have to implement their own cybersecurity.

In follow-up Resolution 56/121, "Combating the Criminal Misuse of Information Technologies," the UNGA strengthened the language of Resolution 56/19.[32] It is recognized in the preliminary paragraphs that the "misuse of information technologies may have a grave impact on all States" as a result of the utilization of ICT to enhance international cooperation and coordination.[33] Further, "gaps in the access to and use of information technologies by States can diminish the effectiveness of international cooperation in combating the criminal misuse of information technologies."[34] The best way forward is "cooperation between States and the private sector in combating the criminal misuse of information technologies . . . [and] the need for effective law enforcement."[35] Thus, in order to preserve the utility of ICT for enhancing international cooperation and coordination, all states must have access to and use ICT while establishing P3s and law enforcement mechanisms to deter the criminal misuse of telecommunications technologies.

As the UNGA suggests in Resolution 56/121, by transferring information technology to developing countries and training local personnel in it use, global efforts to combat the misuse of information technology will be enhanced. It follows that if there is one state that is not able to counter the use of ICT by terrorists in its territory, that state is a weak link in the chain of countering the criminal misuse of cyberspace.

To illustrate the importance of the issue of bridging the digital divide to enhance cybersecurity, it is useful to briefly examine illegal Internet service providers in Africa. Such networks present opportunities for criminal and terrorist organizations to bypass law enforcement efforts.[36] Illegal Internet services are established when the operator of the networks obtains bandwidth needed to create an Internet service provider (ISP) without abiding by national regulations or paying for access to the Internet backbone services. This is possible after bandwidth is diverted by the operators of an illicit ISP from a commercial Internet backbone network to the illicit network. The illicit ISP is then in a position to sell Internet access to interested parties at a significantly reduced cost compared to licit ISPs. The low cost is a result of the illegal ISP not paying the necessary access and regulatory fees, which are typically high in less-developed countries since there is a high demand for and low supply of available bandwidth.[37] Furthermore, telecommunications monopolies are typical in these regions, which is another factor in the high cost of legal ISPs. Thus, illegal ISPs appeal to people since they are able to get the same service offered by the legal ISP for a fraction of the cost.[38]

Some have suggested that illegal ISPs are a good thing since in some cases, such as South Africa, they have helped to demonopolize the Internet industry by competing directly with the legal telecommunications providers.[39] The problem for law enforcement occurs, for example, if one combines an illegal ISP with voice over Internet protocol (VoIP). The result is the negation of legal communication interception methods used by law enforcement.[40] Thus, bridging the technological gaps in developing countries is a crucial element in assuring that the P3 and law enforcement efforts outlined by UNGA's global cybersecurity strategy are not undermined.

In 2004, the UNGA addressed the importance of protecting critical information infrastructures.[41] Critical infrastructures are identified as "those used for, inter alia, the generation, transmission and distribution of energy, air and maritime transport, banking and financial services, e-commerce, water supply, food distribution and public health—and the critical information infrastructures that increasingly interconnect and affect their operations."[42] In this resolution, the role of the government in dealing with the critical information infrastructure is clearer than in previous resolutions. Eleven elements for the enhancement of the protection of critical information infrastructures are proposed in the annex of this resolution.

First, it is urged that emergency warning networks should be established to identify and warn of cyber vulnerabilities, threats, and incidents. General awareness should be raised in order to facilitate understanding of the role that stakeholders play in critical infrastructure as well as in protecting that infrastructure. The resolution further encourages the formation of partnerships between private and public stakeholders to better prevent, investigate, and respond to threats on critical information infrastructures. Communications networks should be in place and regularly tested to assure their effective operation during a crisis situation. For their part, the resolution urges states to develop adequate domestic laws and policies that will allow for the investigation and prosecution of cybercrime, as well as the trained personnel who enable the investigation and prosecution of such misuses. Moreover, states are held responsible for identifying the perpetrators of an attack against critical information infrastructure and sharing this information with affected states. In this regard, appropriate international cooperation should take place in accord with properly crafted domestic laws to assure that the critical information infrastructures are secure. Constant testing of the protection systems and education of the personnel are deemed essential for the success of such measures.

World Summit on the Information Society and Internet Governance Forum

The World Summit on the Information Society (WSIS) is the forum mandated by the aforementioned UNGA resolutions where governments and all interested stakeholders deliberate on what the guiding principles of the emerging Information Society are. This section will focus on those elements in the WSIS's Geneva Declaration of Principles (2003), the Tunis Commitment and the Tunis Agenda (2005), and the outcome of the inaugural Internet Governance Forum (IGF) pertaining to the establishment of a global culture of cybersecurity as laid out by the UNGA.

The first phase of the WSIS, held in Geneva from December 10 to 12, 2003, allowed all relevant parties the chance to formally begin the process of developing the Information Society based on trust and security. The priorities established by GA resolutions, notably 56/121 and 57/239 (described below), were discussed. The meeting resulted in the drafting and adoption of the Declaration of Principles and Plan of Action by "the representatives of the peoples of the world."[43] The Declaration of Principles defines that the Information Society should be organized around a

> common desire and commitment to build a people-centered, inclusive and development oriented Information Society, where everyone can create, access, utilize and share information and knowledge, enabling individuals, communities and peoples to achieve their full potential in promoting sustainable development and improving their quality of life, premised on the purposes and principles of the Charter of the United Nations and respecting fully and upholding the Universal Declaration of Human Rights.[44]

The Information Society is therefore based on democratic principles in which individuals are guaranteed the right to freely create and transmit information and knowledge, as long as their objectives are not against the principles of the UN Charter and the Universal Declaration of Human Rights.

Security is a cornerstone of the Information Society. Paragraph 5 of the Geneva Declaration states that users must have confidence in the Information Society, a framework of trust that includes "information security and network security, authentication, privacy and consumer protection," which must be established to assure that data, privacy, access, and trade are protected.[45] Further, the WSIS recognizes that ICT has the potential for devastation and recommends that appropriate actions at the national and international levels should be taken to secure cyberspace so that ICT is not used "for purposes that are inconsistent with the objectives of maintaining international stability and security, and may adversely affect the integrity of the infrastructure within States."[46] In this regard, the Declaration of Principles calls for all interested stakeholders to have a strong commitment to the concept of "digital solidarity" with governments at the national and international level, and it recognizes that new forms of partnership will be required in order to meet the goals set out in the declaration.

In addition to the Declaration of Principles, participants of the first phase of the WSIS in Geneva negotiated and agreed on a Plan of Action for achieving the goals set therein. In section C5.12, the WSIS defines what actions must be taken to fulfill the objectives contained in paragraph 5 of the Declaration of Principles.[47] Reiterating the importance of security and its role in developing users' confidence with using ICT, the Plan of Action recommends public-private partnerships for the prevention, detection, and response to cybercrime and ICT misuse. For their role, governments are mandated with the task of developing guidelines taking into account the ongoing efforts in these areas.

The main outcome of the second WSIS summit on the Information Society was the adoption of the Tunis Commitment and the Tunis Agenda for the Information Society. Significantly, the Tunis Agenda calls on the Information Society to ensure the "requisite legitimacy of its governance, based on the full participation of all stakeholders, from both developed and developing countries, within their respective roles and responsibilities."[48] Internet governance is defined as "the development and application by government, the private sector and civil society, in their respective roles, of shared principles, norms, rule, decision-making procedures, and programs that shape the evolution and use of the Internet."[49] It does not clearly define the role of each stakeholder, the government in particular, for Internet governance, though the statement clearly indicates that actors other than national governments have a strong role in governing the Internet. Recalling the Aristotelian perspective, the risk in allowing nongovernmental authorities to develop legislation or decrees is that these parties will seek to further their own interests rather than the interests of the community as a whole.

Further, the Tunis Agenda states that "the existing arrangements for Internet governance have worked effectively to make the Internet the highly robust, dynamic and geographically diverse medium that it is today, with the private sector taking the lead in day-to-day operations, and with innovation and value creation at the edges."[50] It is further stressed that there is a "need for enhanced cooperation in the future, to enable governments, on an equal footing, to carry out their roles and responsibilities, in international public policy issues pertaining to the Internet, but not in the day-to-day technical and operational matters, that do not impact on international public policy issues."[51] Hence, the private sector's role is clearly defined by the Tunis Agenda as being responsible for the day-to-day operations of the Internet, and governments should play no role in these technical and operational trivialities. The government's role remains unclear, other than that it should have a significant role in international public policy making.

The views expressed by participants in the inaugural Internet Governance Forum provide further insight into the perception of what government's role should be in provisioning Internet security.[52] Significantly, a market-driven approach was emphasized in which "government's first responsibility is [to] set the benchmark, and ask the private sector to respond."[53] The reasoning is that the main actors in the field are service providers and the software industry and individuals.[54] While it is true that these are the main stakeholders, this viewpoint is tantamount to suggesting that benchmarks be set against certain crimes and that it is the responsibility of nongovernmental stakeholders to ensure that crimes are not committed. Further, it was noted "that better information security practices happen globally, not just nationally through the coordinating role of government but through the activities of industry."[55] The appropriate role for government is thus not one of a critical provider of security. Rather, it is that of a security coordinator setting benchmarks for the private sector to meet. According to paragraph 40 of the Tunis Agenda, prosecuting cybercrime is one area in which the collaborative efforts of stakeholders should take place. Due to the global nature of the Internet, it is recognized that cybercrime that is perpetrated in one country might impact people in another country.

It seems paradoxical that entities other than national governments working under the auspices of international institutions of diplomacy would be tasked with governing any domain, since governance is the responsibility of governments. As Aristotle correctly suggested, the political system exists to eliminate the bias of individuals to the best extent possible. This is not to say that the private sector is guilty of taking advantage of its position as the main engine developing the technology on which the Information Society is based. It is quite the contrary. One must keep in mind that national governments were the chief negotiators of the Declaration of Principles, the Tunis Agenda, and the Tunis Commitment. Therefore, it appears that governments are shirking their responsibilities to provide security, hoping that the private sector and individuals, with some legislative guidance, will do the job for which government is responsible. This becomes apparent when reviewing the United States' National Security Strategy to Secure Cyberspace (NSSSC), which is important since the United States founded the Internet and thus "has important knowledge and experience" in cybersecurity.[56] In the field of the public-private partnership, the NSSSC dictates that

> the federal government could not—and, indeed, should not—secure the computer networks of privately owned banks, energy companies, transportation firms, and other parts of the private sector. The federal government should likewise not intrude into homes and small businesses, into universities, or state and local agencies and departments to create secure computer networks. Each American who depends on cyberspace, the network of information networks, must secure the part that they own or for which they are responsible.[57]

It is therefore apparent that national governments are responsible for putting the responsibility of cybersecurity on the private sector, which has gladly taken up the task. This has been described as a "wonk" approach to cybersecurity.[58]

In the United States, the picture continues to be bleak with regard to public ordering of cybersecurity. On the one hand, the Department of Homeland Security has announced a "Manhattan Project" for cybersecurity. Disappointingly, its aim and scope is solely "to protect the federal domain and ensure the security, resiliency and reliability of the nation's information, technology and communications infrastructure."[59] The view of the private sector and individuals being responsible for their own cybersecurity continues to permeate government thinking. According to Secretary Michael Chertoff,

> The federal government does not own the Internet, thank God, and it doesn't own the nation's cyber networks. You own the Internet and the nation's cyber networks. The federal government cannot be everywhere at once over the Internet or in cyberspace. There is a network that operates within that domain. And as a consequence, the federal government cannot promise to protect every system, let alone every home computer from an attack.[60]

This logic, which is tantamount to saying that everyone is responsible for protecting their own home from attack since the police force cannot be everywhere, continues. Until public law enforcement takes the lead in securing cyberspace, with the private sector playing an important but secondary role, the Information Society will not maximize the utility of networks.

The Perils of Private Ordering: Network Effects, Trust, and Community Harm

Recall Aristotle's abstract conceptualization of the purpose of a polis's rulers to provide legislation and distribute justice to a community, which in the modern era is the Information Society. As discussed above, the Information Society depends on the free flow of information over computer networks. The utility of computer networks rests on the academic concept of network effects. That is, "The greater the size of a network, the greater the benefits."[61] A networked community benefits each time a new user joins that network. People tend to join networks if they can trust that they will benefit as members of the network.

Neal K. Katyal, in "The Dark Side of Private Ordering: The Network/Community Harm of Crime," identifies the main reason for current cybersecurity strategies as being the wrong approach in addressing injustice in cyberspace. This, he argues, is in part due to the focus of criminal justice on the individual impact of a crime, rather than on the harm of a crime to the community at large.[62] In his view, focusing on harm to the community rather than the individual impact of a crime is especially important in cyberspace, as each instance of a cybercrime, no matter how trivial it is, leads to the network's users not trusting the network.[63] With each intrusion, mistrust increases, and the number of users using the compromised network decreases. As a result, the utility of the network to the remaining users decreases.[64] Katyal argues against the common perception as documented in the UNGA resolutions, WSIS, IGF, and NSSSC that "the strong arm of law enforcement has no business when the only harm to a victim is remote and intangible."[65] This view is fallacious, since it focuses only on the individual harmed rather than the harm done to the computer network. Katyal argues that even breaches of computer networks motivated by curiosity seriously damage a community's trust in the network, thereby decreasing the principle of the network effect. It follows that justice in the Information Society can be achieved only if injustice to the community is considered in addition to injustice to the individual. In order for the Information Society to reach its full potential, all cybercriminals should be tracked and punished to the fullest extent possible under the law so as to prevent the loss of trust and increase network usage.

Even if laws exist, this does not mean that the crime will be prevented, since law enforcement authorities must have the capabilities and procedures to prevent, investigate, and prosecute cybercrime.[66] Contrary to the views of the UNGA, WSIS, IGF, and NSSSC, Katyal argues that is the responsibility of law enforcement organizations, not private individuals or corporations, to enforce cyber law and prosecute all infringements. Private ordering efforts, such as proprietary antivirus or firewall software, will not prevent computer crime simply because this software or hardware is purchased and installed by a user, and the interest of private industry is to

> promote sales of anti-virus software, intrusion systems and the like. Yet, the ability to afford and the knowledge to use such technologies will not be distributed equally. Those with fewer resources will not be able to adopt them in the same way that richer individuals and institutions can. Further, because these technologies are often complicated, there will be some who have the resources to purchase them but lack the skills necessary to use them effectively.[67]

Thus, since not all computer users will be able to afford or know how to use protection software, their computers will be prey to attackers. This gap will result in those without protective measures using the network less because they lack the trust in the network to allow for more migration of human activity into cyberspace.[68] Thus, these constraints indicate that private efforts cannot protect every user. Hence, governments must steer clear of the current approach and bear greater responsibility for network protection in order to ensure that the Information Society is a secure environment in which information flows freely.

A further consequence of private industry being given the responsibility of securing cyberspace is that in their effort to assure they meet benchmarks set by the government, connectivity to their networks may be diminished.[69] Put otherwise, if ISPs are burdened with the responsibility to assure that their services are not being used for criminal acts, they might react to any suspicious activity (no matter how slight) by purging users for such actions. This, too, harms open networks overall.

One could argue that Katyal is being overly pessimistic in his view that the private ordering of cybersecurity harms the network and prevents the equal distribution of justice.

However, currently, states are far from achieving this goal.

In his article "Towards a Cyber Security Reporting System: A Quality Improvement Process," Jose Gonzalez examines how such a system could be established. It is argued that the current mechanisms that monitor cyberspace for security violations are not adequate because of overburdened staffs, the ease of anonymity in cyberspace, inexperienced defenders of cyberspace, and the lack of sharing of attack data. While numerous institutions that monitor cyberspace in order to identify threats to security exist, such as computer emergency response teams (CERTs), these centers are not coordinated and do not make generally available the data they collect. This in effect hampers international efforts to secure cyberspace, since general lessons gleaned from successful cyberattacks are not disseminated at a global level. Therefore, a private entity operating in a state with adequate CERT facilities might be aware of an impending cyberattack, but another private entity in a CERTless country will not. Further, the problem with the current CERT system is that private entities do not report all infringements of their cyberspace, as they fear loss of profits. What is required is for a model similar to that monitoring civil aviation to be established to monitor data traffic for attacks. This too requires a P3, however, with the public leading the private. The current state of this field is that it is still in a slow transitory phase. Thus, while the CoE is correct in emphasizing the importance of a 24/7 monitoring network across borders, governments need to make a greater effort to facilitate the establishment of such a network.

Conclusion

The problem of public law enforcement authorities not being able to have a primary role in assuring private entities' information security must be addressed. Cybercrime is a great threat to the Information Society. Computer networks have greater utility to users when there are more users present on a network. Individuals use computers to join networks they trust in order to exchange information with other users. When trust on these networks is compromised, a user will leave the network, thereby diminishing the utility of the network to the rest of the community. Security and trust are the cornerstone of the Information Society. With each unjust network intrusion, these principles are diminished, no matter how trivial the intrusion is.

Currently, the private sector is being held responsible for securing cyberspace, since most of the infrastructure, including the Internet, is not owned by governments. This course is being encouraged by the UNGA, WSIS, IGF, and governments, including the U.S. government. This strategy is misguided. Public policy and governance are the foundation of trust. The roots of this idea stem from the Aristotelian conceptualization of the political partnership, which places the polis at the top of a political hierarchy. Being made up of a political partnership between individuals, households, and villages, the polis is the domain in which the deliberation of legislation happens, law enforcement is organized, and adjudication occurs. Aristotle placed these powers in the public sector since the realm of interests of each of the polis subunits might not seek out the best interests of the community at large. Governments can react and place legal sanctions on a private entity that has failed in its duty to provide a secure digital environment for its subscribers; however, this does not reverse the fact that the crime happened in the first place.

In this regard, the establishment of independent international investigative commissions for cybercrime mandated by the United Nations Security Council with the cooperation of Interpol is one solution. This will enhance the ability of states to investigate cybercrimes and increase the chances of perpetrators being caught. The second proposal is for the establishment of a 24/7 data traffic monitoring and control system run by public law enforcement.

Without the public sector taking an active role in assuring the security of private networks, security in cyberspace will not be distributed equally across the Information Society. A secure cyberspace is possible. This desired end state can only occur with the continuation of the P3 model; however, the public should be in the lead rather than, as it stands, the flip side of this modest proposal.

Countries should not wait until a devastating attack to encourage a robust public sector role in leading cybersecurity.

Notes

1. Marc D. Goodman and Susan W. Brenner, "The Emerging Consensus on Criminal Conduct in Cyberspace," *International Journal of Law and Information Technology* 10, no. 2 (2002): 139–223.
2. International Telecommunication Union, *Research on Legislation in Data Privacy, Security and the Prevention of Cybercrime* (Geneva: ITU, 2006).
3. See, for example, Yale Ferguson and Richard Mansbach, *Remapping Global Politics: History's Revenge and Future Shock* (Cambridge: Cambridge University Press, 2004).
4. Carnes Lord, "Introduction," in Aristotle, *The Politics*, trans. Carnes Lord (Chicago: University of Chicago Press, 1984), 1.
5. Aristotle, *The Politics*, 1252a1–5.
6. Ibid., 1252a1.25–1252b1.30.
7. The starting point, according to Aristotle, "is a cause of those things that are or come about because of it." See Aristotle, *Eudemian Ethics*, 1222b.29–30.
8. Aristotle, *The Politics*, 1253b1.39–40.
9. Aristotle, *Nicomachean Ethics*, trans. Martin Oswald (Upper Saddle River, NJ: Prentice Hall, 1999), 1142a5–15.
10. Ibid., 1253a1, 1287a1–1287b36.
11. Ibid.
12. Aristotle, *The Politics*, 1282b1.16–21.
13. Ibid., 1136a.30–1136b.5.
14. Aristotle, *Nicomachean Ethics*, 1141b25–30.
15. Ibid.
16. Ibid., 1134a.26–31.
17. This hierarchy is expressed by P. Yannakogeorgos.
18. Robert E. Molyneux, *The Internet under the Hood: An Introduction to Network Technologies for Information Professionals* (Westport, CT: Libraries Unlimited, 2003), 29.
19. Gene White, *Internetworking and Addressing* (New York: McGraw-Hill, 1992), 12.
20. This paper focuses on developments in the field of security within this context.
21. United Nations General Assembly (UNGA), "Creation of a Global Culture of Cybersecurity," A/RES/57/239, January 31, 2003.

22 Ibid., Preliminary Paragraph 5.

23 Ibid., Preliminary Paragraph 6.

24 Ibid., Preliminary Paragraph 7.

25 While it is not the scope of this chapter to discuss what techno-geopolitical considerations each state negotiating the UNGA resolutions brought to the table, the reader should keep in mind that states negotiated and adopted the resolution. This is the objective of this chapter.

26 UNGA, "Creation of a Global Culture of Cybersecurity," Operational Paragraph 3.

27 Ibid., annex.

28 Ibid.

29 UNGA, "Developments in the Field of Information and Telecommunications in the Context of International Security," A/RES/56/19, January 7, 2002, Preliminary Paragraph 7.

30 Ibid., Preliminary Paragraph 8.

31 Ibid., Operational Paragraph 1.

32 UNGA, Resolution 56/121 (2002), Preliminary Paragraph 5.

33 Ibid.

34 Ibid., Preliminary Paragraph 6.

35 Ibid., Preliminary Paragraphs 8, 11.

36 Joshua Gordon, *Illegal Internet Networks in the Developing World*, Research Publication No. 2004–03, Berkman Center for Internet and Society at Harvard Law School, February 2004.

37 Ibid.

38 Ibid.

39 Personal communication with Daniel Aghion during the United Nations Institute of Training and Research, Web Seminar Series on ICT Policy Issues for Development, *Broadband Wireless to Bridge the Digital Divide*, United Nations Headquarters, New York, May 17, 2006.

40 Ibid., 5.

41 UNGA, "Creation of a Global Culture of Cybersecurity and the Protection of Critical Information Infrastructures," A/RES/59/199, January 30, 2003.

42 Ibid., Preliminary Paragraph 3.

43 World Summit on the Information Society, Declaration of Principles, para. 1.

44 Ibid.

45 Ibid., para. 5.35.

46 Ibid., para. 5.36.

47 World Summit on the Information Society, Plan of Action, section C5.12.

48 Tunis Agenda, 31.

49 Ibid.

50 Tunis Agenda, para. 55.

51 Tunis Agenda, para. 69.

52 Lines 72–79 of the Tunis Agenda called on the UN secretary general to establish an Internet Governance Forum during which discussions on Internet governance between the multiple stakeholders occurred. The inaugural Internet Governance Forum, held in Athens, Greece, from 31 October 2006 to 3 November 2006, focused on a number of topics relevant to Internet security.

53 Richard Simpson, "Creating Trust and Confidence through Collaboration," Internet Governance Forum, Athens, Greece, October 31, 2006.

54 Henrik Kaspersen, "Creating Trust and Confidence through Collaboration," Internet Governance Forum, Athens, Greece, October 31, 2006.

55 Ken Cukier, "Creating Trust and Confidence through Collaboration," Internet Governance Forum, Athens, Greece, October 31, 2006.

56 International Telecommunications Union, "Research on Legislation in Data Privacy, Security and the Prevention of Cybercrime."

57 George W. Bush, *National Security Strategy to Secure Cyberspace* (Washington, DC: White House, 2003), 11.

58 Greg Garcia, "Forging a Private-Public Partnership: The Wonk-Free Approach to Cybersecurity," *Cutter IT Journal* 19, no. 5 (2006): 21–35.

59 Michael Chertoff, "Remarks by Homeland Security Secretary Michael Chertoff to the 2008 RSA Conference," April 8, 2008, accessed April 9, 2008, http://www.dhs.gov/xnews/speeches/sp_1208285512376.shtm.

[60] Ibid.

[61] Ibid.

[62] Neal K. Katyal, "The Dark Side of Private Ordering: The Network/Community Harm of Crime," in *The Law and Economics of Cyberspace*, ed. Mark Grady and Francesco Parisi (Cambridge: Cambridge University Press, 2006), 193–217.

[63] Ibid., 197.

[64] Ibid.

[65] Ibid., 196.

[66] Ibid., 194.

[67] Ibid., 199.

[68] Ibid., 194.

[69] Ibid., 214.

Cyber Horizons 8

The compass of this chapter is to provide a broad strategic-level assessment of new technologies either currently being rolled out, slowly being adopted, or on the near horizon. Although the chapter focuses on an overview of technological trends that may shape the future cyber environment, as we warned in chapter 3, predicting what the next five years will look like along the cyberspace terrain would be a fool's errand. The pace of development and innovation coming from the private sector, at universities, and in research laboratories is staggering. Many outcomes are the result of structured, calculated design. Other consequences are completely unintended. In either instance, the anticipation of the timing and impact of a disruptive technology is impossible to prophesy. Therefore, a cautionary note about predictions might be appropriate.

In a 1995 *InfoWorld* column, Robert Metcalfe, founder of 3Com, predicted, "The Internet will soon go spectacularly supernova and in 1996 catastrophically collapse." Adding further context to Metcalfe's vision of the future, an anonymous source once opined, "A good forecaster is not smarter than everyone else, he merely has his ignorance better organized." Thus, this chapter aims to focus on only certain changes in core and emerging technologies that define cyberspace. In this discussion, we also hope to predict, with caution, their impact on peripheral technologies where applications will reside, function, and be built. These changes represent a range of new solutions, new threats, and new dilemmas that are technical, societal, and even moral. They will require a new synergy among cross-disciplinary academic fields, subject matter experts from disparate professions, and a new emphasis on public-private partnerships.

Big Data

The term *data mining*, although relevant to discussions on "machine learning" (see below), is a somewhat dated expression. We no longer "mine data"—we are assaulted by it. In truth, we live in the age of big data. Practically everything we do produces data that is tracked and recorded.[1] This data is partially the result of

191

the arrival and explosive growth of the Internet of Things (IoT), which bonds us to the objects and instruments of our daily life, "our cars, our homes, our appliances, our clothing and much more. In the emerging world of the Internet of Things, everything we do, see, use or touch will leave electronic tracks, enlarging further both the potential commercial and social value of such data."[2]

The flood of data generated daily is difficult to comprehend. In scale, it is analogous to the vastness of space or the imagination of the human mind. Sources include news articles and accounts in text and audio forms, imagery, video from security cameras, all types of sensors, GPS systems, smart phones and tablets, new types of media, and LiDAR (light detection and ranging—a remote sensing method used to examine the surface of the Earth, which includes sensor data, modeling/simulation and virtual training, geophysical analyses, and disaster analyses). Some data involves lower quality, such as web data, blogs, forums, and tweets. Adding vagueness to the complexity, much of this information is proprietary and fragmented among numerous private sector actors and is therefore difficult to quantify in terms of the actual size of the Internet or the extent of global cybercrime and cyber espionage.[3]

This data heterogeneity generates increasingly complex questions and will require new processing methods and a workforce of algorithm developers and software engineers.[4] The benefits of harnessing these massive flows will lead to valuable insights that range from finely tailored marketing campaigns and uncovering new ways to detect symptoms of diseases and their spread, to anticipating impending national disasters and political or terrorist events.

In order to understand the virtual incalculability of the data environment, consider the estimate that the planet produces 2.5 exabytes (exabyte = one billion billion bytes) of data daily.[5] Five exabytes is supposedly the sum of all words ever spoken by humankind. A single exabyte of data would fill 1.5 billion CD-ROM discs or three thousand Libraries of Congress. Therefore, by the end of today we will have generated the equivalent of 7,500 Congressional Libraries. By 2025, that number will increase to the point where the digital world is producing approximately 163 zettabytes (1 zettabyte = 1,000 exabytes) per year.

In addition to being immense, data is also heterogeneous, interrelated, and byzantine. As these properties intensify and magnify, computing performance has plateaued. Moore's Law (the axiom which, since 1965, suggests that every eighteen months the number of transistors on a computer chip doubles, driving the expansion of functions on a chip at a lower cost per function) has been declared "dead." The new reliance on computer performance and productivity now, to a large extent, rests on the improvement and development of algorithmic research.[6]

The multidimensional challenge of managing big data comes from the set of problems known as the three Vs—volume, variety, and velocity. Volume is the foundational challenge. The exponential daily growth of data overwhelms our storage facilities, the communication grid that transports it, and our ability to manage it and make it actionable. Compounding the problem of volume is the second issue—variety.

Variety refers to the varying data sources and formats that alternate from simple data to more complex data. Simple data often fits into fields on a spreadsheet or a database application. Examples include fiscal data, sensor data, metadata (data about data), and clickstream data (the virtual stream a user leaves behind while surfing the Internet). More complex data includes biometric data, geospatial information system (GIS) data, encrypted packets, social media data, and other types of data exhaust. These divergent data-generation events discharge clashing categories and formats. Each "event" requires its own analytical method and contributes to, and compounds, the variety problem of big data.

Moreover, a fusion challenge exists when analysts attempt to merge data from hard numerical readings from sensors or databases with softer indicators that articles, photos, blogs, and tweets communicate. To the analyst's world, data is basically divided into **structured data** and **unstructured data**. Structured data, as its name implies, relates to information with a high degree of organization. Information in structured data form is usually organized by tables, spreadsheets, and columns and can be readily searchable by simple and direct search engine algorithms or other search operations.[7] Structured data fits seamlessly within relational databases, which are configured to recognize relations among stored items of information, and therefore agilely lends itself to searches. Information such as records on credit cards, bank accounts, retail purchases, Internet service providers' metadata, air flights, hotel bookings, trade flows, and statistics of all kinds represents a brief list of examples.

On the other hand, unstructured data has no recognizable ordering or identifiable relationships and therefore is not adaptable to databases. E-mails, word processing documents, videos, photos, audio files, presentations, web pages, and many other kinds of images and business documents may have some internal structure, but because this type of information does not have a predefined data model and is not organized in a predefined manner, it is unstructured. Analysis of unstructured data is highly interpretational. What does an image represent? How to gauge the tone of an editorial or social media rant? How to identify and trace the movement of individuals of interest as they traverse geographic boundaries and multiple networks? How to track any entity as it crosses a range of data sets? These are the sorts of questions that unstructured data often poses. Moreover, unstructured data is everywhere and is far outpacing structured data in terms of both volume and growth. Currently, over 80 percent of data is unstructured. As with structured data, unstructured data can be

---

Box 8.1   Data Exhaust

Data exhaust refers to the data generated as trails or information by-products resulting from all digital or online activities. These consist of storable choices, actions, and preferences, such as log files, cookies, temporary files, and even information that is generated for every process or transaction done digitally. This data can be very revealing about an individual, so it is very valuable to researchers and especially to marketers and business entities.

Source: https://www.techopedia.com/definition/30319/data-exhaust.

either machine generated or human generated. Whatever the source, it adds to the burgeoning wave of complex data and the attendant challenges of building resilient and economic databases, as well as formulating efficient algorithms for managing information.

The third V in the big-data triptych is velocity. It is the measure of the flow of data. Increasing computing speeds and pressures of response demand in support of real-time analytics and decision making have strained the transport apparatus. Status updates along the smart grid that previously transpired every two to four seconds are now approaching a rate of ten times a second thanks to new phasor technologies.[8] Meanwhile, high-frequency financial trading and those who depend on situational awareness to perform their duties, such as first responders, national security professionals, and the military, need short date-to-decision cycles. As volume increases and variety mushrooms, velocity is the third coefficient in the big-data problem. The interplay of the three Vs challenges the effort to convert raw data into actionable information.

Withal, the growth of IoT and the explosion of big data will continue to place more pressures on national security and global security regimes for at least the near future. Analysts are often overwhelmed. Existing and future operations depend on a highly educated and technical workforce. Because of a scarcity of talent, many security jobs are not filled. (Edward Snowden, who claimed to earn $200,000 a year as a computer expert, dropped out of high school and took computer courses at a local community college without earning a degree.[9]) Add to these conditions the rigors of the security clearance process in finding qualified people and the range of tasks at the strategic, operational, and tactical levels that persistently feed the pressures of increasing demands.

> As the big-data revolution continues, this list of data sources will grow to include unstructured data feeds, such as ISR and drone footage, passive sonar feeds, gunshot echolocation systems, traffic systems, surveillance footage analytics, text analytics applied to texts, social media—a list that will expand to include novel types of sensors and fused data products as they are created. These sources of data will need to be managed by the national security community to maintain its intelligence edge.[10]

Assuming these problems are resolved, the enhancement of the work of police and intelligence agencies to investigate their suspects and interdict against crime and terrorism can become robust. However, the negative returns are much harder to forecast. Important questions will haunt and bedevil us. How will this thickening network of connected systems complicate security regimes and be an element in the rise of system vulnerabilities? Will privacy concerns clash with security imperatives as state and private actors secure access to private information? What are the limits for abuse for both legitimate and nonlegitimate actors?

To summarize, too much data is being generated at too fast a rate, and from too many different sources. As briefly mentioned above, the ability to manage data by boosting computer performance depends more and more on algorithmic theory and development. New types of analytics have the promise of collecting, managing, and analyzing data from not only tabular sources but also textual, linguistic, and visual feeds. Hence, new knowledge and insight will be drawn through an array of advanced automated technologies and methodologies while accommodating a tsunami of data from a multitude of sources. To this end, artificial intelligence and its subfield, machine learning, are key concepts.

Artificial Intelligence

Artificial intelligence (AI) is often a lax term that generalists sometimes use to merely describe an application that has never been done before. Artificial intelligence is frequently grouped into two categories—**artificial general intelligence** (AGI), also referred to as strong intelligence, and **artificial narrow intelligence** (ANI), or weak intelligence. AGI's base principle is that a machine can be made to think and have the ability to represent the human mind and, ergo, be capable of experiencing consciousness. A computer, robot, or any smart device, therefore, could function in a similar mode as a human brain and, with applicable inputs, outputs, and the appropriate programming, have a mind in exactly the same sense that human beings have minds. If fulfilled, the belief is that machines will be able to reason, think, and do all the functions that a human is capable of doing.

Noam Chomsky described AI research as a field that "analyzes the internal structure of a system that empowers it to perform a task, which computers often perform better and faster than human beings."[11] As a discipline, basically, it refers to a computer system that perceives its environment and takes actions such as learning and problem solving that normally require human or animal intelligence. In order to introduce human reasoning, problem solving, and what we casually call common sense, machines need access to information, categories, and objects such as databases, rules of logic, and sometimes robotics. The enormous power of computers to explore and evaluate massive amounts of data, detect patterns, and reveal connections has already been demonstrated in economics, the natural sciences, and national security.

These cognitive functions are about maximizing the odds of success at any defined goal, which currently include such tasks as visual perception, speech recognition, translation between languages, and decision making. Eventually, the combination of AI and robotics will be making use of their environments to perform even higher cognitive undertakings—such as the naturally instinctual task of building a bird's nest. Its potential is immense, transformational, and speculative. Indeed, much of AI's transformative applications are yet to be addressed.[12] Advancement in artificial intelligence over the past several years has already surpassed expectations. Experts foresee an even greater pace of development and progress for the future.

Researchers at Harvard's Belfer Center for Science and International Affairs, Greg Allen and Taniel Chan, refer to the "Cambrian explosion" as a metaphor for the coming evolutionary change in robotics and autonomous computer systems on which AI resides. The Cambrian Explosion is the relatively brief time event in the earth's history that occurred approximately 540 million years ago. During that span, the pace of evolution momentously changed for both the diversity and complexity of life forms. Most major modern animal phyla appeared during a period in what the author Bill Bryson described as "the moment when complex life burst forth in dazzling profusion."[13]

Today, analogous breakthroughs in algorithmic theory and intelligent agents, such as smart devices and software, are opening an impressive world of knowledge discovery and influencing many aspects of daily life. These **artificial agents** control access to credit, determine capital investment, read news articles, and automate the selection process of what applicant gets a job or who gets paroled. Due to the speed and efficiency it affords, we have increasingly turned over to AI the tasks of decision making and the permission to take actions on our behalf. Moreover, our reliance on artificial agents continues to grow as we empower them. As a result, there is much speculation about the future. These conjectures augur hopeful prospects for the world economy, engineering, national security, biomedicine, and daily life, as well as concerns over individual privacy, job automation, the structural composition of the labor pool, sea changes in business models, the impact on global commerce, the use of lethal autonomous weapons systems, the weaponization of biochemical agents, and the exploitation of the media.

Robotics and AI

Robotics, the subject of many a science fiction plot, is also a fundamentally related field of AI. Robots require AI to manage such tasks as object handling and navigational exercises like motion planning and mapping. Narrow artificial intelligence, the nonsentient branch of AI, works ideally where its function is to run automated tasks that are largely simple and repetitive. Although the potential is still formative, it will be the field of AI that undergoes the most progress over the near term. In contrast to narrow AI and despite the boundlessness of the human imagination and the vast amount of investment funding, the technology of general AI remains nascent and still requires years of serious and collaborative research for it to become "a fully functional reality."[14] However, this more "conscious" branch of AI is the more transformative and the subject of much research and excitement, while at the same time it is fraught with risk for the scientific community, military planners, business strategists, and public policy makers. The tension is public and has at times led to friction between the private sector and the military.

Contrary to strong AGI, narrow artificial intelligence does not attempt to perform the full range of human cognitive abilities. Narrow artificial intelligence is designed to learn and perform a narrow purpose and set of tasks, such as credit scoring, insurance pricing, and anomaly, spam, or fraud detection. It is nonsentient in that it is not aware of its environment except for its rule-based coding and the specific task it performs. Generally, unless retrained with new data and repurposed with new algorithms, a narrow artificial intelligence model designed for speech recognition cannot perform a mapping or motion planning function, because it is restricted by the rules imposed by the programming.

ANI works ideally where its function is to run automated tasks that are largely simple and repetitive. Narrow artificial intelligence pulls data from databases to find correct responses to queries, either by responding vocally to human language interaction or as a guide to navigate through a decision tree. Global Positioning Systems (GPSs), video gaming, and Apple's Siri are examples of narrow or weak artificial intelligence because they can accurately respond with information only from a linked database. Despite appearing complex or intelligent, these types of machine learning algorithms (see below) have no awareness of their environment outside the database. However, the rise of big data, the development of graphic processing technology (as in gaming videos), and breakthroughs in algorithmic methodology have optimized the potential of narrow artificial intelligence. According to Michael Chi of the Australian Strategic Policy Institute, "While many different kinds of AI will be pervasive, they'll be narrow, limited and for a specific purpose. In the next 10 years, 99% of the artificial intelligence you interact with, directly or indirectly, will be nerdily autistic, super smart specialists."[15]

Be it commerce, government, or civic society, advancement in AI has the potential to be game changing. In the security realm, the consequences will be impactful and unpredictable. Autonomous systems will enhance all facets of national security and will increase the effect of force used by both state and non-state actors. In combination with and as an augmentation to cyber, AI will make the non-asymmetrical conflict arena more non-asymmetrical. Digital networking can enable extensive cyber espionage, facilitate crime, help terrorist groups organize online, and exploit media in liberal democracies—and over time, do it more cheaply.

AI and its subfields, machine learning and deep learning,[16] allow systems to not only learn from past data but also observe and self-teach from additional data input. The growing capabilities permit a machine (computer, robot, or weapons system) to make decisions and operate autonomously. The new paradigm will not only enable cyber defense systems to automate the defense of known vulnerabilities, but also to predict emerging threats as the system essentially reprograms itself and improves its functionality. Unfortunately, any adversarial actor with sufficient resources could create or procure an AI exploit capable of automating routine resource-intensive tasks associated with penetrating a target system. As the cost of replicating software declines and the need for highly skilled personnel diminishes, "work factor constraints of entry" for frail/corrupt state actors and nonstate actors ease as well.[17] Hence, while the impact of AI is uncertain, so are the shocks from the power diffusion that could result if these actors acquire the capability to cause significant cyber effects.

Other threats to cybersecurity involve the prospect of automating the discovery of system vulnerabilities and the consequent onslaught of cyberattacks on a grander scale. As computer systems become more complex and learning systems rely on more massive data sets from an ever-expanding universe of big data, hackers find a world filled with opportunity as well. Additionally, implanting "poison data" into training data sets can allow an adversary to corrupt an AI system to not only disable it but also force it to perform inaccurately or counterproductively.[18] AI makes more possible the forgery and alteration of audio and video media to undercut surveillance and intelligence operations. Even if discovered and arrested, such actors have the effect of undermining trust across institutions and sowing panic throughout a population.[19]

Amid this Cambrian era of artificial intelligence, the DoD envisions an integrated web of unmanned systems in its Joint Force program. Systems are developing rapidly for deployment in a multidomain battle space, which will change the way we wage war, operationally and morally. The United States is investing billions to identify targets, pilot unmanned aircraft and land vehicles, navigate its surface and subsurface fleets, and sift through massive waves of data from satellite feeds, intelligence intercepts, social media, news, and literature from all sources. Ultimately, the decision to kill could also be in the control of autonomous weapons systems. These AI efforts are the foundation of the U.S. military's **Third Offset Strategy**, which it foresees as its way to shift the axis of battle in its favor by deploying advanced technologies and forward-thinking operational concepts.[20] The U.S. military is not alone in defense research advancing AI, and some have expressed concern about the emergence of autonomous weapons systems and "algorithmic warfare."

As the technological process marches headlong, government's investment pales in comparison to that of the private sector. The quest for military superiority is only surpassed by the ardor for economic superiority. We invest billions of funds and intellectual capital to build machines and systems to predict the market, refine products, and make trade more frictionless. As an unintended result, we have built machines so complex that, for the first time, we now have inventions that "operate in ways their creators don't understand."[21]

Programs can generate their own algorithms and write their own commands to solve problems and make decisions. Even the software engineers who develop these applications cannot explain entirely the behavior and reasoning behind their operation. The artificial neurons within these systems interconnect across an array of intricate layers in a welter of mathematical functions and variables, which combine with a series of iterations of calculations to form an opaque and nearly inscrutable matrix. Will Knight of the *MIT Technology Review* describes the interplay of calculations within these deep neural networks:

> The neurons in the first layer each receive an input, like the intensity of a pixel in an image, and then perform a calculation before outputting a new signal. These outputs are fed, in a complex web, to the neurons in the next layer, and so on, until an overall output is produced. Plus, there is a process known as backpropagation that tweaks the calculations of individual neurons in a way that lets the network learn to produce a desired output.[22]

We have succeeded in creating machines to perform tasks and make decisions far beyond the scale and scope of our own human capabilities. As a result, we have come to rely on them to organize our lives, make us more comfortable, limit our risk from disease and attack, and predict our futures. Where we have not succeeded is in the ability to find a way to have a conversation. As we give these creations the permission to diagnose our health, improve our daily routines, and make autonomous kill decisions in times of conflict, we should at least consider a means of inserting a human element into the loop, if only to be able to ask, "Why did you do what you did?" Giving voice to these concerns, Stephen Hawking declared in a 2016 interview, "The rise of powerful AI will be either the best, or the worst thing, ever to happen to humanity. We do not yet know which."[23]

Machine Learning

Artificial intelligence and **machine learning** are closely related concepts. They each are categories within the field of computer science, but not without an important functional nuance. Where AI is a branch of computer science that tries to build machines capable of intelligent behavior, machine learning is the science of getting computers to perform without explicit programming. Nidhi Chappell, Intel's head of machine learning, described the difference between AI and machine learning thus: "AI is the science and machine learning is the algorithms that make the machines smarter. . . . So, the enabler for AI is machine learning."[24]

Machine learning algorithms create programs that learn from experience, automatically inferring or "learning" preference models based on empirical observations of users. For example, whenever you do a Google search on things to do in Paris, a list of suggestions will appear, all according to the order of how they are ranked and rated based on your previous recorded searches and/ or those of others. Through these preference modeling methods, more sophisticated machine learning algorithms can also conduct searches that can discover or "learn" things other than merely consumer behavior, such as identifying terrorist precursor crime, epidemiological trends, or how the human genome works.

Principally, machine learning is the study of how algorithms learn from and make predictions on data. Often merged with the term *data mining*, the idea behind machine learning is to formulate algorithms that use input data and statistical analysis to calculate an output value within an acceptable range. What results are analytical models that allow researchers, data scientists, engineers, and analysts from any subject area to produce reliable and repeatable decisions that also reveal previous "hidden insights" from historical relationships and data trends or "hidden structures" from unknown outputs. Additionally, machine learning can iteratively improve or reweight itself as it processes new data. For these reasons, many consider machine learning the most promising method for optimizing the analysis of big data.[25]

Machine learning algorithms generally fall into two distinct classifications. They are either supervised or unsupervised. **Supervised learning algorithms** are the more common. Mathematicians formulate these algorithms via the use of a known data set (called the training data set or labeled data) to make predictions. The training data set includes human-labeled input and known response values of known outputs. After its "training," the supervised learning algorithm applies what it learned to new data and seeks to construct a model off the labeled data to make predictions for a new data set. It gains these insights by "observing" previous examples of data and deriving a model that will be further tested. Therefore, the algorithm is not confined by hard-coded or fixed program parameters, which can result in anti-pattern responses and findings. Rather, it uses the labeled data to solve/infer a classification or regression prediction problem (regression analysis is a statistical process for estimating the relationships among variables). The model makes predictions and refines itself with each iteration. In the supervised algorithmic approach, software learns from data to perform such filtering analyses as how features correlate to actions or events. As the algorithm self-improves over time, it learns through the process of adding larger and more diverse data sets. Examples of applications include a range of predictive analyses from spam filtering and anomaly detection to visual pattern recognition and human behavior analysis drawn from speech and video sources. The U.S. Navy applies supervised learning algorithms to support submarine presurfacing lookout posts. The National Institutes of Health's project on early tumor detection uses the same approach for a molecular tagged imaging application. A remote sensing tool that surveys outer space is a real-life illustration by NASA of how this methodology is put into practice.[26] The objective in a supervised learning algorithm is to map new input data to predict the output variable for that data in order to reveal "hidden insights."

In contrast, **unsupervised learning algorithms** are untrained. This approach uses unlabeled data to infer labels from activities or events. The aim is to generate a model from an unlabeled data set without any predefined response values, categories, or known outputs. The result is a "knowledge discovery" of inferred labels based on structures, relationships, commonalities, trends, patterns, and other ordering schema between inputs.[27] As opposed to the analysis by supervised learning algorithms, unsupervised learning seeks to uncover "hidden structures" from unknown outputs rather than "hidden insights" from known outputs and trends. The algorithm accomplishes this through the use of clustering or association rule learning.[28]

Put briefly, an unstructured learning problem looks for inherent groupings in data and turns these correlations into lead or "theory generations." An illustration of a real-life application that distinguishes unsupervised learning algorithms from supervised learning algorithms would be the example of retail marketing. Market analysts would rely on a structured learning approach to predict consumer trends and consumer demand using data from past sales. On the other hand, the same manufacturer or retailer would use an unstructured algorithmic approach to produce a consumer segmentation model to identify markets based on similarities of buyers. Buyer resistance to price, ranking of product attributes, or classification of consumers as innovators, early adopters, laggards, etc., allows the company to identify and size the market for its product or service.

With 80 percent of data being unstructured, unstructured learning is gaining in importance. Association rule learning winnows out groups based on relations between variables. Clustering maps entities into smaller groups based on shared features. These computing methods offer potential solutions to a broad swath of applications in both commerce and government, while addressing the variety problem of big data. Clustering and association rule learning have been found useful to many fields of research and applications that include not just marketing but also medicine, psychology, sociology, archeology, insurance, security, and virtually any recognized professional or scientific area.

The avalanche of unstructured data, which would otherwise lie inert, can be organized, modeled, and marshaled to serve society and science through machine learning methodology. Machine learning makes possible "the automated processing of 'data exhaust' [mentioned above] into valuable information about social groupings, spending habits, social media sentiments and several other trends and inferences that prove revealing."[29] Summarizing functions and pattern clustering enable analysts to see their worlds through multiple lenses, which can lead to further experimentation and theory design. Machine learning optimizes the functions that computers are designed to do and do best—performing calculations across massive amounts of data. By drawing statistical inferences and constructing models from processed data, computers seem to finish our very thoughts. For example, when we type only a few characters in a search engine, the algorithm "magically" assumes and then completes the entire query field. This is only a small example of how machine learning analytics is all around us—forming new data, creating new predictive tools, enabling knowledge discovery, and often subtly enriching our lives.

The "deep learning" mechanisms, which these tools enable, have proven to be highly effective in predicting diseases and making decisions in finance, manufacturing, and military operations. However, they are also a factor in creating a "black box" process in automated systems, where neither the system, its creators, nor its owners can accurately explain the artificial reasoning behind these machine decisions.

This problem leaves open a moral question of accountability. While the DoD has endorsed restrictions on the use of autonomous and semiautonomous systems exerting lethal force, skepticism among the private sector and the public remains.[30] The European Union's General Data Protection Regulation will restrict automated decision making. The law will take effect in 2018 and touts assurances that it will effectively create a "right to explanation" for a user to demand an accounting if an algorithm decision affects them.[31] But this law has yet to be tested in the courts. Also, is a sufficient explanation technically possible?

Technology has brought us into uncharted territory again. In this instance, the potential for empowerment seems limitless, but the ethical and moral questions are profound. To rely on a deus ex machina to resolve these issues might

Box 8.2   Deep Learning

Deep learning uses structures loosely inspired by the human brain, consisting of a set of units (or "neurons"). Each unit combines a set of input values to produce an output value, which in turn is passed on to other neurons downstream. For example, in an image recognition application, a first layer of units might combine the raw data of the image to recognize simple patterns in the image, a second layer of units might combine the results of the first layer to recognize patterns of patterns, a third layer might combine the results of the second layer, and so on. Deep learning networks typically use many layers—sometimes more than one hundred—and often use a large number of units at each layer to enable the recognition of extremely complex, precise patterns in data.

Source: "Preparing for the Future of Artificial Intelligence," Executive Office of the President, National Science and Technology Council Committee on Technology, October 2016.

mean putting our faith in some impossible hope. Simply yearning for artificial intelligence and machine learning methods to automatically self-improve and reprogram our problems away could tilt our fate toward the perilous direction if we find ourselves on the horns of Hawking's dilemma: "either the best, or the worst thing, ever to happen to humanity."

Third Offset Strategy

As President Harry Truman was leaving office in 1953, America was still suffering from the trauma of World War II. The fragile cease-fire agreement with North Korea was a nonformal treaty, and Soviet threats to the "free world" appeared to be escalating globally. Under the overhang of past turbulence and impending dangers, the National Security Council Report 68 (NSC-68) called for a massive buildup of the U.S. military and its weaponry. Although the recommendations eventually became policy, Truman had concerns about the capacity of the war-weary country's economy to sustain large defense expenditures over a potentially indefinite period.[32] His administration, therefore, called for a strategy to offset U.S. disadvantages in manpower and geographic reach. The logic driving this First Offset Strategy was that, as a deterrence to Soviet or Chinese aggression, the United States could inflict unacceptable losses by retaliating at a place of its choosing—including "Communist heartlands." Explicitly, "this must be based on massive atomic capability."[33]

The nuclear strategy maintained U.S. dominance over the succeeding decades of the Cold War and through the Vietnam era. However, the retreat from Southeast Asia combined with the buildup of Warsaw Pact forces and the Soviet Union's mushrooming nuclear arsenal challenged U.S. superiority. Under Secretary of Defense Harold Brown (1977–1981), the military undertook the development of precision-guided munitions, stealth, and intelligence, surveillance, and reconnaissance (ISR) systems. The array of new-generation weaponry was profusely on display during the 1991 Gulf War. The use of "smart" weapons, which were supported by global positioning navigation systems and the latest IT technology, allowed Allied forces in Operation Desert Storm to outmaneuver the opposition, destroy targets, and limit casualties.[34] This new paradigm was described as another "system of systems," often referred to as C4ISR (command, control, communication, computers, intelligence, surveillance, and reconnaissance). C4ISR combines information collection, analysis, and transmission and weapons systems to create perfected mission assignment—or what others sarcastically have called "precision violence" or "just-in-time warfare."

Today, perceived U.S. advantages in military "great power" competition are gradually eroding. Even "client states" of China and Russia can demonstrate some of the same technological strengths as the United States in advanced weaponry. Peer and near-peer competitors now invest in Second Offset capabilities that are producing a growing symmetry between the United States and its global rivals and regional rising powers.[35] Therefore, in order to maintain its dominance in the continuing revolution in military affairs, the U.S. defense establishment believes it needs to commit itself to a new course—a Third Offset Strategy. This Third Offset Strategy relies on the development of AI to enhance the capability of war fighters and the use of unmanned weapons systems in a multidomain battle space. With the arrival of this new generation of weapons comes a changing face of warfare, a transformation in combat decision making,[36] and an outbreak of moral and ethical questions concerning the use of autonomous weapons.

Machine learning/deep learning is key to the development of future militaries. The asymmetric advantage of unmanned vehicles on land, sea, air, and space relies on artificial intelligence. AI is also critical to human-machine collaboration and teaming in combat. The F-35 Joint Strike Fighter jet (for which Chinese hackers allegedly stole plans equal to over fifty terabytes of data from U.S. defense contractors in 2010; see chapter 4) is an archetype of Third Offset Strategy weaponry.

In addition to stealth capability, the F-35 includes information sharing, sensor fusion, and digital displays.[37] It can be described as a flying sensor that can accommodate massive amounts of data, analyze it, and then display it in the pilot's helmet.[38] The technology allows war planners and war fighters to not only make enhanced decisions but create an integrated electronic attack platform. "The F-35 is an airpower force multiplier—the 'quarterback' of air operations, utilizing its advanced network and sensor suite to distribute information and target allocation across the air picture."[39] As noted by a navy test pilot, "In the future, it may not matter where the weapon comes from. I may pass the data along, or I may fire a weapon and it may come from somewhere else. That is where we are heading."[40]

Yet, as discussed above, this reliance on network technology creates vulnerabilities. The deep learning mechanisms and "black box" process of automated systems create breaches in the system unknown to the creator and operator. These system flaws would most likely not be discovered until after they have been exploited by an adversary. Because of the complexities of algorithms, the hope of monitoring decision-making processes by somehow partnering with machines is an elusive solution—further hobbled by vague definitions and standards for optimal efficiency and certainty. At the same time, the enormous and mounting flow of data, the demands for instantaneous processing, and shorter time-to-decision cycles are overwhelming human capacities in war and peace.

For war fighters, the need for optimal decision and solution resolution, however, is a matter of life or death. Despite the pressures, we still need a human in the loop to assure our moral responsibility and our humanity. The decision to use lethal force in a distributed battle-scape must not be ceded to machines. Yet, in those instances when under attack at machine speeds, as former deputy secretary of defense Robert Work offered in a very human response: "We want to have a machine that can protect us." The dilemma for Third Offset Strategists is that as unmanned systems become more autonomous over time due to technological advances, how do we retain effective and efficient control? Will every human in the decision loop create a friction point that yields a timing advantage to an adversary who has no such compelling sense of accountability that would require human control and verification? There is not a simple path to an "elegant solution." Building unmanned systems with augmented intelligence has profound priority-setting challenges.

Box 8.3   Autonomous Warfare Glossary

Autonomous weapon system: "A weapon system that, once activated, can select and engage targets without further intervention by a human operator. This includes human-supervised autonomous weapon systems that are designed to allow human operators to override operation of the weapon system, but can select and engage targets without further human input after activation."

Human-supervised autonomous weapon system: "An autonomous weapon system that is designed to provide human operators with the ability to intervene and terminate engagements, including in the event of a weapon system failure, before unacceptable levels of damage occur."

Semi-autonomous weapon system: "A weapon system that, once activated, is intended to only engage individual targets or specific target groups that have been selected by a human operator. This includes: semi-autonomous weapon systems that employ autonomy for engagement-related functions including, but not limited to, acquiring, tracking, and identifying potential targets; cueing potential targets to human operators; prioritizing selected targets; timing of when to fire; or providing terminal guidance to home in on selected targets, provided that human control is retained over the decision to select individual targets and specific target groups for engagement."

Source: DoD Directive 3000.09, 2012, https://www.defense.gov/News/Article/Article/1254719/project-maven-to-deploy-computer-algorithms-to-war-zone-by-years-end.

In addition to the above issues, the partnership between the private sector and DoD will be strained and may require forging a new public-private partnership between the government, defense industry, and IT sector. Many companies in the software and hardware sectors of the IT industry have little or no experience working with either the U.S. government or defense industry prime contractors, subcontractors, and systems integrators.[41] They see the rigors and myriad regulations of dealing with the federal government acquisition process as discouraging and would rather sell to the Fortune 100s of the world than cope with the compliance burdens, cost accounting standards, and intellectual property issues that government contracts impose.[42] For its part, the DoD may have to sacrifice some organizational and cultural themes in order to attract talent for a more innovative military.[43] A business model approach to operations might displace traditional military methods of thinking when necessary.

Withal, the United States should also find a way to convince its allies to develop similar high-end technologies. However, the inducement to commit to invest in futuristic weapons could be a difficult sell during times of domestic political and economic uncertainty. In the backdrop to these issues is the fact that we live in uncertain times and will probably dwell there for at least the foreseeable future. In this environment, security forces will have less margin for error than predecessor regimes, as unforeseen swings in power alignments and power dispersions seem to occur regularly and almost naturally.

This chapter opened with a discussion about attempts to predict the future of the cyber terrain. The pace of development within this domain is staggering, unpredictable, and could take us anywhere. A second comment on predictions about the changing cyber landscape and cyber threat might also be fitting, but from another perspective. In his remarks before the Senate Committee on Intelligence, James R. Clapper, then director of national intelligence, said, "Looking back over my more than half a century in intelligence I have not experienced a time when we've been beset by more crises and threats around the globe."[44] It is prudent to be mindful of how changeable are our times. Therefore, when we speak of the cyber threat and global security, we are speaking of concepts, regimes, paradigms, legal codes, standards, and environments in constant flux. These are mutable systems of new complexities with a greater range of state and nonstate actors and a brand of asymmetry never before experienced.

Distributed Ledger Technology

In 2013, U.S. federal authorities seized the website and server of a black market site known as Silk Road. The following year, the FBI took down the same platform a second time after it had reemerged. From 2011 to 2014, Silk Road engaged in the illegal trade of narcotics, malicious software programs, pirated media, fake passports, computer hacking services, and money-laundering schemes. The payment method for these illegal goods and services was the cryptocurrency known as Bitcoin. As briefly discussed in chapter 2, cryptocurrencies are digital assets and a medium of exchange that use cryptology to secure financial transactions. Because they exist outside the traditional banking system, participants in cryptocurrency markets benefit from minimal transaction fees, faster transaction times, and varying degrees of anonymity.

Their popularity has grown in seismic proportions since 2009 when Bitcoin was launched. "Parents are dispensing allowances in Bitcoin to teach their kids to be digital citizens. Marijuana smokers are buying buds from Bitcoin-enabled vending machines. Consumers in emerging markets such as Brazil and Russia are starting to use Bitcoin to hedge their volatile currencies."[45] In 2016, Bitcoin more than doubled its value. In fact, it gained 126 percent in one year, surpassing all world fiat currencies. According to the 2016 Akamai Threat Advisory, the factors contributing to its appreciation were speculation over the instability of national currencies and a flight of cash from the Chinese yuan, which accounted for 98 percent of all Bitcoin trades.[46]

There are many legitimate uses for virtual currencies. Besides reducing transaction costs, they facilitate online micropayments. (Micropayments are very small payment amounts usually incurred when a user accesses an Internet page or service—such as music downloads.) In territories where banking systems are underdeveloped and lacking infrastructure, such currencies can also support and boost local commerce. Virtual currencies abet commerce in the developed world as well. Because they mostly conduct business within their own financial ecosystem, participants in these currency markets not only benefit from the minimal fees and compressed transaction time, but also from the avoidance of economic disruption due to market and currency exchange-rate fluctuations, fiscal policies, and monetary policies. Various leading venture capital firms have invested in virtual currency start-ups for these and other reasons.[47] In 2016, investment funds began offering retirement accounts with individual ownerships in Bitcoin (for the lucky investor, a $5,000 investment in Bitcoin at the end of 2011 was worth $1.2 million at the beginning of 2017).[48]

The core of a cryptocurrency network is **Distributed Ledger Technology** (DTL). Referred to by Bitcoin users as blockchain, it has been described as "a technology for a new generation of transactional applications that helps establish security, trust, accountability and transparency."[49] Not only does the private sector see DTL as an idea and force that will eventually prevail over business models across an array of industrial sectors, but the U.S. government also believes that investment in and development of this technology will be useful as an open-source governance model and a mechanism against cybercrime and espionage operations. "Blockchain technology has the potential to streamline and accelerate business processes, increase cybersecurity and reduce or eliminate the roles of trusted intermediaries (or centralized authorities) in industry after industry."[50] Despite the current allure of cryptocurrencies for criminals and those who wish to evade tax laws or escape detection and interdiction for purchases of illegal goods and services, a main benefit of DLT is also its facility for making transactions transparent and secure, as a way to build trust among peer clients and partners in a digital collective network. Its injection into the bloodstream of commerce has been predicted to be as potentially disruptive as the Internet's impact on communications.[51]

Central to DLT is a **distributed ledger** or database that permits participants (who can be either individuals or institutions) in the network to share and retain identical cryptographically secured records on a peer-to-peer basis.[52] Transactions are recorded one time on a shared ledger and synchronized across the business network, thus eliminating duplication and the need for intermediaries. This manner of interaction allows transactions to occur more efficiently and at lower transaction costs.

Each transaction is a "block" of information containing addresses, dates, times, amounts, and a digital signature, which acts as a tool to certify the authenticity of the transaction (see figure 8.1). The digital signature (see chapter 2), which is generally a hash function, confirms that the entity making the transaction matches their digital identity stored on the ledger. The ledger is maintained over a network of computers, with nodes where information about participants' accounts is not only stored but where a history of transactions is also kept. Each block of information/transaction is mathematically linked to the previous block through an algorithm, hence the term *blockchain*. For a transaction to be entered into the ledger, network members validate the agreement by calculating the correct input to a hash function. The computation also acts as a digital signature. Through this consensus algorithm, known as the **consensus mechanism**, each network participant acts as both a publisher and subscriber.[53] The ledger represents a database of accounts, balances, and a sequential history of transactions, where information is shared, updated, and selectively replicated in real time.[54]

The consensus mechanism means that trust is hard-coded into the system. Intruders cannot modify the records without other members of the exchange noticing the tampering of the blockchain, since each transaction is embedded with a digital signature. A PKI (public key infrastructure; see chapter 2) protocol assures that only valid users are interacting with the ledger. Although identities connected

Figure 8.1 How a Blockchain Works

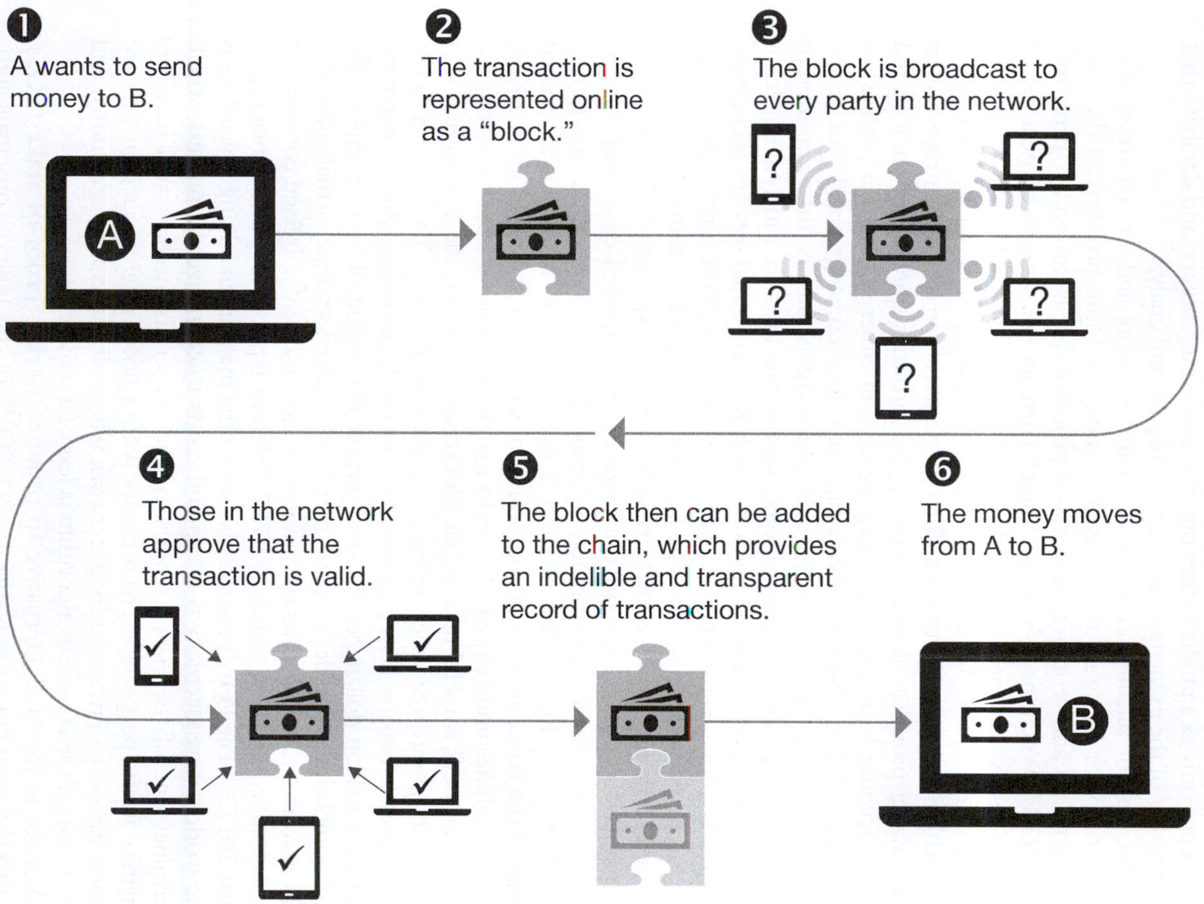

1 A wants to send money to B.

2 The transaction is represented online as a "block."

3 The block is broadcast to every party in the network.

4 Those in the network approve that the transaction is valid.

5 The block then can be added to the chain, which provides an indelible and transparent record of transactions.

6 The money moves from A to B.

Source: Senate Committee on Commerce, Science and Transportation, "The Promises and Perils of Emerging Technologies for Cybersecurity," 115th Cong., 1st Sess., March 22, 2017.

with accounts might be anonymous, digital signatures linked to account transactions are public because the record of activity is shared and all participants have real-time access. Therefore, there can be no double-spending. This consensus platform acts not only as a public ledger but also as a sentry, notary, and database that every member of the exchange can access, monitor, and analyze.

In the case of Bitcoin, users download free software and/or acquire special-purpose computer hardware that is used to solve the input problem to the consensus algorithm and verify transactions—a protocol that is known as **"proof-of-work"** (POW). When they obtain or "mine" currency, participants create a virtual "wallet." These wallets are also the digital addresses that hold, store, and transfer Bitcoins. In addition, wallets contain the private keys, which allow "miners" to interact within the currency network. Bitcoin members can set up their own wallets or use a wallet provider—a separate entity that provides storage and security and maintains account balances. Wallets may be kept in either hot storage (online) or cold storage (off-line). Bitcoin holders can use online exchangers and "wallet services" that perform computations for fees and commissions, or they can attempt the algorithms themselves. Names of wallet service providers are widely available on the Internet as well as companies that offer such Bitcoin-related services as currency exchanges, lending, micropayments, asset management, venture capital, etc.

In proof-of-work, miners vie to add the next block of transactions in the chain by competing to solve an extremely difficult cryptographic puzzle. The first to solve the puzzle is awarded a prize of newly minted coins and a transaction fee. Members usually compete in teams in order to combine computing power. The proposition of this method is that a majority consensus is reached because of the concentration of computing power. Once the problem is solved, all other machines update their ledgers to match the winning team's results.

Proof of work is useful on a public blockchain; however, the downside is that as they scale upward they need massive computational power. This in turn drains electrical power, making it an expensive way to reach consensus. Bitcoin currently consumes a million dollars per day. For further illustration of how enormous the cost of computing is, studies estimate that four hundred separate virtual currencies would need two hundred times the amount of electrical power Ireland consumes.[55] (The website coinranking.com lists 1,757 different types of cryptocurrencies as of August 2017.[56]) The POW protocol also skews the majority of mining toward areas of the world where electricity is cheap and tends to centralize the process, which undermines one of the main strengths of the consensus mechanism. Therefore, anonymity in the public blockchain comes with a price, whereas such an expense is unnecessary on a private business network where all participants are known and dependence on the consensus algorithm is less of a requirement.[57]

A more economical alternative to proof-of-work is **proof-of-stake** (POS). It is also the most common platform after POW. In this type of consensus algorithm, exchange members referred to as "validators" or "forgers" confirm the legitimacy of the transactions. In order to be a validator, participants must hold a certain percentage of the network's total value. In the POS protocol, the odds of being selected to generate the next block depend on the fraction of coins the member owns[58] (in other words, based upon the network member's wealth, or stake in the network). One reasoning beneath this consensus mechanism is that no rational stakeholder would act against their own self-interest by allowing the system to become corrupted.[59]

Box 8.4 — Blockchain Technology

Angus Champion de Crespigny

Blockchain technology has taken the world by storm. Starting with Bitcoin, it has been declared the new Internet, a bank killer, or a Ponzi scheme and the latest "tulip bubble," depending on whom you ask. The reality is somewhere in the middle. The technology is incredibly powerful, but revolutionary technologies take time to mature, and occasionally people's imaginations get ahead of the technology.

Public blockchains enable network participants to record the state of some data at a particular point in time, with no one able to easily restrict or change that data. With Bitcoin, this data is who holds how many of the cryptocurrency Bitcoin. For other blockchains, other data or even code may be shared.

So why is this so powerful? Transferring value has always required a central party to ensure that people are not spending money they don't have, which has led to an enormous centralization of power among a relatively small number of financial institutions that can move that value among a fairly closed network. For many people around the world, this is not a big problem, as we can gain access to that network relatively easily. For others, however, their ability to get access to money is incredibly low.

With blockchains, however, value can move simply like another form of data. If you can access an Internet connection, you can receive value, and you can send it. You don't even need to be a human: machines or software can send and receive value seamlessly. It is a new financial system.

Blockchains can also act as a global data anchor, for example as the digital fingerprint of someone's passport information. A trusted authority may verify that the digital fingerprint matches the original passport, and as long as someone else trusts the trusted authority, they can trust that the digital passport information matches the original. We now have digital passports.

The implications of this technology are huge; however, innovations such as this take time, as there are many obstacles along the way. To begin with, financial systems have many more regulatory hurdles than technical ones, so integrating cryptocurrencies into the financial system is unlikely to open banking up to the unbanked. Additionally, when using it as a data anchor and storing sensitive information on a blockchain, the data will remain on the blockchain forever, which is not ideal even if the data is encrypted, as we don't know if it will remain secure in the future.

Bitcoin and blockchain technologies are ushering in a new future of finance, but it is a long road for it to reach its potential. User-friendly access, consumer protections, and simply time to gain consumer adoption are needed. As this evolves, however, we can expect to see some very exciting things indeed.

Angus Champion de Crespigny is a consultant who leads blockchain strategy for a global professional financial services practice. He is an international speaker and advises governments, media organizations, and start-ups on technical and regulatory issues concerning distributed infrastructure.

POS seeks to address the issue of energy consumption by ascribing validation in proportion to the sum of coins held by a forger. Instead of expending massive amounts of energy to answer POW puzzles, which a majority of POW miners need in order to provide a consensus, a POS forger is limited to validating a percentage of transactions that is reflective of his or her ownership stake. For their services, validators are paid transaction fees. In these types of cryptocurrency exchanges, coins are not mined over an extended period. Rather, all coins come into being at the outset of the exchange network. No further coins are mined after day one. There are other consensus algorithms besides POW and POS, each with its own benefits and shortcomings. The search for faster, more energy-efficient, and less centralized variations continues as the concept of DLT expands and the need for security, trust, accountability, and transparency grows along with it.

DLT can also integrate **smart contracts** over its distributed network. A smart contract is a self-executing, computerized transaction protocol that executes the terms of a contract. Smart contracts autonomously administer trusted transactions and agreements over an arc of disparate, anonymous parties without the need for a central authority, legal system, or external enforcement mechanism. The terms of the agreement between buyers and sellers, lenders and borrowers, or among manufacturers, shippers, agents, retailers, end users, and maintenance providers are directly written into lines of code and therefore can render transactions traceable, transparent, and irrevocable.

Consequently, smart contracts have the potential of eliminating legal contracts. According to Ernst & Young's Financial Services Office, "distributed ledgers enabled with smart contracts could become capable of performing trusted database operations in a distributed environment that today would require a centralized infrastructure."[60] Namely, this would mean that smart contract applications designed for trusts, financing agreements, insurance policies, supply-chain management, and so on, could potentially diminish the need for bankers, lawyers, brokers, agents, and accounting departments.

Additionally, in the security domain, information sharing between the private sector and the government has always been fraught with suspicion and tension about the release of sensitive data. A distributed infrastructure network can combine data into threat feeds that ensure transactional integrity and maintain reputation, while not revealing the identity of the contributor.[61] As the cybercrime threat spreads and spans the globe, DLT can enable interoperability among global law enforcement offices and collaboration between the private and public sectors on a much grander scale.

Among the potential cost savings and societal benefits for providers and consumers, governments and citizens, are the elimination of redundant bookkeeping, contraction of document clearing and settlement times, reduction of risk, simplification of tax and regulatory compliance, a countermeasure against cybercrime and fraud, distributed operations support for war fighters, and a more secure environment to conduct business and maintain daily routines. These innovations offer transformative opportunities that could drastically change business models. However, until standards and practices are established and universally accepted, the technology remains an opening for abuse by criminals, adversarial state actors, and opportunists wishing to game a fluid and unregulated system. The same potential may also hold true for dissidents, insurgents, activists, and whistleblowers.

Conclusion

As these technological advances occur, the process of globalization continually progresses as well. Technology drives globalization, and globalization responds with feedback loops that create and influence a ceaseless chain of cause and effect. Technological evolution and intensifying globalization are concomitant forces that form the social rhythms of innovation, revelation, risk, government policy, public opinion, disruption, and pain. The highly connected system of states and the manner by which populations link economically and politically has resulted in an information age where time and space are compressed, borders blur, power disperses, and alternate spheres of authority rise. Moreover, the monopoly of violence to which states once held exclusive rights is marginalized by the weaponization of information. These elements make twenty-first-century conflict asymmetrical and non-asymmetrical in an arena of state and nonstate actors.

The "sordid boon" of the information age is that while ICT-enabled economic development increases productivity, innovation, and GDP growth, as well as an advanced skilled workforce, it also has an underside. As discussed in much detail above, terrorists recruit, criminals exploit, and adversarial governments can undermine liberal democracies. Yet, despite the perils, no state can resist these forces—even if they so choose. Past data indicates that GDP growth directly relates to increased connectivity to the Internet. Therefore, we lurch onward and consider the losses due to cybercrime and terrorism as essentially a tax on economic growth.[62]

Part of the above discussion also detailed the PRC's and Russia's attempts to use "information security" as a defensive and offensive strategic weapon to further national interests and assure the national dominance of the political elite. However, under the imperative of human rights, the United States also uses its cyber capability to support dissident groups and promote freedom of speech in these countries. The National Security Agency is responsible for not only delivering critical information in support of national defense; it is also expert in cyber infiltration techniques. The Office of Tailored Access Operations (TAO) conducts its work on a 24/7 basis in teams of hackers, engineers, hardware and software specialists, and other technology professionals. TAO tools include the same categories of malware used by U.S. adversaries and implements them with effective deployment and return.

These efforts are viewed as existential threats to China, Russia, and other authoritarian regimes across the globe, and the steps by these governments to resist and retaliate are, in their estimation, morally justified. Hence the efforts to align and coordinate international agreements and treaties to combat terrorism and organized crime and to establish standards on cybersecurity go fallow due to the failure and resistance by states to find common ground.

Meanwhile, other states are trying to emerge as cyber superpowers. In reaction to the Stuxnet, Duqu, and Flame attacks, Iran has responded with a cyber exploit organization going by the name **Tarh Andishan** (innovators). Tarh Andishan targets military installations, research institutes, governments, financial institutions, and critical infrastructure facilities of every sector. Nations with experience against Iran's hacks run a gamut that includes the United States, the United Kingdom, the United Arab Emirates, China, Canada, France, Germany, Turkey, Mexico, Pakistan, Saudi Arabia, Kuwait, Qatar, and South Korea.[63] The group is small but conducts operations within Iran and from locations in the West. Their members are proficient in English and are constantly expanding their suite of exploits.

North Korea and Syria also seek to establish footprints in the battle terrain. Although their attacks are relatively unsophisticated, their intentions are to attract global attention and eventually move on to more grandiose goals. Their actions and objectives are no less similar to other countries with emerging economies who know that their political influence in the world depends on their cyber capabilities and the level of modernization of their industrial infrastructure. In order to assure their hopes of ascent, these societies understand that their commercial and industrial infrastructure must be continuously evolving and resilient. Its defense may require a cyber force that is offensive as much as it is defensive.

In addition to the technologies outlined above, the potential of quantum computing is approaching. Although still nascent and not ready for commercialization, quantum computing offers the capacity for computing large numbers of calculations in parallel. Quantum computers rely on subatomic particles called quantum bits (qubits) to process data. Unlike digital computers that require encoding based on binary digits, quantum computing is imbued with subatomic properties that allow it to exist and function in simultaneous states. The promise they hold for the future is the potential to increase computing power and capability beyond the exponential and perform functions that with today's technology are impossible.[64]

Technology is an irresistible force. We endure the uncertainties and disruption it causes in order to continue to move forward, and because we have no other choice. However, if we imprecisely employ it for the purpose of pursuing vague opportunities or for the satisfaction of being the first to demonstrate a proof to a theory, the real-world results might end in disappointment, skepticism, or something far worse.[65] Hawking's "best or worst thing to happen to humankind" caveat is a dilemma we accept and embrace, knowing our future will be both rewarded and plagued with alternating trials of progress, missteps, and sometimes disaster. The digital transformation now taking place requires that we maintain a very delicate balance between what is efficient and productive and what we also consider to be just and moral.

Key Terms

structured data

unstructured data

artificial intelligence

artificial general intelligence

artificial narrow intelligence

artificial agent

Third Offset Strategy

machine learning

supervised learning algorithm

unsupervised learning algorithm

deep learning

autonomous weapon system

human-supervised autonomous
weapon system

semiautonomous weapon system

Distributed Ledger Technology

distributed ledger

consensus mechanism

proof-of-work

proof-of-stake

smart contract

Tarh Andishan

Notes

[1] Eric Jardine in "Cyber Security in a Volatile World," Global Commission on Internet Governance and Chatham House, 2017, 7.

[2] "Cyber Security in a Volatile World," 125.

[3] Ibid., 22.

[4] "CCICADA and Big Data," 2014, https://www.hsdl.org/?view&did=789070.

[5] Michael Chi, "Big Data in National Security: Online Resource," Australian Strategic Policy Institute, 2017, 3.

[6] Ibid.

[7] https://brightplanet.com/2012/06/structured-vs-unstructured-data.

[8] "CCICADA and Big Data," 5.

[9] Bruce Newsome and Jack Jarmon, *A Practical Introduction to Homeland Security and Emergency Management from Home to Abroad* (Los Angeles: Sage Publications/CQ Press, 2016), 361.

[10] Chi, 16.

[11] Yarden Katz, "Noam Chomsky on Where Artificial Intelligence Went Wrong," *Atlantic*, November 1, 2012, https://www.theatlantic.com/technology/archive/2012/11/noam-chomsky-on-where-artificial-intelligence-went-wrong/261637.

[12] Greg Allen and Taniel Chan, "Artificial Intelligence and National Security," Belfer Center for Science and International Relations, 2017.

[13] Bill Bryson, *A Short History of Nearly Everything* (New York: Broadway Books, 2003), 325.

[14] http://analyticsindiamag.com/artificial-narrow-intelligence-vs-artificial-general-intelligence.

[15] Chi, 11.

[16] https://blogs.nvidia.com/blog/2016/07/29/whats-difference-artificial-intelligence-machine-learning-deep-learning-ai.

[17] Allen, 19.

[18] Ibid., 25.

[19] Ibid., 2.

[20] George Galdorisi, "Designing Unmanned Systems for Military Use: Harnessing Artificial Intelligence to Provide Augmented Intelligence," *Small Wars Journal*, August 27, 2017.

[21] Will Knight, "The Dark Secret at the Heart of AI," *MIT Technology Review* 120, no 3 (May/June 2017).

[22] Ibid.

[23] http://www.bbc.com/news/technology-37713629.

[24] http://www.wired.co.uk/article/machine-learning-ai-explained.

[25] Chi, 8.

[26] http://ewh.ieee.org/cmte/cis/mtsc/ieeecis/Harold_Szu.pdf.

[27] Ibid., 9.

[28] Ibid.

[29] Ibid., 10.

[30] Allen, 21.

[31] https://arxiv.org/abs/1606.08813.

[32] Robert Martinage, "Toward a New Offset Strategy: Exploiting U.S. Long-Term Advantages to Restore U.S. Global Power Projection Capability," Center for Strategic and Budgetary Assessments, 2014, 8.

33 James S. Lay, *A Report to the National Security Council on Basic National Security Policy*, NSC 162/2, Washington, DC, October 30, 1953, sec. 34, paragraph a.

34 Simon Dalby, "Geopolitics: The Revolution in Military Affairs and the Bush Doctrine," *International Politics* 46, nos. 2–3 (2009): 234–52.

35 Katie Lange, "3rd Offset Strategy 101: What It Is, What the Tech Focuses Are," *Defense Media Activity*, March 31, 2016; George Galdorisi, "Designing Unmanned Systems for Military Use: Harnessing Artificial Intelligence to Provide Augmented Intelligence," *Small Wars Journal*, August 23, 2017.

36 Ibid.

37 Martinage, 8.

38 Lange.

39 Jacqueline Schneider, "Digitally Enabled Warfare: The Capability-Vulnerability Paradox," Center for a New American Security, August 2016, 8.

40 Ibid.

41 Peter Dombrowski, "America's Third Offset Strategy: New Military Technologies and Implications for the Asia Pacific" (policy report, Nanyang Technological University, June 2015), 8.

42 Jesse Ellman, Lisa Samp, and Gabriel Coll, "Assessing the Third Offset Strategy" (report of the CSIS International Security Program, March 2017), 8.

43 Ibid., 3.

44 Ionut C. Popescu, "Strategic Uncertainty, the Third Offset, and US Grand Strategy," *U.S. Army War College Quarterly* 46, no. 142 (Winter 2016–2017): 71.

45 Olga Kharif, "Bitcoin: Not Just for Libertarians and Anarchists Anymore," BloombergBusiness.com, October 9, 2014.

46 Benjamin Brown, "2016 State of the Dark Web," Akamai Threat Advisory, 2017, 6.

47 Ibid., 8.

48 Jason Zeig, "Should You Put Bitcoin in Your IRA?," *Wall Street Journal*, January 14–15, 2017).

49 U.S. Senate Committee on Commerce, Science and Transportation, "The Promises and Perils of Emerging Technologies for Cybersecurity," 115th Cong., 1st Sess., March 22, 2017.

50 http://www.ey.com/gl/en/industries/technology/ey-blockchain-reaction-tech-plans-for-critical-mass.

51 Ibid.

52 "Financial Technology: Information on Subsectors and Regulatory Oversight," Government Accountability Office, GAO-17-361, 2017, 40.

53 Manav Gupta, *Blockchain for Dummies*, IBM Limited Edition (Hoboken, NJ: Wiley, 2017), 10.

54 Ibid., 6.

55 "The Promises and Perils of Emerging Technologies."

56 https://www.coindesk.com/short-guide-blockchain-consensus-protocols.

57 Gupta, 17.

58 https://www.coindesk.com/short-guide-blockchain-consensus-protocols.

59 Angus Champion de Crespigny, senior manager, Ernst & Young, LLP, New York, conversation with the author, August 30, 2017.

60 "Implementing Blockchains and Distributed Infrastructure," Ernst & Young, LLP, 2016.

61 "The Promises and Perils of Emerging Technologies for Cybersecurity."

62 Melissa Hathaway, *sic* in Bruce Newsome and Jack Jarmon, *A Practical Introduction to Homeland Security and Emergency Management from Home to Abroad* (Los Angeles: Sage Publications/CQ Press, 2016), 448.

63 James Scott and Drew Spaniel, "Know Your Enemies: A Primer on Advanced Persistent Threat Groups," Institute for Critical Infrastructure Technology, 2015, 13.

64 Steven Grobman, Intel fellow and chief technology officer, Intel Security Group, statement for the record before the U.S. Senate Commerce Committee on the Promises and Perils of Emerging Technologies for Cybersecurity, March 22, 2017.

65 Malcolm Harkins, chief security and trust officer, Cylance Inc., statement for the record before the United States Senate Commerce Committee on the Promises and Perils of Emerging Technologies for Cybersecurity, March 22, 2017.

Appendix

Strategic Military Cyber Concepts

Cyber Law and Policy

Col. Gary Brown and Maj. Israel King

Introduction

Cyber capabilities have opened an entirely new area of warfare. It has been called a revolution in military affairs—evolutionary technological development, and associated tactical and strategic change, altering the character of war.[1]

Many of the same law-of-war issues exist in cyber operations as in traditional military operations. Whether the law of war applies to a particular cyber activity may depend on whether a state of armed conflict exists between the actors. This may be more challenging in cyber, as some basic questions remain unanswered. Perhaps most important, it is not settled when a cyber operation will be considered to constitute a use of force or an armed attack. Despite the uncertainty in policy, if injury, death, damage, or destruction results from a military cyber activity, cyber law practitioners should assume the activity is likely to be considered a use of force under international law.[2]

Even given the limitations noted above, as a matter of policy, the United States complies with the law of armed conflict (LOAC) in all military operations.[3] The fundamental issues arising in cyber operations are no different than those relevant to kinetic military operations. The law of cyber warfare has at its core the same basic principles of military necessity, avoidance of unnecessary suffering (humanity), proportionality, and distinction. One of the greatest challenges in cyber warfare is applying these time-honored principles to actual cyber operations. These issues are set in detail below.

Another challenge is the way cyber warfare freely mixes with aspects of everyday life. Affecting cyber systems can have negative effects on utility systems (such as electricity and water), financial systems (such as banking and paying by credit card), and communications (such as telephone systems and social media networks). Complicating the matter further, cyber warfare techniques are often not very different from the practices of cyber criminals or spies. Because there is significant overlap and different legal regimes apply to the different areas, cyber activities require careful scrutiny from the appropriate lawyers.

The chapter first addresses cybercrime, followed by a discussion of the law applicable to cyber conflict. It discusses both the resort to armed conflict (*jus ad bellum*) and the law that applies during armed conflict (*jus in bello*), focusing on issues of special concern for cyber law practitioners. Next, the chapter looks at espionage. It finishes with a discussion of U.S. policy in the area.

Cybercrime

U.S. Domestic Law

Generally, computer code is considered a form of speech and is protected under the First Amendment. That means encryption technology and cyber "weaponry" both at least potentially enjoy constitutional protection.[4] Some specific elements of computer-related U.S. laws are set out below.

In 1984 Congress passed the Computer Fraud and Abuse Act (CFAA), the first U.S. domestic cybercrime statute. This statute prohibited unauthorized access to defense and financial computer systems in an era when the nation was just starting to awaken to the possibilities of cybercrime.[5] Since then the number and scope of U.S. cybercrime statutes have broadened in response to the rapid expansion of cyber threats, creating a web of prohibitions and penalties designed to criminalize virtually every unauthorized use of a computer network or system.

The CFAA, located at 18 USC § 1030, remains the nation's preeminent cyber-crime statute, criminalizing seven main types of computer-related activity. First, it prohibits the act of obtaining national security information without authorization and then willfully retaining that information or providing or attempting to provide that information to an unauthorized recipient.[6] Second, it prohibits the unauthorized access of information from financial institutions, U.S. government agencies, or any other protected computer.[7] Third, it prohibits trespassing into a federal government computer, even when no information is obtained during such trespass.[8] Fourth, it prohibits the unauthorized access of a protected computer with intent to defraud if the access furthered the intended fraud and resulted in the obtaining of something of value by the unauthorized party.[9] Fifth, it prohibits the unauthorized access of a protected computer that results in physical or logical damage.[10] Sixth, it prohibits a person from trafficking in computer passwords or similar information when the trafficking affects interstate or foreign commerce or may be used to access without authorization a computer used by or for the federal government.[11] Seventh, it prohibits extortion attempts involving a threat to cause damage to a protected computer or a threat to impair the confidentiality of information obtained from a protected computer.[12]

The Wiretap Act, located at 18 USC § 2511, also has expanded to account for the crimes of the computer age. Originally designed to regulate the use of wiretaps to investigate crime, it has come to criminalize other types of unauthorized communication intercepts and disclosures, including "electronic communications," such as those made over the Internet.[13] The core prohibition of the Wiretap Act disallows any person from intentionally intercepting, or attempting to intercept, any wire, oral, or electronic communication.[14] The Wiretap Act also prohibits the intentional disclosure of communications that are known to have been illegally intercepted.[15] Finally, the Wiretap Act

prohibits the use of the contents of any wire, oral, or electronic communication with knowledge or a reason to know that the contents were obtained through an unauthorized intercept.[16]

A plethora of other domestic federal statutes also cover cybercrime, including the following:

- The Electronic Communications Privacy Act, located at 18 USC §§ 2510–2521, protects against the unlawful interception of data in transit.
- The Stored Communications Act, located at 18 USC § 2701, prohibits accessing an electronic communication service provider without authorization and obtaining, altering, or preventing authorized access to electronic communications (such as e-mail or voice mail) while they are in storage.[17]
- The Identity Theft and Assumption Deterrence Act, located at 18 USC § 1028, prohibits the unauthorized use, possession, or transference of a means of identification of another person for purposes of conducting any unlawful activity.[18]
- The Identity Theft Penalty Enhancement Act, located at 18 USC § 1021A, creates a new offense of aggravated identity theft leveraging enhanced penalties whenever a person knowingly transfers, possesses, or uses a means of identification of another person during and in relation to any felony violation of certain federal offenses, such as hacking activities in violation of CFAA outlined above.[19]
- The Access Device Fraud Act, located at 18 USC § 1029, prohibits the production, use, possession, or trafficking of unauthorized or counterfeit access devices, which are any instruments—such as passwords or account numbers—that can be used to obtain money, goods, services, or any other thing of value or that can be used to initiate a transfer of funds.[20]

- The Wire Fraud Act, located at 18 USC § 1343, prohibits the transmittal of any instrument by means of wire, radio, or television communication in interstate or foreign commerce for purposes of obtaining money or property fraudulently.[21] This statute is deemed to apply to Internet transmissions due to an expansive interpretation of the term "wire, radio, or television communication" contained within the statute.[22]
- The Economic Espionage Act, located at 18 USC § 1831, prohibits the receipt and possession of trade secrets without the owner's consent.
- The National Stolen Property Act, located at 18 USC § 2314, prohibits the transportation in interstate commerce of "any goods, wares, securities, or money" valued at $5,000 or more that are known to be stolen or fraudulently obtained. Computerized transfers of funds have been covered by this law.
- Communication Lines, Stations or Systems, located at 18 USC § 1362, prohibits injuring or destroying any of the works, property, or material of any radio, telegraph, telephone or cable, line, station, or system, or other means of communication, operated or controlled by the United States, or used or intended to be used for military or civil defense functions of the United States.[23]

Most states also have computer crime statutes that might be relevant in some situations. In a situation involving computer fraud or damage to or unauthorized access to a computer, it may be worthwhile to research applicable state law.

Given continuing issues with hacking and the proliferation of malicious software, the volume of laws designed to deter and punish cybercrime will most likely continue to increase. In fact, as recently as January 2015, President Barack Obama introduced legislative proposals that would "allow for the prosecution of botnets, criminalize the overseas sale of stolen U.S. financial information like credit card and bank account numbers, would expand federal law enforcement authority to deter the sale of spyware used to stalk or commit ID theft, and would give courts the authority to shut down botnets engaged in distributed denial-of-service attacks and other criminal activity."[24] It remains to be seen how many of these proposals will be added to the burgeoning cybercrime legal regime.

International Law

In contrast to the significant volume of domestic legislation, little international law currently exists to combat the problem of cybercrime. In fact there is only one major international treaty on the matter, the aptly named Convention on Cybercrime (also known as the Budapest Convention), which came into force in 2004.[25]

The core provisions of the Budapest Convention require the convention's signatories (which as of this writing include the United States and 46 other countries) to define criminal offenses and sanctions under their domestic laws for four categories of computer-related crimes: fraud and forgery, child pornography, copyright infringements, and security breaches such as hacking, illegal data interception, and system interferences that compromise network integrity and availability.[26] The convention also requires signatories to establish domestic procedures for detecting, investigating, and prosecuting computer crimes and for collecting electronic evidence of any criminal offense.[27] Finally, and perhaps most importantly, the convention requires signatories to establish a rapid and effective system for international cooperation in the investigation and prosecution of cybercrime, as the convention deems cybercrimes to be extraditable offenses and permits law enforcement authorities in one country to collect computer-based evidence for those in another.[28] Although the Budapest

Convention has nowhere near universal acceptance, evidence would indicate that it is rapidly gaining acceptance, given that 16 of the 47 current signatories have acceded to the convention since 2012.[29]

An additional protocol to the Budapest Convention, criminalizing acts of a racist and xenophobic nature committed through computer systems, came into force in 2006.[30] This additional protocol specifically criminalizes the dissemination of racist and xenophobic material through a computer system, the issuance of threats or insults of a racist or xenophobic nature through a computer system, or the distribution of material that "denies, grossly minimizes, approves or justifies acts constituting genocide or crimes against humanity" using a computer system.[31] Although the number of countries that has signed and ratified the additional protocol currently stands at 24, the United States has not ratified or even signed it.[32] This is believed to be due to concerns that the additional protocol's provisions are inconsistent with U.S. constitutional guarantees, most notably the right to free speech. In fact the principal reason the additional protocol exists is that the United States objected to the inclusion of prohibitions on racist and xenophobic speech in the Budapest Convention.[33] Thus, it is unlikely that the United States will accede to this additional protocol for the foreseeable future.

International Law and Cyber Conflict

Conceptualizing Cyberspace

The word *cyberspace* has been defined in a variety of ways, reflecting different ways of thinking about it. Is cyberspace a shared, consensual hallucination as the originator of the term suggested?[34] Or is it more corporeal, as the Department of Defense (DOD) has determined: "the interdependent network of information technology infrastructures and resident data,

including the Internet, telecommunications networks, computer systems, and embedded processors and controllers"?[35] This chapter will track DOD's definition, leaving aside the human element that is often considered part of the definition of cyberspace.[36] In the future, that may well be an important part of any discussion of cyberspace operations, but for the present, U.S. law, policy, and doctrine are built around a machine-oriented view.

Determining what cyberspace is does not answer the question of its legal status. It has been suggested that cyberspace be treated as a global common, similar to the high seas.[37] Implementing a global commons theory would be problematic, because there seems to be little interest among states in considering cyberspace a freely shared resource. Even if states agreed, there are plenty of nonstate actors who operate to their own benefit and the detriment of others, so for now any meaningful cyber commons remain just a noble ideal.

The majority position is that because the Internet is hosted on infrastructure (routers, cables, servers, etc.) existing on physical territory, cyberspace remains subject to traditional notions of territorial sovereignty. Even taking this most conservative approach raises practical questions. Normally, states are expected to control their own territory, ensuring that criminal and aggressive actions do not emanate from it. Because of privacy, free speech, volume of data, and other challenges, states really do not control cyber activities moving across infrastructure in their territory. It is estimated, for example, that about 25 percent of all command-and-control servers controlling botnets and over 40 percent of malware sites are hosted in the United States.[38] Presumably, the United States would prefer it if this criminal activity with global effects were not occurring, but cyber sovereignty seems to have practical limits. In the future there may be agreement on some modified version of traditional sovereignty, with states assuming responsibility for actions they know about. Under the current system, affecting networks or other computer infrastructure located in a territory of another state might be a violation of sovereignty, although questions remain about exactly when and how virtual intrusions violate territorial sovereignty. Any violation of sovereignty is unfriendly, but violations that cross the threshold of non-interference are most serious. The nonintervention principle mandates that states not take coercive or dictatorial actions that deprive another state of control over a sovereign matter (e.g., military, political, economic, or cultural matters). Violations of this principle could serve as a basis for exercising national self-defense.[39]

The *Jus ad Bellum*: Uses of Force and Self-Defense

For millennia, humankind has struggled to decide when it is appropriate to resort to the international use of military force.[40] Over time, the weight of opinion has swung between allowing the unfettered use of force by states against other states as an instrument of political power to prohibiting any manifestation of international conflict as abhorrent to civilized society.[41] In the modern age, the body of law governing the conditions under which states may resort to conflict with other states, called the *jus ad bellum*, is centered on the Charter of the United Nations (UN), which came into force as a treaty on 24 October 1945.[42]

For purposes of the *jus ad bellum*, the most important provision of the UN Charter is Article 2(4), which states that "all members shall refrain in their international relations from the threat or use of force against the territorial integrity or political independence of any state, or in any other manner inconsistent with the Purposes of the United Nations."[43] States are thus generally prohibited from using force outside of their own borders. The principal means by which the UN enforces this prohibition is through chapter VII of the charter, which outlines certain military and nonmilitary measures that the UN Security Council may take with respect to conduct deemed to be a threat to peace, a breach of peace, or an act of aggression.[44]

Notwithstanding the UN Security Council's role in suppressing illegal uses of force and restoring international peace and security, states that find themselves subjected to an illegal use of force may also defend themselves in the absence of or in conjunction with UN Security Council assistance. Article 51 of the UN Charter codifies this well-established principle when it states that "nothing in the present Charter shall impair the inherent right of individual or collective self-defense if an armed attack occurs against a Member of the United Nations."[45] Although the plain language of Article 51 would seem to indicate that the right of self-defense exists only after a state has been attacked, the weight of opinion on the matter is that states also have a right to defend themselves against an attack that has not yet been prosecuted but is imminent.[46] The degree to which this right extends temporally, prior to the execution of an attack, is the subject of a debate that goes beyond the scope of this chapter.

What remains then is the question of what activities would qualify as a use of force under Article 2(4) that could potentially lead to intervention by the UN Security Council, and what activities would qualify as an armed attack under Article 51 that would allow a state to act pursuant to its right of self-defense. On these points, the UN Charter provides no further guidance. However, for assistance in defining the term "use of force," many authorities turn to Resolution 3314 of the UN General Assembly, which provides examples of acts that would qualify as "acts of aggression." These acts include the following:

- Invading or attacking the territory of another state;
- Bombarding or using other weapons against the territory of another state;

- Blockading the ports or coasts of another state;
- Attacking the land, sea, or air forces or the marine or air fleets of another state; and
- Sending armed bands, groups, irregulars, or mercenaries into another state on behalf of a third state, which carry out acts of armed force of such gravity amounting to the acts listed above.[47]

Further, for guidance on what constitutes an "armed attack," many authorities turn to the decision of the International Court of Justice (ICJ) in its judgment in the *Military and Paramilitary Activities in and against Nicaragua Case*, also known as the *Nicaragua Case*.[48] In this case, the ICJ held that only the "most grave" forms of the use of force would qualify as an armed attack, implying that the "scale and effects" of the act must reach some minimal threshold before it may be elevated above the level of a "use of force."[49] However, some states, including the United States, viewing that allowing a qualitative gap between actions constituting a use of force and those qualifying as an armed attack would create an untenable situation where a nation would be subjected to force and yet would not be able to defend itself, have held that they have the right to respond in self-defense against any illegitimate use of force.[50]

How do actions in cyberspace fit within this framework? Nowhere in the UN Charter or in the classical definitions of "act of aggression" or armed attack are references to cyberspace or cyber warfare to be found. However, does this mean that the actions of a state committed in or through cyberspace cannot be deemed a use of force or armed attack? Not according to the ICJ. In 1994 the ICJ issued its *Advisory Opinion on the Legality of the Threat or Use of Nuclear Weapons*, holding that the principles enshrined in Article 2(4) and Article 51 of the UN Charter "apply to any use of force, regardless of the weapons employed."[51] The United

States has signaled its acceptance of the ICJ's opinion in the context of cyberspace operations in several ways. First, in the 2011 *International Strategy for Cyberspace*, President Obama stated that "consistent with the United Nations Charter, states have an inherent right to self-defense that may be triggered by certain aggressive acts in cyberspace."[52] Also, one year later, at the 2012 USCYBERCOM Inter-Agency Legal Conference, the U.S. Department of State legal advisor, Harold Koh, stated that "cyber activities may in certain circumstances constitute uses of force within the meaning of Article 2(4) of the UN Charter" and that "a State's national right of self-defense, recognized in Article 51 of the UN Charter, may be triggered by computer network activities that amount to an armed attack or imminent threat thereof."[53]

Given that the existing *jus ad bellum* legal framework applies to cyber warfare, specific acts taken in or through cyberspace are subject to examination to determine whether they rise to the level of a use of force or an armed attack.

In 2009 an international group of experts convened in Tallinn, Estonia, at the invitation of the NATO Cooperative Cyber Defence Centre of Excellence to consider this and many other questions relating to the law and cyber warfare.[54] The conclusion this group of experts reached was that "acts that injure or kill persons or damage or destroy objects are unambiguously uses of force."[55] This seems to reflect the official view of the United States, as evidenced by another statement from Koh to the effect that "cyber activities that proximately result in death, injury, or significant destruction would likely be viewed as a use of force."[56] Examples of cyberspace activities that would meet this threshold would include those that trigger a nuclear plant meltdown, open a dam above a populated area, causing destruction, or disable air traffic control services, resulting in airplane crashes.[57]

But what of those cyberspace activities that do not cause death or destruction? While there is agreement that such activities could theoretically also rise to the level of a use of force or even an armed attack, there remains little consensus on where the line separating uses of force from non-uses of force should be drawn.[58] The conclusion of the international group of experts was that in the absence of a clear threshold, states considering a cyberspace operation will do their best to consider "the international community's probable assessment of whether the operation violates the prohibition on the use of force" by analogizing the cyberspace operation to other possible actions, applying a variety of factors that might include the following:

- Severity: The more the consequences of a cyberspace operation impinge on critical national interests, the more they will contribute to the depiction of a cyberspace operation as a use of force;
- Immediacy: Those cyberspace operations that produce immediate results are more likely to be viewed as a use of force than those that take weeks or months to achieve their intended effects;
- Directness: The more direct the chain of causality between the initial cyberspace operation and its consequences, the more likely it will be viewed as a use of force;
- Invasiveness: The more a cyberspace operation intrudes into the target state or its cyber systems contrary to the interests of that state, the more likely it will be characterized as a use of force;
- Measurability of Effects: A cyberspace operation that can be evaluated in very specific terms with respect to the effects of the operation is more likely to be characterized as a use of force than one with difficult to measure or subjective consequences;
- Military Character: A nexus between the cyberspace operation in question

and military operations heightens the likelihood of characterization as a use of force;
- State Involvement: The clearer and closer a nexus between a state and cyberspace operations, the more likely it is that other states will characterize those operations as uses of force by that state; and
- Presumptive Legality: Those cyberspace operations that fall within categories of activities such as propaganda, psychological operations, espionage, or economic pressure are less likely to be considered uses of force as they are not expressly prohibited by international law.[59]

That the United States tends to follow this approach can be discerned once again from Koh's speech, in which he opined that "in assessing whether an event constituted a use of force in or through cyberspace, we must evaluate factors, including the context of the event, the actor perpetrating the action (recognizing challenging issues of attribution in cyberspace), the target and location, effects and intent, among other possible issues."[60] For good or ill, as many uses of cyberspace operations are among those that do not cause outright death or destruction, it is likely that the current state of ambiguity regarding the legality of such operations is likely to continue until states develop a specific treaty concerning cyberspace operations, or international norms develop through repeated state practice and custom in response to such operations.

Case Study: Estonia, 2007. Perhaps the best publicly documented illustration of the threshold at which cyber activity alone could trigger armed conflict occurred in Estonia. In April 2007 the Estonian government announced it was relocating a Soviet-era bronze statue from the center of the capital, Tallinn, to a military cemetery located elsewhere in the city. By the time the actual relocation took place, ethnic Russians had rioted and other instances of violence erupted in response. The night the statue was moved a massive distributed denial-of-service (DDoS) action began against Estonian websites, flooding them with bogus requests and rendering them incapable of performing their intended functions. Other activities included defacing official websites and disrupting the domain name system. For about three weeks, electronic governance and business in Estonia were severely disrupted.[61]

Although at the time some suggested the cyber aggression might be serious enough to invoke Article 5 of the Washington Treaty (which requires NATO member states to engage in mutual self-defense if a member state comes under attack), it was apparently not seriously debated. The Estonian government determined the actions could be dealt with under a law enforcement regime, but it is unclear that anyone was ever held to account for the activity.[62]

Retorsion and Countermeasures

Even if committed to following the law when suffering cyber malfeasance that falls short of a use of force or armed attack, states are not condemned to inaction. There are three potential courses of action they might take.

First, *retorsion* is an unfriendly but lawful response to an unfriendly, but not illegal, action by another state. As acts of retorsion are lawful, they may be punitive or anticipatory.[63] For example, if a state is using an official social media account to spread negative information about another state, the second state could refuse to allow its Internet service providers to be used by the first state.

A second option, *countermeasures*, takes it up a notch. If a state is a victim of unlawful activity, it has the right to engage in countermeasures for the purpose of ending the other state's unlawful behavior. Countermeasures are actions that would be unlawful but for the fact that they are

countermeasures. Countermeasures must be necessary and proportionate.[64] Countermeasures in response to illegality perpetrated with cyber means are not limited to cyber activities, and, conversely, cyber countermeasures are available for kinetic offenses.

As the proper purpose for countermeasures is ending illegality, if the offensive conduct has already ceased, countermeasures are not appropriate. Retaliatory activity does not qualify as countermeasures. Further, anticipatory countermeasures are not permitted. However, both of these situations may be complicated by a planned or ongoing campaign of illegality. If a state has taken steps that are an integral part of the illegal act, even if the act has yet to occur, early countermeasures may be permitted. Similarly, if a particular unlawful act has ceased but was part of a continuing campaign of illegal actions, countermeasures to end the campaign might be lawful.

For example, a state might violate another state's sovereignty by planned intrusions into its territorial seas. The victim state in this case might decide to deny service to the ships' communications systems by overloading them with routine network traffic. Interfering with the ships' systems would be unlawful but for the fact that it is an appropriate countermeasure.[65]

Finally, a third legal framework option a state might use for a response is referred to as the *plea of necessity*. If an essential interest of a state is subject to a grave and imminent peril, a state may respond.[66] Although the action taken would resemble a countermeasure (i.e., normally be unlawful), it would differ in that it would ordinarily be anticipatory.

Case Study: Stuxnet, 2009. The best documented event that clearly constituted a cyber attack is Stuxnet, a cyber attack against Iran's nuclear weapons program that destroyed about 1,000 nuclear centrifuges.[67] Malware specifically designed to target the brand and source of the industrial control system that operated the uranium enrichment facility at Natanz was able to bridge the air gap between the system and the Internet and wreak controlled havoc on the Iranian program.[68] The malware worked by causing the delicate centrifuges to change their rotation rate in a way that exceeded their design. Because the centrifuges were physically damaged, Stuxnet is generally considered to be an example of a cyber attack.

Of course, it is important to note that before any response action is completed, there must be attribution, an assignment of responsibility for the unfriendly activity. Most nefarious activity is designed to disguise the identity of the responsible actor. This can be done in various ways.[69] Fortunately, there is also a variety of technical means to discover who is responsible for carrying out cyber activity. The means may involve analyzing the malware for clues about the author or similarities to previous events. It might also analyze network traffic through a variety of means to discover the original source of the malware.[70]

Given that cyber operations can be launched by individuals acting alone, those sponsored by groups or states, or even by individuals who don't know their sponsor, attribution is rarely absolutely certain. While in some areas of law this might preclude taking action, in international law the standard is reasonableness.[71] If a state believes attribution is reasonably established, it may move forward to considering options.

International Norms in Cyberspace

Because states have been reluctant to agree on how the law applies to cyber operations, norms development has assumed a larger role in the discussion. Norms are "shared expectations among states about appropriate behavior."[72] The United Nations Group of Government Experts, of which the United States is a member, has suggested a series of norms that seem to have fairly widespread acceptance. They include

the following: States should not knowingly allow their territory to be used for internationally wrongful acts and should not conduct or knowingly damage or impair the use of critical infrastructure or the information systems of emergency response teams. States should also cooperate to assist in criminal investigations involving information and communications technologies (cyber).[73]

Although norms are not law, they do begin to define the behavior that might someday, through custom and practice, become international law. Because cyberspace is a new field of operations, states have seemed reluctant to agree to bind themselves legally. More flexible norms and other confidence building measures may be the best option available at this point.[74]

The *Jus in Bello*

Presuming that a state of hostilities already exists between states, the use of cyberspace operations as a tool of warfare will be regulated by a completely different body of law called the *jus in bello*. This body of law, most commonly referred to in the United States as the LOAC, regulates the conduct of the parties in all aspects of armed conflict.[75] Unlike the *jus ad bellum*, the corpus of the LOAC resides within a diversity of treaties, the most significant of which include the following:

- The Hague Convention (II) on War on the Laws and Customs of War on Land (1899);
- The Hague Convention (IV) on War on Land and Its Annexed Regulations (1907);
- The Geneva Convention (I) on Wounded and Sick in Armed Forces in the Field (1949);
- The Geneva Convention (II) on Wounded, Sick, and Shipwrecked at Sea (1949);
- The Geneva Convention (III) on Prisoners of War (1949);

- The Geneva Convention (IV) on Civilians (1949);
- The Additional Protocol (I) to the Geneva Conventions (1977); and
- The Additional Protocol (II) to the Geneva Conventions (1977).[76]

As can be seen, the majority of these treaties came into force more than a half-century ago, and the two Additional Protocols to the Geneva Conventions were promulgated while the Internet was still in its infancy. However, while there is no reference to cyberspace or to cyber warfare within any of the major treaties that compose the LOAC, the weight of opinion is that the principles enshrined within these treaties apply to cyberspace operations in the same way that they apply to other military capabilities. This is through the Martens Clause, proposed by Fyodor Fyodorovich Martens, the Russian delegate to the Hague Convention of 1899, which states that "until a more complete code of the laws of war is issued, the High Contracting Parties think it right to declare that in cases not included in the Regulations adopted by them, populations and belligerents remain under the protection and empire of the principles of international law, as they result from the usages established between civilized nations, from the laws of humanity and the requirements of the public conscience."[77] Similar clauses have been incorporated into every subsequent major LOAC treaty, and this fact has come to mean that the basic principles of the LOAC apply to all means and methods of warfare, regardless of whether they were foreseen in negotiating a particular treaty or not.[78]

What, then, are the basic principles of the LOAC that serve to restrain the use of cyberspace operations within armed conflict? For our purposes, we will discuss five such principles: military necessity, distinction, proportionality, humanity (or unnecessary suffering), and chivalry (or honor). Keep in mind that these principles only apply to cyberspace operations that qualify as "attacks," meaning those actions that have the tendency to result in damage or destruction to objects or injury or death to people.[79] This can make assessing cyber operations for legal compliance more challenging given that cyber capabilities can be used for mischief that does not rise to the level of an attack in the context of armed conflict, making the application of the principles of LOAC, such as distinction and proportionality, uncertain.[80] Disruptive activities might include power brownouts, DDoS, intermittent interruption of communications services, and so forth.[81] As long as these events do not physically damage equipment or injure anyone, they do not qualify as attacks as currently defined.[82] These occurrences have typically been dealt with as law enforcement issues.

Military necessity. The principle of military necessity, which can be found in Article 23(g) of the 1907 Hague Convention, simply requires that the means and methods of warfare used by a combatant to defeat the enemy as quickly and efficiently as possible not be otherwise prohibited by the LOAC.[83] For example, the principle of military necessity would justify those actions deemed inherently necessary by the nature of war, such as using a cyberspace operation to destroy or seize persons and property that are properly objects of attack.[84] Some commentators claim that the principle of military necessity means that only those actions that are actually necessary under the circumstances are permitted.[85] Under this formulation, even if an action is not specifically prohibited by the LOAC, it may still be unlawful if it is deemed to have been unnecessary. The United States has rejected this position as not properly reflecting the state of the law as contained within international treaties or state practice.[86]

Distinction. The principle of distinction, as codified in Article 48 of Additional Protocol (I) to the Geneva Conventions, requires that "the Parties to the conflict shall at all times distinguish between the civilian population and combatants and between civilian objects and military objectives and accordingly shall direct their operations only against military objectives."[87] Military objectives are those "objects which by their nature, location, purpose or use make an effective contribution to military action and whose total or partial destruction, capture or neutralization, in the circumstances ruling at the time, offers a definite military advantage."[88] This delineation is necessary to ensure that all parties have the respect due for civilians and their property, which are supposed to be protected as much as possible from the vagaries of war.[89]

In the cyber context, the application of the principle of distinction would prohibit cyber attacks capable of destroying enemy computer systems directed against ostensibly civilian infrastructure, such as computer systems belonging to stock exchanges, banking systems, and universities. However, many cyber assets are used for both military and civilian purposes, which can complicate the analysis. Such "dual-use" systems are lawful military objectives if they make an effective contribution to the enemy's warfighting efforts.[90] This increasing interconnection between military and civilian cyber infrastructure has rendered civilian systems potentially more at risk. Electrical grids, communications nodes, transportation systems—all are potentially lawful military targets. This is also an issue with kinetic operations, but the reach and scope of cyber capabilities increase the opportunity to actually carry out operations against such objects.

Case Study: Operation Orchard, 2007. Just before launching an air strike on Syrian nuclear facilities in 2007, Israel apparently used cyber techniques to reduce the effectiveness of Syrian air defenses, enabling their jets to carry out the mission unhindered. Integrated air defense systems are clearly valid military targets.[91]

The principle of distinction would also prohibit the use of cyber attacks against civilians. However, civilians who engage in attacks, including attacks of a cyber nature, are deemed to be "directly participating in hostilities," which consequently causes them to lose the protections generally accorded to civilians and become valid targets.[92] Interestingly, the general rule that civilians should not be used to engage in attacks can be difficult to apply in cyber operations.[93] The U.S. policy about which cyber activities amount to an attack is unclear, so determining which activities would qualify a civilian as directly participating in hostilities can be a challenge. Also, the issue with civilians participating in fighting is that they can compromise the safety of nonparticipating civilians. However, as the nature of cyber operations is such that they may be conducted from distant and secure locations, there is no practical additional danger to civilians caused by cyber operators launching cyber attacks. It is possible that civilians conducting cyber operations amounting to an attack could be subject to criminal prosecution either by the enemy or by an international tribunal.

Ultimately, although cyber attacks upon either dual-use objects or civilians directly participating in hostilities would not be prohibited by the principle of distinction, as with attacks on all other valid targets, such strikes still need to be tempered through the application of the principle of proportionality discussed below.

Finally, the principle of distinction would prohibit the use of indiscriminate cyber weapons that cannot be directed at a specific military objective or limited in their effects.[94] For example, combatants could not employ a cyber weapon that strikes randomly once employed and thus could just as easily strike a protected computer system as one constituting a valid military objective.[95] Combatants would also be prohibited from employing a type of malware that is capable of targeting specific military objectives but which, upon striking its objective, spreads uncontrollably and causes harm to purely civilian networks.[96]

Proportionality. The principle of proportionality finds its expression most clearly in Article 57(2)(iii) of Additional Protocol (I) to the Geneva Conventions, which states that parties to an armed conflict are to "refrain from deciding to launch any attack which may be expected to cause incidental loss of civilian life, injury to civilians, damage to civilian objects, or a combination thereof, which would be excessive in relation to the concrete and direct military advantage anticipated."[97] This principle recognizes that civilians and civilian objects, while generally protected from being made the direct object of attack, may, in some situations, be incidentally harmed by a strike conducted against a valid military target.[98] In such situations, however, those ordering a strike should remain mindful of the protections generally afforded civilians and civilian objects and thus take feasible measures to limit the collateral damage that attacks will generate.[99] In the cyber context, for example, it would be important when planning a cyberspace operation against a military computer system to assess the potential for damage to private civilian computers that hold no military significance but just happen to be networked to the military computers that will be struck.[100] In situations where collateral damage may be difficult to quantify or fully predict, the requirement is to consider all apparently reliable information reasonably available at the time.[101]

However, when examining the concept of proportionality in the context of a specific cyberspace operation, keep in mind the distinction between collateral damage and collateral effects. While cyberspace operations may result in death or destruction—collateral damage—that must be taken into account when calculating the proportionality of a strike, cyberspace operations may also result in nondestructive collateral effects, such as inconvenience, irritation, stress, or fear, which need not be considered when determining whether a particular attack was proportional.[102] For example, a minor, brief disruption of Internet services to civilians might result incidentally from a cyber attack against a military objective. The inconvenience caused by this disruption would be a collateral effect that would not need to be measured and compared against the military advantage gained for purposes of a proportionality analysis.[103]

Humanity. The principle of humanity (also known as the principle of unnecessary suffering) is codified in Article 35(2) of Additional Protocol (I) to the Geneva Conventions. Under this provision, parties to a conflict are prohibited from employing "weapons, projectiles, and material and methods of warfare of a nature to cause superfluous injury or unnecessary suffering."[104] Basically, one may only inflict the amount of suffering that is absolutely necessary to accomplish a military objective. Any suffering above and beyond that is inhumane.[105] This principle is most often used to prohibit the use of weapons that are crafted in such a way as to create suffering above and beyond that which is necessary or to prohibit the use of otherwise legal weapons in ways that are calculated to cause such an unnecessary amount of suffering.[106] In the cyber context, for example, if an enemy combatant has an Internet-addressable pacemaker device with a built-in defibrillator, it would be lawful to take control of the pacemaker to kill him or to otherwise take him out of the fight. However, it would be unlawful to conduct the operation in a manner that is intended to cause additional pain and suffering for his own sake, such as stopping his heart and reviving him multiple times before killing him.[107]

In order to ensure compliance with the principle of avoiding unnecessary suffering, the DOD requires a legal review of all weapons before the military is permitted to use them.[108] The DOD's requirement to review weapons predates Additional Protocol I, but the rule observed by other legally compliant states is Article 36 of the protocol. The DOD, in its reviews, ensures that its weapons are not inherently indiscriminate and that they are not calculated to cause superfluous injury. Additionally, the DOD ensures its weapons are in compliance with specific treaties, such as those banning poisoned and biological weapons.[109]

Reviews of kinetic weapons are relatively straightforward; they may involve test firing weapons and field tests. Cyber weapons, on the other hand, are not only difficult to review but also difficult to even define.[110] On the contrary, cyber *methods* of warfare are susceptible to review, and methods of warfare, although less often discussed, are also addressed in the prohibition of unnecessary suffering. Terrorism, starvation, and perfidy (discussed below) are all examples of prohibited means of warfare.[111] For example, as discussed above, methods of cyber warfare that are indiscriminately destructive are unlawful, including the random distribution of malware that damages physical computer components. Of course, the military utility of such a method of warfare seems relatively limited. As technology advances, legal advisors will need to be ready to review new methods for compliance.

The *DOD Law of War Manual* provides little guidance to practitioners regarding the legal review of cyber weapons. It merely notes that "[n]ot all cyber capabilities . . . constitute a weapon or weapons system" and then directs readers to regulations of the various services.[112] Unfortunately, the services have not been especially forward leaning in defining cyber weapons.

The Air Force is the first, and to date only, service to regulate the issue specifically. Air Force Instruction (AFI) 51-402, *Legal Reviews of Weapons and Cyber Capabilities*, defines weapons as "devices designed to kill, injure, disable or temporarily incapacitate people, or destroy, damage or temporarily incapacitate property or materiel."[113] Generally, it is computer code or hacking techniques that form the basis of a cyber attack. Much less often does a cyber attack involve a physical device. So, most of the time, the instrumentality of a cyber attack will not qualify as a cyber weapon under the Air Force's

formulation. The instruction addresses this gap with the term "cyber capability." A cyber capability is "any device or software payload intended to disrupt, deny, degrade, negate, impair or destroy adversarial computer systems, data, activities or capabilities."[114] The definition of cyber capability goes on to exclude "a device or software that is solely intended to provide access to an adversarial computer system for data exploitation."[115]

Once something is defined as a cyber capability (and not intended for espionage), a rigorous requirement for legal review attaches. The Air Force requires that "all cyber capabilities being developed, bought, built, modified or otherwise acquired by the Air Force . . . are reviewed for legality under LOAC, domestic law and international law prior to their acquisition for use in a conflict or other military operation."[116] On its face, this provision requires a new legal review every time a line of code is modified. As this could happen dozens of times during the course of a single operation, and would happen thousands of times during the development process, how the Air Force will actually administer the requirement is unclear.

The *Tallinn Manual* takes a different approach, in that it appears to put more responsibility on the operational legal advisor to ensure compliance with the law, recognizing the speed at which operations may proceed.[117] The *Tallinn Manual* also excludes any requirement for a new review when code is changed in a minor or insignificant way. Finally, the *Tallinn Manual* does not exempt capabilities from legal review based on the motivation behind their intended use but rather focuses on the effect of the capability in the operational context.[118]

Honor. The principle of honor (also known as chivalry) stands for the proposition that the application of the weapons of war should be tempered by "a certain amount of fairness in offense and defense and a certain mutual respect between opposing forces."[119] Basically, as expressed in Article 35(1) of Additional Protocol (I) to the Geneva Conventions, the principle of honor is an explicit recognition that "in any armed conflict, the right of the Parties to the conflict to choose methods or means of warfare is not unlimited."[120] Most commonly, honor prohibits killing, injuring, or capturing an adversary through acts of perfidy, defined in Article 37(1) of Additional Protocol (I) to the Geneva Conventions as "acts inviting the confidence of an adversary to lead him to believe that he is entitled to, or is obliged to accord, protection under the rules of international law applicable in armed conflict, with intent to betray that confidence."[121] The rationale is that such actions would potentially

- Undermine or dilute the effectiveness of the protections afforded by the LOAC,
- Impair the ability of the parties to interact in a nonhostile way, such as through diplomatic negotiations, and
- Damage the basis for the restoration of peace short of the total destruction of one party by another.[122]

For example, in the cyber context, the principle of honor or chivalry would prohibit the use of e-mail to invite the enemy to a meeting with a representative of the International Committee of the Red Cross (an internationally recognized protected symbol) with intent to lead enemy forces into an ambush.[123]

The principle of honor is not intended to prohibit all types of military deception. Article 37(2) of Additional Protocol (I) to the Geneva Conventions expressly allows ruses of war, which are "acts which are intended to mislead an adversary or to induce him to act recklessly but which infringe no rule of international law applicable in armed conflict and which are not perfidious because they do not invite the confidence of an adversary with respect to protection under that law."[124] In the cyber context, such lawful ruses would include the creation of a dummy computer system simulating nonexistent forces, transmission

of false information causing an opponent erroneously to believe operations are about to occur or are under way, bogus orders purported to have been issued by the enemy commander, etc.[125]

In any event, application of this principle in cyberspace may be especially difficult, as the notion of honor in long-range combat is already strained. It seems almost quaint that in cyber warfare, from thousands of miles away, where foes are effectively reduced to electrons and icons on a computer screen, a notion of fair play would be part of the combat equation. Nevertheless, it is included in the *Law of War Manual*.

One particular oddity in the *Law of War Manual*'s discussion of honor is its assertion that there is an obligation to avoid inconvenience to civilians, but only in the case of cyber operations. "[E]ven if a cyber operation is not an 'attack' or does not cause any injury or damage that would need to be considered under the proportionality rule, that cyber operation still should not be conducted in a way that unnecessarily causes inconvenience to civilians or neutral persons."[126] It is not clear why the DOD included this language in the cyber operations chapter when inconvenience isn't a consideration in warfare, as noted elsewhere in the *Law of War Manual*.[127] The principles apply during times of war, when causing death and destruction is lawful, at least under the appropriate circumstances. Under these conditions, the attention due avoiding mere inconvenience is *de minimis*.

Case Study: Republic of Georgia, 2008. The most straightforward use of cyber warfare is when cyber activity is taken in conjunction with kinetic action, and the best known example of this occurred in 2008 when Russia invaded the Republic of Georgia. Concurrent with the movement of Russian troops into South Ossetia (the region of Georgia Russia targeted), the majority of websites in the region were taken down. Additionally, cyber attacks took down Georgian government websites at the same time.[128]

Electronic Warfare[129]

Electronic warfare (EW) has generally been considered separately from cyber warfare, but there is a trend toward combining the two disciplines. This is being driven by a recognition that both areas rely on the electromagnetic spectrum to some extent and that maintaining a false separation is illogical and potentially detrimental to operations in both areas. Unlike cyber warfare, EW has a long history of doctrine and practice that enables it to operate as an integral part of kinetic operations. For example, an airstrike would not be routed over contested territory without suppressing enemy air defenses, which can be an EW mission.

Cyber Espionage and Intelligence Gathering

International Law

It is well established that states commonly use cyberspace to conduct espionage activities against other states and nonstate groups.[130] When used within the context of an armed conflict, espionage activities are permitted, subject to limitations imposed by the LOAC, such as the prohibition on acts of perfidy.[131] Outside of armed conflicts, however, espionage is neither expressly condoned nor condemned by international law.[132] In fact, despite the fact that espionage has been commonly used to gather information since biblical times, there has been little international effort to determine what the limits on acceptable espionage might be or even to note its international legality.[133] States have seemed satisfied to pass domestic legislation prohibiting espionage activities conducted against them, while simultaneously dedicating much time, effort, and resources to conducting espionage against others, both friend and foe.[134] It is clear that in the absence of a direct prohibition in international law on espionage per se, cyber espionage would not rise to the level of use of force under the *jus ad bellum* legal framework discussed earlier.[135]

Although the rule, or lack of rules, is straightforward, the application in cyberspace can be difficult. In physical space, it is generally easy to distinguish espionage and more aggressive action. Traditional combatants wear uniforms and carry weapons openly, and someone using kinetic weapons to wound or kill is unlikely to be mistaken for a spy because the activities are just too different.

Cyber espionage, on the other hand, could easily be mistaken for aggressive activity. Obtaining unauthorized access to a computer or network, elevating privileges from user to administrator, viewing system files, and installing malware for persistent access are examples of activities that would be undertaken in both cyber espionage and in cyber attack operations. This ambiguity has the potential to create confusion over whether a particular cyber operation should be considered aggressive or a use of force. Consequently, the traditional international law position that ignores espionage may not be tenable in cyberspace in the long run.

The United States has long felt that cyber espionage with the purpose of stealing industrial information for profit should be treated less favorably than espionage for national security. There has historically been little support for this position, but in 2015, China, whose cyber-espionage activities are often pointed out as the primary reason for U.S. concerns in the area, appeared to give some ground on the issue. The United States and China agreed that neither country's government would conduct or support cyber-enabled theft of intellectual property with the intent of providing competitive advantage to private companies.[136] There are concerns that Chinese behavior will not change, but even its recognition of a separate class of espionage might be seen as a victory of sorts for the U.S. position.

Case Study: Operation Buckshot Yankee, 2008. In 2008 the DOD's classified military computer networks were compromised by malware. A flash drive preloaded with targeted malware was inserted into a military laptop at a base in Southwest Asia. The malicious code spread from US Central Command's computer network across the DOD information network, infecting both classified and unclassified computers. The purpose of the malware was to discover what information was available on the network, report back to its controller, and then exfiltrate desired information. The DOD concluded the malware was distributed by a foreign intelligence agency.[137]

Operation Buckshot Yankee is an example of an operation that doesn't rise to the level of a use of force or armed attack but is rather an effective demonstration of the value of cyber techniques as tools of espionage. Another example is the Office of Personnel Management hack of 2015, which resulted in the exfiltration of the personal data of millions of individuals who hold security clearances in the United States.[138]

Domestic Law

It should be noted up front that intelligence law is a very specialized area of practice. Legal advisors who do not work in the area regularly should consult with those who do before rendering advice. Classification issues and the large number of organizations involved in the area make it a potentially treacherous field for lawyers.

In the United States, the ability of an intelligence agency to gather intelligence is restrained by laws designed to safeguard the privacy and constitutional rights of Americans.[139] For purposes of intelligence gathering by the DOD, the principal sources of law in this arena are Executive Order 12333, *United States Intelligence Activities*; DOD Directive 5240.01, *DOD Intelligence Activities*; and DOD 5240.1-R, *Procedures Governing the Activities of DOD Intelligence Components*.

The intelligence oversight rules contained within the above documents only apply when members of U.S. intelligence components attempt to collect information

on U.S. persons.[140] For purposes of these procedures, information is deemed to be "collected" only when it has been received for use by an employee of an intelligence component in the course of his or her official duties.[141] Data collected by electronic means is "collected" only when it has been processed into intelligible form. A "U.S. person" is any one of the following: a U.S. citizen; an alien known by the DOD intelligence component concerned to be a permanent resident alien; an unincorporated association substantially composed of U.S. citizens or permanent resident aliens; or a corporation incorporated in the United States, except for a corporation directed and controlled by a foreign government or governments.[142]

Persons or organizations outside the United States are presumed to not be U.S. persons unless specific information to the contrary is received. Also, aliens in the United States are not presumed to be U.S. persons unless specific information to the contrary is received.[143]

In order for a member of an intelligence component to collect information on a U.S. person, that collection must be a necessary aspect of the mission assigned the collecting component, and the information collected must be within one or more of the following categories: information obtained with consent, publicly available information, foreign intelligence, counterintelligence, potential sources of assistance to intelligence activities, protection of intelligence sources and methods, physical security, personnel security, communications security, narcotics, threats to safety, overhead reconnaissance, or administrative purposes.[144]

Collection of foreign intelligence information by DOD components by means of electronic surveillance is subject to additional restrictions. For example, electronic surveillance for foreign intelligence and counterintelligence purposes may normally be conducted in the United States only pursuant to an order issued by the Foreign Intelligence Surveillance Court, and electronic surveillance for foreign intelligence and counterintelligence purposes may normally only be conducted outside the United States pursuant to the approval of the U.S. attorney general.[145] Although DOD 5240.1-R also briefly discusses procedures for conducting signals intelligence, most information dealing with signals intelligence is limited to a classified annex promulgated by the director of the National Security Agency.[146]

U.S. Public Policy on Cyber Warfare

Perhaps more than other areas of DOD practice, U.S. cyber operations are affected by internal government policies and are scrutinized by an intensive interagency review process.[147] This may be because the law in the area is unsettled. Unfortunately, there are only a few public documents relevant to the U.S. view of the international law applicable to cyber warfare. The primary ones are the *International Strategy for Cyberspace* (2011), the legal advisor Harold Koh's speech at the U.S. Cyber Command Legal Conference (2012), and the *DOD Cyber Strategy* (2015).[148]

There is also a chapter on cyber operations in the *DOD Law of War Manual*, but as discussed earlier, it contains little of note. It leans heavily on Koh's speech and adds nothing new, making it necessary to turn elsewhere for more comprehensive guidance. For example, the DOD *Law of War Manual* cyber chapter notes that none of the following would constitute a cyber attack during armed conflict: defacing government web pages; briefly disrupting Internet service in a minor way; briefly disrupting, disabling, or interfering with communications; or disseminating propaganda. These examples are so obvious and limited that they are of little use to legal practitioners in the field.

Turning now to the earliest and broadest of the current U.S. policy documents, the *International Strategy for Cyberspace* is largely an aspirational list of

how things ought to be with cyber operations and international relations relevant to cyberspace. It does, however, provide a useful statement of U.S. policy: "When warranted, the United States will respond to hostile acts in cyberspace as we would to any other threat to our country."[149] This statement, although carefully ambiguous, makes clear that there is a point at which the United States will consider cyber aggression the equivalent of a traditional kinetic attack, earning an aggressive cyber—or even kinetic—response.

The *DOD Cyber Strategy* of 2015 is an update of its 2011 strategy. The original document was almost entirely defensive; the 2015 version offers a bit more of interest to LOAC practitioners. For one thing, it is reportedly the first document in which the United States publicly says cyber warfare is an option for the military in future conflicts. It notes that "the U.S. military may conduct cyber operations to counter an imminent or on-going attack against the U.S. homeland or U.S. interests in cyberspace" and further indicates the military might use cyber operations to terminate an ongoing conflict on U.S. terms to prevent the use of force against U.S. interests or to deter or defeat strategic threats in other domains.[150] Also of interest, the strategy lists "military-related" critical infrastructure as a potential target of cyber operations.[151]

Some other documents that may be of interest to legal advisors include the *National Response Framework* (*Cyber Annex*),[152] the draft *National Cyber Incident Response Plan*,[153] and the memorandum of agreement between the DOD and the DHS regarding cybersecurity.[154]

Conclusion

Cyberspace and the activities that occur in cyberspace continue to grow in importance and complexity. Most state actions in cyberspace are carried out in secret, and states appear to have little interest in agreeing to new treaty law or specific norms of behavior. As a result, cyber operations will continue to be a law-intensive subject, requiring the work of attorneys with deep and broad knowledge of the area as well as an ability to adapt quickly to changing situations. This essay serves as a basic starting point and reference, but in this ever-changing field, continual research is required to remain current.

Notes

This reading was previously published in *An Airman's Guide to Cyberpower*, http://www.airuniversity.af.mil/CyberCollege/Portal/Article/Article/1238536/cyberlaw-and-policy.

1 Steven Metz and James Kievit, *Strategy and the Revolution in Military Affairs: From Theory to Policy* (Carlisle, PA: Strategic Studies Institute, 27 June 1995), http://www.strategicstudiesinstitute.army.mil/pdffiles/PUB236.pdf.

2 See discussion on the notion of attack, *infra*.

3 Department of Defense (DOD) Directive 2311.01E, *DOD Law of War Program*, 22 February 2011, para. 4, http://www.dtic.mil/whs/directives/corres/pdf/231101e.pdf.

4 In *Bernstein v. United States Department of Justice*, in which report, 9th Circuit, 1999, the court protected the dissemination of computer code under the First Amendment.

5 H. Marshall Jarrett and Michael W. Bailie, *Prosecuting Computer Crimes* (Washington, DC: Office of Legal Education Executive Office for United States Attorneys, 2011), 1.

6 18 USC § 1030(a)(1).

7 18 USC § 1030(a)(2).

8 18 USC § 1030(a)(3).

9 18 USC § 1030(a)(4).

10 18 USC § 1030(a)(5).

11 18 USC § 1030(a)(6).

12 18 USC § 1030(a)(7).

13 Jarrett and Bailie, *Prosecuting Computer Crimes*, 59.

14 18 USC § 2511(1)(a).

15 18 USC § 2511(1)(c).

16 18 USC § 2511(1)(d).

17 18 USC § 2701(a).

18 18 USC § 1028(a)(7).

19 18 USC § 1028A.

20 18 USC § 1029.

21 18 USC § 1343.

22 Jarrett and Bailie, *Prosecuting Computer Crimes*, 110.

23 18 USC § 1362.

24 The White House, "Securing Cyberspace—President Obama Announces New Cybersecurity Legislative Proposal and Other Cybersecurity Efforts," White House, 13 January 2015, https://www.whitehouse.gov/the-press-office/2015/01/13/securing-cyberspace-president-obama-announces-new-cybersecurity-legislat.

25 Kristin Archick, *Cybercrime: The Council of Europe Convention* (Washington, DC: Congressional Research Service, 2004), 2.

26 U.S. Department of State, *Convention on Cybercrime*, Treaties and Other International Acts 13174, 1 July 2004, 13174, Articles 7–10.

27 Ibid., Articles 14–22.

28 Ibid., Articles 23–34.

29 Council of Europe Treaty Office, "Chart of Signatures and Ratifications of Treaty 185: Convention on Cybercrime," Council of Europe, 19 October 2015, http://www.coe.int/en/web/conventions/full-list/-/conventions/treaty/185/signatures?p_auth=WRdndSqa.

30 Council of Europe Treaty Office, "Details of Treaty No. 189: Additional Protocol to the Convention on Cybercrime, Concerning the Criminalization of Acts of a Racist and Xenophobic Nature Committed through Computer Systems," Council of Europe, accessed 5 November 2015, http://www.coe.int/en/web/conventions/full-list/-/conventions/treaty/189.

31 Additional Protocol to the Convention on Cybercrime, Concerning the Criminalization of Acts of a Racist and Xenophobic Nature Committed through Computer Systems, 28 January 2003, Articles 3–6.

32 Council of Europe Treaty Office, "Chart of Signatures and Ratifications of Treaty 189: Additional Protocol to the Convention on Cybercrime, Concerning the Criminalization of Acts of a Racist and Xenophobic Nature Committed through Computer Systems," 19 October 2015, http://www.coe.int/en/web/conventions/full-list/-/conventions/treaty/189/signatures?p_auth=WRdndSqa.

33 Archick, *Cybercrime*, 2–3.

34 William Gibson, *Neuromancer* (New York: Ace Books, 1984).

35 JP 1-02, Department of Defense Dictionary of Military and Associated Terms (as amended through 15 October 2015).

36 For example, the Congressional Research Service defined *cyberspace* as "the total interconnectedness of human beings through computers and telecommunication without regard to physical geography." Steven A. Hildreth, "Cyberwarfare," report for Congress, 19 June 2001, https://www.fas.org/sgp/crs/intel/RL30735.pdf.

37 See, for example, Michael Chertoff, "The Strategic Significance of the Internet Commons," *Strategic Studies Quarterly* 8, no. 2 (Summer 2014), http://www.au.af.mil/au/ssq/digital/pdf/summer_2014/chertoff.pdf.

38 Jaikumar Vijayan, "US Tops List of Countries Hosting Malware and Botnets," *Security Intelligence*, 18 November 2014, https://securityintelligence.com/news/us-tops-list-of-countries-hosting-malware-and-botnets.

39 An excellent treatment of the application of the noninterventional principle in a cyber context is Ashley Deeks, "The Geography of Cyber Conflict: Through a Glass Darkly," *International Law Studies* 89 (2013): 1, http://stockton.usnwc.edu/cgi/viewcontent.cgi?article=1043&context=ils.

40 *Internet Encyclopedia of Philosophy*, s.v. "Just War Theory," accessed 5 November 2015, http://www.iep.utm.edu/justwar.

41 Yoram Dinstein, *War, Aggression and Self-Defence* (Cambridge: Cambridge University Press, 2001), 71–80.

42 Ibid., 80.

43 Charter of the United Nations, 26 June 1945, Article 2(4), http://www.un.org/en/sections/un-charter/chapter-i/index.html.

44 Ibid., Articles 39–50, http://www.un.org/en/sections/un-charter/chapter-vii/index.html.

45 Ibid., Article 51, http://www.un.org/en/sections/un-charter/chapter-vii/index.html.

46 Dinstein, *War, Aggression and Self-Defence*, 165–68.

47 UN General Assembly, Resolution 3314 (XXIX), "Definition of Aggression," 14 December 1974, http://legal.un.org/avl/ha/da/da.html.

48 Michael N. Schmitt, ed., *Tallinn Manual on the International Law Applicable to Cyber Warfare* (Cambridge: Cambridge University Press, 2013), 55, https://issuu.com/nato_ccd_coe/docs/tallinnmanual/75?e=0/1803379.

49 *Republic of Nicaragua v. United States of America*, in *International Court of Justice Reports*, 27 June 1986, 101–4, http://www.icj-cij.org/docket/files/70/6503.pdf.

50 Matthew C. Waxman, "Cyber Attacks and the Use of Force: Back to the Future of Article 2(4)," *Yale Journal of International Law* 36, no. 42 (2011): 438, http://dx.doi.org/10.2139/ssrn.1674565.

51 Legality of the Threat or Use of Nuclear Weapons, Advisory Opinion, in *International Court of Justice Reports* (1996), 244.

52 President, *International Strategy for Cyberspace: Prosperity, Security, and Openness in a Networked World* (Washington, DC: White House, 2011), 10, https://www.whitehouse.gov/sites/default/files/rss_viewer/internationalstrategy_cyberspace.pdf.

53 Harold Hongju Koh, "International Law in Cyberspace" (address, USCYBERCOM Inter-Agency Legal Conference, Fort Meade, MD, 18 September 2012).

54 The resulting *Tallinn Manual* identifies international law applicable to cyber warfare and sets out 95 rules with accompanying commentary. It represents the opinion of the international group of experts who drafted it and isn't necessarily reflective of the positions of NATO or any member state.

55 Schmitt, *Tallinn Manual*, 48.

56 Koh, "International Law in Cyberspace."

57 DOD General Counsel, *Department of Defense Law of War Manual*, 12 June 2015, 998.

58 Schmitt, *Tallinn Manual*, 48.

59 Ibid., 48–51.

60 Koh, "International Law in Cyberspace."

61 Eneken Tikk, Kadri Kaska, and Liis Vihul, *International Cyber Incidents: Legal Considerations* (Tallinn, Estonia: Cooperative Cyber Defence Centre of Excellence, 2010), 15–25.

62 Ibid., 25–26.

63 *Tallinn Manual*, rule 9, comment 13.

64 *Tallinn Manual*, rule 9, comment 2.

65 For a discussion of countermeasures in cyber, see Geoffrey Corn, Rachel E. VanLandingham, and Shane R. Reeves, eds., *U.S. Military Operations: Law, Policy, and Practice* (Oxford: Oxford University Press, 2015), 139–46.

66 UN General Assembly, Resolution 56/83, Responsibility of States for Intentionally Wrongful Acts, Article 25, 12 December 2001, http://legal.un.org/ilc/texts/instruments/english/draft_articles/9_6_2001.pdf.

67 There are at least two other examples of destructive attacks, including the following: a 2014 cyber attack on a German steel plant that gained access to the industrial control system and caused a blast furnace to explode. R. A. Becker, "Cyber Attack on German Steel Mill Leads to 'Massive' Real World Damage," *Nova Next*, 8 January 2015, http://www.pbs.org/wgbh/nova/next/tech/cyber-attack-german-steel-mill-leads-massive-real-world-damage. The other was a cyber attack on an oil pipeline in Turkey in 2008 that disabled sensors and over-pressurized the oil to cause an explosion. Jordan Robertson and Michael Riley, "Mysterious '08 Turkey Pipeline Blast Opened New Cyberwar," *Bloomberg Business*, 10 December 2014, http://www.bloomberg.com/news/articles/2014-12-10/mysterious-08-turkey-pipeline-blast-opened-new-cyberwar. Neither of these events is as well documented as Stuxnet.

68 Kim Zetter, *Countdown to Zero Day* (New York: Broadway Books, 2014).

69 One popular method of masking identity on the Internet is through the use of TOR (The Onion Router). See https://en.wikipedia.org/wiki/Tor, accessed 4 December 2015.

70 Neil C. Rowe, "The Attribution of Cyber Warfare," in James A. Green, ed., *Cyber Warfare: A Multidisciplinary Analysis* (New York: Routledge, 2015), 61–72.

71 Monroe Leigh, "Kenneth B. Yeager v. The Islamic Republic of Iran," *American Journal of International Law* 82, no. 2 (April 1988): 353–62, http://www.jstor.org/stable/2203199.

72 Roger Hurwitz, senior rapporteur, *A Call to Cyber Norms* (March 2015), 1.

73 Report of the Group of Governmental Experts on Developments in the Field of Information and Telecommunications in the Context of International Security (22 July 2015), http://www.un.org/ga/search/view_doc.asp?symbol=A/70/174.

74 Paul Meyer, "Another Year, Another GGE? The Slow Process of Norm Building for Cyberspace," IC for Peace Foundation, August 2015, http://ict4peace.org/wp-content/uploads/2015/09/CyberG-GEICT4PCommentAug2015aa.pdf.

75 International Committee of the Red Cross (ICRC), *International Humanitarian Law: Answers to Your Questions* (Geneva: ICRC, 2014), 8, https://www.icrc.org/en/publication/0703-international-humanitarian-law-answers-your-questions.

76 Ibid., 14–15.

77 Rupert Ticehurst, "The Martens Clause and the Laws of Armed Conflict," ICRC, 30 April 1997, https://www.icrc.org/eng/resources/documents/misc/57jnhy.htm.

78 Ibid.

79 Schmitt, *Tallinn Manual*, 106–7.

80 See, for example, William H. Boothby, *The Law of Targeting* (Oxford: Oxford University Press, 2012), 370: "Issues of proportionality do not of course arise where there is no attack"; and *DOD Law of War Manual*, para. 16.5.1: "If a cyber operation constitutes an attack [it] must comport with the requirements of distinction and proportionality."

81 Gary D. Brown and Owen W. Tullos, "On the Spectrum of Cyber Operations," *Small Wars Journal*, 11 December 2012, http://smallwarsjournal.com/print/13595.

82 The clearest definition is found in the *Tallinn Manual*, Rule 30. DOD's position in the *Law of War Manual* (para. 16.5.1) is vague but appears to be consonant with the *Tallinn* formulation.

83 DOD General Counsel, *DOD Law of War Manual*, 52.

84 Ibid., 52–53.

85 Gary G. Solis, *The Law of Armed Conflict: International Humanitarian Law in War* (Cambridge: Cambridge University Press, 2010), 258.

86 DOD General Counsel, *DOD Law of War Manual*, 57.

87 Protocol Additional to the Geneva Conventions of 12 August 1949, and Relating to the Protection of Victims of International Armed Conflicts (Protocol I) (8 June 1977), Article 48.

88 Additional Protocol I, Article 52(2).

89 ICRC, International Humanitarian Law, 47.

90 Rule 8, *ICRC Customary International Humanitarian Law Study*, accessed 8 November 2015, https://www.icrc.org/customary-ihl/eng/docs/v1_cha_chapter2_rule8.

91 Jason Rivera, "A Theory of Cyberwarfare: Political and Military Objectives, Lines

of Communication, and Targets," *Georgetown Security Studies Review*, 10 June 2014, http://georgetownsecuritystudiesreview.org/2014/06/10/a-theory-of-cyberwarfare-political-and-military-objectives-lines-of-communication-and-targets.

92 Ibid., 118–22.

93 "Combat operations" are considered an inherently governmental function performable only by military personnel, according to DOD Instruction 1100.22, *Policy & Procedures for Determining Workforce Mix*, encl. 4, ¶ 1(c)(1) (12 April 2010). For a discussion of some of the issues surrounding civilians engaging in combat, see Joshua P. Nauman, "Civilians on the Battlefield: By Using U.S. Civilians in the War on Terror, Is the Pot Calling the Kettle Black?," *Nebraska Law Review* 91, no. 2 (2013), http://digitalcommons.unl.edu/cgi/viewcontent.cgi?article=1176&context=nlr.

94 Ibid., 145–46.

95 Ibid.

96 Ibid.

97 Protocol Additional to the Geneva Conventions of 12 August 1949, and Relating to the Protection of Victims of International Armed Conflicts (Protocol I), 8 June 1977, Article 57(2)(iii).

98 Solis, *Law of Armed Conflict*, 274.

99 Ibid.

100 DOD General Counsel, *DOD Law of War Manual*, 1004.

101 *Tallinn Manual*, rule 51, para. 10.

102 Schmitt, *Tallinn Manual*, 160.

103 DOD General Counsel, *DOD Law of War Manual*, 1004.

104 Protocol Additional to the Geneva Conventions of 12 August 1949, and Relating to the Protection of Victims of International Armed Conflicts (Protocol I), 8 June 1977, Article 35(2).

105 The noble but somewhat vague concept of "unnecessary suffering" can be difficult to apply in kinetic contexts; applying it to cyber activities is downright daunting. In the virtual world itself, few actions rise to the level of suffering. Suffering would seem to require a physical or psychological effect; "injury" might have been a better term to capture the intent of the provision.

106 ICRC, *International Humanitarian Law*, 48.

107 Schmitt, *Tallinn Manual*, 143–44.

108 DODD 5000.01, *The Defense Acquisition System*, 20 November 2007, para. E1.1.15.

109 DOD *Law of War Manual*, para. 6.4.

110 Gary D. Brown and Andrew O. Metcalf, "Easier Said Than Done: Legal Reviews of Cyber Weapons," *Journal of National Security Law & Policy* 7 (2014): 115, http://jnslp.com/wp-content/uploads/2014/02/Easier-Said-than-Done.pdf.

111 Suffering would seem to require a physical or psychological effect, and some experts have suggested "injury" would have been a better term to capture the intent.

112 *DOD Law of War Manual*, para. 16.6.

113 AFI 51-402, *Legal Reviews of Weapons and Cyber Capabilities*, 27 July 2011, 6.

114 Ibid., 5.

115 Ibid. This appears to be an indication of a level of discomfort in logically distinguishing between military operations and espionage.

116 Ibid., para. 1.1.2.

117 *Tallinn Manual*, rule 48.

118 Ibid., para. 8–9.

119 DOD General Counsel, *DOD Law of War Manual*, 66.

120 Protocol Additional to the Geneva Conventions of 12 August 1949, and Relating to the Protection of Victims of International Armed Conflicts (Protocol I), 8 June 1977, Article 35(1).

121 Ibid., Article 37(1).

122 DOD General Counsel, *DOD Law of War Manual*, 67.

123 Schmitt, *Tallinn Manual*, 181.

124 Protocol Additional to the Geneva Conventions of 12 August 1949, and Relating to the Protection of Victims of International Armed Conflicts (Protocol I), 8 June 1977, Article 37(2).

125 Schmitt, *Tallinn Manual*, 184–85.

126 *DOD Law of War Manual*, 1005.

127 Ibid., 242, footnote 306.

128 Jeffrey Carr, ed., *Inside Cyber Warfare*, 2nd ed. (Sebastopol, CA: O'Reilly Media, 2012), 17.

129 DOD defines electronic warfare as "[m]ilitary action involving the use of electromagnetic and directed energy to control the electromagnetic spectrum or to attack the enemy." Joint Publication 1-02, *Department of Defense Dictionary of Military and Associated Terms*, 15 October 2015.

130 DOD General Counsel, *DOD Law of War Manual*, 999.

131 Schmitt, *Tallinn Manual*, 193–94.

132 Daniel B. Silver, Frederick P. Hitz, and J. E. Shreve Ariail, "Chapter 20: Intelligence and Counterintelligence," in *National Security Law*, 2nd edition, ed. John Norton Moore

and Robert F. Turner (Durham, NC: Carolina Academic Press, 2005), 965.

133 Ibid.

134 Ibid.

135 Schmitt, *Tallinn Manual*, 50.

136 White House Fact Sheet, *President Xi Jinping's State Visit to the United States*, 25 September 2015, https://www.whitehouse. gov/the-press-office/2015/09/25/fact-sheet-president-xi-jinpings-state-visit-united-states.

137 Ellen Nakashima, "Defense Official Discloses Cyberattack," *Washington Post*, 24 August 2010, http://www.washington-post.com/wp-dyn/content/article/2010/08/24/AR2010082406495.html.   Operation Buckshot Yankee was a motivation behind the 2009 U.S. decision to establish USCYBERCOM.

138 David E. Sanger and Julie Hirschfeld Davis, "Hacking Linked to China Exposes Millions of U.S. Workers," *New York Times*, 4 June 2015, http://www.nytimes.com/2015/06/05/us/breach-in-a-federal-computer-system-exposes-personnel-data.html?_r=0.

139 DOD 5240.1-R, *Procedures Governing the Activities of DOD Intelligence Components That Affect United States Persons*, December 1982, 13.

140 Ibid., 15.

141 Ibid.

142 Ibid.

143 Ibid.

144 Ibid., 16–18.

145 Ibid., 24–25.

146 Ibid., 29.

147 U.S. Senate, "Advance Questions for Vice Adm Michael S. Rogers, USN, Nominee for Commander, United States Cyber Command," 11 March 2014, http://www. americanrhetoric.com/speeches/PDFFiles/ advanceqsadmrogers031114.pdf.

148 DOD, *The DOD Cyber Strategy*, April 2015, http://www.defense.gov/Portals/1/ features/2015/0415_cyber-strategy/Final_ 2015_DoD_CYBER_STRATEGY_for_ web.pdf.

149 *International Strategy for Cyberspace*, 2011, 14, http://www.whitehouse.gov/sites/ default/files/rss_viewer/international_ strategy_for_cyberspace.pdf.

150 *DOD Cyber Strategy*, 5.

151 Ibid., 14.

152 *National Response Framework Cyber Annex*, Federal Emergency Management Agency, FEMA.gov, accessed 1 November 2015, https://www.fema.gov/media-library/ assets/documents/25556.

153 *National Cyber Incident Response Plan*, draft, accessed 7 November 2016, https://www.us-cert.gov/sites/default/files/ncirp/NE%20 DRAFT%20NATIONAL%20CYBER%20 INCIDENT%20RESPONSE%20PLAN%20 20160930.pdf.

154 Department of Homeland Security to DOD, Memorandum of Agreement, accessed 1 November 2015, http://www.acq.osd.mil/ mibp/dpac/DOD-DHS%20Memorandum %20of%20Agreement%20Sept%202011.pdf.

North Korean Cyber

Adam Albarado

Proponents of cyber as an effective tool of statecraft argue such attacks are ethical because cyber weapons are able to specifically target certain systems to produce desired effects.[1] Opponents of such claims argue that there are too many limitations to its usage for cyber to be truly effective.[2] The reality is that cyber is most effective as an element of statecraft when used in conjunction with a whole-of-government approach to coercion or deterrence where the state maintains escalation dominance. Such capability normally resides with the stronger state. Yet weak states continue using cyber as a tool of statecraft in attempts to coerce and deter adversaries. North Korea (DPRK) is an example of such a country.

In addition to its tepid economy, it is also weak in most other forms of traditional statecraft. I define traditional forms of statecraft as the elements of DIME, that is, diplomatic, information, military, and economic. The outlier here is that, while most of North Korea's military equipment is outdated, it maintains one of the world's largest militaries with over one million active duty and eight million reserve personnel.[3] Its artillery holds Seoul, South Korea's capital, under constant threat of annihilation, making the North's military a credible threat despite questionable capability in conventional force-on-force engagement. Thus, its military can be used in conjunction with cyber to assist with coercion efforts. While other weak states may not have such military capability, what matters is that there is another element of state power that can be brought to bear.

Another characteristic of North Korean statecraft is its willingness to eschew international norms. One example of this is Pyongyang's continued nuclear testing in the face of international acceptance of the Nonproliferation Treaty (NPT) and despite multiple United Nations Security Council (UNSC) resolutions intended to punish the DPRK for its nuclear program.[4] Another example is North Korea's persistent ballistic missile tests, which are also repeatedly condemned and sanctioned by the UNSC.[5] UNSC resolutions are binding to all UN member states, which includes North Korea. However, North Korea continues to ignore such objections to its behavior, weakening arguments that cyber norms can effectively deter state-sponsored cyberattacks and act as a stabilizing influence in cyberspace.[6]

Pyongyang has launched numerous cyberattacks since 2009, with some estimates claiming North Korea perpetrates as many as 250 million cyberattacks per day against South Korean online entities.[7] Given the lack of Internet access to the general population, this activity indicates Pyongyang understands the importance of cyber as an asymmetric alternative and has invested heavily in its cyber warfare proficiency. With an aging military infrastructure and limited sources of national power, the DPRK has used cyber in an effort to exert pressure on stronger, more capable adversaries and retain its global relevance.

North Korea, under the leadership of both Kim Jong-Il and his successor, Kim Jong-Un, has developed cyber capabilities since the 1990s in hopes of building cheaper asymmetric options to use against more powerful adversaries.[8] Before the advent of the Internet, North Korea was limited to conventional military options to support its campaigns of coercion and deterrence, aimed mostly at South Korea. According to the International Telecommunications Union, South Korea had the highest ICT development index (IDI) score, of all 167 countries measured in 2015. With such reliance and integration of all aspects of cyber into the national makeup, South Korea is one of the most vulnerable countries to cyber threats. The U.S. is not far behind at 15.[9]

North Korea stands at the other end of the ICT spectrum. Although sufficient data is not available to calculate a valid IDI score, it is estimated only a handful of elites out of the state's 25 million people have regular Internet access. Such limited connectivity provides North Korea with the advantage of limited cyberattack vulnerability when compared to more powerful nations whose economies and command and control systems are more dependent upon stable and reliable ICT systems.

Despite Seoul's vulnerability to cyberattack, Pyongyang has been unable to translate its cyber aggression against its neighbor into noticeable state benefit. While some DPRK cyber activities arguably fall within a deterrence framework, other actions are better characterized as geopolitical protests or proof-of-concept demonstrations to refine future cyber capabilities. Cyberattacks against South Korea's financial sector and government in 2009, 2011, and 2013 created significant inconvenience for South Korean citizens, erasing bank files for some, and contributing to overall public unease. Although these actions did not result in any obvious concessions to North Korea, they also did not result in effective actions in retaliation against Pyongyang.

Outside of the 2014 Sony Pictures Entertainment (SPE) hack, little has been written regarding possible motives or objectives for some of the more significant attacks over this period. While Pyongyang's persistent cyber aggression likely furthers overall goals associated with the technical state of war between the two neighboring states, cyberattacks offer the North a tool that can be used in peacetime and wartime with little risk of consequence. Since the elevation of Kim Jong-Un in December 2011, the young leader has embarked on a recurring cycle of aggression across various domains in order to stabilize his regime and obtain leverage over the South through coercion and intimidation. The cyberattacks of 2013 and 2014 provide context to draw conclusions regarding Kim Jong-Un's objectives during these events.

Overview of Notable North Korea Cyberattacks

If press reports are accurate, South Korea is under daily attack from DPRK hacker units.[10] Although North Korea has one of the poorest economies in the world, the reclusive regime maintains 17 cyber warfare organizations comprised of approximately 5,100 personnel who carry out research and development in addition to cyber espionage and cyberattacks against various entities.[11] Since 2009, North Korean hackers have persistently targeted South Korean media, financial, and political institutions.[12]

Pyongyang continues aggressive actions in cyberspace despite being ostracized from the international community and deprived of the economic benefits of globalization. What makes North Korea difficult to defend against is its disregard for international law. This disdain for international law makes North Korea unpredictable and weakens normal methods of deterrence and coercion. What follows are overviews of two of the more significant North Korean malicious cyber actions. An examination of these events and the responses by international actors lend insights into the effectiveness of cyber as an element of statecraft and potential deterrence responses by the victims.

20 March 2013 DarkSeoul Attack

On 20 March 2013, the networks of three of Seoul's main television broadcasters (KBS, MBC, and YTN), along with three South Korean banks (Shinhan, Nonghyup, and Jeju) were attacked by "DarkSeoul" malware suspected of being distributed by Bureau 121 hackers from North Korea.[13] The attacks resulted in the networks of the affected companies being frozen, with some customers of affected banks being unable to withdraw money from ATMs and news broadcasting crews unable to access computers. Unlike the distributed denial of service (DDoS) attacks South Korea experienced in the past, DarkSeoul malware was specifically designed to defeat popular Korean antivirus software and hit the targeted networks. Notably, all the victimized businesses had been previously cited as potential targets by Pyongyang. It is obvious Kim Jong-Un was trying to send a message. The *New York Times* suggested the North's leader was demonstrating that "[North Korea] can reach into Seoul's economic heart without blowing up South Korean warships or shelling South Korean islands."[14]

The outages in each affected network only lasted a few hours before bank and computer services were restored. None of the television broadcasters' programming was interrupted.[15] On 10 April 2013, the South Korean government announced North Korea was behind the attack and had evidence the attacks had been planned for at least eight months.[16] While it is ultimately unknown why the 20 March cyberattacks against South Korea occurred, awareness of some of the events surrounding the incident provides context within which to gauge possible DPRK objectives.

The year, 2013, was a low point in North-South relations on the Korean peninsula. In just his second year of power, Kim Jong-Un was still consolidating his position as North Korea's Supreme Leader and possibly looking for opportunities to demonstrate strength to a domestic audience. On 12 February 2013, North Korea conducted its third nuclear test with the detonation of what it claims was a miniaturized device, giving fuel to fears it was closer to weaponizing a nuclear warhead with which to arm a ballistic missile.[17] The test violated the UN NPT, to which North Korea was a signatory member until formally withdrawing in 2003, and blatantly disregarded international norms on nuclear testing.[18] The nuclear test also occurred on the same day President Obama delivered his State of the Union address for 2013 and coincided with threats several days earlier from DPRK news outlets to retaliate against the U.S. and South Korea for cyberattacks it claims to have suffered.[19]

In addition to the nuclear test, the South inaugurated its first female president, Park Geun-hye, on 15 February, roughly one month prior to the 20 March attacks. The inauguration occurred approximately two weeks prior to the 1 March commencement of the annual FOAL EAGLE combined field training exercise involving over 210,000 U.S. and Korean military forces. The multi-week FOAL EAGLE exercise, conducted by the Combined Forces Command, has been a source of friction between the North and South for years. The North routinely proclaims the exercise to be a provocation to war. On 8 March, in the aftermath of fresh sanctions against Pyongyang for its nuclear test and in the run-up to FOAL EAGLE, North Korean news agencies announced the nation had "scrapped" the 1953 armistice. It also threatened military retaliation against Seoul and the U.S., and cut off a Red Cross hotline between the two governments on 11 March, the same day the annual U.S., ROK computer-assisted command post exercise, KEY RESOLVE, began.[20]

In response, U.S. Secretary of Defense Chuck Hagel announced the U.S. would place 14 additional ground based interceptor (GBI) missiles in Alaska as a deterrent to North Korean threats. The U.S. also deployed four additional guided missile destroyers (DDGs), stationed B-52 bombers in Guam, and brought F-22 Raptors to participate in the final part of the exercises. Finally, the North continued provocations by staging an unusually aggressive military exercise of their own, within their own borders.[21]

2013 North Korean Objectives and Results

Under the rule of Kim Jong-Un's father, Kim Jong-Il, North Korea routinely conducted a predictable cycle of brinksmanship that usually resulted in concessions from the United Nations or South Korea in exchange for a cessation of the North's provocative behavior. In exchange for halting activity at its Yongbyon Nuclear Scientific Research Center, or other incendiary behavior, the North received economic aid or other forms of dispensation, strengthening the Kim family's hold on power.[22] After the death of Kim Jong-Il in December 2011, Kim Jong-Un attempted similar behavior by launching a long-range ballistic missile in December 2012. While the launch served a military research and development purpose, it is likely the younger Kim anticipated similar concessions, which he could use for domestic consumption and subsequently consolidate his hold on power.

North Korea is also known to posture before each KEY RESOLVE/FOAL EAGLE (KR/FE) set of exercises in an attempt to coerce the U.S. and South Korea into canceling the exercise. As stated, the North equates the annual exercise to war preparations by its adversaries. In the past Pyongyang has offered to suspend nuclear tests and return to Six Party Talks on denuclearization in exchange for a halt to joint U.S., Korean exercises.[23]

Early 2013 provided an optimal time for Kim Jong-Un to attempt to coerce concessions from South Korea's new president given her recent inauguration; fresh UN sanctions as a result of the North's December 2012 ballistic missile launch; threats of new sanctions as a result of a third nuclear test in February; and the upcoming KR/FE combined exercise. Each of these events can be viewed as attempted coercion by deterrence and coercion by compellence. On the one hand, through its actions the DPRK was attempting to deter the South from conducting KR/FE. On the other, Kim was likely also attempting to coerce concessions (e.g., increased humanitarian aid and possibly increased dialogue with the international community) to solidify his domestic position and increase his legitimacy. The computer attacks on South Korea's financial and media networks were intended to signal an escalation in coercion attempts. North Korea likely chose computer attacks because it was one of its few options left for escalation.

While North and South Korea have been at a stalemate since the official end of hostilities in 1953, both enjoy what academics term the stability-instability paradox. Such a situation is said to exist when there is enough overall deterrence for either side to engage in all-out warfare, but not enough deterrence to prevent minor provocations. Stephen Haggard and Jon R. Lindsay cite the Cold War as such an example. During the Cold War, the risk of nuclear warfare and mutually assured destruction deterred nuclear and large-scale conventional war between the U.S. and the Soviet Union. However, this threat did not deter proxy wars between the two nations, or minor conventional conflicts. Haggard and Lindsay conclude their analogy by saying, "The use of threats to attenuate the risks of general war . . . can incentivize lower-level aggression."[24] In the case of North and South Korea, this situation exists because, while U.S. and South Korean forces enjoy overwhelming conventional advantages, South Korea's major economic and population centers are well within range of the North's excessive conventional capability. While South Korea might win any prolonged military engagement with the DPRK, the possibility of such conflict turning into a regional war and the devastating damage it would cause prevent such conflict, but is not enough to prevent lesser forms of aggression, such as the March 2013 cyberattacks.

Ultimately, Kim's efforts in 2013 failed to produce coercion by compellence or deterrence and his added use of cyber aggression can be viewed as an attempt at escalation in order to achieve his strategic objectives. However, Kim was not able to duplicate the cycle of brinksmanship used by his father, which had periodically resulted in successful coercion. Nor did Kim have other viable options at escalation short of provoking an unacceptable response.

North Korea's actions did not result in any humanitarian, financial, or other concessions to the regime, nor was KR/FE canceled. Three important points can be drawn from this analysis. First, internationally accepted norms deterring nuclear testing and proliferation as well as emerging norms prohibiting cyber interference in a state's financial systems did little to deter state-sponsored cyberattacks or strengthen the coercive effects of such an attack. Second, cyber, while an available form of statecraft to be used in attempts at coercion, was not used in isolation, but as part of a broader escalatory effort. Finally, in this case, the cyberattacks were the last available form of escalation short of provoking a response that would result in either diminished domestic prestige for Kim or a larger conflict that would almost certainly result in defeat. In other words, Pyongyang did not maintain escalation dominance.

November 2014 Sony Pictures Entertainment (SPE) Hack

The November 2014 cyberattack on SPE is another example of the DPRK's use of cyber as an element of statecraft. In this case, North Korea attempted to deter a private U.S. company from showing a film, *The Interview*, depicting the murder of its leader, Kim Jong-Un. While Pyongyang did not directly threaten the U.S. government, it likely knew the U.S. would respond to any coercive attempts against SPE over U.S. networks. This may have been the impetus on 25 June 2014 when the North Korean Ministry of Foreign Affairs appealed to the Obama administration not to support release of the film, before any cyberattack took place.[25]

As the Christmas release date for the film approached, and it became apparent SPE would release the film, entities attributed to North Korea hacked into the Sony network and began stealing sensitive data to include e-mails, movie scripts, and other sensitive information before launching a "wiper" attack on 24 November.[26] SPE employees were made aware of the attack through messages displayed on screens of Sony terminals proclaiming the Guardians of Peace (GOP) carried out the attack. Over the next several days the personal data of SPE employees, along with embarrassing emails from SPE executives and scripts of several movies still in development, were leaked online. The Guardians of Peace escalated its rhetoric on 16 December, posting an online threat to carry out 9/11-type attacks on theaters showing *The Interview*.[27]

In response to the threat of terrorism, SPE indefinitely postponed the release of *The Interview* on 17 December, the same day U.S. officials blamed North Korea for the attacks. The GOP cyberattacks appeared to end the next day, 18 December. The FBI confirmed the GOP's link to Pyongyang on 19 December, the same day President Obama, during his year-end address, said SPE made a mistake canceling the release and announced the U.S. would respond proportionally. The president's announcement was also the first time the U.S. named a foreign government responsible for a cyberattack and promised to punish it. Two days later, SPE representatives reversed course and announced *The Interview* would be released.[28]

2014 North Korean Objectives and Results

Unlike the innuendo during increasingly tense relations on the peninsula amid the 2013 financial and entertainment network cyberattacks, North Korea was specific and vocal regarding its intent in 2014. It made this apparent through GOP statements and DPRK official channels. The objective of the 2014 SPE attack was to deter Sony from releasing *The Interview* and, barring that, deter theaters from showing the film. While Pyongyang initially succeeded in coercing SPE to cancel the release, its triumph turned into failure once the U.S. government stepped in.

Despite its eventual failure and relative ineffectiveness, the 2014 SPE attack demonstrates the potential value of cyber as a coercive tool when dealing with entities below the state level. SPE executives were quick to cave to hackers' demands just three weeks after the initial breaches of the company's networks and one day after being threatened with 9/11-style attacks on theaters showing the film. As mentioned, the attacks by the GOP appear to have ended after Sony's announcement of postponement. This can be viewed as successful use of cyber means for deterrence.

Two additional characteristics of the 2014 SPE hack are worth noting. First, the pairing of other forms of statecraft with the SPE cyberattack is present. The SPE cyberattacks contained elements of diplomacy (e.g., statements by the Ministry of Foreign Affairs), information (e.g., statements through official DPRK media), and economic (e.g., the publishing of unreleased movie scripts online in attempts to affect SPE income). Each would have been more effective if carried out with the initial knowledge that the acts were supported and perpetuated by the North Korean government. For example, by confusing attribution at the outset, North Korea limited potential use of military or economic provocations to threaten escalation and elicit potential concessions from SPE or other involved governments. Obscuring attribution also arguably limited any future attempts to halt the film's release through diplomacy, though the June 2014 attempts had already failed. Instead of blunting retaliation by the victim, attribution issues limited the options of the attacking government.

Second, the 2014 SPE cyberattack represented another example of North Korea ignoring norms of international behavior. In this instance, Pyongyang violated U.S. law as well as U.S. territorial sovereignty by conducting a cyberattack that resulted in theft and damage to a computer network resident within the U.S. These violations fall into what have been deemed "internationally wrongful acts," as decided by the UN Group of Governmental Experts recommendations.[29]

Finally, while the GOP attacks appear to have ceased after SPE announced the postponement of *The Interview*'s release, the exact cause for this termination is debatable. The cessation of North Korean cyber hostilities can just as easily be linked to President Obama's escalation through his 19 December announcement naming North Korea as responsible for the attacks and promising a U.S. response. The fact that there was no reported retaliation by Pyongyang after the 21 December announcement by SPE that *The Interview* would indeed be released supports the argument that cyber is not as effective a tool of coercion if the attacker does not maintain escalation dominance. The declaration by the president represented an escalation in the conflict; and the U.S. maintains escalation dominance over North Korea in all elements of statecraft. North Korea, having been blamed by the U.S. for the SPE attack risked further escalation were it to have continued cyberattacks.

North Korea provides U.S. policy makers useful insight on how to deal with weaker nations for whom norms and international law mean little. As a weak nation, North Korea has been mostly unsuccessful when using cyber for deterrence and coercion primarily because it does not maintain escalation dominance against the state actors it is targeting. In instances where it did maintain escalation dominance (e.g., in the SPE hack, before U.S. government intervention) it achieved some success. Other weak states are likely to find similar results when using cyber as a form of statecraft. While reinforcing state action in cyberspace with other forms of statecraft may enhance a deterrence campaign's effectiveness, the use of cyber will remain limited as a form of statecraft as cyber tools mature. Issues with attribution and credibility also weaken the effectiveness of cyber as a form of statecraft.

The establishment of international cyber norms may help limit escalation among near-peer competitors, but will not have a similar effect on weaker states looking for an advantage in the international community. While outside the scope of this paper, the pursuit by revanchist powers like China and Russia to create a parallel international system through the establishment of such institutions as the Asian Investment Bank and organizations based on non-Western principles also limit the effectiveness and establishment of such norms. The Joint Chiefs of Staff reinforce this in *Joint Operations Environment (JOE) 2035. JOE 2035* highlights the evolution of parallel international institutions that might legitimize state actions the current Western-led international order views as illegitimate.[30] At best, cyber norms may prevent a state from taking actions that could result in sanctions or damage to its reputation. At worst, states may not care about norms if they feel their sovereignty is threatened or if they seek to challenge the Western-led international order.

Notes

A version of this reading has been published elsewhere as "When Norms Fail" (white paper, Air Force Cyber College Policy Brief, March 2018).

[1] "Talking Foreign Policy: A Discussion on Cyber Warfare," *Case Western Reserve Journal of International Law* 47, no. 3 (Spring 2015): 319–342, 325.

[2] Hyeong-Wook Boo and Kang-Kyu Lee, "Cyber War and Policy Suggestions for South Korean Planners," *International Journal of Korean Unification Studies* 21, no. 2 (2012): 85–106, 89–90.

[3] James Hackett, ed., *The Military Balance 2010*, International Institute for Strategic Studies (London: Routledge, 2010).

[4] *Treaty on the Non-Proliferation of Nuclear Weapons*, United Nations Office for Disarmament Affairs, United Nations, 1 July 1968, https://www.un.org/disarmament/wmd/nuclear/npt/text; Anna Fifield, "Punishing North Korea: A Rundown on Current Sanctions," *Washington Post*, 22 February 2016, https://www.washingtonpost.com/news/worldviews/wp/2016/02/22/punishing-north-korea-a-run-down-on-current-sanctions/?utm_term=.8db1b327826f.

[5] Edith M. Lederer and Eric Talmadge, "UN Security Council Strongly Condemns North Korea Missile Test," *Chicago Tribune Online*, 13 February 2017, http://www.chicagotribune.com/news/nationworld/ct-north-korea-missile-test-20170213-story.html; Taehoon Lee and Ben Westscott, "Failed North Korean Missile Exploded 'Within Seconds,' US Says," *CNN World Online*, 22 March 2017, http://www.cnn.com/2017/03/21/asia/north-korea-missile-test.

[6] Private and public entities, such as Microsoft Corporation, the United Nations, and the European Union, have claimed that internationally accepted cyber norms and confidence-building measures will deter state-sponsored malicious actions in cyberspace and serve to decrease the risk of conflict and misunderstanding. See NATO Cooperative Cyber Defense Center of Excellence, "OSCE Confidence-Building Measures for Cyberspace," 20 December 2013, https://ccdcoe.org/osce-confidence-building-measures-cyberspace.html; Angela McKay, Jan Neutze, Paul Nicholas, and Kevin Sullivan, *International Security Norms: Reducing Conflict in an Internet-Dependent World*, Microsoft, December 2014; and Patryk Pawlak, *Cyber Diplomacy: Confidence-Building Measures*, European Parliamentary Research Service, October 2015.

[7] Chico Harlan and Ellen Nakashima, "Suspected North Korean Cyber Attack on a Bank Raises Fears for S. Korea, Allies," *Washington Post*, 29 August 2011, https://www.washingtonpost.com/world/national-security/suspected-north-korean-cyber-attack-on-a-bank-raises-fears-for-s-korea-allies/2011/08/07/gIQAvWwIoJ_story.html?utm_term=.c5b3ed73fc08; "N. Korea Steps Up Hacker Attacks on S. Korean Firms," *Chosun Ilbo*, 30 August 2011, https://www.english.chosun.com/site/data/html_dir/2011/08/30/2011083000444.html.

[8] "N.Korea's Highly Trained Hacker Brigades Rival CIA," *Chosun Ilbo Online*, 5 May 2011, http://english.chosun.

com/site/data/html_dir/2011/05/05/2011050500392.html.

9 *Measuring the Information Society Report 2015*, International Telecommunications Union, 2015, 60. The IDI takes into account several measures of ICT penetration into a society (e.g., Internet usage, broadband subscriptions, data availability, households with a computer, etc.).

10 "N. Korea Steps Up Hacker Attacks," *Chosun Ilbo*.

11 Son To'k-ho, "Pyongyang Hacking Support Personnel Increased by 900," *Chosun Ilbo*, 29 April 2015, accessed online at Open Source Center, https://www.opensource.gov/portal/server.pt/gateway/PTARGS_0_0_200_0_0_43/content/Display/KPR2015050125607748?returnFrame=true.

12 David Lee, "Bureau 121: How Good Are Kim Jong-Un's Elite Hackers?," *BBC Online*, 29 May 2015, http://www.bbc.com/news/technology-32925503.

13 "Broadcasters, Banks Recover Networks after Suspected Cyber Attacks," *Yonhap*, 21 March 2013, http://english.yonhapnews.co.kr/news/2013/03/21/55/0200000000AEN20130321003500315F.HTML; Graham Cluley, "DarkSeoul: Sophos Labs Identifies Malware Used in South Korean Internet Attack," *Naked Security by Sophos*, 20 March 2013, https://nakedsecurity.sophos.com/2013/03/20/south-korea-cyber-attack.

14 Choe Sang-hun, "Computer Networks in South Korea Are Paralyzed in Cyberattacks," *New York Times*, 20 March 2013, http://www.nytimes.com/2013/03/21/world/asia/south-korea-computer-network-crashes.html.

15 Ibid.

16 "South Korea Blames North for Bank and TV Cyber-Attacks," *BBC Online*, 10 April 2013, http://www.bbc.com/news/technology-22092051.

17 David Chance and Jack Kim, "North Korea Nuclear Test Draws Anger, Including from China," Reuters, 12 February 2013, http://www.reuters.com/article/us-korea-north-idUSBRE91B04820130212.

18 Kelsey Davenport, "Chronology of U.S.-North Korea Nuclear and Missile Diplomacy," Arms Control Association, October 2016, https://www.armscontrol.org/factsheets/dprkchron.

19 Choe, "Computer Networks in South Korea Are Paralyzed."

20 Choe Sang-hun, "North Korea Declares 1953 War Truce Nullified," *New York Times*, 11 Mar 2013, http://www.nytimes.com/2013/03/12/world/asia/north-korea-says-it-has-nullified-1953-korean-war-armistice.html.

21 Thom Shanker, David E. Sanger, and Martin Fackler, "U.S. Is Bolstering Missile Defense to Deter North Korea," *New York Times*, 15 March 2013, http://www.nytimes.com/2013/03/16/world/asia/us-to-bolster-missile-defense-against-north-korea.html.

22 Ibid.

23 "Change in N. Korea Does Not Mean Regime Change: Senior U.S. Diplomat," *Korea Times*, 5 February 2015, http://www.koreatimes.co.kr/www/news/nation/2015/02/485_173053.html.

24 Stephan Haggard and Jon R. Lindsay, "North Korea and the Sony Hack: Exporting Instability through Cyberspace," *Asia Pacific Issues*, no. 117 (May 2015): 3–4.

25 Choe Sang-Hun, "North Korea Warns U.S. over Film Mocking Its Leader," *New York Times*, 25 June 2014, https://www.nytimes.com/2014/06/26/world/asia/north-korea-warns-us-over-film-parody.html?_r=0.

26 Ellen Nakashima, "Why the Sony Hack Drew an Unprecedented U.S. Response against North Korea," *Washington Post*, 15 January 2015, https://www.washingtonpost.com/world/national-security/why-the-sony-hack-drew-an-unprecedented-us-response-against-north-korea/2015/01/14/679185d4-9a63-11e4-96cc-e858eba91ced_story.html.

27 Lori Grisham, "Timeline: North Korea and the Sony Pictures Hack," *USA Today*, http://www.usatoday.com/story/news/nation-now/2014/12/18/sony-hack-timeline-interview-north-korea/20601645; Ellen Nakashima, "Why the Sony Hack Drew an Unprecedented U.S. Response against North Korea," *Washington Post*, 15 January 2015, https://www.washingtonpost.com/world/national-security/why-the-sony-hack-drew-an-unprecedented-us-response-against-north-korea/2015/01/14/679185d4-9a63-11e4-96cc-e858eba91ced_story.html.

28 Ellen Nakashima, "Why the Sony Hack Drew an Unprecedented U.S. Response against North Korea," *Washington Post*, 15 January 2015, https://www.washingtonpost.com/world/national-security/

why-the-sony-hack-drew-an-unprecedented-us-response-against-north-korea/2015/01/14/679185d4-9a63-11e4-96cc-e858eba91ced_story.html; Haggard and Lindsay, "North Korea and the Sony Hack"; Lori Grisham, "Timeline: North Korea and the Sony Pictures Hack," *USA Today*, http://www.usatoday.com/story/news/nation-now/2014/12/18/sony-hack-timeline-interview-north-korea/20601645.

29 United Nations, General Assembly, *Group of Governmental Experts on Developments in the Field of Information and Telecommunications in the Context of International Security*, A/70/174, 2015, 2/17, available at www.un.org/ga/search/view_doc.asp?symbol=A/71/172.

30 *Joint Operating Environment (JOE) 2035: The Joint Force in a Contested and Disordered World*, 14 July 2016, 7–8.

Normalizing Cyber Disruption as an Element of National Power

Sam Kidd and Pano Yannakogeorgos

Cyber capabilities have great potential as power-projection tools across the spectrum of statecraft. Today, however, command and control of cyber options are as tightly controlled as nuclear weapons. This, we believe, is due to the focusing of cyber capability development in a military context and a lack of strategic thought in the area of disruptive cyber operations. This can be blamed on two things. First, is the position that "the classification of cyberspace solely as a domain of conflict has contributed to this theoretical stagnation, limiting policymakers' understanding of the ways in which cyberspace can be leveraged for broader applications of statecraft." Second, is the argument that international law regime governing "uses of force short of war has fallen in desuetude." We argue here that *disruptive* cyber operations offer varied and potentially graduated means of operationalizing each of the diplomatic, information, military, and economic (DIME) instruments of power against state and non-state actors to exact costs on transgressors, deter aggressors, and project power in a humanitarian, non-lethal manner. Our purpose is to agitate U.S. national security and foreign policy discussion regarding employing disruptive cyber operations as legitimate non-lethal means of shaping the behavior of adverse foreign decision makers.

Definitions and a common lexicon are the basis of all debates on warfare. Participants in debates about air, land, sea, and space power all know what they mean by armed attack and the use of force. What little argument that takes place about definitions in traditional warfighting domains usually revolves around two or three assertions that more or less mean the same thing. As argued elsewhere more extensively,[1] clarifying definitions for cyber conflict will permit for the informed establishment of policy tools to utilize cyber operations to project power. Developing clear and widely accepted distinctions between access, disruption, and attack is critical. A cyber lexicon that does not label every non-defensive action as an attack, and analogizes cyber operations to the recognized international tools of statecraft discussed below, has the potential to recast current rhetoric within the milieu of statecraft and inform workable policy and strategy.

A conflation of definitions has led to an over emphasis on cyber war. This has resulted in a wealth of thought validating the application of *jus ad bellum* and *jus in bello* to cyberspace actions which meet the definition of "use of force" or "armed attack." Yet, there are other tools of statecraft recognized and regulated by international law which may be employed in the cyber domain. Utilizing the term "disruptive cyber operations" to describe coercive or influential cyber actions that do not cross the "armed attack" threshold more adequately shifts the discussion away from the attack rhetoric than the commonly used term "computer network attack." It is also less demonizing than the also commonly used "cyber-enabled malicious activity." Recognizing that most cyber activities fall within the spectrum of disruptive cyber operations may help drive foreign policy decision makers to analyze such actions under the rubric of existing customary international law governing coercive measures rather than the armed force or attack construct.

Disruptive cyber actions undertaken by states may be categorized as retorsion, countermeasures, or reprisal. These are tools of statecraft generally recognized in customary international law, with the one caveat being armed or forceful reprisal actions taken outside the context of an armed conflict. Some commentators argue that this form of reprisal is no longer acceptable due in large part to the UN Charter prohibition on the "use of force." Yet, the majority opinion on the UN Charter framework, which finds that a gap exists between the "use of force" and "armed attack" thresholds, has a tendency to undermine the concept of "an international security regime" designed to keep "violence within tolerable levels."[2] It significantly shrinks "the room [for states] to maneuver—to push, shove and struggle with one another—for the redress of grievances."[3] The application of retorsion, countermeasures, and reprisal as tools of cyber statecraft may prove to be effective at deterring potential adversaries and punishing those who violate international obligations.

Retorsion is distinguishable from reprisal and other forms of countermeasures because it describes actions that are inherently lawful, but "unfriendly." Countermeasures and reprisals are actions taken that would otherwise be in violation of law or an obligation to the state against which the action is taken, but are justified as a means to compel that state to terminate its own "internationally wrongful acts or omissions." Because cyberspace is still a relatively permissible environment with few normatively prohibited actions, a whole host of disruptive cyber operations leveraging the diplomatic, information, or economic instruments of power would qualify as acceptable forms of retorsion. Limited rules apply to retorsion actions because the conduct is not inherently unlawful.

Economic sanction is a generally accepted form of retorsion under international law when the sanction does not contradict other legal obligations. It is commonplace in today's discussion of cyberspace to analogize cyber actions with concepts existent in the traditional air, land, maritime, and space domains, resulting in frameworks for thinking about cyberspace that vary in their efficacy.

Analogizing disruptive cyber operations with economic sanctions appears to present a valuable analytic tool for strategists to determine what types of coercive, but non-forceful, cyber actions will be justifiable under the international law concept of retorsion. Temporarily denying an offending state the ability to transfer data across certain information and communication technology infrastructure inside or outside the borders of the offending nation may be a legitimate form of reprisal.

Disruptive cyber operations, or the threat of such operations, that would violate international obligations, such as the principle of non-intervention, may also be utilized by states if the actions qualify as countermeasures. To qualify as countermeasures, disruptive cyber operations must not cross the "use of force" threshold, and be "undertaken by an injured state in response to another state's internationally wrongful conduct,"[4] in order to "bring about cessation of or reparation for the illegal conduct."[5] Cyber countermeasures as a means of responding to a computer network attack have been analyzed by Michael Schmitt and other commentators.[6] Countermeasures are a tool that may operate as an extension of any of the United States' (U.S.) four instruments of power, although Schmitt argues that countermeasures are neither punitive or deterrent tools.[7] This restrictive view of countermeasures effectively eliminates peacetime reprisal from the quiver of legitimate countermeasures available for policy makers.

The problem with accepting the existence of a gap between the use of force and the armed attack thresholds is the lack of legitimate options to proportionally respond to a use of force that does not amount to an armed attack. As Schmitt states, "In particular, it incentivizes treating such operations as armed attacks in order to justify a response by the injured State."[8] Schmitt argues for the efficacy of countermeasures as a means by which states may respond to "harmful cyber actions in a manner more robust than retorsion, but less provocative than a use of force."[9] Yet, he also recognizes the reality of this restriction on countermeasures: "It has the consequence of leaving a state facing cyber uses of force [or any use of force for that matter] that do not rise to the armed attack level unable to respond in kind." The concept of armed reprisal in peacetime is the most controversial of these three tools, but could be overcome provided the state is subject to a threat or use of force in cyberspace or otherwise has the authority to respond proportionally without escalating the matter to an armed attack in order to respond in self-defense.

A reprisal, different from retorsion, is an act that is "per se illegal under international law" but is justified "as a response to an unlawful act by another state."[10] Thus reprisal is generally consistent with countermeasures, except that the term *reprisal* is most often associated with forcible acts. There is disagreement among scholars as to the legality of the forcible reprisal.[11] The *Tallinn Manual* recognizes that a minority of international law experts hold the opinion that "proportionate countermeasures could involve a limited degree of military force in response to circumstances below the Article 51 threshold of 'armed attack.'"[12] Normative acceptance of this minority opinion would solve the problems created by the "use of force/armed attack" gap. Categorizing these forcible countermeasures as reprisals would provide additional utility, especially in the cyberspace context. Reprisals, unlike self-defense actions, "can be taken at a time and place different from the pivotal event (although not at a completely remote time)."[13] Reprisals can also be directed against individuals or non-state actors as well as against states.[14] The attribution problem in cyberspace presents a situation where a victim state may not know who is responsible for a use of force committed against that state sufficient to meet the immediacy requirement to respond in self-defense. In addition, the

potential exists for a use of force in cyberspace to be committed by a non-state actor or unacknowledged proxies. Policies which help resurrect the legitimacy of reprisal and articulate the willingness of the U.S. to take action against states or non-state actors who use or threaten force against the U.S. would most likely be in the best interests of U.S. national security. President Obama's statements after the Sony hack, that the U.S. will "respond proportionally . . . in a place and time and manner that we choose,"[15] and in response to the possible use of chemical weapons by the Assad regime the U.S. would use airstrikes to "impose a price" for such actions,[16] are examples of what such policy statements might look like.

The need for non-lethal, but potentially forceful, coercive and punitive options in international relations, as a means of preserving international order and preventing escalation to armed conflict, has been demonstrated throughout history. In today's environment, every aspect of the DIME has become digitized and thoroughly interconnected. The demand for operationalizing cyberspace across the whole of government to leverage the digital DIME to meet national security objectives already exists and will grow in importance as adversaries, of both the state and non-state variety, pose more complex and sophisticated threats. A lack of effective tools is evident in the fact that the U.S. has been relatively willing to employ strategic bombing or devastating economic sanctions as coercive or punitive implements, despite their history of limited success. There has been little discussion as to how the U.S. might utilize cyber, retorsion, countermeasures, or reprisal in response to aggressive foreign actions such as Russia's invasion of Ukraine or China's island building in the South China Sea. U.S. foreign policymakers and strategists have the opportunity to reset the cyber lexicon and continue fleshing out existing normative international law structures through cyberspace policy, strategy, and acknowledged state practice in order to provide the president with viable non-lethal, smart power options for defeating adversary strategies.

Notes

1 http://nationalinterest.org/commentary/keep-cyberwar-narrow-8459?page=2.
2 Charles W. Kegley Jr. and Gregory A. Raymond, "Normative Constraints on the 'Use of Force' Short of War," *Journal of Peace Research* 23, no. 3 (1986): 213.
3 Ibid.
4 Katherine C. Hinkle, "Countermeasures in the Cyber Context: One More Thing to Worry About," *Yale Journal of International Law Online* 37 (2011): 12.
5 Ibid., 14.
6 See Michael N. Schmitt, "'Below the Threshold' Cyber Operations: The Countermeasures Response Option and International Law," *Virginia Journal of International Law* 54 (2014), and Hinkle, "Countermeasures in the Cyber Context."
7 Schmitt, "Below the Threshold," 715–16.
8 Ibid., 730.
9 Ibid.
10 Georg Kerschischnig, *Cyberthreats and International Law* (The Hague: Eleven International Publishing, 2012), 123.
11 Ibid.
12 Michael N. Schmitt, ed., *Tallinn Manual on the International Law Applicable to Cyber Warfare* (New York: Cambridge University Press, 2013), 38.
13 Kerschischnig, *Cyberthreats and International Law*, 123.
14 Ibid.
15 Katie Zezima, "Sony 'Made a Mistake' by Pulling Movie after Cyberattack," WashingtonPost.com, December 19, 2014, https://www.washingtonpost.com/news/post-politics/wp/2014/12/19/obama-to-hold-his-end-of-the-year-press-conference-friday.
16 Jeremy Rabkin and John Yoo, "A Return to Coercion: International Law and New Weapon Technologies," *Hofstra Law Review* 42, no. 4 (2014), 1118.

ISR and Cyberspace

Maj. Robert Johnson, USAF; Capt. Daniel Votipka, USAF;
TSgt. Danielle Dye, USAF; Maj. Trevor Stutting, USAF;
Capt. Jamie Blummer, USAF; Ms. Tiffany Harbour, DAF;
Capt. Laura LeFevre, USAF; and Capt. Thomas Shew, USAF

Introduction

The Air Force conducts its core mission of global integrated intelligence, surveillance, and reconnaissance (ISR) in and through cyberspace. This new domain represents an ever-expanding source of intelligence data vital to the full range of joint military operations. At the same time, cyberspace represents both new avenues to apply force against adversaries and increasing vulnerabilities for them to do likewise. ISR is a critical enabler of the offensive and defensive operations the Air Force conducts in cyberspace. This chapter will explore ISR in cyberspace and those ISR actions that enable cyberspace operations.

Defining ISR in Cyberspace

Chairman of the Joint Chiefs of Staff Joint Publication 3-12 (R), *Cyberspace Operations*, defines cyberspace ISR as:

> ISR activities in cyberspace conducted to gather intelligence that may be required to support future operations, including offensive cyber operations (OCO) or defensive cyber operations (DCO). These activities synchronize and integrate the planning and operation of cyberspace systems, in direct support of current and future operations. Cyberspace ISR focuses on tactical and operational intelligence and on mapping adversary cyberspace to support military planning.[1]

This definition provides only a limited description. A complete discussion of cyberspace and ISR must examine those surveillance and reconnaissance operations to collect intelligence in cyberspace, as well as those ISR activities that enable cyberspace operations.

Consider cyberspace ISR as a three-legged stool. The three legs are exploit, attack, and defend. Cyberspace ISR activities exploit cyberspace to collect intelligence about adversaries from the information that transits and is stored on their digital networks. Cyberspace ISR activities also enable cyberspace attack on adversary computer networks as well as activities that allow us to defend our own networks. Underpinning these three legs is the foundation laid by cyberspace intelligence preparation of the operating environment (C-IPOE) that provides a thorough understanding of the cyber battlespace. The remainder of this chapter will describe in further detail these cyberspace ISR activities.

There are a few foundational points that help inform the discussions that follow. First, intelligence collected from cyberspace informs the full range of joint operations, not only cyberspace operations. Second, the preponderance of cyberspace activities involves the collection of intelligence. Third, cyberspace operations are critically dependent upon ISR to characterize the operating environment, determine access points, develop avenues of attack, and identify threat vectors. Last, cyberspace operations rely on all intelligence disciplines, not just intelligence collected in cyberspace.

Cyberspace Intelligence Preparation of the Operating Environment

A critical first step for any joint operation is defining and understanding the operating environment.[2] This is no different for cyberspace operations. Cyberspace intelligence preparation of the operating environment characterizes adversary cyberspace by providing a detailed understanding of the cyber terrain through extensive network mapping utilizing all intelligence disciplines.

Network Mapping

Cyberspace can be deconstructed into five layers—the identity, cyber-persona, logical, physical, and geographical layers—each with their own unique characteristics.[3] It is the objective of C-IPOE to understand each of these layers to enable collection or OCO/DCO. Many times the initial vector to map adversary networks begins with the identity and cyber-persona layers. The identity layer describes the person/group acting in cyberspace, and the cyber-persona layer describes the "digital representation of an individual or entity."[4] Characterizing the identity layer of cyberspace involves naming the actual people, state/nonstate groups, and their affiliations as well as describing their capabilities and patterns of behavior as it relates to the physical world. Mapping the cyber-persona layer includes tying these named person(s)/group(s) to their associated e-mail addresses, Internet protocol (IP) addresses, handheld devices, and/or computers, to name a few. Cyber-persona layer mapping also includes linking identities to signatures in nonmalicious or malicious code, detailing individuals' search histories and noting websites where individuals visit or contribute.[5]

The identity and persona layers tell us who is operating in cyberspace. The logical and physical layers tell us *how* they are operating in cyberspace. Protocols in the logical layer tell the digital information

where and how to flow through a network architecture. The logical layer also describes abstract entities: "not tied to an individual, specific path, or node. A simple example is any website that is hosted on servers in multiple physical locations where all content can be accessed through a single uniform resource locator (URL)."[6]

Analyzing the logical layer is similar to reading the postmarks on the outside of an envelope. Cyberspace ISR analysts investigate this layer by analyzing and unwrapping packets of information traversing the network and tracing the routes on which they flow in order to develop a comprehensive understanding of the network. Physical layer analysis complements this by determining the hardware through which this information flows. A logical network map can be developed to graphically represent this data, detailing information flow paths (links) and network devices used for routing and storing digital information (nodes).

Mapping the physical layers and geographic layers of the network links the abstract portion of the cyberspace domain to its physical manifestation in the natural domains. The physical layer refers to actual network elements, that is, the infrastructure. This network infrastructure includes the links, wired links (cable), and wireless links (satellite ground stations and/or terrestrial relay towers) as well as the intermediate connectors and nodes, "routers, switches, servers and computers."[7] The geographic layer represents the specific location of the elements of the network in the natural domains of land, sea, air, or space.[8]

The order with which these five layers are presented in this chapter should not imply that mapping the cyberspace terrain necessarily proceeds sequentially or linearly to a finite point. Information collected in any one of these layers can provide a linkage to one layer to enable further mapping of another layer. This mapping process is an iterative, cross-feeding analytical process. Further, cyberspace is constantly changing, often rapidly and erratically. Thus C-IPOE must be constantly refreshed. It is a continual activity of first establishing an adversary network baseline map and then continually updating this network map through a process of identifying distinct, relevant changes to an adversary's tactical and/or strategic network state. Any network changes are characterized for the purpose of making the appropriate adjustments to friendly strategy and tactics to maintain access and freedom of movement and maneuver in adversary networks.[9] C-IPOE characterization efforts must be dynamic, using broad systematic tools, such as high-speed logical sensors and advanced automated analytical support systems.[10] With these sensors and systems, analysts are equipped to characterize the rapidly evolving cyberspace terrain.

Multi-Intelligence Support for C-IPOE

C-IPOE is reliant on the full range of intelligence disciplines. Signals Intelligence (SIGINT) may identify a signal or communication in an area of interest vital for C-IPOE. For example, an intercept from voice communications may provide network login credentials needed to enable further cyberspace mapping. Geospatial Intelligence (GEOINT) can detail locations and types of various telecommunications cables, radio/cellular relay towers, satellite ground stations, and large data storage centers.[11] Intelligence collection from human sources (HUMINT) such as debriefings (interrogations) and document exploitation can provide information relevant to C-IPOE, such as network administrator names and daily routines (identity layer); e-mail, phone numbers, and passwords (cyber-persona layer); and network design plans (logical and physical layers). Similarly, intelligence collection from open sources (OSINT) such as social media websites or other various websites can detail cyber-persona, logical, and/or physical layers. Website IP addresses as well as other metadata from open sources assist in detailing logical layer information as well as information useful in identifying and geolocating physical elements of such adversary networks. Pictures and video from open sources can show buildings or other distinct physical terrain landmarks that support geographic layer mapping. Ultimately, C-IPOE activities require a planning, collection, and analysis process integrated with all relevant intelligence disciplines to successfully synchronize and optimize ISR support for cyberspace.[12]

C-IPOE is a critical precursor to all other cyberspace operations, and it is often the most difficult and time consuming. It can take months and years of detailed investigative and analytic work.

ISR from Cyberspace

Using the foundation laid by C-IPOE, network elements as well as access vectors can be identified to enable focused collection of intelligence data from cyberspace. In digital networks, this data exists in one of two states: "in motion," transiting between two devices in the network, or "at rest," stored on one of the devices in the network. Therefore, cyberspace data collection activities can be divided based on the state of the data. Passive collection activities target and collect data that transits the wired or wireless links between computers for analysis. Active collection, computer network exploitation, targets dormant data on individual computers and servers. This section will describe each type of collection in detail.

Passive Cyberspace Collection

An analogy to HUMINT can be useful to better understand passive collection in cyberspace. During a HUMINT collection activity, an agent might go to a location where two targets are known to meet and listen in on their conversation. Doing likewise in cyberspace can be more complicated. Eavesdropping on this conversation through passive collection as it transits in cyberspace on links between computers can be difficult due to the volume of data transiting. A conversation can easily be "buried" due to the link being saturated with messages back and forth between the multiple applications running in the background emanating from multiple computers sending and receiving information on the Internet. This situation would be akin to the HUMINT collector trying to hear that same conversation standing in a busy subway stop at rush hour. Additionally, with the use of modern encryption techniques, communicants often encode the message into a language only discernible by the sender and receiver who hold the key to decrypt the information. Passive collection can be relatively easy to execute with little OPSEC risk given it is hard to identify the listener in a crowd, but it is inherently limited in the data that can be collected based on what the targets are willing to communicate within earshot. This limitation requires the second type of collection: active collection, i.e., computer network exploitation (CNE). It is very common to see passively collected information used to inform subsequent active exploitation. Conversely, CNE operations typically gain the initial accesses on links as a precursor to passive collection operations.

Active Cyberspace Collection: Computer Network Exploitation

CNE describes both "enabling operations and intelligence collection capabilities to gather data from target computer systems."[13] CNE takes advantage of flaws in network infrastructure and/or individual computer systems to gain access and actively collect information stored "at rest" in the computer systems. Using the previous HUMINT example, this would be like an agent dressing like an employee and getting a fake office ID to get into a closed office space or sneaking in at night

past all the security cameras by moving through all the spots not covered by the cameras' view. However, whenever collection is enabled by vulnerabilities in the network, if discovered by the target, software can quickly be corrected, closing not only that network to future collection, but also in every other network using that software, once a fix is published.

The Product of Cyberspace Collection/Analysis: DNI

The data obtained through passive and active cyberspace collection, processed, and then analyzed becomes an analytical product called digital network intelligence (DNI). The production of DNI to satisfy intelligence requirements is a SIGINT function conducted under Title 50, United States Code, by the National Security Agency/Central Security Service (NSA/CSS).[14] DNI can also be produced by units under the command of a joint force commander when authorized by an EXORD or when delegated temporary SIGINT operational tasking authority by NSA/CSS.[15] DNI may be used to focus further collection as well as used to satisfy strategic, operational, or tactical intelligence requirements to support operations in any domain. An example of a strategic intelligence requirement satisfied by DNI could be a product resulting from the exploitation of digital information describing an adversary nation's political leadership's intent to develop nuclear weapons. An operational example can be digital information collected from an adversary's military command, control, communications, computers, and intelligence (C4I) systems that outlines impending troop, weapon system, and/or munitions movements. Finally, a DNI product satisfying tactical intelligence requirements can include an increase in C4I system network traffic, as indicated from passive collection, indicating changes to enemy alert levels such as integrated air defense system activations. DNI production specifically for cyberspace operations describes cyberspace

ISR activities that enable OCO and DCO. The following sections will explain these activities in greater detail.

ISR for OCO

Cyberspace Targeting

The ability to deliver cyberspace effects requires three critical elements: target identification/characterization, access to that target, and tools to deliver the intended effects. Cyberspace targeting enables all three. Cyberspace targeting links desired effects with adversary cyberspace vulnerabilities to deny, disrupt, or destroy adversary capabilities. Cyberspace targeting relies on intelligence detailing system vulnerabilities to identify where and how to direct cyberspace fires by answering the question of whether current characteristics or changes to the adversary system topography open up a path for generating fires effects or close off a path being used previously. Cyberspace targeting must consider an update to a computer's operating system, the connection to a supervisory control and data acquisition (SCADA) system, a change to system security policies, and/or the addition of antivirus or other security products. In most cases, this data is collected by actively probing adversary networks regularly with messages specifically crafted to elicit responses that provide information about the topography of the network and running programs on each machine in the network. This is commonly referred to as scanning the network. Additionally, exploitation may be required to identify changes that are intentionally hidden from active scanning, like the list of installed antivirus tools or attached physical devices. Finally, for the target computer system, analysts compare current network characteristics or any changes to offensive cyberspace tools to determine whether these current characteristics or changes give the opportunity to use an offensive tool, take a tool off the table, or change the risk decisions associated with specific techniques used by the tool.

Mission Planning and Execution

Once the cyberspace "target folder" (i.e., detailed targeting solution) has been developed, cyberspace ISR analysts and operators develop the mission plan. Mission planning takes mission objectives and translates these into tactical tasks for execution. In addition to targeting information, ISR input to mission planning will include expected threats, neutral actors, and/or other friendly forces operating in the target network space. ISR analysts will identify potential vulnerabilities to offensive tools as a result of these expected threats and/or other actors operating in the space. ISR analysts will provide detailed timing as well as approach vectors discovered during the analysis of the target adversary network to help choreograph mission execution. ISR analysts also assist in the development of contingency options should automated network responses, adversary actions, and/or other actor actions precipitate the need for an alternate course of action. During mission execution, cyberspace ISR analysts provide real-time situational awareness and threat warning. Finally, after the completion of a mission, ISR analysts will support mission debriefing and lessons learned. ISR analysts will characterize adversary tactics, techniques, and procedures (TTPs) employed in response to friendly actions as well as any other adversary network intelligence gathered as a result of the operation in order to improve future cyberspace missions.

Intelligence Gain/Loss Assessments

The joint targeting process incorporates intelligence gain/loss (IGL) assessments to weigh the risk targeting operations have on future intelligence collection activities. In striking a particular target in the natural domains, future collection may be denied as a result of the loss of that target which had been providing lucrative intelligence. This is particularly critical for cyberspace operations. Whereas in the natural domains the elimination of a target (e.g., radio communication tower) can prevent future collection in a localized area of operations due to the absence of the target, in cyberspace, the use of a cyberspace tool to create effects on a C4I target can eliminate the future use of the cyberspace tool for future intelligence collection or attack missions *globally*. A cyberspace operation (OCO or CNE) utilizes specialized tools that require extensive resources, time, and tradecraft to develop and depend on specific network vulnerabilities to ensure undetected and continual access to deliver effects or collect information. Thus, a cyberspace operation could "potentially compromise (future) intelligence collection activities" and future use of an offensive tool by exposing this sensitive technology and tipping adversaries to their network vulnerabilities that allowed the cyberspace tool to penetrate and then attack or collect.[16] When such network vulnerabilities are patched to counter a cyberspace tool, the patches can be made available worldwide. Thus, many cyberspace tools carry the risk of having utility for only a few uses or just one use before adversary countermeasures eliminate its use worldwide. Therefore, IGL assessments within the cyberspace domain take into account the extreme perishable nature those cyberspace capabilities suffer when exposed. The assessment must weigh whether or not the cyberspace tool might have utility for a potentially higher-priority operation or intelligence collection effort where subsequent loss of the capability is acceptable.

ISR for DCO

Indications and Warning (I&W)

While friendly actors attempt to exploit and attack adversary networks, adversaries are doing likewise to friendly networks. Defending against exploitation and attacks requires a detailed understanding of adversary cyber actors and their capabilities and constant vigilance. Cyberspace I&W focuses on predicting, detecting, analyzing, and alerting of adversary cyberspace actions and threats. *Joint and National Intelligence Support to Military Operations* (JP 2-01) defines I&W, in general, as a process that analyzes and integrates operations and intelligence information to assess the probability of hostile actions and provide sufficient warning to preempt, counter, or otherwise moderate their outcome.[17] Due to anonymity and relative freedom to maneuver our adversaries enjoy in cyberspace, cyberspace I&W may only recognize adversary cyberspace operations triggers with relatively short windows of opportunity to respond.

Cyberspace I&W data can be organized into two types of observations, those that occur in real time at network speed, and the fusion of all other sources of information prior to a predicted attack or espionage event. Those observations of enemy activity prior to a delivered cyberspace effect follow what is termed the cyberattack kill chain. This chain of adversary actions produces many potentially observable events that may start with adversaries conducting initial target research (e.g., probing network systems) followed by attempts to gain increasing access through testing. Adversaries then use this gained knowledge to tailor (weaponize) code specific to the target system. Finally, the adversary selects a delivery methodology (e.g., e-mail with link or attachment) that installs the malicious attack code as well as any command and control code intended to manage exfiltration of data if the intent is also espionage.[18] Unlike the physical domain, the transition from delivery to attack/exploitation can transpire in seconds. However, prior to weapon delivery, initial phases of adversary cyberspace targeting development generate observable warning data over an extended period of time to enable friendly forces the ability to alert of an impending adversary network penetration seeking to create adverse network effects or espionage. For example, increases in adversary research into military organizational structures, personnel, network infrastructure, and workplace procedures, followed by network probing, spear phishing e-mails, or social engineering attempts, may occur days, weeks, or even months before any network-level adverse effects exist. Furthermore, as the attack moves into the intermediate phases of gaining and expanding accesses, observations will include those that occur at network speed. For this reason, one of the most crucial elements of a cyberspace-warning system is the capability to recognize, collect, and profile network anomalies related to all the phases of a potential network attack to facilitate the systematic identification of suspected and actual malicious activity.[19] Cyberspace I&W systems provide support to DCO through the monitoring, detecting, analyzing, and alerting of threats to both the DODIN and national critical infrastructure.

Attribution and Mitigation

If cyberspace ISR is not able to predict an attack to enable proactive defense, it can play a critical role in determining key information after an attack. Attribution consists of "determining the identity or location of an attacker or an attacker's intermediary."[20] Attribution of cyberpersonas is an extremely difficult endeavor due to the size, composition, and governance of the Internet. In addition, determining the intent/motive behind an attack is an equally important part of attribution because it allows leaders to determine possible trends or issues that need to be addressed from a defensive standpoint to predict/prevent future attacks.

Through the analysis phase following an attack, defenders can often discover adversary tactics, techniques, and procedures, new attack vectors, and unknown network vulnerabilities to support mitigation, recovery from the current attack, and

actions necessary to prevent future attacks. The intelligence gathered during this analysis enables the development of new countermeasures (e.g., security patches or updated policies) to prevent future successful attacks. In the cases where attribution of major attacks is achieved, the intelligence can be used to inform DCO response actions: information gathered about the source, method, or purpose of an attack to develop counterattack cyberspace tools to create proportional effects outside the DODIN on the adversary's networks.[21] Analysis leading to successful network countermeasures (e.g., vulnerability patching) and/or responsive actions on adversary networks helps achieve deterrence through communication of network resiliency (denial of future benefits from attack) and fear of retribution.

Conclusion

Communications have transitioned from a radio frequency–dominated paradigm to an IP-dominated paradigm. Further, information has shifted from being stored in hardcopy print form to being stored digitally. As a result, cyberspace presents an ever-increasing source of intelligence about our adversaries as well as an increasing area of vulnerability to our own operations. Cyberspace ISR activities are described via three primary missions: exploit, attack, and defend, all of which require the foundation laid by C-IPOE. Exploitation activities enable access to and intelligence collection from adversary information networks. Data collected from cyberspace that is processed and analyzed results in the production of what is called digital network intelligence. DNI supports the full range of military operations, not just cyberspace operations. When conducting offensive cyberspace operations, ISR operations are critical for target development and mission planning as well as weighing costs versus benefits of using extremely perishable cyberspace tools. Adversaries also seek to exploit and attack friendly networks. Thus, cyberspace ISR activities detect, predict, and/or mitigate enemy intrusions into our networks. Finally, ISR for cyberspace operations requires a multi-INT planning, collection, and analysis approach to synchronize and optimize intelligence support for cyberspace.

Notes

This reading was previously published in *An Airman's Guide to Cyberpower*, http://www.airuniversity.af.mil/ CyberCollege/Portal/Article/Article/ 1238539/isr-and-cyberspace.

[1] Chairman of the Joint Chiefs of Staff (JCS), Joint Publication (JP) 3-12 (R), *Cyberspace Operations*, 5 February 2013, II-4–II-5, http://dtic.mil/doctrine/new_pubs/jp3_12R.pdf.

[2] JCS, JP 2-0, *Joint Intelligence*, 22 October 2013, I-17, http://www.dtic.mil/doctrine/new_pubs/jp2_0.pdf.

[3] Ibid., I-2, but extended from three layers to five layers for clarity.

[4] Ibid., I-3.

[5] Ibid., I-4.

[6] Ibid., I-3.

[7] Ibid., I-3.

[8] Ibid., I-2, I-3.

[9] Rewording of the JP 3-12 definition of event detection and characterization on pages II-8 and II-9 to give the topic more clarity.

[10] William J. Lynn III, "Defending a New Domain: The Pentagon's Cyberstrategy," *Foreign Affairs*, September/October 2010, accessed 10 August 2015, 15, https://www.foreignaffairs.com/modal_forms/nojs/link-form/pdf/1113238.

[11] JP 3-12, *Cyberspace Operations*, IV-3.

[12] John C. Koziol, "Contesting the Information Battlespace," *Joint Force Quarterly*, 3rd Quarter 2007, 71, http://dtic.mil/doctrine/jfq/jfq-46.pdf.

[13] Department of Defense, JP 1-02, *Department of Defense Dictionary of Military and Associated Terms*, 31 January 2011, 73.

[14] Air Force Annex 3-12, *Cyberspace Operations*, 30 November 2011, 23, https://www.doctrine.af.mil/download.jsp?file-name=3-12-Annex-CYBERSPACE-OPS.pdf.

[15] JP 3-12, *Cyberspace Operations*, II-4–II-5.

[16] Ibid., II-9.

[17] JP 2-01, *Joint and National Intelligence Support to Military Operations*, 5 January 2012, III-44, http://dtic.mil/doctrine/new_pubs/jp2_01.pdf.

[18] Sergio Caltagirone, Andrew Pendergast, and Christopher Betz, "The Diamond Model of Intrusion Analysis," 7 May 2013, accessed 21 August 2015, 31–32, www.dtic.mil/get-tr-doc/pdf?AD=ADA586960.

[19] Brian Fuller, "Federal Intrusion Detection, Cyber Early Warning and the Federal Response" (SANS Institute Reading Room, 2003), 7, accessed 15 August 2015, http://www.sans.org/reading-room/whitepapers/warfare/federal-intrusion-detection-cyber-early-warning-federal-response-1095.

[20] Jeffery Hunker, Bob Hutchinson, and Jonathan Margulies, "Roles and Challenges for Sufficient Attack Attribution" (Institute for Information Infrastructure Protection, 2008), 5, accessed 10 August 2015, http://www.theip3.org/docs/publications/350.pdf.

[21] JP 3-12, *Cyberspace Operations*, II-2, II-3.

Abbreviations

AGI artificial general intelligence

AI artificial intelligence

ANI artificial narrow intelligence

APNIC Asia Pacific Network Information Centre

APT advanced persistent threat

ARPA Advanced Research Projects Agency

BTC Bitcoin

BYOD Bring Your Own Device

CA certificate authority

CAN computer network attacks

CAUSE Cyber-attack Automated Unconventional Sensor Environment

CCDCoE Cooperative Cyber Defense Center of Excellence

CCP Chinese Communist Party

CDMA Cyber Defense Management Authority

CDMB Cyber Defense Management Board

CERT Cyber Emergency Response Team

CFAA Computer Fraud and Abuse Act

C4ISR command, control, communication, computers, intelligence, surveillance, and reconnaissance

CII critical information infrastructure

CIO chief information officer

CIS Commonwealth of Independent States

CISO chief information security officer

CoE Council of Europe

COTS commercial off-the-shelf

CPC Communist Party of China

CSIS Center for Strategic and International Studies

CSL Cyber Security Law

C2 command and control

DARPA Defense Advanced Research Projects Agency

DDoS distributed denial of service

DHT distributed hash table

DNI Directorate of National Intelligence

DNS Dynamic Name System

DOS denial of service

DTL Distributed Ledger Technology

ECC elliptical curve technology

ENISA European Network and Information Security Agency

FARC Fuerzas Armada Revolucionarias de Colombia

FIS foreign intelligence service

FISS foreign intelligence and security service

FSB Federalnaya Sluzhba Bezopasnosti

GCC global culture of cyber security

GFW Great Firewall of China

gTLD generic top-level domain

GWOT global war on terrorism

HMI human-machine interface

HTML Hypertext Markup Language

HTTP HyperText Transfer Protocol

HUMINT human intelligence

IAB Internet Architecture Board

IARPA Intelligence Advanced Research Project Activity

ICANN Internet Corporation for Assigned Names and Numbers

ICC International Criminal Court

ICS industrial control system

ICT information and communication technology

IED improvised explosive device

IETF Internet Engineering Task Force

IGF Internet Governance Forum

IMP interface message processor

IP Internet Protocol

ISAC information Sharing and Analysis Center

ISO   International Organization of Standards

ISP   Internet service provider

ISR   intelligence, surveillance, and reconnaissance

ITU   International Telecommunications Union

I2P   Invisible Internet Project

IW   information warfare

LiDAR   light detection and ranging

LOC   line of code

MAC   media access control

MAD   mutually assured destruction

MMOG   massively multiplayer online games

NCPH   Network Crack Program Hacker

NIST   National Institute of Standards and Technology

NSF   National Science Foundation

NSSSC   National Security Strategy to Secure Cyberspace

OPM   Office of Personnel Management

OSI   Open Systems Interconnection

PKI   public key infrastructure

PLA   People's Liberation Army

PLC   programmable logic controller

POS   proof-of-stake

POTS   plain old telephone system

POW   proof-of-work

PRC   People's Republic of China

PTN   public telecommunication network

RBN   Russian Business Network

RIS   Russian Intelligence Service

RMA   Revolution in Military Affairs

SCADA   supervisory control and data acquisition

SCM   software configuration management

SMB   social media bot

SNMP   Simple Network Management Protocol

SQL   Structured Query Language

SQLi   SQL injection

SSF   Strategic Support Force

SWIFT   Society for Worldwide Interbank Financial Telecommunications

TAO   Tailored Access Operations

TCP   transmission control protocol

THS   TOR hidden services

TOC   transnational organized crime

TOR   the Onion Router

TRB   technical reconnaissance bureaus

UNGA   UN General Assembly

URL   Uniform Resource Locator

VC   Virtual Currency

VNSA   violent nonstate actor

WiMAX   Worldwide Interoperability for Microwave Access

WSIS   World Summit for the Information Society

Index

About the Authors

Jack A. Jarmon is the author of *The New Era in U.S. National Security* (Rowman & Littlefield, 2014) and co-author of *An Introduction to Homeland Security and Emergency Management* (2015). He has taught international relations courses at the University of Pennsylvania, the John C. Whitehead School of Diplomacy and International Relations at Seton Hall University, and Rutgers University, where he was also associate director of the Command, Control and Interoperability Center for Advanced Data Analysis—a Center of Excellence of the Department of Homeland Security (Science and Technology Division). He was USAID technical advisor for the Russian government in the mid-1990s. During its economic transition period, he worked for the Russian Privatization Committee and with such organizations as the U.S. Russia Investment Fund, the European Bank of Reconstruction and Development, and various money center banks. His private sector career includes global consultant firms, technology companies, and financial institutions. He was a manager with Arthur Andersen in Moscow and director of strategic alliances at Nortel Networks, Brampton, Ontario. He studied Soviet and Russian affairs at Fordham University and the Harriman Institute at Columbia University. He is fluent in Russian and holds a doctorate degree in global affairs from Rutgers University.

Pano Yannakogeorgos is the founding dean of the Air Force Cyber College. His expertise includes the intersection of cyber power, national security, and military operations; international cyber policy; cyber arms control; global cyber norms; and Eastern Mediterranean security. He was lead researcher on a Chief of Staff of the Air Force–directed study published as "The Human Side of Cyber Conflict." In addition, he has edited several books and written monographs, articles, and chapters including "Keep Cyber War Narrow" (*National Interest*); "Chinese Hacking Only Part of the Story" (CNN Online); "Internet Governance and National Security" (*Strategic Studies Quarterly*); "Challenges in Monitoring Cyber Arms Control" (*Journal of Information Warfare and Terrorism*); "Pitfalls of the Private-Public Partnership Model," in *Crime and Terrorism Risk: Studies in Criminology and Criminal Justice*; and "Cyberspace: The New Frontier and the Same Old Multilateralism," in *Global Norms: American Sponsorship and the Emerging Pattern of World Politics*. He has also published in *The Atlantic*, *The National Interest*, CNN Online, and *The Diplomat*. Prior to joining AFRI, Dr. Yannakogeorgos was a member of the faculty at Rutgers University, Division of Global Affairs, and he has served as an advisor within the United Nations Security Council on issues related to nuclear nonproliferation, the Middle East (including Iran), Al-Qaeda, and Internet misuse. He holds a PhD and MS in global affairs from Rutgers University and an ALB in philosophy from Harvard University.